Thinking Faith after Christianity

SUNY series in Theology and Continental Thought
Douglas L. Donkel, editor

Thinking Faith after Christianity

A Theological Reading of Jan Patočka's
Phenomenological Philosophy

Martin Koci

Cover photo: The Wotruba-Kirche in Vienna, Austria. Photograph by the author.

Published by State University of New York Press, Albany

© 2020 State University of New York

All rights reserved

No part of this book may be used or reproduced in any manner whatsoever without written permission. No part of this book may be stored in a retrieval system or transmitted in any form or by any means including electronic, electrostatic, magnetic tape, mechanical, photocopying, recording, or otherwise without the prior permission in writing of the publisher.

For information, contact State University of New York Press, Albany, NY
www.sunypress.edu

Library of Congress Cataloging-in-Publication Data

Names: Koci, Martin, 1987– author.
Title: Thinking faith after Christianity : a theological reading of Jan Patočka's phenomenological philosophy / Martin Koci.
Description: Albany : State University of New York Press, 2020. | Series: SUNY series in theology and continental thought | Includes bibliographical references and index.
Identifiers: LCCN 2019028105 | ISBN 9781438478937 (hardcover) | ISBN 9781438478920 (pbk. : alk. paper) | ISBN 9781438478944 (ebook)
Subjects: LCSH: Patočka, Jan, 1907–1977. | Philosophical theology. | Phenomenological theology. | Philosophy and religion.
Classification: LCC B4805.P384 K63 2020 | DDC 199/.437—dc23
LC record available at https://lccn.loc.gov/2019028105

10 9 8 7 6 5 4 3 2 1

Contents

Acknowledgments — vii

List of Abbreviations — ix

Introduction — 1

Chapter 1 *Philosophia ancilla theologiae?* Jan Patočka and the Theological Turn — 19

Chapter 2 *Sola ratione?* On the Spiritual Crisis of Modernity — 47

Chapter 3 After Metaphysics? Patočka's Deconstruction of Metaphysics and the Postmodern Overcoming of Ontotheology — 93

Chapter 4 Faith and/as Metaphysical Thinking: A Theological Reading of Patočka's Negative Platonism — 119

Chapter 5 Deconstruction or Heresy: Reconsidering the Un-thought of Christianity — 149

Chapter 6 The Call to Responsibility: Derrida's Reading of Patočka's Christian Thinking — 175

Chapter 7 Sacrifice for Nothing: The Movement of Kenosis in Patočka's Thought — 199

Conclusion Thinking Transcendence, Living Transcendence   227

Notes   239

Bibliography   273

Index   287

Acknowledgments

I wish to thank Professor Lieven Boeve and Dr. Joeri Schrijvers from Leuven who supported me in the course of working on this book. I am grateful to my other friends and colleagues from Leuven, especially the members of the research group Theology in a Postmodern Context, for stimulating discussions we had over the years. Thanks must go to Colby Dickinson, who always treated my work with a profound respect, and to Justin Sands, who never hesitated to ask questions out of his genuine interest in the work of others. I am extremely grateful to both of you for academic collegiality and friendship.

I am very indebted to the Institut für die Wissenschaften vom Menschen in Vienna, for granting me a Junior Jan Patočka Fellowship. The six months I spent at the IWM were in many ways decisive for the production of this book. Thanks must go to the academic staff of the IWM, especially to Ludger Hagedorn, the head of the philosophy program and Patočka Archive in Vienna, for his detailed comments on previous versions of this work. However, thanks also belong to the administrative staff of the IWM for their care, which enabled me to focus only on my writing.

Over the years, many people critically assessed the results of my research. Those who deserve to be mentioned are Ivana Noble, Peter DeMey, František Štěch, Virgil Brower, Gábor Ambrus, and Prokop Brož.

I am grateful to Daniel Leufer and Tim Morgan for introducing me to the peculiarities of the English language. Their educated insights made the text of this book much better.

Last but not least, I would love to give special thanks to my wife Katka, who knows what it means to write an academic book. The family life of two scholars is a complicated thing. Experiences of our relatives as well as our own experiences are telling. Katka, thank you for your willingness to live with me the life in problematicity, a truly Patočkian movement, on an everyday basis. And I also have in mind our children, Noemi and Elias, who are the inspiration for thinking more than they realize and who can constructively interrupt the flow of ideas when necessary.

An earlier version of chapter 4 was originally published in the *International Journal of Philosophy and Theology* 79, nos. 1–2 (2018): 18–35, DOI: 10.1080/21692327.2017.1402692, and the previous version of chapter 7 appeared in *Modern Theology* 33, no. 4 (2017): 594–617, DOI: 10.1111/moth.12357. Last but not least, I am grateful for the generous financial support that made this work possible. This project was conceived within the framework of the project Christianity after Christendom (PRIMUS/HUM/23) and was written and completed with the generous financial support of the Austrian Science Fund (FWF) for the project Revenge of the Sacred: Phenomenology and the Ends of Christianity in Europe (P31919).

Abbreviations

Jan Patočka's Texts

CN — *Le christianisme et le monde naturel.* Translated by E. Abrams. *Istina* 38 (1993): 16–22.

HE — *Heretical Essays in the Philosophy of History.* Translated by E. Kohák. La Salle: Open Court, 1996.

NP — *Negative Platonism.* In *Jan Patočka: Philosophy and Selected Writings.* Translated by E. Kohák. 175–207. Chicago: University of Chicago Press, 1989.

NW — *The Natural World as a Philosophical Problem.* Translated by E. Abrams. Evanston: Northwestern University Press, 2016.

PE — *Plato and Europe.* Translated by P. Lom. Stanford: Stanford University Press, 2002.

SS 1 — *Sebranné spisy Jana Patočky, vol. 1. Péče o duši, I: Stati z let 1929–1952; Nevydané texty z padesátých let.* Edited by I. Chvatík and P. Kouba. Praha: Oikoymenh, 1996.

SS 2 — *Sebranné spisy Jana Patočky, vol. 2. Péče o duši, II: Stati z let 1970–1977; Nevydané texty a přednášky ze sedmdesátých let.* Edited by I. Chvatík and P. Kouba. Praha: Oikoymenh, 1999.

SS 3 — *Sebranné spisy Jana Patočky, vol. 3. Péče o duši, III: Kacířské eseje o filosofii dějin; Varianty a přípravné práce z let 1973–1977; Dodatky k Péči o duši I a II.* Edited by I. Chvatík and P. Kouba. Praha: Oikoymenh, 2002.

SS 4   *Sebranné spisy Jana Patočky, vol. 4. Umění a čas, I: Soubor statí, přednášek a poznámek k problémům umění.* Edited by D. Vojtěch and I. Chvatík. Praha: Oikoymenh, 2004.

SS 6   *Sebranné spisy Jana Patočky, vol. 6. Fenomenologické spisy I: Přirozený svět; Texty z let 1931–1949.* Edited by I. Chvatík and J. Frei. Praha: Oikoymenh, 2008.

SS 7   *Sebranné spisy Jana Patočky, vol. 7. Fenomenologické spisy II: Co je existence; Publikované texty z let 1965–1977.* Edited by P. Kouba and O. Švec. Praha: Oikoymenh, 2009.

SS 10   *Sebranné spisy Jana Patočky, vol. 10. Komeniologické studie II: Texty publikované v letech 1959–1977.* Edited by V. Schifferová. Praha: Oikoymenh, 1998.

SS 12   *Sebranné spisy Jana Patočky, vol. 12. Češi I: Soubor textů k českému myšlení a českým dějinám.* Edited by K. Palek and I. Chvatík. Praha: Oikoymenh, 2006.

SS 13   *Sebranné spisy Jana Patočky, vol. 13. Češi II: Soubor textů k českému myšlení a českým dějinám; Nepublikované práce.* Edited by K. Palek and I. Chvatík. Praha: Oikoymenh, 2006.

SS 20   *Sebranné spisy Jana Patočky, vol. 20. Dopisy Václavu Richterovi.* Edited by I. Chvatík and J. Michálek. Praha: Oikoymenh, 2001.

Other Texts

GD   Jacques Derrida. *Gift of Death.* Translated by D. Wills. Chicago: University of Chicago Press, 1995.

NYP   *The New Yearbook for Phenomenology and Phenomenological Philosophy XIV. Religion, War and the Crisis of Modernity: A Special Issue Dedicated to the Philosophy of Jan Patočka.* Edited by L. Hagedorn and J. Dodd. London: Routledge, 2015.

PSW   Erazim Kohák, *Jan Patočka: Philosophy and Selected Writings.* Chicago: University of Chicago Press, 1989.

QCT   Martin Heidegger, *The Question Concerning Technology.* In *Basic Writings*, edited by D. F. Krell, 307–342. San Francisco: HarperCollins, 1993.

Introduction

Not only to live faith, but also to think it.

—Jan Patočka

In a letter addressed to a theologian of his acquaintance, the Czech philosopher Jan Patočka suggests that faith is more than practice. Faith, which in Patočka's writings always means Christianity, concerns thinking. What does it mean to associate Christianity with thinking? Does Patočka ever express his personal views concerning belief? Is he accidentally pronouncing a theological idea here? Does the proposition contain a programmatic statement? Is this a provocation indicating that faith does not think (enough)? Or, should we understand it as a challenge to think more about faith, or to think about faith in a different way? This book is launched from the midst of these questions and is to some extent an extended reflection on this single enigmatic utterance. It seeks to explore Christian faith and theology in their proximity to philosophical-phenomenological reflection and its way of thinking. The central thesis is that Patočka's thought offers a wealth of insights that both challenge and inspire theology in its own task of thinking.

Some readers may be surprised by my choice of principal interlocutor. Patočka is neither a theologian nor a philosopher of religion. If we had to describe him in a single word, it would most likely be "phenomenologist." Scholars have been interpreting Patočka's philosophical work for many years and examining him from various perspectives: as phenomenologist, political thinker, interpreter of ancient philosophy, follower of Husserl and Heidegger, expert on Comenius, philosopher of history. Patočka is variously presented as an academic philosopher of the classical school, a civil rights activist, a passionate critic of modernity, a prolific writer, the Socrates of our times, the champion of life in truth, a thinker of shocking thoughts concerning the First World War, a heretic, and perhaps even as a forerunner of postmodernity. Patočka has many faces and his readers find many voices in his voluminous output, but rarely, it appears, the voice of theology. The motivation that lies behind this present work is to accept the challenge of finding that voice and to read, interpret, and appropriate Patočka's thought from a distinctively theological perspective.

I believe these reflections will provide an alternative and complementary perspective to the resurgence of religion and the reconsideration of Christianity in the present-day context, something otherwise described and debated as the "theological turn" in contemporary continental philosophy. The book is divided into seven chapters, each of which can be read separately as a discussion of a particular theologoumenon in Patočka, but which taken together gradually unfold the overall argument concerning the task of thinking, that is, and to paraphrase Patočka, the task not only of living Christianity but also of thinking it.

Chapter 1 tackles a long-debated question: Are theology and philosophy discrete disciplines that *font deux*? Sometimes conceived as the relationship between faith and reason, this question is scrutinized in light of Patočka's thought. The theological turn initiates a return to the question in a new context. Traditionally, theologians have reclaimed philosophical concepts for the sake of theological arguments. Now, the key players are philosophers, who retrieve theological issues and thus challenge the traditional doctrine of *philosophia ancilla theologiae*—philosophy as the handmaiden of theology. As a phenomenological philosopher, Patočka firmly rejects theological imperialism and the (mis)uses of philosophy. His early publications betray an especially polemical undertone regarding theology, and the influence of Heidegger appears indisputable in this respect. What is yet more interesting is that Patočka's apologetic for the autonomy of philosophy resembles the later critique of the theological turn in (French) phenomenology formulated by Dominique Janicaud.

That said, Patočka's thought significantly changes over the years. While anxious to identify and clarify the vocation of philosophy, Patočka increasingly acknowledges the importance of theology. He reads the prominent theologians of the day such as Rudolf Bultmann; he discusses theological issues with academic theologians, mostly of the Barthian orientation, such as Josef Lukl Hromádka and Josef B. Souček; he presents lectures for students of theology on themes such as "Christian faith and thinking"; and he is fascinated by concepts of high theological importance such as conversion, faith, the soul, and sacrifice. Ultimately, just as it is among certain representatives of the theological turn in contemporary phenomenology, Patočka's phenomenological philosophy is open to the structures of theological thinking. Chapter 1 therefore argues for drawing Patočka into the field of theology as a complementary voice in the debate concerning the relationship between theology and philosophy, and it demonstrates that Patočka's thought opens possibilities for a theological reading and may even present a constructive critical impetus for theology and its own task of thinking.

Having established a link between the philosopher and the proposed theological reading of his work, chapter 2 presents a detailed account of the context from which Patočka speaks, namely, modernity. In Patočka, we do not find a univocal language concerning modernity, although his focus, following Husserl, is rather critical and, in the footsteps of Heidegger, perhaps even negative. Although the tone of chapter 2 echoes Patočka's critical outlook, it has to be said that the Czech philosopher is well aware that modernity represents a mass of heterogeneous ideas, varied modes of thinking, competing rationalities, and positive developments. Rather than aiming at a summary of the totality of Patočka's reflections on modernity, I therefore propose a series of "windows" that offer a variety of insights into its multifaceted nature. But there is one thread that unites these various lines of thought and provides us with a clearer perspective, and that is Patočka's perennial struggle with the idea of crisis. Although the modern crisis has numerous facets, I will confine myself to considering what I see as the three most relevant: the crisis of rationalism, the crisis of metaphysics, and the crisis of religion.

In chapters 3 and 4, I explore Patočka's critique of metaphysics in detail. Can metaphysics be overcome? Is theology possible after the demise of metaphysics? These questions are common to both the theological turn and Patočka's oeuvre, although for Patočka, the process of overcoming does not result in nonmetaphysical or even antimetaphysical closure. Chapter 3 is concerned mainly with problematizing ready-made postmetaphysical theories, especially in the field of contemporary theology. Here I will turn to the examples of Jean-Luc Marion and John D. Caputo. In dialogue with these prominent authors, it will become clear that, while rejecting metaphysical philosophy, Patočka reconsiders metaphysical thinking and thus proposes an alternative to the recent theological turn. To reinforce the claims proposed in chapter 3, chapter 4 analyzes Patočka's essay *Negative Platonism*, written in the 1950s. This work, which predated the theological turn and entered the debate as a concept, represents a unique attempt to develop a metaphysical thinking beyond the ontotheological lapsus. The question guiding our inquiry concerns the theological significance of Patočka's metaphysical thinking. Without preempting the answer here, it is worth noting that the principal impact of Patočka's reconsideration of metaphysics is likely to be found in the field of the theology of faith, and that our insights will lead us to the question: What kind of Christianity can we associate with Patočka?

Chapter 5 tracks Patočka's deconstruction of classical Christianity and sketches the broad contours of the kind of Christianity that belongs in the past, that is, the Christianity we now find ourselves "post." But Christianity is by no means irrelevant or unimportant in a post-Christian age. On the contrary, our present context calls for a reconsideration of Christian themes. I will therefore be taking a closer look at Patočka's notion of demythologized Christianity, which for Patočka means a Christianity beyond myth and enlightenment and emancipated from both ancient *religio* and modern rationalism. I will also explore the idea of "the un-thought" and therefore aim at "thinking Christianity after (the end of) Christianity," that is, Christianity as something that is still on its way and unfolding in the future.

By the same token, Jacques Derrida engages with Patočka's *Heretical Essays in the Philosophy of History*. His provocative reading suggests that Patočka should be considered a Christian thinker and, in this sense, a crucial figure in the debate concerning religion in the contemporary world. Chapter 6 examines both Derrida's reading and the readings of Derrida's reading. Derrida draws on Patočka's thesis that the essence of religion in general and Christianity in particular, as the religion par excellence, is responsiveness to the Other and to others. In this sense, Derrida reveals and supports the thesis that for Patočka, Christianity is a particular form of (philosophical) thinking rather than a confessional religion.

Finally, chapter 7 explores the idea of sacrifice, an idea that is at the heart of Patočka's later works. Is it mere coincidence that the philosopher who paid the ultimate price for his opinions—the same price as Socrates, the model of philosophical life—reflected on sacrifice in the final period of his professional life? A fascinating idea of kenosis and kenotic sacrifice represents the pinnacle of Patočka's interest in Christianity and in theological issues. Such insights will certainly provoke the formulation of numerous challenges to theology and how it functions in the context of the theological turn. I will advance the thesis that the Christianity that comes after the end of Christianity—after its kenotic death—is a particular mode of thinking, namely, the task of thinking faith.

I thus intend first to examine the somewhat neglected perspective of considering the thought of Patočka as it relates to religion and theology and thereby to make something of an original contribution to Patočka studies. I will also, however, consider Patočka in relation to what has become known as the theological turn in contemporary continental philosophy and as a forerunner of this movement, with a particular contribution to recent developments in phenomenology. Second, the theological perspective of the book will go beyond a mere description and classification of the theological motifs in Patočka and develop a genuine theological reading that will contribute to the general scholarship on Jan Patočka, but it will also unfold unexpected possibilities for Christian thinking as such—what is traditionally called theology. In this sense, as I argue in the conclusion, such an engagement with Patočka will contribute to the discussion concerning the close but always complex relationship between theology and philosophy while at the same time opening up a refreshing approach to "thinking" and "living" transcendence.

The Contexts and Contours of Patočka's Thought

Patočka studies are flourishing today. His phenomenological interpretations of and elaborations on the works of Edmund Husserl and Martin Heidegger and his thought-provoking analysis of the idea of Europe and the philosophy of history hold center stage in much recent scholarship. The burden of this present offering is to lay out a further perspective—a theological one. Is it a coincidence that Patočka's very first published work and his final finished work both concern religion and theology? Although almost fifty years separate his short essay "Theology and Philosophy" (1929) and the more lengthy "On Masaryk's Philosophy of Religion" (1977), we discern a gradually developing interest in Christianity throughout Patočka's philosophical activity.

Jan Patočka was born in 1907 in northern Bohemia, at that time part of the Austro-Hungarian Empire. He studied philosophy in Prague and in Paris, where he met Edmund Husserl. This encounter was to set Patočka's philosophical orientation and see him develop a genuine interest in phenomenology. In 1931, Patočka earned his doctorate in philosophy, defending a thesis on *The Notion of Evidence*,[1] and began his academic career as an assistant professor at Charles University in Prague. Thanks to a Humboldt scholarship, Patočka was able to study in Berlin and Freiburg from 1932 to 1933. Although he arrived in Germany at the invitation of Husserl, the most decisive moment for Patočka's later philosophical development was his encounter with Martin Heidegger. Patočka concurs with Heidegger's notion of being-in-the-world and the idea that the human subject is a historical being—a being that is radically different from the being of objects. After his time in Freiburg and after witnessing significant political changes in Germany, Patočka returned to Prague where he cofounded Cercle philosophique de Prague and became its first secretary. The movement emerged as a critical reaction to the (neo)positivist philosophical mainstream of the time and hosted Husserl's Prague lectures in 1935. The following year, Patočka finished his *Habilitationsschrift* on *The Natural World as a Philosophical Problem*.[2] A promising academic career was interrupted when Nazi Germany invaded Czechoslovakia in 1939 and closed the Czech universities. After the war, Patočka returned to Charles University but did not stay long. The communist coup of 1948 led to purges against all "classes," including the intelligentsia. As a humanist-democratic philosopher, Patočka was expelled from the university and worked at various minor research positions and later as a librarian at the Czechoslovak Academy of Sciences. The Prague Spring, an attempt to democratize socialism in Czechoslovakia in the late 1960s, enabled Patočka to renew his academic career. In 1968, he was named a full professor in Prague and three years later received an honorary doctorate from the University of Aachen. His third spell at the university lasted only four years, however. The Soviet occupation and fresh purges at all levels of society forced Patočka into retirement and he was expelled from academia for the final time. Despite this misfortune, Patočka remained active and participated in the underground activities of the intellectual opposition to the communist regime. What began on a small scale—one philosopher and his students meeting in private to discuss philosophy—developed into Patočka's very public involvement as a spokesperson for Charter 77, a human rights movement that protested oppression by the totalitarian state. Because of his very public acceptance and performance of this responsibility, Patočka died in dramatic circumstances in 1977.

Hypotheses concerning Patočka's continual intellectual struggle with religion, and the importance for theology of that struggle, might seem somewhat controversial considering the standard interpretation of his multilayered work. The usual approach to Patočka tends to focus on one or another of his principal areas of interest and his major writings from a particular period of his life. Patočka's early engagement with phenomenology between the wars is typically represented by *The Natural World as a Philosophical Problem* (1936). Faced by a neopagan Nazi ideology that represented the tragic eruption of a particular manifestation of modernity that would be revealed in all its horror during the Second World War, Patočka set about the grandiose project of reinterpreting the origins of modernity and modern rationality. Patočka did not finish "his great book," however, but left us with numerous drafts, published posthumously under the editorial title *Andere Wege in die Moderne* (Other ways to the modern age).[3] After the war, Patočka gave himself to serious reflection on the demise of metaphysics and dedicated much of his time to developing alternative patterns of thought. The highlight of this period is the corpus of texts knowns as *Negative Platonism*.[4] In the later years of his philosophical life, Patočka elaborates on two interrelated ideas. First, he develops his own general philosophy of history. Second, and more particularly, he reflects on the notion of Europe, its end, and what is to come. Two monographs sum up these philosophical endeavors: *Europe and Post-Europe* and *Heretical Essays in the Philosophy of History*.[5] His research led Patočka to reconsider some of his previous phenomenological positions and to republish *The Natural World as a Philosophical Problem* with a new postscript "*The Natural World* Remeditated Thirty-Three Years Later." Here, Patočka presents his idea of human existence as a movement. In fact, he talks about three movements of existence: the movement of acceptance, the movement of defense, and the movement of truth, also described as the movement of transcendence. This interpretation of human being-in-the-world is generally taken as "Patočka's most original contribution to philosophy."[6] The pressing political situation also motivated Patočka to explore the Platonic idea of caring for the soul and on this basis to formulate a spiritual response to the unpleasantness in society, something that is still relevant today.[7]

It is not possible to do justice to the complexity of Patočka's thought in so short a volume. That his work is so multifocal and unsystematic has both advantages and disadvantages. The advantage is that Patočka can be interpreted from many different angles. Phenomenological interpretations come first, of course,[8] but Patočka is becoming an increasingly important figure in political philosophy in our contemporary post-European world,[9] especially in relation to the discourse on the philosophy of history, the importance to Europe of the Greek legacy, and Christianity and the tradition of metaphysics. Finally, Patočka is understood as the interpreter of the crisis of modernity and, in this sense, also of the crisis of rationality. The chief drawback of the rather scattershot nature of Patočka's work is that his "big ideas" tempt the interpreter to focus, as we have already suggested, on a particular period or a particular set of writings. Those who take this approach can easily overlook the lines of thought that developed more gradually and that become apparent only when his oeuvre is considered as a whole, from the very earliest writings of his youth to the great works of philosophical maturity.

So, what is usually considered to represent the core of Patočka's work? Erazim Kohák, biographer and translator of Patočka's essential writings into English, summarizes the three most common ways of classifying the thought of the Czech phenomenologist: (1) philosophy without a kernel (*Philosoph ohne Mitte*), (2) the philosophy of humanism, and (3) existential phenomenology.[10] The first approach claims that Patočka's work lacks thematic coherence and skips from one topic to another according to the historical context. Dramatic historical changes and challenges certainly influenced Patočka's philosophical focus. The geopolitical situation in postwar Europe stimulated numerous philosophical reflections on the idea of Europe, including Patočka's own. It is possible, however, to trace Patočka's interest in this problem to his very first engagement with Edmund Husserl and his *Crisis of European Sciences and Transcendental Phenomenology*.[11] It can very easily be argued, therefore, that Patočka is being coherent in following the theme of Europe and the crisis of Europe throughout most of his professional life.

The second reading places Patočka as the successor of the humanistic philosophical tradition prevalent at the beginning of the twentieth century in the Czech philosophical context. Following Tomáš G. Masaryk, Patočka published numerous studies on social and political issues that were in line with the Enlightenment tradition of republicanism and democracy. His later engagement with the work of Jan Amos Comenius, whom Patočka interprets as a representative of an alternative modern humanistic tradition in contrast to, for example, Descartes, supports the view that Patočka was a modern humanist. His involvement in Charter 77 seems to confirm his lifelong humanistic orientation, which he inherited from Masaryk in the interwar period.

The humanistic line is interrupted by the Second World War, however, after which Patočka draws ever closer to Martin Heidegger. Some of his ideas even echo the dark language of Friedrich Nietzsche—the title of the sixth heretical essay reads, "Wars of the Twentieth Century and the Twentieth Century as War." The fact is, however, that Patočka had engaged with Heidegger as early as the 1930s, so reading his work through the lens of existential phenomenology—the third of Kohák's trilogy of approaches to Patočka—has relatively long roots. It is quite clear, furthermore, that the postwar texts lean much more on Heidegger, and that the Husserlian line of thought fades into the background.

Paul Ricoeur offers an alternative classification and identifies two focal points in Patočka's thought: (1) the phenomenology of the natural world and (2) the philosophy of history.[12] In this sense, Ricoeur follows more the Husserlian and Heideggerian line of thought in Patočka's work. According to Ricoeur, Patočka never lost sight of phenomenology and developed phenomenological issues beyond his great German teachers. He notes that in his thesis on "the natural world," Patočka expresses a certain dissatisfaction with Husserl's conclusions, which are still "too modern" in holding on to the dualism of subject and object. Heidegger seems to offer a way beyond this impasse, but, as Patočka's later phenomenological studies clearly show, the philosophy of *Dasein* is also inadequate. For Ricoeur, this is the moment Patočka introduces his teaching on the movements of existence and on being as a movement. Patočka's phenomenology of movement does not refer to the typical meaning of moving from one place to another. What Patočka has in mind is better described as "emerging." Movement informs beings, or in Patočka's words movement is "that which makes being what it is."[13] The bottom line of Patočka's argument is to overcome the polar division between objectivity and subjectivity, or as Ricoeur puts it: "Movement as an actualization on the way is not more subjective than objective. The being in motion is happening."[14]

The second central facet of Patočka's thought according to Ricoeur is the philosophy of history. The question of the meaning of history is present throughout Patočka's oeuvre, but interestingly enough this line of questioning in Patočka does not seek an objective answer. For him, it is not possible to say that the meaning of history is this or that, in other words, "this" or "that" thing. Rather, the meaning of history is something that is constantly at stake in the drama of human freedom. Concretely, Patočka finds the meaning of history in realizing its problematicity, that is, in the "shaking" of presupposed meaning. The Czech word *otřes* that Patočka uses in this context is very strong. It carries the meaning of being moved or shocked not only emotionally but existentially; the German word *erschüttern* also expresses Patočka's idea more faithfully than the English word *shake*. Because Patočka talks about "being shaken" in his widely read *Heretical Essays*, secondary literature often associates this term with those who experienced wars, totalitarian regimes, and other dramatic events of recent history, but were able to resist despite having no real power.[15] Ivan Chvatík nonetheless suggests a different context for the phrase. For Chvatík, Patočka is referring to the epochal shock caused by "the death of God and the collapse of metaphysics."[16] This brings us back to the intuition behind this book. In my hypothesis, Patočka's thought has high theological relevance, especially at a time when Christianity is once more indisputably an issue in continental philosophy.

It is true that the so-called theological turn in French phenomenology appeared on the scene only after Patočka's death—at least if we regard the publication of Jean-Luc Marion's *Dieu sans l'être* (1982) as the symbolic breakthrough that initiated the debate.[17] But this has not stopped some authors listing Patočka alongside Jean-Luc Marion, Michel Henry, and Jean-Yves Lacoste as the forerunners, and even the authors, of the theological turn in continental philosophy:[18]

> Patočka is one of the few thinkers who already in his time conceived the crisis of modernity not just in terms of its cultural and scientific dimensions, but explicitly analyzed the need for a reassessment of religion, and, in the European context, particularly of Christianity. From the very early writings until the late *Heretical Essays* there runs a core of untimely thoughts that are as provocative and heretical to the Christian tradition as they are to the triumphant secularism of modern times. This philosophical venture makes him stand out as an important forerunner of and critical counterweight to the contemporary resurgence of religion in scholarly and intellectual discourse.[19]

Although this point of view is rare and not widely accepted, the present volume adopts it as its point of departure. To justify an exploration of the potential theological implications of Patočka's work, we will now briefly explore the assertion that Christianity is central to his work.

Patočka and Christianity

Patočka was baptized in the Roman Catholic Church but raised in a secular, anticlerical family. Like many of his fellow citizens, after the founding of the free Czechoslovak state in 1918, Patočka left the church in order to make a symbolic break with the Catholic Habsburg monarchy. Interestingly, he returned to Catholicism a year later but did not become a practicing believer. A serious intellectual engagement with Christianity was mediated for Patočka through his Protestant friends and colleagues at university. Although Patočka was discouraged from converting to Protestantism by Protestant theologians themselves, the fascination of what he saw as the energizing Protestant thinking of the twentieth century very much stuck in his mind. Nonetheless, in later life, Patočka would rediscover the depths of Catholicism, mostly through literature.[20] Although it is difficult to say on the basis of biography alone whether Patočka was closer to Catholicism or Protestantism, whether he was a non-Christian or truly a Christian thinker,[21] the present volume nonetheless puts forward the thesis that thinking concerning Christianity is an integral part of Patočka's phenomenological philosophy. In *Heretical Essays*, Patočka writes enigmatically about Christianity: "Christianity remains thus far the greatest, unsurpassed but also un-thought-through human outreach that enabled humans to struggle against decadence."[22] It would not be stretching the point to say that this book is all about that one sentence, which will launch us into a theological reading of Patočka's thought, into laying out the possible meanings of Christianity as something "great," "unsurpassed," but also "un-thought-through" in Patočka, and into focusing on the possibilities of rethinking theology against this background. In other words, the main object of this book serves a double purpose: to describe, systematically, the theological motifs in Patočka and to draw out the implications for theology of Patočka's thought.

First, however, it is necessary to consider what Patočka actually has to say about Christianity, and here the preceding English translation is somewhat misleading. The main problem is with the word "outreach," which Kohák uses for the Czech word *vzmach*. An alternative rendering could be "upswing," but this seems equally inadequate.[23] The French *élan* and the German *Aufschwung* in the respective translations of Patočka's work[24] do much better than either of the English variants.

Vzmach is not a word used in everyday conversation. It is a carefully thought through philosophical notion. In the context of the Christianity portrayed in *Heretical Essays*, it seems that for Patočka *vzmach* refers to a sense of transcendence.[25] This transcendence does not, however, point to an otherworldly reality but to the freedom of human being, which transcends the world as a world of things that appear to us. Followers of Heidegger would say that Patočka uses *vzmach* to point out the ontological difference between being human and the being of entities; *vzmach* is what enables us to struggle against decadence, to cope with the forgetfulness of the fundamental difference between being human and other beings, but also to deal with forgetfulness concerning the position of being-in-the-world as historical beings. *Vzmach* is therefore a dynamic driving force, something that transcends limits and crosses boundaries. It seems much more plausible to use the French word *élan* in place of *outreach*, even in English editions, otherwise what Patočka has in mind when he uses the word *vzmach* is literally lost in translation.[26]

There is another problem with our sentence. Kohák's translation reads "Christianity remains the greatest . . . human outreach," or, in our proposed version, "human élan." The Czech original, however, says only that "Christianity is thus far the greatest, unsurpassed but also un-thought-through élan . . ."[27] The word "human" is missing. Although Kohák suggests that Christianity remains a "human" driving force against decadence, Patočka in fact leaves his statement regarding the status of Christianity with a degree of ambiguity. "Christianity is . . . the élan that enabled humans to struggle against decadence," says Patočka. Now that we have exposed these subtle differences, we can turn our attention to the most interesting question concerning Patočka's enigmatic sentence, a question we will scrutinize very closely: What is Patočka's Christianity all about?

The provocative suggestion of the un-thought-through-ness of Christianity and its unfinishedness has led interpreters to various speculations. What might a fully thought-through Christianity look like? Is it a demythologized Christianity? Is it a secular Christianity without religion? Is it an immanent Christianity without transcendence? What does the "un-thought" of Christianity ultimately mean?

Patočka's relationship to Christianity is both complex and wide ranging. What we find wrapped up in a single sentence in *Heretical Essays* is present, and develops gradually, throughout Patočka's oeuvre. Theological issues seem to be a neglected axis of his philosophical work, but one possible approach to researching the topic is to apply a historical—chronological—perspective. Jindřich Veselý follows this path in his essay "Jan Patočka and Christianity," where he outlines four distinct periods over which Patočka developed his interest in Christian matters.[28]

The first stage, between the wars, represents Patočka's philosophical beginnings as a phenomenologist and disciple of Husserl, a time when he clearly saw his role as an apologist for philosophy. Indeed, Patočka dedicates numerous studies to methodological questions in which he explores the field of philosophy, the vocation of the philosopher, and the context of philosophical reasoning. Patočka's passion for the cause is extraordinary and it is no surprise that whenever philosophy encounters theology, Patočka resolutely defends his discipline and seeks to protect it from any potential "theological imperialism."

The perspective shifts in the years immediately following the Second World War. Although Patočka was largely prevented from publishing during this period, it was a significant one in his intellectual development. Having come face to face with the neopagan totalitarian ideology of National Socialism, Patočka does not hesitate to defend Christianity as being among the most prominent intellectual forces in European thought and Western civilization. Having seen Europe under serious threat, Patočka makes an intensive study of the history of philosophy, which brings him to the question of a post-European—or equally a post-Christian—epoch. From this moment forward, the pressing issue of Christianity after (the end of) Christianity remains uppermost in Patočka's mind.

Following the philosophical mainstream of the 1950s, Patočka then, in Veselý's third phase, explores the possibilities of philosophy after the alleged end of metaphysics. He develops the idea of negative Platonism and sketches out a larger work under the same title, which in many respects resembles later attempts to overcome ontotheology in the context of the theological turn. Veselý reminds us that Patočka explicitly acknowledges that philosophy and theology share a concern with metaphysics and its critique.[29] Here, Patočka's elaboration on the notion of faith prefigures the position concerning Christianity that he developed in the later years of his philosophical career.

In Patočka's opinion, faith is a particular mode of thinking and of living in openness to the future.[30] His output in the 1960s and 1970s—the final phase in Veselý's scheme—offers several variations on this main idea. Although the vast secondary literature on the final period of Patočka's output focuses on themes such as caring for the soul and the movements of existence, here we will consider the neglected but highly significant questions concerning the un-thought of Christianity, Christianity as the religion of responsibility, and the scandalous idea of kenotic sacrifice.

Veselý's chronological perspective on Patočka and Christianity reveals two things. First, that over the years, Patočka moves from polemicizing against Christianity to engaging with an interpretation of its possibilities in the context referred to as post-Christian. Second, and perhaps more important, Patočka shifts from acknowledging Christianity as a significant force in Europe to thinking about the importance of Christianity after (the end of) Christianity, and about Christianity as thinking. We are again reminded, therefore, about the key idea that faith is something to be thought about, that faith is thinking. This leads us to a thesis that takes Patočka's thoughts on Christianity as being present throughout his life's work. Patočka's constantly growing interest in Christian and even theological issues points to a carefully thought-through goal of thinking beyond the limits of Christianity. If we read Patočka's works from all stages of his professional life from this perspective, we find that his reflections on Christianity after (the end of) Christianity, and thus his reflections on the possibility of transcendence from the point of view of being-in-the-world, is a golden thread—although often a slender one—in his lifelong philosophical inquiry. The preconditions for such an inquiry can already be detected in his early writings:

> Part of the finitude of our actual life is to experience a need for some external support, for salvation. Salvation is the sustenance of our life by an external, absolute power. . . . It is not possible to rely on the gods, because the absolute is not outside but within us. Man stands in a closer and more intimate relation to God than is either safe or pleasant.[31]

Is this theology, or the philosophy of religion? Probably neither. Patočka is a phenomenologist, so in line with his philosophical upbringing he "perceives" Christianity, meaning he sees Christianity as the possibility of thinking about God/transcendence within us. Interestingly, Patočka generally uses negative—apophatic—language to describe the experience of transcendence as he is keen to resist proposing positive definitions. For Patočka, therefore, faith represents more than knowledge and convictions or adherence to a set of opinions and confessions.[32] Faith, as noted earlier, is thinking, that is, thinking and questioning about the truth of life and life in truth. The field of thinking seems to be the common ground where philosophy and theology meet. The aim I pursue in this book, therefore, is not primarily to present Patočka as a thinker with a strong affiliation to theology but to develop a Christian thinking that draws inspiration from Patočka, and thus to contribute to what Jean-Yves Lacoste has recently described as the shift from theology to theological thinking.[33] Without employing theological imperialism, thinking faith after Christianity seems in Patočka to be one embodiment of *philosophia vera*—which is not the same as Christian philosophy—but not the only one. In summary, this challenge to adopt the task of theological thinking offers the opportunity to challenge theology to open itself to a neglected form of phenomenological philosophy and at the same time to have an impact on theology from within. Interacting with Patočka leads us away from the safe haven of theology and to becoming sensitive to the task of (theological) thinking.

Toward an Appropriation of Patočka's Philosophy in Theology

Because Patočka presents Christianity as something that is the "greatest," which is "unsurpassed," but which is also "un-thought," this way of presenting the issue directly concerns theological thinking. Recent theological scholarship has inquired into philosophical interpretations of religious issues and Christian topics proposed by the authors of the theological turn with the intention of drawing inspiration for our understanding of faith in the contemporary—postmodern—context.

The number of works on Patočka's thoughts on Christianity is constantly growing, both among individual philosophers—Ludger Hagedorn, Eddo Evink, and Nicolas de Warren[34]—and in collective works. A special issue of the *Journal for Cultural and Religious Theory* (no. 15, 2015) is almost entirely dedicated to reflections on Patočka's work on "religion and the gift."

Despite the fact that philosophers—albeit a limited number—acknowledge Patočka's challenging interpretations of Christianity as a significant component of his overall work, it is striking that theologians are yet to give serious consideration to Patočka's thought. Why should this be? First, there is the issue of language and the availability of sources: analysis of Patočka's original works requires knowledge of his mother tongue, Czech, which is certainly not the easiest language to master. But this cannot be the whole case. Excellent translations of Patočka exist in French and German, and the English corpus of texts is constantly growing. It is certainly possible to initiate a theological discussion with Patočka on the basis of sources available in the principal world languages. Second, and perhaps more important, Patočka's work has not been met with unbounding enthusiasm by Czech theologians. There is a general lack of dialogue between theology and phenomenology in the Czech theological world[35] and somewhat of a negative attitude in Patočka's philosophical disciples toward any attempt to seek out his theological relevance.[36] The aim of the present work is to remedy this lack in the philosophical and theological fields and to offer a novel and integral interpretation of Patočka's phenomenological philosophy. Thus, my taking—or perhaps dragging—Patočka into the theater of theological debate is intended as a humble contribution to theology's traditional adagio of *fides quaerens intellectum*—faith seeking understanding.[37] We will soon see that Patočka himself values this theological statement and contrasts it with another part of theological tradition, that is, *philosophia ancilla theologiae* (chapter 1).

For Patočka, Christianity is a matter of thinking. Yet as many of his reflections show—for example, his ideas about Europe after Europe, and the task of philosophy after the end of metaphysics—Patočka likes to think "beyond" the presupposed meaning of things. His call for thinking consists in pointing beyond itself and therefore contains a certain sense of transcendence. I therefore propose a reading of Patočka that makes possible a novel understanding of Christianity after (the end of) Christianity. On one level, we can interpret our situation as the completion of the shift from Christendom to a post-Christian age. Religion has ceased to be the principal reference point for interpreting our existence in the world. Modernity removed the sacred canopy, and this allowed for rapid development in many fields, especially science and technology. However, the emergence of enlightened humanity also has its dark side. For Patočka, the crisis of modernity can be deemed a spiritual crisis (chapter 2). And as every crisis is also an opportunity, instead of uselessly lamenting the loss of Christian privileges, Patočka's critical account of modern rationality leads us to think of the Christianity that is to come—"after Christendom."

On another level, reflecting on Christianity after Christianity can also mean heeding the call to a thinking that is never complete but always emerging. Patočka's deconstruction of metaphysics in order to give way to metaphysical thinking (chapter 3) motivates us to think of the deconstruction of the timeless religion of reason. In this sense, Christianity after Christianity is a reference to thinking faith beyond ontotheology and the *religio* of myth (chapters 4 and 5).

This search for Christianity after Christianity, and thus for a theological appropriation of Patočka's thought, is based on an investigation of the entire corpus of Patočka's writings, including some lesser-known texts that remained unpublished during the philosopher's lifetime or that remained only as the drafts of great and ambitious but unfinished projects. The inquiry reveals the proximity of Patočka's thought to the current debate on the theological turn. I intend to prove this hypothesis using three interrelated themes: (1) the deconstruction of Christianity in Patočka, (2) Derrida's reading of Patočka as a Christian thinker, and (3) Patočka's eminent interest in the motif of kenotic sacrifice. This focus on the un-thought of Christianity in Patočka's deconstructions does not necessarily lead to a purely negative theology—as many postmodern engagements with Christianity seem to do.[38] Rather, it unfolds a positive conception of Christianity as the amplitude of life (chapter 5). In this sense, Christianity after Christianity appears to represent the call to responsibility (chapter 6) manifested in the figure of kenotic sacrifice (chapter 7).

Any thesis that supports Patočka's relevance for theology risks accusations of heresy. A theological engagement with Patočka will surely be condemned by defenders of pure phenomenological orthodoxy—just as the French phenomenologists Marion, Henry, and Chrétien were criticized by Dominique Janicaud for their interest in religion.[39] As much as it challenges mainstream conceptions of Christianity as a metaphysical *vera religio veri Dei*, the proposition of thinking faith after Christianity could certainly be called heretical. Nonetheless, drawing on Patočka's own method of heretical thinking, that is, his "shaking" and interrupting of the supposed nonproblematic meanings, and following Patočka's creative use of his sources and his pushing their interpretation to their limits, I aim to question and challenge both the standard interpretation of Patočka as a philosopher who has little to say about theology, and the theology that shows little interest in the contemporary contextual sensibilities that have been well captured in the critical consciousness of recent philosophy.

Chapter 1

Philosophia ancilla theologiae?
Jan Patočka and the Theological Turn

How are we to understand the relationship between philosophy and theology? Is philosophy merely the handmaiden of theology, or is it rather theology freed from superstition and irrational ideas such as revelation? Phenomenology has had little to say in this respect. The resolute opposition to any intermarriage between the two disciplines had been on the table since Husserl: a methodological atheism is certainly among his axioms.[1] Heidegger does not deviate from this position and clearly distinguishes philosophy from the positive science of theology. Despite the oft-cited statement from Heidegger's interview with *Der Spiegel* late in his professional life that "only a god can still save us,"[2] the distance between philosophy and theology remains a dictum for the German philosopher. This does not, however, prevent theologians from reading and interpreting phenomenology, especially Heidegger's phenomenology, from their own perspective. Theology has never hesitated to read and use philosophy for the sake of theological arguments. It can thus be assumed that the answer to the question with which we opened this chapter depends on one's perspective.

More recently, however, phenomenology has undergone a significant turn. Christian religious and theological issues have become a crucial field of interest for the so-called new phenomenologists: Emmanuel Levinas, Jean-Luc Marion, Michel Henry, and Jean-Louis Chrétien have all produced works of great theological relevance. What is most significant about their engagement with theology is that it is deliberate and explicit. As such, the meaning of theology in these works departs significantly from traditional understandings precisely because of their phenomenological perspective: "It is a radically renewed sense of theology—a sense made discernible only by phenomenology," says László Tengelyi.[3] Although the theological turn is not accepted by all phenomenologists, the engagement with theological thinking is without doubt a component of phenomenological philosophy that is progressing rapidly.

Dominique Janicaud, for example, considers the theological turn to be an irregular development that violates the basic principles of phenomenology, namely, the limits of the phenomenon. For Janicaud, phenomenology and theology cannot be considered a single unifiable discipline; they "make two" (*font deux*).[4] The shift from the apparent to the unapparent respects neither the tradition nor the phenomenological method. Paradoxically, the same can be said from a theological perspective. The unorthodox thinking of the theological turn challenges the metaphysical conception of transcendence, God, faith, and other issues. Yet current debates over the relationship between theology and philosophy are influenced largely by the discourse of the theological turn in (French) phenomenology.

Jan Patočka stands somewhere in the middle, that is, between Husserl/Heidegger and the theological turn. At the beginning of his career, Patočka follows the traditional path and resolutely closes the door on theology: "The philosopher never helps the theologian."[5] He moves entirely within the sphere of immanence, and his primary interest is that which appears: phenomena.[6] He also, however, elaborates on the phenomenological tradition in order to liberate thinking from the impact of metaphysics, thus placing himself in closer proximity to thinkers of the new theologically oriented phenomenology. So, while Patočka demonstrates a traditional methodological aversion to theology, his own (re)interpretation of phenomenology nevertheless takes him in the direction of the theological turn.

Jeffrey Bloechl has recently argued that phenomenology "presents itself as a new *ancilla theologiae*."[7] Patočka would most likely disagree with such a claim and repeatedly defends philosophy's distinctiveness from theology.[8] A closer reading, however, reveals that his phenomenology is not entirely alienated from theology and can even be considered proximate to the structures of religious-theological thinking that have once again found their way into philosophical discourse. As such, Patočka appears well worth approaching from the theological perspective. Although he never explicitly set about the task of renewing theology, his reflections on the boundary between the two disciplines are not necessarily opposed to theology. On the contrary, Patočka provides us with the thought-provoking impetus to think theologically about the question of whether philosophy and theology are two discrete disciplines.

Against the background of this hypothesis, this chapter will follow two intertwining threads: the relationship between theology and philosophy in Patočka and an assessment of the theological discourse in contemporary phenomenology. First, I will present Patočka's criticism of the theological misuse of philosophy. Early on, he holds the opinion that there is a clear lack of relation between the two disciplines. To clarify this position, I will also engage with the work of Martin Heidegger and Dominique Janicaud and raise questions concerning Patočka's fundamental views on the task of philosophy. I will closely investigate certain essays of Patočka's that elucidate his understanding of the philosophical endeavor, namely, "Some Comments Concerning the Extramundane and Mundane Position of Philosophy" (1934) and "Chapters from Contemporary Philosophy" (1936). I will also argue that Patočka's preoccupation with his own discipline paradoxically challenges his initial viewpoint concerning theology. Finally, I will show that Patočka's position on the relationship between theology and philosophy not only develops over time but also challenges certain current views and opens the door for an entirely new understanding of the relationship between these two modes of thinking.

Are Theology and Philosophy Two Separate Things?

It is significant that Patočka begins his writing career with a publication that explicitly addresses the relationship between theology and philosophy. The essay, simply entitled "Theology and Philosophy" (1929), reveals the fighting spirit of an enthusiastic young scholar who refuses any mixing of these two disciplines.[9] Philosophical reasoning must be protected from the pretentious reductionism and unwarranted imperialism exercised by theology. In other words, Patočka aims to refute the claim that philosophy is merely the whipping boy of *sacra doctrina* and to insist that it is, rather, an autonomous critical voice. What is it, then, that separates the two disciplines from one another? Patočka's primary argument against blurring the boundary is methodological: philosophy searches for the truth whereas theology receives it; unlike theology, philosophy does not posit its truth from revelation. For the philosopher, the truth is always disputable and questionable, it is never simply given, as it is for the theologian.

Patočka describes the philosophical method as a conglomerate of three moments: (1) the descriptive, (2) the critical, and (3) the constructive or metaphysical.[10] The first moment concerns immediate sensual experience: phenomena appear and are processed. The second moment unfolds the first: it involves the phenomenon of experience itself and raises the question of how phenomena appear. Finally, in the third moment, philosophy formulates hypotheses concerning the world as a whole, which manifests itself in experience. Patočka is clear, however, that the interpretation of phenomena is more than the examination of experience. Although philosophy cannot proceed without knowledge acquired from concrete historical experience, its aim is to transcend the experiential in order to formulate holistic claims about meaning, truth, the good, and the world—about the whole. Overall, philosophy represents a three-dimensional act of thinking permanently on the way to wisdom that continually escapes full possession because of new appearances.

Theology is different. Patočka illustrates the gap between philosophy and theology with the example of distinct approaches to the idea of God.[11] Philosophically, God can surely be treated as a phenomenon in experience. The idea of a personal transcendent absolute has occupied the human mind from time immemorial. Similar to the critical phase, God functions as the postulate of rational thinking. As such, the idea of God provides the explanation for experience itself. Finally, philosophical reasoning can accept God as either the foundation—the base—or the first principle—above all—that grounds the whole. Although Patočka has difficulty allowing the presence of God into philosophical discourse at all, reference to God is philosophically plausible insofar as the idea of God is used as a concept: "The God of philosophers is entirely different from the God of theologians. Our God is a hypothesis, a datum, and an object. The God of theologians speaks, gives orders, and commands what one has to believe without giving reasons for such belief."[12] The philosopher can accept only a silent God. When God becomes a noetic principle, philosophy betrays its vocation and becomes a quasi-theological travesty. In contrast, for the theologian, God functions as a noetic principle quite legitimately. Interestingly, Patočka associates the notion of "noetic principle" with God as if it were understandable per se and without the need of further explanation. In Patočka's view, the philosopher is forbidden from beginning to think from the perspective of faith, that is, from the presupposition regarding God and his revelation as the grounding and teleological principle of knowledge. This would result in the philosophically irregular adoption of a kind of theological pretension over philosophy. I assume, therefore, that Patočka uses this term for conceptions that conceive God as the possessor of answers before the questions are asked. In this sense, the task of theologians would be to uncover these answers and make them visible. Hence, philosophy can never support theology because the task of philosophical thinking must start from the perspective of the world, that is, from the situation of being-in-the-world.

For Patočka, theology clarifies a world—down here—full of uncertainties while receiving a certain level of knowledge from heaven above. God is present as the possessor and giver of truth. Theology represents the truth too quickly and provides the answer before the question is even asked. The dilemma is resolved for us but without us. For this reason, Patočka states that the philosopher cannot help the theologian. Philosophy is not the handmaiden of theology; philosophy and theology must remain discreet disciplines.

To his statement, "The philosopher knows that he must eternally walk on earth," Patočka adds a question: "But what is the earth? It may be that its peaks touch the stars. It may be that its abysses contain the deepest mystery."[13] The statement is clear. Philosophy continually discloses new problems, new questions. The answers are always formulated in new and unfamiliar sentences that are hopefully without contradictions. Hence, philosophy never reaches the ultimate point. One question that does need to be asked is whether Patočka closes the door on any possibility of the mutual enrichment of philosophy and theology. A follow-up question suggests that philosophy is by no means sealed within the Nietzschean *human, all too human*. Quite the opposite. Philosophy focuses on a number of questions that overlap with theology. These questions concerning "the stars above" and "the deepest mystery within" are, however, approached from a different perspective. But what was it that influenced the young Patočka in his critical point of view regarding the incommensurability of philosophy and theology?

From Heidegger to Patočka

Heidegger insists that theology is a positive science, an argument he developed in his lecture "Phenomenology and Theology," delivered first in Tübingen (1927) and again in Marburg (1928).[14] It is widely held that this essay contains Heidegger's most detailed discussion on the relationship between theology and philosophy.

Heidegger presents the relationship between theology and philosophy as a question of two types of science: the ontic and the ontological.[15] Ontic sciences inquire into entities, objects, things. They are interested in given beings. As such, the ontic sciences have their positive content (*positum*), which makes them, for Heidegger, positive sciences. In contrast, ontological science concerns Being as such.[16] It shifts from the being of entities (*Seiendes*) to Being (*Sein*). Heidegger argues that the only science capable of this task is philosophy (not surprisingly, his own domain). In other words, Heidegger does not formulate the relationship between theology and philosophy in terms of the agreement or disagreement between faith and reason. The question is methodological: What is the relationship between theological and philosophical rationality?

From this perspective, theology necessarily falls into the category of positive science. But what is the *positum* of theology? What being is given for theology? Heidegger answers these questions as follows: "*Presupposing* that theology is enjoined on faith, out of faith, and for faith, and *presupposing* that science is a *freely* performed, conceptual disclosure and objectification, theology is constituted in thematizing faith and that which is disclosed through faith, that which is 'revealed.'"[17] Heidegger draws our attention to theology as a form of conceptual knowledge concerned with revelation accepted in faith: "All theological knowledge is grounded in faith itself, originates out of faith, and leaps back into faith."[18] This suggests that theology has a positive content given by the external agent called God. It was of little importance to Heidegger whether such revelation happened in history. What matters is the idea of believing, and thus of partaking in the disclosed event of Christianity. At the same time, the scientific character of theology must be clarified. Heidegger notes that theology is not objective knowledge of God. It is neither an investigation into the relationship between human beings and God nor an examination of religious experience. Theology as a positive science is a conceptual inquiry into Christian existence.[19] In this sense, theology cannot be compared to the natural positive sciences, although it remains an ontic science of beings and must therefore be distinguished from philosophy as the science of Being. The ultimate purpose of theology, unlike that of philosophy, is the cultivation of faith already disclosed and received through revelation. By contrast, philosophy, and here Heidegger means phenomenology, is not grounded in anything constitutive. For the philosopher, there is no script to be followed. The only concern is the question of Being.

After stating that theology is a positive science that is distinct from other ontic sciences, Heidegger comes to the central question of his 1927/8 lecture. What is the relationship between theology—a positive science—and philosophy? At first sight, Heidegger's position appears resolutely negative: "There is no such thing as a Christian philosophy; that is an absolutely 'square circle.' "[20] Faith does not need philosophy. On the other hand, theology, as the positive science of faith, needs philosophy as "the ontological corrective of the ontic."[21] This means that in order to remain scientific and autonomous, theology uses philosophical concepts that precede the notions deduced from faith—faith being considered a mode of existence in the world and an understanding of the world. Heidegger explains this through the example of guilt and sin.[22] The former is a pre-Christian ontological notion that precedes the Christian concept of sin, which makes sense only in the context of faith. Clearly, theology finds philosophy useful but it is not, Heidegger insists, philosophy. The science of Being is fully autonomous and devoid of faith—and any other *positum*. By implication, Heidegger urges philosophers to accept methodological atheism and not to compromise phenomenology with faith.

Despite the clear-cut division between philosophy and theology presented in Heidegger's lecture, it still seems possible to argue that the divide between phenomenology and theology is not unbridgeable. For example, Matheson Russell reminds us that Heidegger's early works propose a phenomenological analysis of faith,[23] a faith Heidegger recognizes as having two forms: (1) ontotheology and (2) faith in the sense of original or primitive Christianity.[24] Ontotheology conceptualizes God and his revelation as the positive content of Christianity. God is present as the highest being (*causa sui*) that grounds the being of everything. Conversely, being relates to the highest being and deduces its meaning from the ground of being. This is what Heidegger later calls the ontotheological constitution of metaphysics.[25] For theology, the result is a theistic metaphysical faith that (mis)uses philosophical argumentation for its own apologetics. Against this misconception, the philosopher is obliged to protest.

Apart from ontotheology, which has become the mainstream understanding of Christian faith, Heidegger highlights an alternative conception that he considers to be scriptural and therefore more authentic. This can be illustrated by the reference to Saint Paul—who designates philosophy as foolishness—and the subsequent line of thought in Augustine, Luther, and Kierkegaard. What Heidegger finds in these figures can be stated as the shift from God as the object of faith to faith itself. This theology of faith is conscious of the ontotheological burden of Christianity. With this in mind, Heidegger places a boundary between theology and philosophy. The claim for the total emancipation of philosophy from theology must be understood in the context of his case against the God of ontotheology, which is clearly mirrored in his later "Phenomenology and Theology."[26] However, what is true of the positive theological science is not necessarily true of the whole of theology:

> Likewise, the theological transparency and conceptual interpretation of faith cannot found and secure faith in its legitimacy, nor can it in any case make it easier to accept faith and remain constant in faith. Theology can only render faith more difficult, that is, render it more certain that faithfulness cannot be gained through the science of theology, but solely through faith.[27]

True, one can argue that Heidegger's interest is purely phenomenological and inherently nontheological. However, his series of lectures on the *Phenomenology of Religious Life* (1920/1) and the groundbreaking *Being and Time* (1926) constantly recourse to theological matters.[28] In *Phenomenology of Religious Life*, Heidegger outlines the basic experience of human life. The task of philosophy, and particularly of phenomenology, is to cultivate this experience. Interestingly, Heidegger draws inspiration from a Christian way of life that offers protection from a certain type of theological manipulation he calls the positive science of God. Does Heidegger's critique imply a ban on theology altogether? It seems rather that the destruction (*Destruktion*) of positive theology opens the way for *thinking* both theology and philosophy anew. Later, we will see how Patočka's contribution can be helpful in this respect. For Heidegger, the only credible theology is one that seriously considers human concreteness and facticity in the world.[29] In other words, authentic theology is not the science of God and faith but the struggle for everyday existence in authenticity. Hence, the point of Heidegger's critique is undoubtedly a theology that posits faith and renders it as a static content to be believed, that is, adopted by knowledge. This critique does not, however, close the door on another mode of theology that saves the event of faith. And as Heidegger surprisingly proclaims: "Without this theological origin, I would never have arrived at the path of thinking."[30]

It is unlikely that while writing his essay "Theology and Philosophy" Patočka relied directly on Heidegger's "Phenomenology and Theology." Evidence suggests that Heidegger's text was published only in 1969;[31] Patočka did not meet Heidegger until 1933 while studying in Freiburg.

Lack of direct influence notwithstanding, Patočka could have been aware of the early texts in which Heidegger developed his critique of ontotheology. Although Patočka does not cite Heidegger in his polemic with theology, it seems reasonable to conclude that Heidegger's position lies in the background of Patočka's criticism. Heidegger's "Phenomenology and Theology" and Patočka's "Theology and Philosophy" coincide on their main point: that the relationship between these two disciplines is one of confrontation, conflict, and fruitful polemic. Theology and philosophy are indeed distinct domains and it is phenomenology that draws the boundary.

Countertheological Turns

Dominique Janicaud was the author and tireless defender of the statement that theology and phenomenology are two separate domains (*font deux*). Janicaud argued his point in a critical report on the development of French phenomenology, originally delivered at the Collége international de philosophie in Paris and later published under the title *Le tournant théologique de la phénomenologie française* (1991).[32] Janicaud especially targets Emmanuel Levinas, Jean-Luc Marion, Jean-Louis Chrétien, and Michel Henry, pejoratively calling them "new phenomenologists" and accusing them of opening phenomenology to the theological and thus committing a fatal error that has transformed all phenomenological thinking.

Janicaud decries the new phenomenology for the turn from appearances to the unapparent, from intentionality to the given, from the immanent to the transcendent. The original project of phenomenology, understood as the description of phenomena and their essences, is replaced by an inquiry into the essence of phenomenality. For Janicaud, this development, this abandonment of phenomenological reduction and eidetic insight, is a lethal heresy against Husserl's idea of phenomenology.

To use Patočka's vocabulary, the purity of the phenomenological method depends on philosophy remaining "on earth." Or, as Janicaud puts it in his review of the origins of the French debate on the theological turn in phenomenology, "between the unconditional affirmation of Transcendence and the patient interrogation of the visible, the incompatibility cries out; we must choose."³³ Two avenues in phenomenology can therefore be distinguished: "intertwining" and "aplomb."³⁴ Intertwining, represented by Merleau-Ponty and Paul Ricoeur, remains faithful to the immanent principles of phenomenology and thus sits squarely in the field of phenomenological competence.³⁵ Although Merleau-Ponty, for example, introduces the theme of invisibility into phenomenological research, he never detached the invisible from the visible, that is, from phenomena. In short, the visible and the invisible intertwine. In contrast, aplomb admits an absolute invisibility and, in this sense, a nonphenomenological, metaphysical desire: "The dice are loaded and the choices made; faith rises majestically in the background. The reader, confronted by the blade of the absolute, finds him- or herself in the position of a catechumen who has no other choice than to penetrate the holy words and lofty dogmas."³⁶ The new phenomenology and its theological turn could be defined as the introduction of the sovereign Other into phenomenological philosophy. For Janicaud, all the major figures, from Levinas, through Henry, and up to Marion, succumb to this temptation. Their interest is not purely philosophical but quasi-theological. For instance, Levinas's exploration of the Other (*l'Autre*)—though he claims to distinguish his Talmudic interpretations (theology) from his philosophical writings (phenomenology)—is undoubtedly informed by the God of biblical tradition. Janicaud opines that in this way the theological thematic is abruptly revisited in the field of phenomenology and, consequently, the task of philosophical thinking is obliterated. Janicaud seems to formulate his criticism in a manner analogous to that of Patočka's. The notion of God/ the Other/Transcendence rises majestically but illegitimately as a noetic principle of the new phenomenology. Interestingly, Janicaud and Patočka nevertheless part ways when it comes to the cause of the irregular relationship between theology and phenomenology. Whereas Patočka defends his discipline against theological misuse and misinterpretation, Janicaud accuses fellow philosophers of dishonesty.

The person held personally responsible for the heresy of the theological turn against Husserlian orthodoxy is Martin Heidegger,³⁷ the same who influenced Patočka's apology for philosophy. Janicaud suggests that Heidegger's phenomenology of the unapparent is the key source of the theological turn. Moreover, his fight against ontotheology and his later expressions concerning the openness of phenomenology to the "divine" made Heidegger the champion of the new phenomenologists. The end of metaphysics, proclaimed by Heidegger, has become a commonplace among contemporary authors. As a result, phenomenology remains the only plausible method of philosophical thinking that is also applicable to theology as a philosophical propaedeutic. That said, Janicaud raises important questions: Is the coming of a postmetaphysical era as clear as it is presented? Does phenomenology stand in direct and complete opposition to metaphysics?[38]

Janicaud distinguishes two forms of metaphysics: (1) *metaphysica generalis*, the being of beings, and (2) *metaphysica specialis*, the foundation of being. The former refers to philosophy, the latter to theology. Concerning the relationship between these two forms of metaphysics, Janicaud says: "It is evident that if Husserl brackets *metaphysica specialis* and initially dismisses ontology, he does not do the same in regard to *metaphysica generalis*."[39] Perhaps, Janicaud concludes, a genuine phenomenology can be only metaphysical.[40]

To sum up, Janicaud's concern is the methodological purity of phenomenology. Moreover, he suggests that "phenomenology is not all of philosophy. . . . [Phenomenological philosophy] owes its interest and its scope to the respect of its proper rules as well as to the audacity of its breakthroughs."[41] The problem with the theological turn is that it misuses phenomenology and consequently alienates it from the original intentions of its founder. In other words, the damage caused by the theological turn is the loss of a concern for rigor. Janicaud's point is nothing less than a reiteration of the demand of Husserl's "Philosophy as Rigorous Science" (1911).[42] The phenomenological reduction applies to everything without exception, including the idea of God. Only phenomenology, in its Husserlian setting, enables us to avoid both scientific objectivism and speculative metaphysics. Put another way, a methodologically orthodox phenomenology allows a certain intertwining but excludes abrupt intermixing.

Despite this, Janicaud claims that his critique is not antitheological.[43] His goal seems to be to safeguard the autonomy of both theology and phenomenology. In this sense, Janicaud agrees with the early Heidegger, that theology "is a positive knowledge absolutely different from philosophy, inasmuch as its *positum* is Christian faith."[44] Faith holds on to invisible things. Phenomenology cannot but articulate its findings from the perspective of being-in-the-world: "Phenomenology and theology make two (*font deux*)."[45]

FIDES QUAERENS INTELLECTUM

We can now see that Patočka's "Theology and Philosophy" retrieves many of Heidegger's points and precedes the critique formulated by Janicaud some decades later. The boundary between theology and philosophy must be maintained. But Patočka concludes his "apologetic" on a striking note: "*Philosophia ancilla theologiae*—this was never plausible and never will be. In my opinion, the thesis *fides quaerens intellectum* formulated by Saint Anselm is the most accurate refutation of the previous."[46] Philosophy's servitude to theology is resolutely rejected. Surprisingly, however, Patočka uses not a philosophical but a theological proposition to argue his case. Faith that seeks understanding contradicts the reduction of philosophy to being the handmaiden of theology. One plausible reading of this passage in Patočka, despite his being, like Janicaud, a phenomenologist who is defending his discipline, is that he argues, unlike Janicaud, for the possibility of an intertwining between theology and philosophy. Precisely what the relationship between the two disciplines should be, Patočka does not say. Nevertheless, the very fact that Patočka does not close the door completely challenges the theologian to propose an interpretation.

Traditionally, the axiom *fides quaerens intellectum* refers to the unity of theology and philosophy.[47] The unity avoids the extremes of the univocity proposed by theological imperialism and the radical separation traceable in the Enlightenment and in post-Enlightenment modernity and finds an equilibrium between reasoning from the senses and reasoning from faith.[48]

From a theological perspective, theology cannot do without philosophy. If it is not to degenerate into an ideological travesty, faith requires understanding. One example of such overturning is the ontotheology that was until recently very much a part of theological discussions. It seems possible that Patočka's critique is not directed at theology as such but at particular schools of the theological manipulation of philosophy. In contrast to the severest critics of any intertwining of theology and philosophy—Heidegger and Janicaud, for example—Patočka shows that the relationship between philosophy and theology is highly complex. Patočka admits the plausibility of *fides quaerens intellectum* and advises that it is impossible to read such a relationship as an unconditional opposition.

We have therefore concluded that certain elements of Patočka's phenomenology—already detectable in his radical and youthful passion for his discipline—can be interpreted as an opening up to the theological. His position cannot, however, be identified with the theological turn in contemporary phenomenology. It is important to stress that Patočka always formulates his thoughts from the perspective of being-in-the-world. The sense of transcendence and its manifestations is inherently linked to the world we live in. So, whereas Marion, Lacoste, and Henry revived "God-talk" in a postmodern context from a phenomenological perspective, thinkers such as Patočka prepared the way for conceptualizing theology anew, that is, a theology from below, from the midst of our being-in-the-world. The theological turn in French phenomenology resurrected a God who had seemed dead and renewed the status of religion as a privileged philosophical topic, but this may only have been possible because its predecessors went through the dark night of modernity that killed and buried God but did not forget the important task of theological thinking. This cautious distance, but not separation, from theology made it possible to argue that philosophy and theology are indeed two different domains (*font deux*) but that the boundary between the two is porous.

Philosophy: Questioning the Absolute

Patočka unfolds his point of view on philosophy and its relation to theology in a series of essays written in the 1930s and 1940s. The writings are primarily concerned with the vocation of philosophy and should be read as an apology for philosophical thinking in contrast to the failures of other forms of reasoning. To introduce his theme, Patočka offers a strident criticism of the scientific knowledge that emerged in modernity:

> Science replaces the idea of knowing "*the whole*" with the idea of knowing *all there is*; replaces the idea of knowing the world with the idea of knowing the world's contents; the idea of knowing the essence of things with the idea of a formal system of thought about things; the idea of understanding with the idea of research.[49]

Modern science exceeds its competence because it confuses knowledge of the whole—what we might call *holism*—with the knowledge of everything—or *totalism*. Theology, the science of faith, fails in a similar way because: "in place of a transition from the level of existents to somewhere else, [it] posits a primordial, irreducible, and incomprehensible difference between two ontic levels; it posits the transcendent in place of transcendence."[50]

The problem at stake is the confusion of transcendence with a transcendent object. Theology, suggests Patočka, postulates an object that can be epistemologically exhausted by the power of knowledge. In this sense, theology imitates modern science. A second problem, one we have already highlighted, is theology's claim to penetrate an objective reality that grounds meaning and knowledge and to represent the *telos* of all meaning and knowledge.

It is clear that Patočka formulates this criticism in the wake of Heidegger's *Being and Time*. Theology forgets about the ontological difference. Instead of opening up access to the question of Being, theological speculations focus on beings. This suggests that the world of beings is subordinated to the highest being. Everything becomes an object representable in knowledge. God, the world, and human beings become *things* among other things. The task of theology, therefore, is to formulate eternal, unchangeable truth claims about every*thing*. For this reason, says Patočka, theology is a kind of "transcendental oppression."[51]

In contrast, philosophy unties the chains of subordination and reverses the situation. Patočka elaborates on this in the essay "Chapters from Contemporary Philosophy" (1936), which does not, paradoxically, address the philosophical debate of the time, as one would suppose, but raises the difficult question concerning the nature of philosophical endeavor in general.

Patočka meditates on the thesis of Plato and Aristotle that philosophy has a concern for universal and true knowledge. Contradicting these philosophical giants, Patočka suggests that universal truth is neither placed in the external realm (Plato) nor inscribed within nature (Aristotle); philosophy does not unfold the truth already present but challenges the notion of unchanging and constant truth that may become our possession:

> [Philosophy] is a matter of commitment to an uncertain thing. It is the bet on a possibly false and unrealizable hope. The philosopher must be able to remain on somewhat shaky ground throughout his life. He can never completely eradicate his basic decision by some achieved certainties because all achieved certainties are dependent on his philosophical background and on the method by which he approaches the problem of the whole. This method is itself a particular form of his active decision that forms an integral unity with the philosopher.[52]

Two assertions appear paramount in Patočka: philosophy does not pretend to formulate universal and eternally valid objective truths; philosophy, rather, always interprets the world from a certain perspective. I call this the "default position."

What is it that shapes the default position of philosophy? For Patočka, the default position consists of the historical context and the conscious decisions that are elaborated on the basis of experience and rational reflection, but it also consists of the hidden depths of the philosopher him- or herself. It is formed, therefore, by two components that Patočka designates as basic philosophical a priori: the individual-personal, and the socio-contextual;[53] genuine philosophy must take account of both. The historical circumstances—the socio-contextual a priori—form the background against which it is possible to raise, unfold, and understand problems. The individual-personal a priori is complementary and unavoidable but also limited. The limitation is not an obstacle, however, but a necessary condition for realizing that philosophical questions cannot be resolved simply by absolute claims to universal knowledge: "That which is reveals itself only when we have found a suitable subjective attitude to it. Each problem and each solution has its original spiritual climate in which it alone can be unfolded."[54] In sum, the situation of concrete historical conditions, a concrete time and place, and the fact that "I" find myself in this context, shapes the perspective before "I" gaze at phenomena that appear to me. The philosopher is existentially involved in his or her philosophy: "Genuine philosophy can never be understood in isolation from its author. In contrast, science is in its essence anonymous." And, we could add, science stands in contrast to theology, which is dependent upon the object of God: "Philosophy is never like that."[55]

Here, Patočka sounds like a disciple of Nietzsche, who says, "There is *only* a perspective seeing, *only* a perspective knowing."[56] And perspectives relate to the language of seeing, perceiving things. A perspective comes from the encounter with the visual that appears. Thus, Nietzsche also writes: "There are no facts, only interpretations."[57] Although Patočka seems close to this point of view, his position is more nuanced. He does not reject the existence of facts but differentiates between two kinds: the natural and the social. The former group is examined by science, such as when physics observes the motion of cosmic elements and then interprets the results. These results are more or less descriptive without a direct effect on the nature of the discipline itself. Physics thus remains the examination of physical phenomena whose existence is taken for granted. This is not the case with social facts, which for Patočka are unpredictable human realities that simultaneously happen and interpret themselves. The interpretation is hardly neutral, therefore, but rather tied to a default philosophical perspective that is not necessarily explicitly phrased or consciously realized.

The interpreter participates in the interpreted whether or not he or she is aware of it. In other words, Patočka argues, a neutral perspective, the gaze without affection, prejudice, or predisposition—*theória* in the Aristotelian sense—is impossible.[58]

What is philosophy, then? It seems that the correct answer is contained within the question. For Patočka, philosophy maintains the tension between the particular and the universal. The meaning of the particular is a subjective perspective employed in any philosophical reflection. The universal is then a never-ending conflict within philosophy, that is, philosophical polemics that touch on universal knowledge but always from a particular standpoint. As such, philosophical questioning never arrives at the ultimate point. In Patočka's neat summary: "Philosophy is then joyful resignation; recognizing the absolute, yet not absolutely."[59]

The sense of transcendence, reaching the unreachable absolute, could be deemed the common ground where philosophy meets theology, or, from the opposite perspective, to which theology invites philosophy. Patočka presents this point of view in "On the Letter of Timotheus," his response to the Protestant theologian Bohuslav Pospíšil, published in 1946. Here, the tone of Patočka's engagement with the question of the relationship between philosophy and theology is rather different from what we find in the 1929 essay "Theology and Philosophy." Patočka approaches the problem by raising the question of the necessary conditions for cooperation between the two disciplines.[60] He lists three.

First, philosophy can engage with theology if its notion of the absolute does not contradict Christian faith. Which is to say that philosophy cannot postulate an absolute that is conceivable by rational means alone. Second, and formulated in positive terms, philosophy and theology are compatible when the dialogue between the two makes sense. For this to be the case, philosophical terms must elucidate and interpret Christian faith without losing their philosophical autonomy, and philosophy must not be (mis)used for offering "proofs" of faith. Third, the truth of philosophy should not be presented as the final "objective" truth; philosophy therefore contrasts with theology's claims to bear witness to the truth of faith. The question now is: Has Patočka changed his position on theology? Is he proposing an intertwining of the two disciplines? The following suggests an answer:

> It is clear that no philosophy can find support for its arguments in revealed religion. It is also clear that philosophy cannot be

the basis for faith or apologetics. However, the relation between philosophy and theology may be both compatibility and incompatibility. Certain philosophies may have room for faith.[61]

As we have already seen, Patočka rejects *philosophia ancilla theologiae* but leaves the door open for *fides quaerens intellectum*. It seems that he now explains what the latter is all about: philosophy that acknowledges the moments of unknowing within itself is structurally open to theology, which by the same token confesses that no human being is capable of grasping the ultimate truth. The words compatibility and incompatibility then point to the fact that philosophy can by no means consider theology—the science of revealed faith—as the foundation for its argumentation; similarly, theology cannot render any particular philosophy as the foundation of faith. Philosophy and theology are compatible, but distinct.

Reconsidering the Intertwining of Phenomenology and Theology

Twenty years after the publication of "Theology and Philosophy," Patočka returns to the same theme but does not repeat his critique of the subordination of philosophy to theology according to the claim *philosophia ancilla theologiae*. The essay "Hromádka and Philosophy" is Patočka's response to the challenge of philosophy formulated from the perspective of theology.[62]

The main point of departure from "Theology and Philosophy" is a summary of the charges against philosophical reasoning. Philosophy, according to its theological critics, formulates questions and problems concerning the absolute but seems incapable of proposing answers concerning absolute meaning. Patočka takes this objection seriously. Instead of repudiating the criticism, however, he reflects on the importance of Christian faith in the history of Western civilization and suggests that "the spiritual capital of Christianity" reflected in theology is the foundation of thinking. But this is more than the traditional appeal to the cultural and intellectual achievements of Christianity. Many universities, libraries, and galleries perhaps owe their existence to our Christian roots, but Patočka points out something more crucial. For Patočka, Christian thinking—theology—is essentially responsible for understanding meaning as something deeper than "the sum of the angles of the triangle [being] 180 degrees."[63]

In other words, the way we think, and the fact that this way of thinking transcends the objectivity of natural science, is the result of theological thinking, which goes beyond the sensual, measurable, and countable.

Patočka then elaborates on his definition of theology.[64] The default position of theology is faith. It means embracing "divine meaning," which is not, however, entirely penetrable and which cannot be grasped unambiguously. Even for theology, therefore, questions remain open. All attempts to shed light on "the essence of the thing" and to enter the depth of meaning fall short. Faith and reason, or theological thinking and rational reflection, are always in tension:

> The role of the theologian is extremely difficult. Theology is the greatest human thinking. The theologian has nothing solid at hand. What he has, however, is the "criterion" of historical concreteness. It is only in a particular historical situation, in the moment of decision-making concerning the entire direction and meaning of life, that the highest addresses us and requires our resolute answer. But we can only understand the *fact* of being addressed; its *content* can never be fully understandable to us humans. No dogma, no formula, no proposition helps us in this respect, because all of them are only forms that must be filled with specific contents.[65]

Theological thinking does not focus primarily on positive content with the aim of saying that this or that is objective truth. This does not mean that theology cannot claim something to be true. Patočka's aim is to point to the unfinished nature of all theological statements. Theology's primary task is to search for ways of transcendence. How does transcendence intertwine with our concrete situation, that of immanence? This is where the paths of theology and philosophy meet, with the proviso that theology is the most difficult thinking. Philosophy knows about the element of transcendence within a human being and within the world, although it is reluctant to name it concretely. Nonetheless, the question itself removes philosophical reasoning from the immanent point of view.

Now it becomes clear that in Patočka's interpretation, a certain negativity concerning objective thinking is shared by both theology and philosophy. Theology questions transcendence without providing the final word. Philosophy knows about transcendence, but its approach to questioning can make transcendence neither the argument nor the proof.

Philosophy is therefore immanent thinking, but it is by no means indifferent to the transcendent aspect of being. Theology, in turn, is oriented to thinking transcendence, yet always from a concrete situation embedded in immanence:

> Philosophy can certainly not be transformed into the voice of faith. Nevertheless, philosophy must be able to construct, at its utmost boundaries, the possibility of meaning that is not purely human and that transcends human understanding. For this possibility, philosophy must supply thoughts, frameworks, categories. Or, it must show, at least, which ideas are insufficient for this task and why they cannot be used. Indeed, theology always uses philosophical terms, though in a different way from philosophy.[66]

THE *RELIGIO* OF PHENOMENOLOGY

Rocco Gangle and Jason Smick are among the few who make an explicit link between Patočka's phenomenology and the theological turn.[67] Although their interest is primarily theological-political and political-philosophical, they claim that Patočka shares with the theological turn the orientation to what we called earlier "the absolute." According to Gangle and Smick, Patočka develops "the *religio* of phenomenology," which implies an intertwining with the infinite.[68] In other words, they contend that Patočka's phenomenology displays a proximity to theology.

Gangle and Smick find two elements that unite theology and philosophy in Patočka: (1) openness and (2) criticism. Philosophy and theology open new possibilities of understanding and delineate new horizons of experience. For both ways of thinking, the possibility of the unexpected, the alternative, and the new is constantly open and interrupting what is deemed certain, traditional, and accepted as given. The authors remind us that this is, of course, not true of the whole of philosophy and theology. They have in mind "Patočka's praxis of phenomenology," which challenges its contextual opponents of positivism, objectivism, and metaphysical rationalism.[69] By the same token, not all theology can be defined as openness to possibility. If any theology suits the argument of Gangle and Smick, it is the theology that "is this positive valuation of possibility—and the transcendence and freedom that opens humanity to possibility—that in

Patočka's view distinguishes religious and philosophical worlds from other cultural worlds."[70]

The second element that unities phenomenology and theology is criticism, or more precisely, critical thinking. Both ways of thinking declare war on monologist narratives and finite answers. Theology and phenomenology stand in the way of our falling prey to totalizing conceptualizations; they prevent us from becoming possessed spiritually, intellectually, or materially. Gangle and Smick argue that, in Patočka, philosophy emerges from "a shaking of all possessions as well as the certainties of those possessions with respect to the meaning of the world."[71] Similarly, theological thinking fights against "a demonic possession."[72] In this sense, the demonic should be understood in terms not of myth—of fighting ghosts and demons—but of the critique of overwhelming metanarratives that deceitfully shroud the multiple and enigmatic meaning of the world.[73]

This interpretation of Patočka emphasizes the fact that both philosophy and religion, in their genuine forms, call everything into question. Phenomenology stands in contrast to metaphysical objectivism. Religion, reflected by theology, struggles against idolatry. The joint effort of criticizing purportedly universal monolithic stories and exposing hegemonic narratives and thought patterns appears to be another meeting point of the two disciplines. Furthermore, characteristic of both phenomenological philosophy and theological thinking is an openness to transcendence that exceeds monologic possession and, in this sense, entails freedom. In contrast to metaphysics and ontotheology, which attempt to resolve the disturbing nature of the open space of a multiplicity of interpretations and replace it with the univocal, Gangle and Smick find in Patočka a conception of philosophy and religion that is capable of the kind of reflection that leads to self-critical inquiry and consequently to a reevaluation of the status quo.[74] For example, rather than offering them doctrine to be followed, Socrates challenges his listeners. In the case of religion, mysticism provides a constant corrective to doctrinal theology. In short, the tension between questions and answers is crucial, and this is what Gangle and Smick call "the *religio* of phenomenology" in Patočka.

It is clear that the religion about which Gangle and Smick speak should be expressed as "religion," in quotation marks. It is a different "religion" from an orthodox Christian understanding but also from that referred to in the scientific-anthropological study of religions. Gangle and Smick's interpretation of Patočka appears to argue for a particular kind of phenomenological theology. This could be considered heretical by both theology and phenomenology. As the title *Heretical Essays* suggests, Patočka was never troubled by crossing boundaries. But the question must be raised: Does the concept of the *religio* of phenomenology—and phenomenological theology—do justice to Patočka's thoughts on the relationship between theology and philosophy?

Two things appear to be central to this kind of phenomenological theology: criticism, and the desire for truth. We cannot associate "religion" with a system of beliefs and doctrines, with a set of norms. It is rather a mode of critique that deconstructs false gods. Phenomenological theology is a permanent reminder of crisis, that is, of the tension between questions and answers, propositions and objections, the "already" and the "not yet." In short, phenomenological theology is critical thinking.

With regard to the second point, the uniting element of theology and phenomenology is the search for truth. The truth at stake, however, is not reducible to correctness (*adequatio rei et intellectum*). This is not to say that this approach must necessarily be avoided or even discarded as implausible. The content of truth claims is not negligible. On the contrary, the criterion of adequacy is taken into consideration. What must be stressed, however, is that it is not the only criterion. The point is that the theory of adequacy does not—paradoxically—aptly or adequately depict the problem of truth.[75] In this sense, phenomenological theology is not so much concerned with the content of truth claims, at least not most importantly, but with the path that leads to truth claims. This reminds us of the classical theological distinction between *fides qua creditur* and *fides quae creditur*. In other words, there is a difference between *how* we believe and *how* we come to the truth and the conceptual apparatus of *what* is believed or considered to be truth. Once again, phenomenological theology places the two in tension.

As Patočka's views on the relationship between theology and philosophy shifted from harsh criticism to the claim that theology is the most rigorous form of thinking, it is not likely that he would object to phenomenological theology as we have described it. However, to associate any kind of theology with Patočka would create something of a surprise. For some, such an association is unconvincing or even unacceptable.[76] Others admit that Patočka has a particular interest in Christianity but remained faithful to his initial position that rejected any intertwining of phenomenology with theology.[77] Gangle and Smick are not alone, however, in their intuition concerning the religious orientation of Patočka's thoughts. Hagedorn and Evink suggest that religious topics are a constant theme of Patočka's voluminous philosophical output.[78] They find the hints of philosophical-religious or even philosophical-theological reflections in the figure of self-opening and in Patočka's treatment of sacrifice, which is an idea of great theological significance:

> The question of religion never left Patočka. For him, this problem was closely associated with the great theme of his philosophy, that is, the loss of the meaning of life against the background of the modern world. It seems that he continually monitored the theological debates of his day and certainly read the classical Christian thinkers of the past.[79]

Although numerous authors sympathize with a theologizing reading of Patočka's thought, none goes so far as to propose that his phenomenological engagement with theological issues can be interpreted as the religion of phenomenology. There is a common feeling, one I agree with, that Patočka is first and foremost a phenomenologist. Although some of the overlap between phenomenology and recent postmetaphysical theology is striking, it cannot be claimed that Patočka developed a particular kind of phenomenological theology. Whether his thought at least allows for a phenomenological theology, however, is a different question. Perhaps this is the appropriate approach to Patočka in the context of our exploration into the relationship between philosophy and theology.

Philosophy, Theology, and the Task of Thinking

The previous discussion connected Patočka's critical point of view regarding theology with Dominique Janicaud, the French phenomenologist and severe critic of the theological turn. Here, we will introduce both Janicaud and one of the main protagonists of practicing theology phenomenologically, Jean-Yves Lacoste, whose call for a shift *From Theology to Theological Thinking* elucidates the possibilities of Patočka's thought in a theological context.

Lacoste argues that theology and philosophy belong together. That is not to say that they are one (*uno*) but that they form a unity (*unio*). The history of theology and philosophy describes such a mutual intertwining that it is barely possible to draw a clear boundary between the two. Theology and philosophy share one and the same task—the task of thinking.

These two facets—the assertion of porosity and the task of thinking—are what underpin Lacoste's argument.

For Lacoste, philosophy and theology share a common frontier: the *positum* of theology undoubtedly interests philosophy, and philosophical questions are relevant for theology.[80] Premodern, modern, and postmodern epochs all bear witness to such mutual concerns. Whether it be the Church Fathers engaging in dialogue with Greek philosophy, medieval Scholastics learning from Aristotle, modern rationalists turning to God as the grounding pillar or the postulate of their philosophical systems, or recent new phenomenology undergoing a theological turn, philosophy and theology are regularly to be found hand in hand—although they do sometimes attack one another. By the same token, Patočka feels obliged to critically comment on theological writings that concern philosophical questions and also to write on theological issues: transcendence, the absolute, sacrifice. Lacoste reminds us of Heidegger's contention that philosophy is capable of dealing with every question. He notes that for Heidegger, this establishes the main difference between philosophy and theology, as theology is concerned only with the question of God/faith. Nevertheless, Lacoste observes that philosophy—including Heidegger's philosophy—never forgets to ask about that domain that strictly speaking belongs to theology.[81] Is it possible to separate theology and philosophy in Augustine, Thomas Aquinas, Pascal, or Kierkegaard? What is the argument of the philosopher and what belongs to the confession of the theologian? Although some figures of the theological turn—Levinas, Derrida, Henry—claim that they distinguish their philosophy from their theology, most acknowledge the porosity—Chrétien—or admit that they write on the boundary—Marion, Falque. Even those who claim to respect the boundary are not entirely convincing. When interpreting Levinas, Derrida, and others, one can take them as both philosophical minds and authoritative interpreters of theological archives. Patočka's own opinion concerning the nature of philosophy assents to the argument of porosity, "recognizing the absolute, yet not absolutely,"[82] and acknowledges that the axis of philosophical thinking focuses on nature, the community, life, death, and God.[83] It is no accident that Filip Karfík called his book on Patočka *Becoming Infinite through Finitude*.[84]

The link between the task of thinking and philosophy was made by Heidegger, for whom the end of metaphysics challenges philosophy to seek a new beginning. This beginning provokes thinking—a way of thinking defined by Heidegger. For Lacoste, the situation is different. History knows plenty of new beginnings that call for thinking after many ends of metaphysics.[85] Meister Eckhart, John of the Cross, Pascal, and Kierkegaard all attempt to think, and, considering their historical conditions, they do think anew.

But the task of thinking suggests there is still something un-thought. Would theology not be the primary engine of thinking in this respect?[86] Lacoste raises the question, and Patočka seems to point to an answer. First, his *Heretical Essays* represent reflections on "the new beginning" after the end of (modern) metaphysics, which is perhaps not surprising for a disciple of Heidegger. Second, and this is indeed striking, Patočka refers in this context to Christianity as "the un-thought-through" project.[87] This could mean that Christianity must be complemented by some thoughts after the end of metaphysics. Or, and this seems more likely, Christianity manifests the task of thinking, that is, the approximation to the un-thought. If this is so, can we still draw a clear line between theology and philosophy?

Lacoste argues for the prudent abolition of boundaries.[88] Perhaps Heidegger is right, and we are facing a new beginning. The end of onto-theology, as it appears from the perspective of theology, and the end of metaphysics, as philosophy experiences it, set the task of thinking. For Lacoste, however, the new does not have to be entirely novel. The past—tradition—teaches us how to deal with this new task. For Lacoste, this means *vita philosophica et theologica*, that is, thinking that is both theological and philosophical.[89] Lacoste describes this symbiosis at length in the first chapter of his programmatic book. His argument, in short, is built on the difference between *theória* and theory.[90] *Theória* pertains to a contemplation of phenomena that is traditionally common to both philosophy and theology. Theory is the product of the mathematization of nature and the modern rationalism and scientific knowledge that promote calculating reason. The (re)turn to *theória*—and thus the search for meaning instead of deducing and predicting—is a task common to philosophy and theology, and it marks the beginning of thinking. What interests us most in this respect, however, is Patočka's point of view.

Significantly, Patočka describes theology by using the category of thinking. We have seen that he does not hesitate to call theology the most difficult task of thinking. Moreover, in a letter to Josef Souček, the Protestant theologian with whom Patočka enjoyed a lifelong friendship, Patočka writes that our task is "not only to *live* faith but also to *think* it." Yet he continues: "However, to think faith does not mean to conceive it as a mere object; it does not mean to grasp faith psychologically or even moralistically. What is at stake is the extension of faith to the field of thinking."[91]

To think faith, theology needs philosophy and its concepts, notions, findings, and theories. For Patočka, philosophy sets the framework of thinking against the background of particular historical situations. Yet theology participates in thinking on its own, from the perspective of faith embedded in concrete historical conditions. In this sense, Patočka's thought dismantles the sharp boundaries between the two autonomous yet interrelated disciplines. Theology and philosophy are united in their methodological aim—to go beyond static objectivistic thinking—and in their task—to exercise the thinking of that which transcends human being, the world, and finitude. Perhaps not all philosophy and theology share these interests, but phenomenology and theology that is sympathetic to philosophy certainly do.

We have seen that Patočka resolutely claims that philosophers never help theologians. He is clearly reacting to theological recuperations of philosophical questioning, especially in traditional Catholic forms of Aristotelianism via Scholasticism and modern Neo-Thomism.[92] The critique is also applicable to the idea of the separation of philosophy and theology as exercised in modern Protestant theology—especially in its post-Barthian modification. Interestingly, the present debate registers a reverse situation. It is no longer philosophers who are taken on board by theologians but theologians who are asked to help contemporary philosophers to *think* certain ideas: the absolute, transcendence, life, death, and God. The theological classics from the Apostle Paul, Augustine, Meister Eckhart, Teresa of Avila, and other mystics to recent authors such as Hans Urs von Balthasar are common interlocutors of the new phenomenologists who are claimed to be responsible for the theological turn. For example, in his thought-provoking book *Crossing the Rubicon: Exploring the Borderlands of Philosophy and Theology*, Emmanuel Falque argues for the "tiling" of philosophy and theology.[94] He also claims that absolute separation is meaningless and that the philosopher is allowed to think as the theologian and then return to philosophy. The same holds for the theologian, who is welcome to venture into the land of philosophy and then return to his own kin. Reading Patočka in this context, we have finally arrived at the conclusion that his phenomenology and theology are in mutual proximity.

Two points must be emphasized. First, the heart of Patočka's criticism concerning the intertwining of theology and philosophy is not the (im)possibility of such intertwining but the argument that God, from a philosophical perspective, cannot be taken as a noetic principle. It seems that in the 1920s, Patočka had already argued for something we find in the theological turn: God is not an object that grounds being—the principle at the beginning—or that absorbs all beings—the ultimate goal. I argue that Patočka's initially critical point of view can be interpreted as the prefiguring of the theological turn that addresses theological issues after the end of ontotheology and metaphysics. This is not to say anything about the plausibility of such claims. I will closely examine "postmetaphysical conditions," if such exist, in chapter 3. Second, Patočka's elaboration on the vocation of philosophy (phenomenology) and his turn to a critically constructive appreciation of theology suggest that phenomenology and (certain types of) theology are united in their attempt to overcome objectivistic reasoning and to practice thinking. Or, to paraphrase Heidegger, theology both reveals and urges the task of thinking. Taken together, this proximity allows me to suggest that "phenomenology is theology." What seems at first to be something of a scandalous statement in fact suggests a more modest reading of Patočka in contrast to that of Gangle and Smick's *religio* of phenomenology.

As I have previously detailed, phenomenology has an interest in the domain of theology: it considers the phenomena of the absolute, finitude, transcendence, and God. Of course, these phenomena are approached from the perspective of being-in-the-world, and phenomenology never draws a conclusion; phenomena never become objects in possession. In this sense, and perhaps only in this sense, phenomenology is a fundamental theology. Traditionally, fundamental theology thinks about *God* from below. It does not begin with the mystery of revelation but rather with experience, from where it climbs up to the mystery—the revelation of God. The theological turn provides an opportunity to reread and rewrite, as Lacoste would put it, fundamental theology according to the challenges of phenomenology—as *thinking* about God. And as Falque suggests, "we have no other experience of God than the human's."[94]

Yet, phenomenology is not theology in the sense that phenomenology—or any other philosophy—would constitute theology or that theology would constitute phenomenology. Phenomenology cannot, Patočka holds, cross the line and accept orders from God/revelation. Both theology and philosophy follow their respective criteria and aims but constantly influence one another. The major impetus of this influence, however, is the tension that ceaselessly challenges both disciplines to *think* anew and then to think *anew again*.

In short, Janicaud and Lacoste are both correct. Although Patočka did not read either of them, he enhances the fruitful tension between theology and phenomenology, which are united in the task of thinking. It does not surprise us that what is called the theological turn emerged within phenomenology. Nevertheless, before the explicit intertwining of the theological and the philosophical as we see it in the new phenomenologists, thinkers such as Patočka needed to exercise caution and to elaborate on the relationship between philosophy and theology very carefully. *Fides quaerens intellectum* is both an argument against the theological takeover of philosophical discourse and also an open space for the intertwining of theology and philosophy. The theological turn resurrected (the question of) the God who had been pronounced dead. This may only have been possible, however, because its predecessors went through the dark night, when God lay silently in his grave, but kept theological thinking in their minds.

Our engagement with Patočka's early works has demonstrated the deconstruction of *philosophia ancilla theologiae*, but this does not result in the total separation of theology from philosophy. If Patočka rejects the subordination of philosophy to theology—as we find in Catholic Thomism—he is critical to the same extent of the separation between the two—as we find in Protestant dialectic theology. Patočka remains open to thinking along the lines of *fides quaerens intellectum*. Now we see the meaning of Saint Anselm's proposal: theology thinks faith, and to think faith requires philosophical wisdom. Or as Lacoste puts it, theology and philosophy think together without boundaries.[95] Theology is not, any more than philosophy, first and foremost proving, objectifying, clarifying, calculating, predicating, theorizing, analyzing, examining, conceptualizing. It may and does include some of these practices to a certain extent, but not only these. Theology (and philosophy) is thinking. So, are theology and philosophy two separate things (*font deux*)? Yes, they are, but the boundary between the two is so porous in both directions that it is sometimes impossible to recognize where one ends and the other begins.

Chapter 2

Sola ratione?

On the Spiritual Crisis of Modernity

What is modernity? Interpretations of the origin, meaning, and evaluation of modernity are riddled with ambiguity and equivocity; comprehensive, watertight definitions are difficult to come by. To paraphrase Aristotle, modernity is said in many ways. Jan Patočka is well aware of the complexities of approaching the question of modernity and for this reason hesitates to propose clear and distinct explanations. The struggle with modern ideas and modes of thinking is a constant adagio of Patočka's thought. His life's work could be considered one great volume on the problem of modernity—a volume he never wrote. Perhaps the impossibility of covering the whole story unambiguously is what prevented Patočka from completing this task. His vast oeuvre does, however, consider diverse perspectives on the matter and make plain the multiplicity and problematicity of modernity.

In everyday language, the word *modern* is generally deemed to be something entirely positive. We speak of modern culture, modern literature, modern music, modern art. In science and scholarship, we think of being up to date, of generating the most recent findings by using the most recent methods. We expect doctors to treat us with modern medicine. Modern means of communication and transportation are taken for granted. We rely on modern trends in all areas of life because we want to be modern. Who wouldn't? Modern people are not laggards. They have their finger on the pulse of the present moment. Opposite the modern is the traditional, the archaic, the outmoded. From this perspective, modernity refers to a period of paradigm change, progress, and emancipation from the old bonds of religion, aristocratic governments (ancien régime), and dogmatic thought patterns such as metaphysics. This process consists in the development of the natural sciences, the establishment of a new political order, and secularization. In short, modernity fundamentally changes human life.

Historians argue about the origins of modernity. Some situate its beginnings in the Enlightenment; others think of the Reformation or even the Renaissance. Chronological mappings are diverse. We can differentiate between "Early Modernity," "Enlightenment Modernity," "Late Modernity," and perhaps even "Postmodernity" as a radicalized version of modernity, or as the epoch that substituted, deconstructed, and transformed modernity. One way or another, the term signifies a plurality of ideas and ideals, beliefs and convictions. Among modern ideas we could mention the autonomy of the freethinking human subject, the expectant development of society into a fully rational civilization, and the belief in the unlimited possibilities of human reason, and therefore in the almost omnipotent powers of *modern* humans. Modernity brings a new kind of universality, ultimate solutions, and the totality of knowledge. The position we take in relation to the modern is thus often the same as the position we take in relation to ideological standards. Nonetheless, between full rejection and naive acceptance runs the gamut of possibilities. The common feature is a critical point of view, so it is not surprising that despite the bright future promised by the modern project, most influential interpretations of modernity operate with the notion of crisis.

The aim of this chapter is to interpret the relationship between crisis and modernity in Patočka's thought. Proclamations of crisis have been proposed from early accounts of modernity up to the present day.[1] When we read Marx, Nietzsche, or Freud, we sense that the phenomenon of crisis is pivotal to their respective reflections on the modern ethos, although not all of them name their observations the *crisis of modernity*. The first to actually point out the situation of modernity as one of crisis is the French philosopher and poet Paul Valéry. His essay *La crise de l'espirt* published in 1919 offers a noticeable diagnosis of modernity in terms of spiritual crisis.[2] Husserl, who is among the first to extensively question the state of modernity philosophically, follows a similar track. In *The Crisis of European Sciences and Transcendental Phenomenology* (1936), Husserl raises a question that troubles us even today: What happened in modernity and how did it change us? Despite the indisputable progress of humankind, we ask ourselves whether the other side of the coin is not a serious crisis of human identity. As one of the last students of Husserl,

Patočka elaborates on the question raised by his teacher and develops his own perspective, suggesting that it is not only a question from the past we are dealing with but one that is highly pertinent to the present day.

What is crisis? The original meaning of the Greek verb *krinein* is to judge or to decide. Thus, *krisis* is a decisive moment, a time of judging and distinguishing possibilities, and, finally, deciding. The hour of crisis yields a titanic struggle because the world does not appear in black and white. Crisis is both a threat we fear and an opportunity we can render fruitful. As a result, crisis can both lead toward a rupture with the past and open the way to an entirely new future. Alternatively, crisis can strengthen previously held positions and find them to be correct. One way or another, crisis is not something we deliberately choose. Rather, we find ourselves in crisis. Heidegger is stronger: we are thrown into crisis.

For Patočka, crisis inherently belongs to the dynamic aspect of human life.[3] Awareness of crisis reminds us that we are not gods high up on Olympus, detached from the happenings of the world; we are not omnipotent observers but active players. We are always on our way in the world.[4] It is against such a background that Patočka reflects on modernity and its outcomes.

Patočka observes the modern development of humankind through the prism of a reconfigured idea of reason. On the one hand, this opens a positive crisis of rationality, which can be understood as the appearance of critical thinking and is filled with a number of enlightening possibilities. On the other, Patočka meditates on the demonic in modern reason, which manifests in war, totalitarianism, and the machinery of violence. The fact that people find themselves in the midst of impersonal powers that drive their lives—even though a widespread narrative claims that they live in the Age of Reason—indicates a serious crisis that conditions not only the personal lives of individuals but also those of the community, of society, and of all humanity. For Patočka, therefore, the crisis of modernity is a fundamental challenge from which there is no escape. To understand modernity is to understand our present crises.

In this chapter, I will examine the issue layer by layer and look for the core of modernity and for what it is that lies behind the modern crisis. First, I will address the development of reason and the paradigm shifts of modern thinking in Patočka's interpretation. Second, I will turn to four great modern philosophers who represent important sources of inspiration for Patočka in his own reading of modernity and its crisis. I will then focus on modernity from a cultural perspective and propose a close reading of Patočka's *La surcivilisation et son conflict interne*, written in the 1950s but published only decades after his death. Finally, I will address modernity as a spiritual crisis and attempt to point out possible ways it may be overcome, if any such ways exist. The hypothesis behind this inquiry is that Patočka's thinking offers a constructive engagement with modernity and in a sense points toward something we could call postmodernity.

The Modern Project of Reason

For Patočka, modernity is a mosaic of heterogeneous factors, ideas, and concepts. To draw a unified line of modern thought would be an impertinent reduction. Thus, to engage with modernity means to enter a discussion with a set of diverse projects based on certain regulative ideas. These projects are often translated and described in common language as *-isms*. The title of Patočka's "Humanism, Positivism, Nihilism, and Their Overcoming" summarizes some of these from a philosophical perspective.[5] Elsewhere, Patočka lists other examples: subjectivism, objectivism, metaphysical dogmatism, Romanticism, Cartesianism, idealism, Titanism, Neo-Thomism. Of course, this list is not exhaustive and can be complemented with other projects—other *-isms*—from the sociopolitical realm such as capitalism, socialism, liberalism, or with the religious systems of Catholicism and Protestantism that have accommodated themselves to modern standards. Given such a litany of *-isms*, it sounds increasingly as though modernity is not only a heterogeneous phenomenon but also an arena full of contradictions, conflicts, and competing narratives. Patočka suggests, nonetheless, that it is possible to draw a line to a single unifying project behind the internal plurality of modernity: *the project of reason*.

Modernity changes the paradigm. For Patočka, it all began with the Renaissance,[6] which shifted the human being from the periphery to the center of thinking. It was only the seventeenth-century Enlightenment, however, that established the concept of rationalism as the determining social factor.[7] Here, Descartes's philosophy caused a revolution and established a discontinuity with the preceding tradition. Cartesianism redrew the map of thinking and consequently the map of nature as it introduced a completely new perspective on how to perceive things. Reason emancipated itself from its religious grounding and became an abstract *ratio* based on experiments, observations, and facts. These were the roots of the nineteenth-century radicalization of rationalism that subsequently led to the conception of technical reason, objectivism, and science as technique. Looking from the other side, modern developments generated the discovery of the subject. The subjectivist perspective challenged the categories of meaning, truth, and the good and questioned what in previous eras had been deemed entirely unquestionable. All this happened against a background of the struggle for emancipation from metaphysics and its speculative reasoning.

Modernity presents itself as the Age of Reason and as bringing in a scientific revolution for the sake of human flourishing. Optimistic rational modernity also, however, led to the agony of wars and conflicts and to the creation of an unprecedented machinery of violence. Understanding what happened in modernity is the *sine qua non* of understanding not only the recent past but also the present.

Husserl argues that science alienated itself from its rigorous foundation and in modernity went down the misleading path of objectivism.[8] Heidegger suggests that the progress of science altered our perspective on the essence of "what a thing is" and "what is" in general.[9] It seems that these (r)evolutions of rationality have far-reaching consequences. Patočka considers both authors and their insights while narrating his own version of the story of modern reason and the crisis of modernity. In what follows, I will present Patočka's interpretation of the modern project, which puts forward the thesis that ultimately the crisis of modernity and the crisis of reason are one and the same thing.

A Reconfigured Idea of Reason

Patočka classifies modernity as a particular mode of thinking based on a reconfigured idea of reason:

> What is reason? This is a question invented by that age [modernity]. All earlier ages had thought that they knew what reason is, and though there had been skeptics who doubted man's capacity to grasp the truth, such skepticism always expressed doubt only as to whether man is truly a rational being, rather than doubt concerning the conception of reason itself as the direct organ of seeing and articulating the truth.[10]

The preceding historical epochs were based on the conception of speculative reason, drawn from the metaphysics of Plato and Aristotle and their respective notions of being. Both philosophers understood the world as an eternal harmonious Universe—as the One. Reason participates in this *Unum* and explores its *Logos*, principles, causal laws, and eternal ideas, in short, the truth. The Christian conception, following the Platonic and Aristotelian rationale, understands reason as the participation in divine reason, the divine *Logos*, the origin of all things—God himself. In one way or another, reasoning is a contemplative *theória*. This means an essentially ahistorical endeavor that pertains to what is eternal and unchangeable because, it is assumed, what is eternal and unchangeable is true. Philosophy and science form a unified knowledge, one and the same rationality that explains the truth of the whole. This premodern conception presupposes the unity of beings derived from the highest being, whether that be a god or a set of eternal ideas. Modernity challenged this idea of reason with an entirely different conception; philosophy and science (and also theology) parted ways and a completely new idea of reason was born:

> In the seventeenth century, however, an entirely different conception of reason became prevalent . . . one for which what is basic is not what is one and harmonious but rather what is clear and distinct. . . . Only now "objective reason" is born, seeking only a simple reconstruction of reality according to its own means, given once and for all. Unity, harmony, integrity cease to be the goals of knowledge and the marks of truth.[11]

The key difference lies in the change of emphasis. The main interest of rational reflection is not participation in the One and its eternal forms. The modern mind looks for objective knowledge—*clear and distinct*—in a world of observed facts. The method of acquiring correct knowledge is not contemplation or intellectual insight into the whole but objective science. The founding fathers of this reconfigured conception of reason are René Descartes and Galileo Galilei.

Galileo announces the end of the ancient cosmos.[12] He is convinced that his mathematical method makes things clearer and more explicable. The change he brought is then reflected in Descartes's philosophy, which sets the course of the following centuries. Descartes's distinction between *res extensa*—the mathematically conceived primary domain of knowledge—and *res cogitans*—a mental substance—is not only a shift of paradigm but a rupture with the preceding tradition, which prepares the way for the mathematization of nature and the conception of human being as the owner and master of all knowledge.[13] Patočka traces the tendencies of mathematization from ancient Greek philosophy but interprets this ancient endeavor as a break with mythical thinking based on givens, on certainties. The philosophical science of the ancient world is the origin of questioning that emerged from the wonder of what-is. In Patočka's opinion, modern Cartesian mathematization is something different:

> Thus, while the Greeks managed to establish islands of rational thought—capable of accounting for one of its regions—amid a sea of naively presented reality, modern thought laid claim to an entire landmass of rationality and sought to found one single whole of unified knowledge, embracing all without exception.[14]

Contrary to popular belief, the difference between ancient and modern science is not therefore a simple opposition between concepts and facts. The key difference is the *manner* in which concepts and facts are treated.[15] It is the idea of a world presented as *res extensa* that paves the way for the final takeover of the rational objectivism that prevails in the modern ethos. Patočka illustrates this with the example of the gradual objectification of nature:

> Modern thinking undermined the medieval system entirely from scratch and brought a completely new way of understanding nature. Now nature is observed and construed but not assessed. All moral and aesthetic considerations are put aside. The only decisive thing is the certainty, completeness, and accuracy of observation. Mathematics stepped out from its episodic role . . . and became "the language of the book of nature."[16]

The world is a thing that can be grasped. This is something radically new. For the Greeks and medieval thinkers, the world is not an object, a thing present at hand, but rather the whole where things appear.[17] Reason can participate in the whole in two senses. First, by means of analogy that mirrors the truth. Second, by means of wonder at the fact that it all could be otherwise. Patočka says, "that is how the concept of reason and understanding had been understood for a thousand years . . . reason was essentially a speculative reason, the seeker of unity, analogy, and harmony."[18] This ends with the rise of modernity.

Cartesianism argues for the supreme authority of the objective reason of the natural sciences, especially mathematics and geometry.

Husserl shows that modern scientific rationalism turns the world into an idealized unit full of causal relations and causal laws.[19] In Patočka's reading, this absolute formalization of all reality is the core of the crisis identified by the founder of phenomenology.[20] Heidegger refers to this outcome of modernity as the mathematical projection.[21] In his opinion, *the mathematical* has become "the fundamental presupposition of the knowledge of things."[22] The assumption behind this reconfiguration of reason is that everything—*every-thing*—can be converted to numbers that can subsequently be mastered by calculation.[23] The modern project of scientific rationalism, "a uniformity of all bodies . . . requires a universal uniform measure as an essential determinant of things, that is, numerical measurement."[24]

To summarize, once nature is understood in mathematical and mechanistic terms, the same fate soon befalls human beings. Although human beings are considered the masters of nature, they become part of the world of objects and are objects in themselves. Modernity challenges and subsequently changes not only the understanding of reason but also the self-understanding of human being. Although embedded in human beings as the capacity that distinguishes them from animals (Descartes), reason is taken as an objective impersonal force that rules over *everything*. We see, therefore, that the ambition of modernity—the Age of Reason—is to replace contemplative speculations about Being as One and its hierarchy (*theória*) with one reason as an objective examiner of beings (*theory*).

The Rise of Scientific Reason

The modern project of rational objective thinking influences the shape of modern culture, and its consequences are visible in the everyday life of modern society. The most obvious change is that science takes the lead and becomes the privileged arbiter of "what is" and "what truth is." Coincident with the emancipation of the scientific reason of the Enlightenment, religion withdraws from its traditional position and ceases to be a formative element and the guarantor of identity. This is the process known as secularization.

Arguably, modern secularization does not result in the complete elimination of religion. Nevertheless, authority in and control over the public domain is possessed and exercised by different agents. The preference is given to science and its canon of univocal objective knowledge:

> One of the main components of [modern] capital ideas can be identified by the words *science* and *scientism*. A science arises here no longer as a philosophy, that is, not as shaking the naive confidence that being is directly accessible and meaningful and as an attempt to restore that confidence and meaningfulness, but rather as an effective knowledge that intends to be guided solely by what is and to let mere objectivity dictate its theses, come what may. Gradually, science also becomes a specialized mode of knowing, one which applies that tried and proved formal schema of objectivity to ever-new regions of being and new aspects of experience.[25]

Patočka points out several characteristics and outcomes of objective scientific reason: (1) scientific reason pursues universal formalizations using abstract mathematical and linguistic schemas as means of expression; (2) knowledge is deemed effective and only what is effective is deemed knowledge; (3) science is a specialized knowledge and systematic expertise that suppresses other forms of knowledge; and (4) the humanities are legitimate sciences only if they are based on observed measurable facts, or, where nothing measurable is accessible, on critically and presumably objectively reconstructed reality.[26]

Having said that, Patočka stresses that the rise of scientific reason is not utterly negative. Medicine, as a technical science par excellence, is one of the greatest successes of objective reasoning.[27] Patočka also thinks of the introduction of critique to all possible realms of human knowledge, from biblical criticism to the critique of criticism itself.[28] What had always been deemed solid and unquestionable is suddenly now challenged. Human life is exposed to questions and problems raised from new perspectives. The rise of scientific reason seems like a *kairos*, a blessed time for humanity. Nevertheless, the modern mind is not patient, and instead of dwelling in problematicity and seeking new questions for the sake of deeper knowledge, it rushes to substitute old riddles with new certainties.

Let us take the example of biblical criticism to illustrate the fact that scientific—critical—reasoning can be a good servant but a terrible master. Certainly, the historical-critical method in biblical studies is an invitation to study the historical context in which a biblical text originated. In this respect, theology finds a great number of elucidating findings that help us to better understand the content and its context. But if biblical criticism postulates conclusions based on a formally reconstructed—fictional—text according to artificially created rules, then this science of the Bible becomes the perfect example of formalization. For example, the notion of *lectio difficilior potior*, one of the main principles of textual criticism in biblical studies, suggests that the original reading of a particular text is the one that seems to be the more unusual. In other words, the difficult reading is the more plausible. On this basis, a manuscript is evaluated and later published in what is deemed to be its original version. The question is why the application of the rule of the more unusual reading is more scientific than the opposite.

Kohák summarizes Patočka's point as follows: "The new conception of the universe and of man's place therein replaced the idea of God with that of nature, and reason as the ability to grasp the *ratio* of the whole with reason as the ability to perceive, clearly and distinctly, particulars and their association."[29] The notion of clear and distinct reasoning is a crucial problem of modernity that brings us back to Descartes and his famous proposition *cogito ergo sum*, where all enlightening brightness and obscuring darkness begin. Patočka explains the manifold importance of Descartes's creed, interpreting it as the argument for the fundamental certitude of the modern subject and simultaneously as the foundation of objective rationalism.[30]

Cogito ergo sum is a foundational assumption for conceiving truth as corresponding to certitude. This change of perspective, which begins as a hypothesis and ends as a prerequisite, alters the quest for truth and the questioning of truth in a decisive way: certitude defines truth and the truth is defined by certitude.

Modernity, as we have already noted, is a conglomeration of heterogeneous projects and ideas in which Cartesianism gradually became the leading force. The rise of scientific reason, which Husserl later identifies as *crisis* and Heidegger describes as the techno-scientific rationalism of modernity, took place against a background of other forms of modern rationality. Patočka reminds us of these tensions and inner conflicts in order to preserve fruitful polemic as a positive side of modernity.

Two Senses of Reason

Patočka outlines two senses of reason in modernity:[31] Enlightenment rationalism and Romanticism. The first line of reasoning equates to the objective sciences of mathematics, logic, and geometry; the second line retrieves the idea of harmonious nature and the idea of the whole. There are a number of important differences between the two, but most important for Patočka is their distinctive and competing picture of the world.

Enlightenment rationalism conceptualizes nature as a system. In line with the Cartesian worldview of *clare et distincte*, all propositions about reality must be objective and scientific, calculable and predictable. The world is fragmented, and questions are turned into equations. In comparison to the rational ideal of premodern times, *theória*—insight into everything that is—is replaced by *theory*—the explanation of everything that is.

Romanticism, on the other hand, restores the conception of universal harmony and thus the sense of the whole. Although this seems to suggest a return to the intuitions of premodern rationalities, this is not the case. As Patočka notes, the mystical rationalism of Romanticism and its *Naturphilosophie* originates from the changed conditions of modernity. In other words, the Romantic seeking of harmonious unity is in fact rooted in the ideal of modern scientific knowledge rather than in an appeal to the ancient tradition of reason.

Romanticism and Enlightenment rationalism generally take place in the same environment, however, so there are a number of similarities between the two. For Patočka, the most obvious and interesting of these is their struggle against a common enemy: the metaphysics of Christianity.[32]

In the context of Enlightenment rationalism, Patočka uses Kant to illustrate this antagonism. Kant develops a critique of metaphysics and proposes a religion within the limits of bare reason. For Kant, Enlightened reason is the key difference between God and human beings. Kant situates reason on the side of the latter, not on the side of God, who is identical with being and does not need to reflect on "what-is." It is not possible, therefore, to talk about God because God is an inaccessible transcendental idea. Practical reason needs God only as a somewhat passive guarantee of moral order, but it is always reason that reveals the content of morality. Mainstream Enlightenment rationalism finds satisfaction in the removal of the sacred canopy from the world and thus in the formulation of a new understanding of nature based on facts, experiments, objectivity, and technical reason without intervention from the extramundane realm.

For Patočka, Herder provides the clearest example of Romanticism. As a modern thinker, Herder accepts the Newtonian point of view but takes it not as objective law but as the ground of universal harmony.[33] The ultimate goal of Romanticism is to unfold the unity, analogy, harmony, and correspondence of particulars and the whole. In this sense, nature is the divine in Romanticism; the sense of reason in Romanticism is not sober but poetic.

Patočka argues that the tension between the two strains of modern reason is something to be valued and preserved as the heritage of modernity. The modern trust in the abilities of reason is without doubt the overriding evolution that results in numerous positive developments, such as the aforementioned development of sciences. Furthermore, the fact that reason becomes a question in modernity is an opportunity and a challenge that must be taken seriously. However, although Romanticism is itself embedded in modernity, it expresses a major critique with regard to the limitations that are intrinsic to Enlightenment reasoning.

The problem Patočka finds with both senses of reason is their tendency to overrule one another. Enlightenment rationalism evolves into technical reason and overweening objectivism; Romanticism represents a highly questionable attempt to draw holistic conclusions from the fusion of modern natural science and modern mysticism. Neither conception of reason is successful in addressing the most important question regarding human being; both forget what Heidegger would later call the question of being.[34]

For Patočka, the mutual tension between the two senses is capable of opening a space for the questioning of being, not simply asking questions about beings. Once again, we see that Patočka's critique of modernity is not antimodern but embodies the dialogue between different senses of modern rationality.[35] Patočka is much more concerned, however, about late modernity and what he sees as its tragic outworkings.

Closed Reason

Enlightenment rationalism takes the lead in late modernity; reason becomes scientific objective reason. It is worth quoting at length from Patočka's explanation of this process:

> Science becomes a *technē*, the technique of a precise calculation of nature, which would not be bad in itself were it done fully consciously—if humans were aware, at each step, of just what they are doing, cloaking the primordially given world, subjective and unprecise, in an ideational garb that transposes it into a precise universe of truths for all and so makes it calculable. The erroneous impression that we are thereby also reaching

the truth and ultimate true being in itself arises because the fundamental tools of rationality—mathematical concepts and theories—were from the start of this process of rationalization taken over from an unquestioned tradition, technically evaluated, while the question of their meaning and origin remained forgotten.[36]

In Patočka's reading, this is the crisis of modernity: rationality is closed in on itself. Drawing on the early modern thinker Jan Amos Comenius,[37] a Protestant theologian and bishop but also a philosopher and a contemporary of Descartes, Patočka elaborates on the crisis of Enlightenment rationality, which evolved into techno-scientific reason, in terms of the opposition between the open soul and the closed soul.[38]

In Patočka's terminology, modern reason is an expression of the closed soul. As noted in the preceding extract, the borders of modern rationalism are clearly delineated. This implies that there is no place for others, the Other with a capital "O," or the otherwise. What does this mean? First, the closed reason of modernity neutralizes what comes from outside and rephrases it according to its own standards and methods. Following Newton and Galileo, the privileged methods are mathematics and geometry: everything is transformed into numbers, calculable equations, and manageable problems. We are reminded of Leibniz's exclamation: "Let us calculate!"

Second, modern reason excludes the Other that would escape objectification. Even God, if there is a place for God, is the object of *clear and distinct* knowledge. True, Descartes accounts for God in his philosophical system, and despite all the objections modern reason can raise against theism, Cartesianism does not surrender its adherence to God. But what kind of God do we encounter here? For Descartes, God is necessary as the guarantee of his philosophical system, but he is hardly the Other beyond objectification.

Third, modern scientific reason does not allow us to think the otherwise. Reason works with concepts and theories, and what is not translatable into these two cornerstones of rational thought is considered irrational and therefore not worthy of interest. Modern scientific reason rules out the very possibility of thinking differently. In this sense, it seems to me that Patočka points out that modern reason is closed in on itself and falls prey to a blind belief in technique, science, and objective rationality as the only access to truth—objective truth.

In contrast to modern rationalism, the open soul, or open reason, does not dwell in such givens and self-certainty concerning its mission. The aim of open reason is the search for wisdom (*sapientia*), and wisdom for Patočka is something more than the power of arguments based on experiments and calculations. Patočka uses art to illustrate the sapiential character of open rationality.[39] Art constantly offers new images in order to respond to phenomena but never reaches an end with the answers it offers. Looking with an open mind at a piece of art can reveal new dimensions and enrich the viewer's grasp of certain aspects of wisdom, exposing him or her to the subtle polyphony of sensory excitation.[40] In contrast, closed rationality never finds the ardor or the touch of wisdom in the contemplation of paintings, in the recitation of poetry, in the strains of music, because it is blinkered by its clear criteria that decide what is worth seeing and what is supposed to be seen.

To switch from the domain of art to the field of philosophy, the opposition between open and closed rationalities can be rephrased as the opposition between the insight of *theória* and the explanations of scientific theory. The former can incorporate the latter, but the latter must exclude the former. Again, for Patočka, the crisis of modernity lies in this closure to any form of rationality besides techno-scientific objectivism.

Interestingly, the current so-called postmodern critique of modernity formulates something similar. Modernity is considered a closed rationalism, so philosophy looks for alternative, more open-thinking structures. The break with closed rationalism is found in the turn to religion and its thought patterns. By the same token, Patočka realizes the importance of Christianity and Christian thinking for dealing with the crisis of modernity and its rational culture. Religion breaks with the modern enclosure precisely because it allows the others, the otherwise, and, last but not least, the Other to enter the discussion.

I suggest that Patočka's critique of modernity significantly precedes the recent turn to religion and thus opens the way to the theological turn. However, before examining the relationship between modern rationalism and Christianity, I will explore the other principal sources of inspiration for Patočka's critical account of modernity.

Four Figures of Crisis

This section will examine the relationship between crisis and modernity against a background of Patočka's reading of four key figures in modern philosophy: Tomáš G. Masaryk, Friedrich Nietzsche, Edmund Husserl, and Martin Heidegger.[41] All four formulate theses on the crisis of modernity, but each is associated with a different image of such crisis. Masaryk and Husserl place the origins of crisis at the beginnings of modern thought; Nietzsche and Heidegger consider the situation of advanced modernity. Here I will focus on the features most typically associated with each of these critics of modernity: subjectivism and religion (Masaryk), the death of God and nihilism (Nietzsche), the crisis of reason and the problem of objectivity (Husserl), and the problem of techno-scientific rationalism (Heidegger).

Masaryk on Subjectivism and the Crisis of Religion

Tomáš Garrigue Masaryk is best known as president of the "First Republic" of Czechoslovakia after the First World War. His political career, however, was preceded by a successful academic career in the fields of philosophy and sociology. Patočka is interested in Masaryk the philosopher for at least two reasons. First, Masaryk is a thinker who analyzes the modern mind and the changes of paradigms and anticipates the development of modern culture. Second, Masaryk's political and state-forming work was rooted in his philosophical and sociological analysis. In consequence, the (re-)creation of the Czechoslovak state was not merely a political act based on diplomatic endeavors and participation in the technocratic apparatus but a momentous philosophical act rooted in profound rational reflection.[42] The intellectual informs the political—an uncommon development indeed.

Masaryk studied philosophy under Franz Brentano in Vienna, where he also met Edmund Husserl, Patočka's later teacher, who also studied under Brentano. No wonder Patočka elaborates on both these thinkers, whom he considered two different incarnations of the modern spirit.[43] Patočka respects Masaryk, reads him sympathetically, and defends him against his critics,[44] but he often finds himself uneasy with Masaryk's philosophical conclusions and positions, and his attitude to the father of the Czechoslovak nation changes down the years against a background of changing historical circumstances. For example, Kohák argues that for a long time Patočka inclined toward Masaryk's optimistic vision of the humanistic-democratic development of Europe and its political context. After the Second World War, however, Patočka turned to a more Nietzschean and Heideggerian position, characterized by the search for "Europe after Europe" and Christianity after (the end of) Christianity.[45] Regardless of these changes, Masaryk and Patočka always diverged sharply in one respect: their conception of the modern crisis.

Masaryk localizes the crisis of modernity in the crisis of religion. For Masaryk, religion embraces the whole of human life and society. Religion is an integrative element and the foundation of moral order and ethics. Undoubtedly, Masaryk relies here on Friedrich Schleiermacher and Immanuel Kant, from whom he also draws inspiration for his own definition of religion: "Religion is a life *sub specie aeternitatis*—it is a conscious relation to the world, it is the realization of the meaning of life, it is trueness."[46]

Masaryk's religion, via Schleiermacher, is a feeling of dependence on the divine and on effective providence. This position is balanced, via Kant, by the suggestion that religion provides us with a rational and practical orientation in life. Dogmas and liturgical celebrations are put aside in order to open a space for piety, love of one's neighbor, and the hope that overcomes fear.[47] In fact, Masaryk left the Roman Catholic Church to become a Protestant as he felt the hierarchical nature of Catholicism suppressed those elements of religion that were rational and oriented to the practical life. Masaryk embraced the key principles of the liberal theology of the beginning of the twentieth century—with the exception of subjectivism. Masaryk's religion is objectivistic and authoritarian. Although Patočka differentiates the subjective and objective components in Masaryk's concept of religion, the subjective stands only for the obligation of human beings to respond to the objective Providence.[48] For Masaryk, theism is objective, and its objectivity preserves order, which means religion embodies the important practical purpose of maintaining the stability of society; the loss of religiosity poses a great danger. Who is speaking here? A philosopher or a statesman? One way or another, for Masaryk, the crisis of modernity is the crisis of religion.

Modern subjectivism undermines the position of religion and consequently the solidity of modern society, which is what Masaryk seeks to show in his *Habilitationsschrift* on suicide.[49] He observes the increased number of suicides in modern society and asks why this is happening in the progressive conditions of modernity, characterized by the significant development of humanity and all its possibilities. After a sociological analysis of the changes that have taken place in modernity, he finds the reason for the higher suicide rate in the decline of piety and the crisis of religion. Without the presence of eternity and God's providence, humanity loses its sense of meaning and sinks into skepticism. The point Masaryk is making is to emphasize the importance of religion.[50] Shall we thus unfold the sacred canopy above modern humanity and overcome the crisis?

Of course, Masaryk's modern mind by no means suggests a return to traditional religiosity. Quite the contrary. Masaryk proves himself to be a modern thinker par excellence, drawing inspiration from Comte's positivism and American pragmatism. The theological and metaphysical stages have been overcome once and for all. The break with Catholicism and the emphasis on the scientific study of society symbolize these steps in Masaryk's life and work. In fact, Masaryk substitutes the three phases of positivism with a philosophy of two stages: the uncritical-authoritarian and the critical-empirical.[51] Traditional dogmatic theology, speculative metaphysics, and theocracy, combined with feudalism on the political level, are the emblems of the former; philosophy, critical-empirical science, and democracy are the key attributes of the latter. Notwithstanding, the critical stage reckons with religion.

The religion of Masaryk is religion within the limits of bare reason. Such religion provides a moral code of life, sets boundaries and moral rules, and offers guidance for modern human beings. The crisis of religion is therefore the loss of a certain *savoir-vivre*, the art of life, as a result of modern subjectivism. Even worse, subjectivism gives birth to Titanism, the modern belief in the almost unlimited possibilities of human beings—the *Übermensch*.[52] Thus, Masaryk says, society based on the subjectivist creed—society without religion—sooner or later falls into nihilism. Nietzsche's philosophy could serve as a red flag in this respect.

Patočka suggests that Masaryk's evaluation of subjectivism is one-sided, however. Subjectivism can be understood in many ways: as radical individualism and relativism with regard to all values, or as an emphasis on a thinking and a rationality that reflect the individual subject. In other words, the conception of the self as a human subject conditioned by its story and its history in all cases and all situations of life is not the same as the ideology of the absolutely autonomous modern subject.

Patočka finds a similar problem with Masaryk's proclaimed objectivist approach to the world and reminds us of two possible meanings of the objective. The first is related to the realm of epistemology and the question of truth. In this sense, so-called objective truth is what is accessible to all subjects. This is not the same, however, as the second meaning of objectivity, which is that objective entities are supposedly independent of all subjects. For Patočka, Masaryk also commits the fatal error of confusing the two. Objective truth, and thus the real objectivity, is by no means independent of the subject. On the contrary, the subject is a *conditio sine qua non* for objective truth:[53] "A purely objective truth that pretends that subjectivity does not exist is a lie."[54]

Patočka's final assessment of Masaryk's philosophy of the modern crisis sounds somewhat harsh. He interprets Masaryk as a theistic metaphysician, despite Masaryk's self-perception as a critical scientist-philosopher who develops his thinking on the basis of empirical facts. Patočka suggests leaving Masaryk's belief in objectivity behind and reassessing a genuine subjective philosophy. This is where Nietzsche seems to be a true source of inspiration. Who, after all, can provide a better alternative to the great modern statesman than the one who announced the modern crisis?

Nietzsche, Nihilisms, and the Death of God

Nietzsche, prophet of the death of God, makes an inevitable appearance in our account of Patočka's understanding of modernity. For Nietzsche, the evolution of the modern spirit reveals the worst of humankind, and the pinnacle of this negative development is the idea of nationalism. However, Nietzsche sees the problem not so much in the political realm but in the modern story of emancipation and the march toward universalism and uniformization.[55] Modernity is about the eradication of the diversity that had been a part of European tradition from its very beginning. Hellenism, Roman culture, Judaism, and Christianity are but the main mutually interacting narratives. The process of unification is not the invention of modernity itself, however, but is indebted to the continual growth of a Christian morality that is presented as universal. Nietzsche's criticism of modernity is therefore linked to his critique of Christianity.

Nietzsche's understanding of crisis contrasts sharply with that of Masaryk. Whereas Masaryk claims that the crisis of religion causes a loss of meaning, Nietzsche calls for emancipation from religion in order to free humanity from the bonds of absolute meaning.[56] For Nietzsche, Christianity gives birth to skepticism and nihilism because it is a religion of escape. Although Christianity promises a better world, the fulfilment of this promise is conditional on obedience to a supposedly universal set of morals given by God. This orientation to otherworldliness can only produce crisis. How are we to deal with this unpleasant situation? God must step aside and make way for a new man—the *Übermensch*.

Nietzsche contends that the concept of the superhuman or "overman" represents a moral ideal capable of emancipating us from the slave morality of Christianity. The *Übermensch* is the concept of "this-worldliness," being in the world, and standing firmly on the earth in a manner that is diametrically opposed to Christianity's reliance on external realities: "I love those who do not first seek behind the stars for a reason to go under and to be a sacrifice, who instead sacrifice themselves for the earth, that the earth may one day become the over-man's."[57] When Christianity is left behind, it is the task of the *Übermensch* to set new values. Can modern rationalism and the power of techno-science assist us here? Nietzsche's answer is no. In fact, in his religion, modern scientific rationalism meets the same fate as God. Nietzsche sees the arrival of nihilism as a moral crisis and all-consuming catastrophe that ultimately leads him to embrace it.[58] How should we make sense of what seems at first to be a contradiction?

With Nietzsche, everything is ambiguous, especially so when we consider his concept of nihilism, of which Patočka distinguishes the following forms, starting with Nietzsche's own:[59] (1) Nietzsche's creative and joyful nihilism—nihilism as the opposition to absolute metaphysical claims; (2) the mainstream concept of nihilism, which is not Nietzsche's at all but rather a relativism of "anything goes"; (3) the nihilism of surrender to objective powers—this version of nihilism stands in stark contrast to Nietzsche's position and finds its manifestation in various historical appearances of totalitarianism in the twentieth century; and (4) the nihilism of resignation and idleness—this mode of being is characteristic of certain streams of life after modernity, such as the life of consumerism, which is sometimes wrongly interpreted as the meaning of philosophical postmodernism.[60] In fact, this last form represents the ultimate version of nihilism, which prolongs the modern agony that started with the objectification of human beings.

Patočka is anxious to point out that Nietzsche's nihilism must be not confused with other forms of thinking that bear the same name. Arguably, those other forms of nihilism are what Nietzsche fears the most. The last of the four, the nihilism of resignation, is actually the essence of crisis. Patočka quotes the following from Nietzsche's *Nachgelassene Fragmente*: "Our European culture has been moving in agonizing tension for a long time, and decade after decade heading toward a catastrophe: restlessly, nonviolently, hastily; it is like a stream that wants to be at the end, and already does not think, and is afraid of thinking."[61] Despite all the criticism Patočka directs at Nietzsche, he considers the German philosopher correct in his vision of the future of Europe and its impending crisis. Modernity promotes objective rationalism but forgets thinking. Patočka values the fact that Nietzsche provokes us to think once more, which can be aptly illustrated using one of Nietzsche's most provocative yet enigmatic ideas: the death of God.

The pronouncement of the death of God can hardly be interpreted unarguably as the great achievement of modernity in Nietzsche's eyes. It is certainly a *consequence* of modernity, but the question remains: Is the death of God, for Nietzsche, a blessed moment of emancipation for humankind or a tragic and irreversible loss? The scene where a madman comes to the marketplace and preaches the death of God reveals this ambiguity:

> "Where is God?" he cried; "I'll tell you! *We have killed him*—you and I! We are all his murderers. . . . What were we doing when we unchained this earth from its sun? Where is it moving now? Where are we moving to? Away from all suns? Are we not continually falling?"[62]

The cry, "We have killed him," sounds not a little frightening. It is as if Nietzsche was suggesting that the loss of Christianity, the loss of God, meant the loss of something pivotal; as if without God, human beings were not completely human. Does Nietzsche's equivocal philosophy suggest that the crisis of modernity is related to the crisis of religion? Although it would be an interesting discussion, it is not our task to decide this question here. In any case, the death of God instigated a fundamental change and the stage is set for someone else to come: the over-man. This insight is crucial for Patočka's interpretation of the crisis of modernity. Patočka stretches Nietzsche's point further and claims that the rise of the superman—the *Übermensch*—creates a supercivilization. We will discuss this point in detail in the next section, where we will suggest that in Patočka's opinion the death of Christianity is not without serious consequences. Before that, however, we need to consider the two thinkers who influenced a great many of Patočka's views on modernity: Husserl and Heidegger.

Husserl's Crisis of Reason and the Problem of Objectivity

Husserl's *Crisis of European Sciences and Transcendental Phenomenology* offers a serious engagement with modernity and formulates a thoughtful and provocative critique. Husserl does not link the modern crisis with religion. He does not deal with religious questions in the way of Masaryk and does not follow Nietzsche in formulating any bold assertions about the changed status of religion. Religion neither plays a significant role in nor causes the crisis of modernity. Patočka reminds us that "religion remains for [Husserl] an entirely emotional and conceptually inadequate version of profound philosophical motifs."[63] Husserl's position therefore remains purely philosophical, and when it comes to the essence of the modern crisis, he lists the following areas: (1) the crisis of the exact sciences, (2) the crisis of the human sciences, (3) the crisis of culture, and (4) the crisis of philosophy.[64]

Husserl is convinced that the privileged position of Europe, which came about because of reason, "constitutes the central axis of its history."[65] Europe is the birthplace of philosophy, understood as the vocation to rational reflection and the search for truth and responsible life. Modernity, as Husserl sees it, represents a break with this tradition of rational reflection. The core of modernity is thus the crisis of reason and therefore the crisis of Europe.

How can Husserl speak of a crisis of reason after the Enlightenment, the Age of Reason? How can irrationalism appear amid a general belief in science and the progress of humankind based on the constant development of scientific knowledge? Returning to Patočka's two senses of reason mentioned earlier, Enlightenment rationalism prevailed in modern discourse and shaped modern life. Moreover, the modern sciences present themselves as heirs of the European tradition, a tradition of rational reflection. Why then does Husserl, the champion of European reason, detect a crisis?

To demonstrate the key problem, Husserl makes a thorough analysis of the development of modern rationalism.[66] After reviewing the basic characteristics of the modern emphasis on scientific reason, he identifies the breaking point of modern rationalism with Galileo's conception of mathematical science and Descartes's philosophy of rational certitude. Patočka neatly summarizes Husserl's point of view: "Science becomes an infinite endeavor and infinite are its tasks, even though this science is gripped by a uniform bond of rational deduction, which means that it is no longer particular mathematical doctrines but one universal formal mathematical science that takes the lead."[67] Husserl sees science as having been unified on the basis of formal mathematical principles. In contrast to the tradition of different realms of knowledge that participate in a universe they seek to explain, there is suddenly one universal mathematical science that pretends to grasp the universe, to formalize all its relations, and even to deduce them in advance. The hypothesis is that mathematical science and the transposition of nature into numbers produces objective facts free from relative subjective experiences and leads us to both objectivism and naturalism in science.

Objectivism means that "human beings and the natural world are essentially non-apparent objective entities or facts . . . hidden behind the humanly subjective 'veil of appearances.'"[68] Only exact sciences are able see beyond the subjective impressions and experiences of the world. Sciences thus point out what is certain and knowable. Likewise, naturalism claims that only exact sciences are entitled to interpret the facts of the natural world and human life. In this respect, scientific rationalism becomes a mere technical operation for "realizing forces for action and domination, for ordering the world, for the transformation of things for purposes foreign to them; they come to be understood purely as a means which humans have not only a right but also a duty to exploit and expand."[69] This scientific analytic mainstream or *static scientism* is the fundamental problem of the modern, post-Enlightenment era, which continues up to the present day.[70]

Patočka rephrases Husserl's crisis of European science as the crisis of meaning: "This crisis appears to be the loss of the meaning of life. Science has nothing to say about our life's difficulties and anxieties because it is just an 'objective' disengaged science based on pure facts. Fact-based sciences, however, make fact-based people."[71]

Science withdraws from the question of meaning and is therefore, in Husserl's opinion, in crisis because of the orientation of modern rationalism toward the goal of being effective rather than meaningful. Modern science simply prefers *doing* things instead of *understanding* things. To paraphrase Marx, premodern tradition merely interpreted the world, but the point is to change it.[72] For Husserl, modern objectivistic science switches the order and places its methods of observation above the real world that is being observed. Formalistic mathematical science is then mistakenly seen as reality, whereas the real is overlooked and outplayed as too subjective. Modern rationalism simply assumes that science—especially the exact sciences—presents real things as they are, as if scientific rationality were the default perspective for any kind of rational reflection.[73] Husserl interprets this development as a shift from a natural lifeworld to a world *more geometrico*. Patočka uses the example of measuring to explain Husserl's point. For the modern mind, geometry is one of the foundations of objectivity. The objectivity of results means they are universally accessible. Those who lived in previous ages were able to measure in precisely the same manner as those who will measure in the future. In short, measuring looks for timeless exactness. But absolute precision is an unthinkable and unreachable ideal because measurements are always conducted from a certain perspective. Modern rationalism changes the paradigm and argues for a different perspective. Modern geometry makes both objectivity and precision reachable and present at hand:

> The purity of geometric forms then gives birth, in the realm of general philosophic reflection, to a purity of ideas, and both pursue the same ideal of a truth-in-itself, a truth no longer relative to a world of perspectives and approximations, a life-world, but a truth that is absolute in the sense of the ideal of non-relativity and precision.[74]

The geometric world creates the geometric human. This notion of mathematically formalized ultimate truths has nothing to say about the fundamental questions of life. Quite the opposite. Modern rationalism provokes a skepticism that human beings are merely measurable objects among other measurable objects. For Husserl, irrationalism and the loss of faith in reason are logical outcomes of this modern rational culture.

Husserl's aim, however, is not only the deconstruction of scientific rationalism. His confession, his vocation (*Beruf*), is philosophy, understood as critical rational reflection. Husserl believes in reason and in the rational abilities of human beings.[75] Thus the criticism he formulates in *Crisis* also has reconstructive ambitions. Husserl attempts to renew the Enlightenment, to rehabilitate the position of science, and to draw it out from the dead ends of objectivism and naturalism. Husserl believes that genuine science should be grounded in philosophy.[76] And philosophy, as previously noted, is the search for truth and responsible life. In short, Husserl is interested in clear and distinct knowledge that is in close relation to the human subject, the carrier of knowledge. The method he chooses for this purpose is transcendental phenomenology, which turns from the objectivist foundation of science to the question of subjectivism. Husserl's goal is a new *theória*, a new conception of reason based on the subjective foundation of philosophy that serves as the propaedeutic for science.[77]

Husserl is convinced that his conception of rigorous science restores what modern objectivism forgot, which is a fundamental metaphysical questioning of meaning and a perennial philosophy based on real life in the world. Patočka notes that Husserl's ambition should not be confused with a return to the unity of science and philosophy proposed in ancient Greece. Husserl's *Crisis* is very much a *modern project*:

Husserlian theory of modern science is nothing other than a reflection on the perils of fruitfulness, on the ruses of genius, on the irrationality which rationality itself engenders—not, to be sure, necessarily, yet not wholly accidentally, either. (Might not this shadowy side of rationality, this negative aspect of science, lie at the roots of certain specific evils that not only occasioned the catastrophe that Husserl sought to prevent with his reflections but are also, unfortunately, still very much with us.)[78]

Patočka is convinced that Husserl's analysis is still relevant, and that perhaps its relevance has "grown rather than diminished with the passage of time."[79] Husserl was writing *Crisis* shortly before the Second World War. He sensed a catastrophe but could hardly have predicted all its consequences—the spread of totalitarian regimes, the atomic bomb, the Cold War and the bipolar division of the world, to name but a few of the most striking examples. Patočka, a direct participant in and observer of these historical evolutions, sees the ambivalence of modern science and the dark side—the demonic side—of reason. Europe once enjoyed a monopoly on rational culture, but this rational supercivilization then very nearly committed suicide.

Patočka finds Husserl's portrait of crisis correct,[80] and his own description of the story of modern reason is more or less dependent on Husserl's analysis.[81] Perhaps the most important lesson Patočka draws from Husserl is the distinction between modern techno-scientific rationality and reason as a dynamic category, in other words, the difference between reason that formulates knowledge and reason that seeks meaning and understanding.[82] Patočka nonetheless considers the solutions Husserl offers in response to the crisis to be failures.[83] Furthermore, Patočka notes, "[Husserl] is deeply convinced that with the resolution of the theoretical question of a unitary foundation of philosophy and science we have achieved what was most important for the resolution of the crisis."[84]

Husserl wants to achieve the reconstruction of scientific knowledge by the retrieval of the phenomenological method through which the subject relates without prejudice to things as they are. In other words, Husserl seeks the solution to crisis in a radical theory, an ultimate rationalization that brings total clarity. For Patočka, this is not possible as the problem of modernity is not the crisis of scientific reasoning but the crisis of rational thinking itself. According to Patočka, science that is based on mathematics, logic, and geometry—which is the case with modern science at least from Galileo onward—turns out to be a technique with the single purpose of mastering nature. Nature refers here to both its possible meanings: the natural surroundings of human beings, for which Patočka uses the term "lifeworld," and the nature of human beings, that is, the essence or the inner core of living subjects. What is needed, Patočka suggests, is not a better, more scientific method of elucidating the totality of beings by means of radicalized objectification, but the renewal of a meaning-giving rationality that is opposed to modern technical rationalism.

Patočka agrees with Husserl that modernity completely reshaped rationality, cutting reason off from the search for meaning and replacing it with purposive service,[85] and points out that modern technical rationalism and its emphasis on purpose rather than meaning had a profound effect on modern anthropology. Human beings have become objects to be manipulated, parts of a system subordinated to the objective laws of nature. Up to this point, Patočka follows his mentor. Ultimately, however, he finds that Husserl's analysis falls into the trap of the modern project of rational elucidation and clear knowledge. As Sroda aptly notes, "Unlike Husserl, Patočka is not looking for an absolute certainty but teaching us how to live without it."[86] Patočka does not subscribe to Husserl's goal of making from philosophy a rigorous science and thus *philosophia prima*, the basis for other sciences. He therefore turns to Heidegger to question the essence of modern techno-scientific reason and in this sense goes beyond Husserl.

Heidegger and the Danger of Technology

Heidegger's philosophy follows up on Husserl's analysis and shares many aspects with the philosophy of his predecessor and colleague from Freiburg; their overall perspectives are essentially different, however. Husserl interprets the modern crisis in terms of a crisis of reason caused by the technical domination of all forms of scientific reflection. Heidegger does not blame scientific rationality as such. Rather, he points out the complex etymological origin of the word *technē*, which is at the root of technology. He shows that *technē* originally belongs not only to the realm of technical skills but also to the realm of fine art. Thus, *technē* is partly *poiēsis*, a poetic endeavor. Furthermore, *technē* is linked to a certain "know-how," expertise, a way of understanding, and thus to a mode of rationality. In short, *technē* is a knowledge (*epistēmē*) and as knowledge it is "a mode of *alétheuein*."[87] This means that for Heidegger technology is a means of revealing truth.

The question Heidegger raises is whether this view of the inner complexities of technology is also applicable to the modern version of techno-scientific rationality. The answer is both yes and no. Although modern technology continues to "reveal" truth, the essence of that revealing is significantly changed. Modern technology loses the poetic component, which is replaced by a mode of challenging (*Herausfordern*):

> Such challenging happens in that the energy concealed in nature is unlocked, what is unlocked is transformed, what is transformed is stored up, what is stored up is in turn distributed, and what is distributed is switched about ever anew. Unlocking, transforming, storing, distributing, and switching about are ways of revealing.[88]

Heidegger offers the example of a dam on the River Rhine built for the purpose of producing electricity. The meaning of the river is challenged and ultimately changed because of the new power plant. Heidegger contrasts this with the poetic point of view represented, for example, by Hölderlin's poem "The Rhine."[89] What used to be a flow of water in the landscape now "makes sense" from a techno-scientific instrumental mode of revealing. In this respect, Patočka asks whether the modern change and challenge can be taken as a step forward, toward a more mature humankind, and as a development that extends the possibilities of human reason.

Technology delivers great power into the hands of humanity and develops a truly universal perspective that is relevant to all domains of life. But the danger to which Heidegger's analysis draws our attention lies precisely here. Everything is on demand. Every-thing can be ordered. Every-thing—including material things and human beings—is at our disposal. Modern technology creates an illusion of the unequivocal clarity of all beings because they can be mastered and possessed—in knowledge. In turn, the definition of truth is also challenged and changed. To recall the example of the Rhine, the truth of the river is dependent on its purpose. The truth seems to be something that is possible to master. Patočka thus says that "not technology as such but technology in its relation to that in man which is capable of truth represents a danger that needs to be confronted."[90] He spells out the problem as follows:

And therein precisely lies the danger. The uncovering that prevails at the essential core of technology necessarily loses sight of uncovering itself, concealing the essential core of truth in an unfamiliar way and so closing man's access to what he himself is—a being capable of standing in an original relation to the truth. Among all the securing, calculating, and using of raw materials, that which makes all this possible is lost from view—man henceforth knows only individual, practical truths, not the truth.[91]

Heidegger's reflection on the danger of technology refers to both the question of and the conception of truth. Modern scientific rationalism, which is in essence technology, reveals what-is and what is true in its way. What is this conception of understanding, the revealing of what-is? Heidegger argues that the technique of technological revealing is *Gestell*—enframing. But what is *Gestell*?

Heidegger provides his explanation in the essay "The Question Concerning Technology."[92] *Gestell* is the techno-scientific lens through which the world appears to be explicable and controllable within categories—in the frame—of mathematical operations, mathematical sets, and a formal scientific language. The German word *Gestell* comes from the verb *stellen*—to stand. In *Gestell*, everything is a standing reserve and may stand on order. Things are transformed into manageable quantities and the objects of universal order. The truth of things is to be found in their purpose and the purpose of things is equal to their meaning. In other words, in the logic of *Gestell*, what is good is good for its purpose.

The idea of *Gestell* is perhaps the most influential source of inspiration for Patočka's own interpretation of modernity and the modern crisis:

> Now we see the danger . . . Gestell is not any kind of society or the state of energy, and so on, it is a certain way of understanding what is—the revealing of things. . . . Gestell means, in fact, that what rules is not things or orders but *understanding*. Indeed, the understanding and elucidation of things is the universal power of technology and its essence as well as the essence of human beings.[93]

The point is that *Gestell* challenges the understanding of things, but it also, in consequence, challenges the understanding and self-understanding of human beings. The world reveals itself by means of *Gestell*. *Gestell* is the essence of modern technology, the world in the shape (*Gestalt*) of enframing (*Gestell*). For Heidegger, therefore, it is not technology per se but the essence of technology that represents a danger, the danger, for humankind. Patočka summarizes Heidegger's argument as follows:

> In Gestell, the time of universal order, the alienation of human beings culminates up to the point that everyone is basically just a function and the performance of this function. . . . A human being becomes one-dimensional, is deprived of its totality, is reduced to an object, in fact, it is not even an object. A human being has not become a thing that can further be viewed from a different perspective and complemented. . . . All this disappears, and human beings become only an "object" of the order.[94]

What is the way out of this dangerous reduction of the world and humanity? Heidegger finds the redemption (*das Rettende*) in recourse to the original and, in his opinion, richer understanding of *technē*. He recalls the poetic element of technology and presents fine art as something that breaks with *Gestell*.[95] For Heidegger, art cannot be reduced to mere supply and demand. It is a way of understanding whereby the understanding of meaning is not lost but revealed. Heidegger favors the art of the word—poetry. Lines of poetry are opening, revealing, questioning, and thinking. The point of art, therefore, is not primarily an aesthetic experience but a return to the multiple revealing, a return to the fundamental question of truth.

What has Patočka learned from Masaryk, Nietzsche, Husserl, and Heidegger and their interpretations of the modern crisis? First, there is a consensus that modernity is (in) crisis, although this statement means various and sometimes contradictory things. Second, Patočka refines his view of crisis on the basis of reading these four thinkers and concludes that crisis has something to do with the rise of scientific rationality (Husserl) and the spirit of technology (Heidegger). True, we know this already from Patočka's narration of the modern development of reason. Nonetheless, he now adds another perspective—the perspective of religion.

Although Patočka does not fully agree with Masaryk and Nietzsche, he takes the question of religion, perhaps under their influence, as one of the key problems of modernity. The evolution of reason in modernity influences the position of religion, and vice versa. The importance of this issue will become apparent as we consider the consequences for culture and civilization of the crisis of modernity—something that Husserl and Heidegger rather neglect.

The Crisis of Modern Rational Culture and Its Inner Conflict

Modernity is a promising project that envisions the significant development of culture and society. Whether we interpret modernity as an unfinished project or advocate a thesis concerning the end of modernity, one thing is certain: modernity changed and challenged the conception of rationality. Now we must ask: What are the aims of modernity? In this respect, Patočka goes beyond Husserl and Heidegger—who are predominantly interested in describing the theoretical level of the modern crisis—and reflects on the practical consequences and outcomes of the modern reconfiguration of reason. The change and the challenge are not restricted to philosophical circles but have a huge impact on culture and society in general. The notion of modernity does not after all represent only a chapter in the history of ideas—its general understanding refers to a particular step in the development of culture. Thus far we have addressed the rational side of matters. Now we turn to the cultural aspects of modernity and to civilization. Patočka explores these aspects in his investigation of modernity as a particular civilization based on the idea of reason—a rational civilization.

This is the subject of Patočka's "Supercivilization and Its Inner Conflict," an essay that merits a thorough reading by anyone seeking to understand the interpretation of modernity in terms of crisis.[96] Here I propose to offer a more complete picture of the problem and to focus on the position of religion in the modern crisis of civilization as presented by Patočka. I will proceed in four steps. First, I will introduce the shift from premodern civilizations to modern supercivilization. Second, I will present the two versions of modernity that appear in Patočka's analysis—the moderate and the radical. Third, I will focus on the status of religion in each of these versions. Finally, as will become clear in the conclusion of this section, I will suggest that the disenchantment of the world and the loss of religious ways of reasoning are among the primary causes of the modern crisis.

From Civilization to Supercivilization

Patočka's fascinating exploration of supercivilization was published posthumously in the first volume of his collected writings. The exact year of writing is unknown, but most commentators situate it somewhere in the 1950s. Timing is important as it has a bearing on the purpose of the essay.

Johann Arnason suggests that "Supercivilization" represents an attempt by Patočka to critically assess Communism—which unlike the prevailing intellectual accounts of the time is portrayed as a form of totalitarianism—and to search for alternatives.[97] Although it is doubtful that the unpleasantness of Czechoslovakia's situation behind the Iron Curtain left Patočka untouched, I believe that the essay goes beyond this and concerns more general questions. I agree with Marek Skovajsa that Patočka offers an overall interpretation of modernity and its crisis, but that his project must be situated in concrete historical events.[98] What this means is that although Patočka relies on particular examples from his context, his intention is to formulate conclusions that are valid for the modern situation of crisis in general. Patočka interprets modernity in terms of a civilizational paradox: modernity is a "cultural-historical formation that on the one hand extends the scope of traditional civilizations, and on the other is, in contrast to these civilizations, incomplete."[99] For Patočka, modernity forms a civilization alongside others, such as the Christian, Greek, or Roman civilizations, but at the same time is a different concept of civilization, namely, a supercivilization, sometimes translated as over- or hypercivilization (*sur-civilisation* in French, or *Über-Zivilisation* in German).

But what does it mean to interpret modernity as a *supercivilization*? And what exactly is the "conflict" within modernity referred to in the title of Patočka's essay? To answer these questions, we must first consider Patočka's general definition of civilization: "Every civilization is the accumulation and the organization of power, although it is not just that. Originally, it is a turning point in addressing foundational questions of life such as *how* and *why* one should live."[100] For Patočka, civilization is first a form of power that organizes and controls people. Second, and more importantly, civilization is a framework for rational reflection on the purpose of life. Civilization creates the conditions for raising questions and proposing answers concerning the means and the meaning of life. Nevertheless, the purpose or meaning of life is often based on irrational postulations. Here, the irrational does not refer to something negative. On the contrary, it points to a depth of existence that exceeds the rational. What Patočka has in mind is simply that which is beyond objective rationalization. The prime candidate seems to be religion. From this perspective, most civilizations have an irrational core, a core based on a particular set of beliefs.[101]

Modern belief lies in reason. The religion of modernity is rationality; its core is fully rational and fully objective. This represents a radical difference from premodern civilizations. In this sense, modernity forms a supercivilization because it seeks ultimate universalization by means of complete rationalization. Modernity's belief must be certain and stand above all other beliefs. In other words, modernity accentuates the question of *how* and neglects the question of *why*. An alternative name for this process is secularization. The position of both religion and philosophy is weakened, and the birth of the supercivilization has serious consequences in leaving behind the two most significant traditions of Western thought—Christianity and metaphysics.

Moderate Modernity / Radical Modernity

Modernity represents an attempt to create a universal supercivilization, but the process of universalization by means of intensified rationalization is not univocal. Patočka identifies two versions of the modern project of supercivilization—two related but distinct or even competing paths to the ideal of modern reason.[102] First there is *moderate rationalism*. This version of supercivilization is limited to the rational organization of the system and has no pretension to master the totality of life and the world (that is, the lifeworld). Second, in Patočka there is *radical rationalism*. As the word *radical* indicates, this instance of supercivilization aims to transform society, culture, and human life in its totality. In short, modernity is explained in terms of two versions of rational supercivilization that differ in the scope they assign to reason. Moderate supercivilization postulates that the lens of modern reason offers privileged but not unique access to the world. Radical supercivilization on the other hand absolutizes modern, scientific rationalism and employs it in all domains of life. In other words, both versions of modern supercivilization are based on the modern reconfiguration of reason. They operate with objectification, instrumentalization, performative effectivity, calculability, the accumulation of knowledge, and other typical modern features.[103] The difference between the two lies in their respective attitudes to means (instrumental rationality) and ends (substantial rationality), to the questions of *how* and *why*. Patočka's definition of moderate and radical rationalism is as follows:

[A moderate rationality] is conscious of its limitations. This project realizes that its organizational skills, accomplishments, and universalism do not consist in its desire and will to take over the whole of life. On the contrary, its essence is the abstraction from the whole.

The second version of rationalism is totally radical. It proposes a rational organization as the key to *all* questions.... In this radical version of rational civilization, one finds the solution to all of life's questions. There is no problem that could not be cured in this culture.... This radicalism institutes the rule of the last sense-giving rationality, the absolute in the midst of the ordinary and the rule of the human absolute.[104]

Radical rationalism dreams of the total domination of beings. Moderate rationality affirms the power of reason but does not pretend to exhaust the question of the meaning of life. The moderate version does not in fact raise this question as it orients itself in terms of the instrumental *how*. Radical rationalism, however, does not hesitate to formulate ultimate answers regarding meaning. In this sense, radical supercivilization dissolves the question of meaning completely because it fills in the answers and closes the open space of questioning with a total content, or, as Patočka puts it, with "the absolute in the midst of the ordinary."[105] According to Marek Skovajsa, this radicalism is based on the "fallacious presupposition that rationalism is total and that it gives ready-made answers to concrete practical issues as well as to the meaning of life."[106] For Patočka, radical supercivilization is the rule of a hegemonic reason that is presented as the last instance.

Patočka then makes an interesting point regarding religion. Although the general goal of modernity is to overcome the irrational—religious—core of traditional civilizations, radical supercivilization falls into the trap of becoming a para-religious dogmatic structure. How can this be compatible with the claim concerning the absolute position of reason? As we have already noted, Patočka finds religion in the core of (almost all) civilizations. This irrational element of belief is considered not as something negative but as something beyond pure reason. We can call it the depth of existence that is mirrored on the civilizational level. We have also seen that radical supercivilization excludes this profundity and replaces it with all-encompassing reason. Yet the purely rational foundation is analogical to the irrational foundation of any other civilization. In other words, a particular belief is still at work in the radical supercivilization, so the system created on this basis resembles religious structures. We will go on to show in what respect this is so, but first it is necessary to briefly refer to moderate supercivilization.

Moderate modernity acknowledges its limits. Although moderate supercivilization claims instrumental rationality for itself and believes in the modern imperative of effectivity, which supposedly results in a better society, it leaves space for others to enter the field of sense-giving rationality. Who are these others? Patočka thinks of Christianity and philosophy (metaphysical thinking). This is not to say, however, that moderate rationality gives priority, for example, to Christian thinking over science. Moderate supercivilization is a version of modernity and as such it undoubtedly favors secularization. Religion and philosophy do not belong to the order of performative effectivity but to the order of personal and, by definition, private views.

In any case, the fact that Patočka realizes the importance of religion in general and Christianity in particular for his interpretation of modernity deserves our attention. What follows is an inquiry into the relationship between religion and supercivilization in Patočka's essay.

Religion and Supercivilization

Patočka says that structurally, Christianity "belongs to the moderate supercivilization."[107] What does he mean by this? Is he proposing that Christianity is swallowed up by the moderate version of modernity? Or that Christianity is an effect of moderate rationalism? To understand Patočka correctly, we must first approach the matter from the perspective not of modernity but of Christianity.

The sentence we have just quoted reads in full as follows: "being conscious that the Kingdom of God is not of this world, [Christianity] *structurally* belongs to the moderate supercivilization."[108] In other words, Christianity contains an element of distance, something that is beyond the reach of human beings. Patočka wants to say that Christianity bears witness to a realm that cannot become an object in our possession. Against the background of modern rationalism, Christian thinking appears as a mode of thought that is not exhausted in rational mastery but rather transcends it.

We can now look at Christianity's belonging to moderate supercivilization from the perspective of modernity and see what Patočka meant. For

Patočka, moderate supercivilization rises from Christian culture. Or rather, the idea of a rational and universal civilization is the fruit of Christianity and the Christian worldview.[109] In this sense, Christianity continues to live in the secular context of modernity and in fact functions as an important corrective to the excesses of rationalism.

Before we explore in detail the importance of Christianity in Patočka's analysis of modernity, we need to clarify its relationship to radical supercivilization. Despite its structural connection to moderate supercivilization, Christianity is also imprinted in radical supercivilization.[110] Although radical rationalism enhances a rigorous form of secularization in order to diminish religion, it also—somewhat surprisingly—shows signs of religious or at least para-religious structures.

First, radical rationalism formulates grand narratives that resemble civilizational myths. These myths go beyond narration and expand into cults. Patočka mentions the cult of Reason of the French Revolution, and Comte's positive religion and its narrative concerning the development of humankind from a primitive religious status of believing in gods to a positive society with rational convictions. Second, these myths and cults evolve into secular eschatological beliefs. For example, the "gospel" of the eternal progress of humankind, in terms of both the increasing possession of knowledge and material possession, promises "a paradise" in a purely immanent horizon. Interestingly, radical supercivilization reckons with the notion of *kairos*, reconfigured into a secular version of the fullness of time. Third, and related to the previous point, radical supercivilization embodies a whole mechanism of switching from the ordinary to the festive. Secular feasts such as Labor Day divide the time for work from the time for recreation and celebration. Fourth, the aspiration to total determination—the ultimate key to all problems and questions—and the absolute sense-giving enterprise in radical supercivilization are analogous to the constitution of a universal "church," a religious institution. Like certain ecclesiological perspectives, radical supercivilization lays claim to all domains of personal and social life. And since from a radical rationalist perspective total redemption happens inevitably in the world, and that redemption is projected as a total and radical social change, "politics, as the result of this totalization, acquires a sacred meaning."[111] In other words, what was expelled from the public sphere under the name of secularization returns in the form of quasi-political religion. To be sure, this religion contains both orthodoxy and orthopraxy. Feuerbach's thesis that religion belongs to human nature and is inseparable from it still seems to be at work in this version of modernity despite its explicit hostility toward the religious thermalizing of transcendence. Without any explicit intention, in its attempt to overcome religion once and for all, radical supercivilization actually imitates and counterfeits religion.

The banners of radical supercivilization state that *ut omnes unum sint*.[112] However, the meaning of this phrase, which in its original biblical context stressed unity in diversity, here refers rather to a collectivist effort to create uniformity. If unity is mentioned in the context of this version of modernity, it is the unity of the system and its organization. Patočka's negative evaluation of radical supercivilization does not, therefore, come as a surprise. Considering the context of the essay, Patočka's account of the radical version of modernity is an insightful critique of totalitarianism as oppression on the level of both politics (Communism) and thinking (materialism and "scientific atheism").

We now return to the link between Christianity and moderate supercivilization. In contrast to radical rationalism, which suppresses Christianity and replaces it with a secular counterfeit, moderate rationality keeps the Christian element in place. In Patočka's words, the moderate supercivilization preserves *vertical thinking*.[113]

Vertical thinking, as the term suggests, acknowledges something beyond a purely immanent horizon. Reason is not everything. Knowledge cannot be exhausted by means of objectivistic epistemology. Transcendence has a say. Patočka suggests that vertical thinking means to think relationally: I (the subject) and God; I and other human beings; I and other beings. In contrast, the horizontal perspective of radical supercivilization encourages us to think objectively: one object in relation to other objects.[114] Moderate supercivilization inherited vertical thinking from the Catholicism and Protestantism of Western Christianity. Patočka is convinced that these incarnations of Christianity provide structures for the development of modern society and modern rationality, which are critical of religious dogmatism, fundamentalism, and hegemonic thought patterns but are not necessarily hostile to faith in transcendence. Moreover, the modern emphasis on the autonomy of the human subject is rooted in the Christian conception of personhood and the Christian struggle for the equality of all people before God and on earth.[115] The Reformation is a radicalization of this emancipation that is already present in medieval Catholicism and ultimately traceable in the origins of Christianity, such as in the Pauline epistles. Although all the achievements of moderate supercivilization are interpreted through the lens of *ad maiorem gloriam spiritus humani*,[116] they are indebted to its older foundation in the nontotalizing universalism of Christianity.

Golfo Maggini explains the meaning of the search for a nontotalizing universality.[117] For Maggini, moderate supercivilization as depicted by Patočka accepts difference but affirms the power of reason. However, reason in moderate supercivilization is not the sole governing instance but the judge that safeguards a free search for truth. Maggini calls this *rationality*. In contrast, radical supercivilization dreams of hegemonic universalism and total domination over beings. Maggini calls this *rationalism*. In other words, both versions of supercivilization share universalist tendencies, but only the nontotalizing universality of moderate supercivilization, rooted in Christianity, acknowledges that freedom and truth, the two basic values of modernity, can be realized only on the condition that they transcend the purely immanent and horizontal system of rationalism.

Interestingly, Patočka finds similarities between the collectivism of radical rationalism and a combination of Eastern Christianity and the techno-scientific mentality. The mystical elements of Orthodoxy (*sobornost*), with their emphasis on total unity, and a blurred relationship between the Church hierarchy and political organizations (*caesaropapism*) make an explosive cocktail when combined with the bureaucratic machinery of a totally secular rationalism.[118] The result is a hegemonic supercivilization. It is not our task to decide whether Patočka's association of Orthodox Christianity with radical supercivilization is accurate. Given the context of this particular idea—the context of Soviet totalitarianism that emerged from the "Orthodox" East—Patočka's point of view seems to be explicable.

However, the point of our discussion is that Patočka considers Christianity to be a decisive element in modernity.[119] He stresses vertical thinking as a sign of genuine modern supercivilization and in this sense as a constructive solution to the modern crisis.

Lost in Truth, and Self-Limited Universalism

Underlying the crisis of modernity is the conflict between two competing versions of supercivilization and their respective rationalities. For Patočka, this conflict is a clear sign of decline, and "the decline lies in that we are lost in the question of truth."[120] What is Patočka suggesting when he says we are lost in truth? The inner conflict of supercivilization brings confusion regarding the questioning of truth because it goes hand in hand with the conflict of two competing ideas of what is and what is not the truth.[121] In the radical supercivilization, an essentialist notion of truth prevails:

truth is irreversible, unchanging, and eternal. Truth has a static content; it is an axiomatic principle; it is objective. In other words, truth is the result of mathematical calculations and objective experimentations. The danger here is that truth can become an ideology to which everything and everyone must accommodate.

Patočka does not of course dismiss the fact that truth has a content. His intention is to introduce the search for truth as a dynamic process in opposition to the uncovering of ready-made truths regardless of whether these are eternal ideas, natural laws, or mathematical principles.

Moderate supercivilization on the other hand has the potential to develop a nonhegemonic conception of truth. As we have seen, Patočka claims that the two greatest values of the moderate version of modernity are truth and freedom. This version of modernity thus contains certain aspects of negative thinking and a self-reflective, self-critical distance with respect to reason.[122] For Patočka, rational reflection and inquiry into the truth is never final. Moderate supercivilization bears witness to this concept of thinking again and again. In contrast to radical supercivilization, moderate modernity does not pull the truth down from heaven but opens the way for an independent seeking after the truth whereby truth can manifest itself:

> Truth is not merely a "theoretical question" addressed by objective methods and objective means. . . . [Truth] is the internal struggle within human beings for their essential freedom, which is at the core of being human essentially but not factually. Truth is the question of the truthfulness of human beings because the essence of being human is that one might have truth that includes essential care for the truth.[123]

Ilja Šrubař calls Patočka's approach "self-limited universalism."[124] Moderate modernity allows the application of such nonhegemonic universality because it is skeptical of all absolute universalist tendencies and leaves space for a truthfulness of its own and the truthfulness of others by means of self-limitation. As I see it, this is a kenotic moment within rationality. The method of constant questioning, which is strictly applied and yet open to diverse interruptions, paves the way for both particular truths (objective truths) and, more importantly, *truthfulness*.

Milan Hanyš challenges this perspective and suggests that radical supercivilization is in some ways even more indebted to Christianity than is its moderate counterpart.[125] Hanyš supports his view with an analysis of the theology of the Pauline letters of the New Testament. The essence of his argument is that the Apostle Paul is the founder of a universalism that ties salvation not to the acts of law but to faith in the Gospel. Paul therefore withdraws from orthopraxis (the emphasis in Judaism) in favor of orthodoxy (right thinking, right opinions). Hanyš identifies Christianity that is oriented toward orthodoxy with the radical supercivilization that requires everyone to assent to its doctrine unconditionally. This argument runs counter to Patočka's notion of Christianity as a differentiating element between two versions of modern supercivilization, and it emphasizes the hegemonic tendencies inscribed within Christianity itself.

I agree that in its theoretical aspect, radicalism indeed pushes forward its doctrine and orders this doctrine as a truth that must be accepted. Nevertheless, as we have seen, radical supercivilization is primarily oriented to a political agenda and seeks to reshape society according to its objective ideology. What I suggest is therefore that on the civilizational and cultural level, radical modernity does not in fact care about orthodoxy and its doctrine. The only thing required and controlled is a proclaimed orthodoxy that must, however, be followed by strict observation of proper orthopraxis. What do I mean by this? In his essay "The Power of the Powerless,"[126] Václav Havel presents the figure of an ordinary greengrocer in a totalitarian society—a radical supercivilization—who displays a poster bearing the slogan: "Workers of the World, Unite!" The content of the poster is less important than the greengrocer's behavior. He displays the poster without thinking. He may be neither in full agreement with the slogan nor disgusted by it. He probably has no clue as to what is written there and in fact cares very little about it. And he is not alone in this attitude. The lady who regularly buys tomatoes in his shop does not read the poster either, even though she has just displayed a similar slogan in the window of her kitchen. Havel concludes that in a totalitarian society, 90 percent of people behave like this. They all do what they are expected to do; they do not think about it, because nobody asks them to think. In other words, from the perspective of radical supercivilization, what is important is how people act, not what they think. What matters is observance of the prescribed orthopraxy. No one is concerned with orthodoxy; law has replaced faith.

If what Havel suggests is true, radical supercivilization is indeed lost in the question of truth. Truth is objective. It cannot be questioned, so no one thinks about the question of truth anymore. In contrast, moderate supercivilization, based on Christianity and its idea of there being a distance to absolute truth, preserves the possibility of asking questions and searching for truth as *truthfulness*. In this sense, Christianity offers the means for creatively making a way through the modern crisis. In short, Patočka sees Christianity as a foundation for a deeper conception of rationality.

The Loss of Vertical Thinking and the Crisis of Modern Supercivilization

The project of modernity aims to establish a universal rational culture, a supercivilization. The moderate and radical means toward this goal represent two faces of the same project. Taking into consideration the previous discussion and accepting that the main point of Patočka's essay leads us to discovering the conflict within modern civilization itself, it seems clear that radical supercivilization aims to situate itself *above* other civilizations. But it also seems plausible to interpret the moderate version of supercivilization as a civilization *between* its twin sources of Christianity and modernity. Perhaps the ideal of moderate rational supercivilization has never yet existed; perhaps it is between all extremes.

Václav Bělohradský, a student of Patočka's, would disagree here. For Bělohradský, moderate modernity is a lie and Patočka is wrong to place his hope in moderate supercivilization. To deal with the crisis of modernity, what is needed is a truly radical radicalism. Bělohradský understands Patočka's objections to radical supercivilization, but he suggests that what Patočka is criticizing is rather a new breed of metaphysics in the clothes of radical rationalism: "A presupposed direct attitude to the knowledge of reality and the whole of the world."[127] For Bělohradský, this rationalism is not radical at all because it seeks to overcome metaphysics by setting a foundation on a universal religion of reason, institutionalized terror, and the ultimate mechanization of its revolution on the rule of the absolute in the midst of the ordinary.[128] Real radicalism must leave all foundation behind and thus overcome religion and metaphysical violence.

As I see it, however, Patočka is arguing for the very opposite. It is precisely the loss of religion, that is, the loss of Christianity—we can also add the loss of the metaphysical thinking that belongs to Christianity—which is the main reason behind the modern crisis and its tragic consequences: hegemony and terror. By the "loss of religion," Patočka is not referring to the loss of piety, as in Masaryk. What he has in mind is the loss of a particular mode of thinking—"vertical thinking"—the loss of any ability to see beyond the horizon of what is given and accessible by means of objective reason. Moderate modernity preserves this possibility of vertical thinking, whereas radical supercivilization discards everything beyond the horizon of rationalism. Vertical thinking, which is an inseparable part of modernity, therefore opens the way to overcoming the demonic reign of the enlightened rationalism of the absolute, which is the other side of the modern heritage. The map of the modern crisis is drawn as a battle between two competing rationalities. One side of the inner conflict of modernity has its roots in Christianity and ancient philosophy, the other is the outcome of modern science. One side acknowledges the limits of reason, the other promotes absolute rationalism. From that perspective, it makes sense to phrase the problem as a *spiritual crisis*.

Modernity as Spiritual Crisis

We have explored the meaning of modern challenges and changes in some detail, and this has brought us to the claim that these paradigm shifts result in a spiritual crisis. The question is, what does this mean for our interpretation of modernity? Should we keep to the path of modernity despite its obvious problems and failures? Should we adopt an antimodernist attitude? Or should we look for a third way—a *via tertia*—and read Patočka's diagnosis as postmodern, neither completely modern nor entirely antimodern, and concerning itself with the questions and problems of modernity—its crisis—from a different perspective?

Kohák summarizes Patočka's position as follows: "Modernity, as Patočka sees it, raised no new questions but only lost the ability to trust the old answers."[129] Kohák seems to suggest that Patočka's assessment of modernity is somewhat negative and therefore antimodern. Elsewhere, Kohák claims that Patočka forms a bridge between two great traditions of modern philosophy: Husserl's phenomenology and Heidegger's thinking.[130] In this respect, modernity seems to be a dialogue between those two lines of thought, and Patočka's philosophy occupies the central ground between the two. For Kohák, Patočka even translates the inner dialogue of modernity into a meaningful project. From this perspective, Patočka appears to be a critical modern who elaborates upon his predecessors. Thus, Kohák provides us with two if not contradicting then at least competing interpretations. Which one is correct? And are they indeed at all accurate? I argue that Kohák, otherwise a great interpreter of Patočka and someone whose work was largely responsible for making the philosophy of the Czech phenomenologist available to an English-speaking audience, is misleading in both cases. Patočka is neither antimodern nor modern but in a certain sense of the word "postmodern."

We have seen throughout this chapter that Patočka is clear about one thing: modernity has its question, the question of reason. Dealing with modernity therefore requires us to deal with the story of reason. And if we are concerned about the crisis of modernity, we must explore the crisis of rational thinking. If, in fact, "we suggest that the cause of the European crisis appears to be a shallow and mechanized rationalism that cannot give rise to anything living on the land of its artificial world, we have to ask whether it is possible to cure *rationalism* with anything else but *reason*."[131] Reason and crisis are inseparable in modern discourse and in any discourse on modernity. Despite his critique of modernity, Patočka is a champion of reason and rational thinking. He reads the question of reason, a modern question par excellence, through a complex lens and rejects simplification and reductionism. The situation is an intricate one because rationality is the only imaginable way in which the crisis of modernity can be approached and addressed. The modern crisis is a paradoxical patchwork in which rationalism and the fall into irrationalism often stand side by side. For example, the essay "European Reason" (1941) is a reaction against the irrationalism of the Nazi regime, which in Patočka's eyes represents a combination of the pathetic rhetoric of civilizational myths and the complete rationalism of technological developments and technique. By the same token, Patočka criticizes the complete rationality of means that ends in the ultimate irrationality of radical supercivilization—a "philosophical name" for totalitarianism.

It therefore seems clear that the core problem of modernity for Patočka is the reduction of reason to a mere *ratio*, a technology in service of the total rule of humankind over nature, the world, and human beings. Nevertheless, technical rationalism is not all of reason, and neither is reason as *technique* the totality of reason. I propose that this caveat must be understood in line with the Kantian differentiation between *Verstand* (understanding) and *Vernunft* (reason). An analytic-experiential reason—rightly applied in scientific discourse—should not be confused with a greater synthesizing rationality that seeks meaning and understanding.[132] For example, a work of art can be analyzed from the scientific analytical-experimental perspective.

Such analysis will provide us with interesting and important information such as the work's chemical composition or the date of its creation. This information may help toward an interpretation of the painting but will not provide a complete understanding of it because such understanding does not equal the sum of this information. For Patočka, rational understanding, in contrast to modern technical rationalism, refers to insight into meaning. To continue with our example from the field of artistic interpretation, the truth of art is revealed not when we apply certain techniques but when we think through the meaning of art. This truth can never be final but will provoke thought again and again. Moreover, when it comes to art, the issue at stake is not only the truth of the object before our eyes but the truth of our existence mirrored in the piece of art. In other words, the truth of art is not objective but is "revealed" to us, the viewers and interpreters, and challenges our self-understanding.

A similar illustration can be found in the field of natural science. Werner Heisenberg, the Nobel laureate in physics in 1932, suggests that, for example, describing the motion of particles and formulating physical laws based on analytical-experiential methods is not the same as understanding the meaning of particle motion or any other physical event.[133]

The interpretation of Patočka proposed in this chapter shows that the interplay between scientific reason and the rationality that strives for understanding has been lost in the modern orientation toward technological rationalism. Patočka arrives at this conclusion through his engagement with key insights from the great modern philosophers. He follows Masaryk and Husserl in their unconditional emphasis on the rational. From Nietzsche and Heidegger, he has learned the true complexity of the question of reason and that it is necessary to go beyond rationalism. But ultimately, Patočka's position differs from the solutions proposed by his forerunners. Patočka looks for a deeper conception of rationality that breaks with the logic of technical rationalism. In fact, he challenges the need to find an ultimate solution at all. The key to understanding this lies in Patočka's conception of crisis—*krinein*.

We are now back to our initial question: What is the crisis of modernity all about? It is clear that Patočka's interest in the modern crisis goes beyond the critique of reason as an instrument. Crisis applies to the situation of human beings as individuals as well as in society. Patočka thus returns to the ancient understanding of crisis as something dynamic, a moment of decision-making, dealing with problems, and the consciousness of problematicity: "Our life, to the point it lasts, is, after all, constantly in crisis, in the act of deciding, in a yes-no situation, in a kind of equivocal twilight."[134] Life is a constant *krinein*, and crisis belongs to human beings and to being human.[135] Crisis is the condition of life, not an obstacle to be overcome once and for all. Scrupulous attentiveness to the jargon of crisis in current accounts of modernity is endangered by neglecting the central issue, which is looking not for the solution to crisis but rather for its creative integration into our thinking.

Modern crisis as presented by Husserl and Masaryk reverses the order. In this respect, modern thinking is misleading as it attempts to rub out the situation of crisis using the solution to crisis; the philosophical method of questioning is transformed into problem-solving. In this respect, Patočka points out that modernity opens many possibilities, great opportunities for the spirit, but these options are constantly threatened by closed hegemonic thought patterns that lay claim to total knowledge. For this reason, I propose to interpret Patočka's critique as an alternative that goes beyond this impasse—that we find a special kind of postmodern thinking in Patočka.

The figure of post-thinking or after-thinking (*nachdenken*) can be traced through Patočka's entire oeuvre. It is especially explicit in his reflections on Europe, by which he means not a geographical unit but a mode of rationality and philosophical thinking. Against the background of the modern crisis, Patočka posits a *post-European epoch*.[136] If Europe refers to rationality, post-Europe is logically a form of postrationality. In this respect, the postmodern thinking I associate with Patočka is the search for a reason after reason, that is, a rationality that takes into account modern challenges such as the question of reason and the crisis of rationalism, which includes premodern speculative insight—the search for the truth of the whole—and opens possibilities for going deeper and further beyond—the distinction between knowledge and understanding. If we return to our initial claim that Kohák's portrait of Patočka as a critical modern or even antimodern is misleading, we see now that Patočka is indeed rather a postmodern. We must now return to the question of where Patočka finds the foundation of such a postmodern rationality, a rationality that is the basis for creative engagement with the modern spiritual crisis.

I have already pointed out that I find a crucial distinction between rational thinking and technical rationalism. Rational thinking is the human ability to ask fundamental questions and a mode of seeking wisdom, which for Patočka is the foundation of Europe. In contrast, rationalism is the travesty of wisdom and the reduction of thinking to a technique.

The former is philosophical (metaphysical) reason; the latter is known as technical rationalism. But Patočka adds a further element to the distinction in his essay on European reason[137]—Christian reason.

Philosophical-metaphysical speculative reason has its origin in ancient philosophy. Socrates raised the question of the Good, and ever since, philosophy has continued to question all presupposed meaning in order to broaden the understanding of existence. Patočka evaluates this rationality positively as a holistic approach to being. In contrast, technical reason reformulates the world according to causal laws and mathematical principles—reasoning *more geometrico*—and thus presents everything as calculable, predictable, and logical. The understanding of being is replaced by the knowledge of being in the sense of owning the truth about being. In other words, *clare et distincte* is not the result of *theória* (insight) but the dictate of theory. In this respect I agree with James Mensch, who interprets the rise of modern rationalism as a change of emphasis from being to knowing.[138] Against this background, Patočka indicates that Christian reason is "the reason of the heart." Unfortunately, Patočka offers no elaboration on this puzzling idea but the merest hint:

> For if religion includes reason, this reason is definitely more than just the theoretical logos we encounter in science, the logos that seeks to cope with reality, and it is definitely more than the reason of philosophy, which seeks to penetrate the essence of reality. Religion can become a part of the process of rationalization and even significantly contribute to it. Nevertheless, religion contains an atheoretical core—something philosophers are always likely to distort in their interpretations.[139]

What does it mean that religion—Christianity—contains an atheoretical element? Patočka is not to my mind suggesting that Christianity is irrationalism. Christian reason belongs to the domain of rational reflection. Moreover, Patočka affirms the significant contribution of Christianity to the process of rationalization that ultimately resulted in the modern project of rational culture. Although modernity is often at odds with Christianity, we have seen that even explicitly antireligious streams of modern thought tend to maintain certain (para-)religious structures, whether consciously (Comte) or unconsciously (the radical supercivilization of absolute rationalism). Patočka suggests, moreover, that the moderate supercivilization of modernity is directly indebted to Christianity. So, to resolve the riddle of the Christian "reason of the heart," I propose that Patočka is thinking here about a reason that goes beyond rationalism, that the atheoretical core of Christian rationality refers to what we called earlier *vertical thinking*, that is, the ability to reflect rationally and to speculate beyond the horizon of reason based on what is experiential, given, and objectively available.

If the crisis of modernity can be understood in terms of a spiritual crisis, I argue that what Patočka has in mind is simply the loss of vertical thinking. This oblivion or exclusion causes the forgetting of the fundamental questions of life: the question of meaning, of truth, of Being. These questions and indeed the entire exercise of questioning, thinking from question to question, is replaced by technical rationalism—reason as a technology that is ready to give the answers that are deemed necessary. Drawing on Heidegger, Patočka describes this set of modern circumstances as *Gestell*, a universal order in which everything is reduced to an entity that is present-at-hand. Just as we used the example of art earlier, Heidegger offers fine art as the redemption from *Gestell*. The essay "The Symbol of the Earth in K. H. Mácha," in which Patočka interprets the work of the Czech romantic poet Karel Hynek Mácha, follows the Heideggerian line and raises the question of whether a deeper conception of reason can be found in poetry.[140]

For Patočka, the poet is concerned with the most profound questions of being. Poems are meditations on the contrast between the day and the night of life. To embrace crisis, to go through questioning, and to acknowledge problematicity are the main lessons offered by art in general and by poetry in particular. Poems are the very opposite of the texts of rationalism.

Interestingly, Patočka does not fully agree with Heidegger's appreciation of art as the means of redemption from the modern crisis: his suggestion is seen as plausible but insufficient. For Patočka, poetry is concerned with personal-existential crisis; it represents an individual's search for meaning against the background of crisis. Patočka is seeking to understand civilizational crisis, the crisis of modern culture in its entirety. In this respect, poetry must be complemented by rational thinking. But we have seen that for Patočka, reason is not one. In fact, Patočka is critical of the modern development of reason. As such, if we place modern techno-scientific and objectivistic reason to one side, what kind of reason remains to execute thinking? Patočka puts his trust in two rationalities: the philosophical-metaphysical and the Christian. Of course, these are broad terms that require qualification, and this will be provided in chapters 3 and 4 (metaphysics) and chapters 5, 6, and 7 (Christian thinking).

To conclude our discussion on modernity, it seems that Patočka's conception of a spiritual crisis has pointed out the vertical thinking of Christianity as a crucial break with the modern logic of the spirit of technology. In this sense, I propose to read Patočka's critique of radical supercivilization and its rationalism as the search for a reason that takes into account "the reason of the heart." The reconceptualization of modern rationality does not, therefore, depend only on the shift from science to poetry but also on the shift from poetry to Christianity (and philosophy).

This leads us to the final point regarding Patočka's account of the spiritual crisis of modernity and modern reason. Patočka does not seek to return to premodern times. His critique of modernity is not an expression of hostility but the manifestation of modern challenges and their binding legacy. The point he is making is that reason does not exhaust itself in the consideration of objective facts. Facts are undoubtedly an important part of the story, but for Patočka, the story of reason is the *history* of thinking, and history is not merely a fact to be observed but an event to be lived through. The reconceptualization of modern reason is therefore a shift from facts to events. Now we can understand Patočka's concept of the reason of the heart, which is irreplaceable in this respect. The tension between the objective in science and the subjective in Christianity is what ultimately makes *thinking* possible. The reconstitution of this tension is the postmodern position that I associate with Patočka. Not postmodern in the sense that we leave the modern heritage behind once and for all. Rather, Patočka's search for transcending the modern self-enclosure opens the door to a postmodern thinking that does not hesitate to turn to theological thought patterns in response to the thorny questions and challenges raised in modernity.

Chapter 3

After Metaphysics?

Patočka's Deconstruction of Metaphysics and the Postmodern Overcoming of Ontotheology

In the wake of postmodern theological turns to religion, it has become de rigueur to claim that we are living after metaphysics. Patočka's question is what is to be done after "the demise of metaphysics" and can philosophy survive it?[1] It is certainly a question that needs to be asked at a time when professing a critical attitude toward *ontotheology* and elaborating on its *overcoming* is the rule of the day.[2] In this chapter, I therefore propose to read Patočka's critical account of metaphysical philosophy against a background of postmodern attempts to overcome metaphysics and ontotheology.

A variety of motivations lie behind the desire to define oneself as postmetaphysical, nonmetaphysical, or even antimetaphysical. The most oft-repeated of these is in fact theological. Although it is usually formulated by professional philosophers, we hear repeatedly that God, or transcendence, must be portrayed authentically. For example, Jean-Luc Marion argues that God can be properly understood only without being. Gianni Vattimo claims that "Jesus Christ has freed us from the Truth [of metaphysics]."[3] Richard Kearney criticizes an ontotheological reading of God's revelation (in Ex 3:14) as the revelation of *esse ipsum subsistens* and proposes an ontoeschatological interpretation of "God who may be."[4] John D. Caputo leaves the question open and asks who it is that comes after the God of metaphysics.[5]

Although as a phenomenologist Patočka is not particularly well known for having theological issues on his agenda, I will make two related arguments: first, that his thinking provides an alternative point of view to the usual postmodern (postmetaphysical) discourse; and second, that Patočka's philosophy offers a theologically more plausible solution for a reconsideration of God in the wake of the arguments of metaphysics.

I will show this in four stages. First, I will review Patočka's interpretation of metaphysics and its development in the history of philosophy. This analysis will show that metaphysics, according to Patočka, is said in diverse manners and that, ever since its origins in ancient Greece, we have experienced numerous turns, changes, and developments along the way. On this basis, a crucial distinction between *metaphysical philosophy* and *metaphysical thinking* will appear. Patočka's criticism is directed at the former, and what he has in mind under this rubric bears a striking resemblance to Heidegger's analysis and critique of the ontotheological constitution of metaphysics. For this reason, as a second step, I will turn to Heidegger and his argument regarding the problem of ontotheology. Heidegger's critique is unavoidable because it sets the stage for so many current attempts at "overcoming" metaphysics and provides some of the background to Patočka's critical approach. We could even say that the movement of the theological turn and its attempt to go beyond metaphysics is a radical elaboration of Heidegger's critical position toward ontotheology. Third, therefore, I will present two concrete examples of the postmodern tendency to seek to overcome metaphysics and to leave it behind, namely, Marion and Caputo. I will show that to use the critique of ontotheology for postmetaphysical or even antimetaphysical goals misses the point concerning the demise of metaphysics. Finally, I will return to Patočka and suggest that he does not in fact completely or inevitably "undo" metaphysics but rather opens the possibility of genuine metaphysical thinking that could eventually overcome postmodern attempts at overcoming metaphysics. In this respect, Patočka will prove to be an insightful interlocutor of the kind of theology that accepts that we are living in a world after metaphysics, but which also feels uneasy about leaving all metaphysical thinking behind.

From Metaphysical Thinking to Metaphysical Philosophy

Patočka opens his overview of "Metaphysics in the Twentieth Century" with the following definition: "Metaphysics is a philosophical doctrine of the last foundation of world being, of what-is and of what being is in itself."[6] As such, metaphysics emerged in antiquity and became the prevailing philosophical tradition of Western thinking, even though it originally represented only a single chapter in the lengthy tome of ancient Greek philosophy. As the title of Patočka's later essay "Democritus and Plato as the Founders of Metaphysics" suggests, metaphysics has a double origin, although Patočka is anxious to point out that the two metaphysical traditions arise from the same foundation, that is, the venture into the experience of mathematical and geometrical knowledge, which subsequently leads to "total, consistent, and uniform reflection on life and things . . . while penetrating what is eternal and permanent."[7] Metaphysics therefore aims at an explanation of the whole and at determining the ultimate being, which is understood as the divine.[8]

Despite the same general orientation, the two metaphysical traditions differ significantly from one another. The Platonic line, in which Patočka includes Aristotle, is more spiritual, oriented toward *logos*, and concerned with notions such as the "care for the soul." The atomistic tradition of Democritus on the other hand is materialistic. For Patočka, Democritus represents the prelude to the modern techno-scientific mentality, or, to put it the other way round, modern philosophy oriented toward matter and fascinated by technology replays the atomist metaphysics of Democritus. It is hardly surprising, therefore, that Christianity, as the religion of the West, appropriated the Platonic-Aristotelian line of thought and preserved it as Western philosophy. But first things first. Metaphysics predates Christianity, so in order to understand the present crisis of metaphysics, and before we consider Christian metaphysics, we must take a step back—a long step, to the time before Plato and Aristotle. For Patočka, the story begins with Socrates. Whether Socrates is "a literary myth or an historical reality" is unimportant.[9] The point is that he plays a decisive role in the formation of both metaphysical thinking and metaphysical philosophy.

Socrates is the originator of philosophical questioning, the one who made the later metaphysical tradition possible. Socrates's context, as Patočka reminds us, is a concern for the whole, an astonishment with being, and an emphasis on the perplexity of being. In other words, Socrates looks at the world just as it appears, with all its "problematicity." In this way, he opposes the Sophists, who are not afraid of manipulating beings as mere things or tools, and who therefore follow purely pragmatic goals in order to make human life more comfortable. Socrates's maieutic method, on the other hand, reveals the compelling paradox of human existence: that the natural desire for the whole—the knowledge of the whole—can be adequately phrased only as the knowledge of nonknowing. As Patočka observes:

> So Socrates, in contrast to the ordinary mode and direction of life, reaches a new level on which it is no longer possible to formulate objective, factual, positive assertions. . . . He formulates his new truth—since the problem of truth is what is at stake—only indirectly, in the form of a question, in the form of skeptical analysis, of a negation of all finite assertions.[10]

Socrates challenges positive formulations and pretensions to absolute knowledge of the totality of being. For Patočka, as Kohák succinctly puts it, "philosophy in the Socratic sense [is] asking the question about the whole . . . about being as such, being as a whole."[11] This is the basic metaphysical question that according to Patočka is constantly to be thought through. In other words, the true task of metaphysical thinking is "thinking questioningly."[12]

Metaphysical philosophy appears only after Socrates's metaphysical thinking. Plato, Aristotle, and Democritus fall prey to the temptation of "ordinary, finite, and utilitarian practical knowledge" and offer ready-made answers to any questions raised.[13] For Patočka, these followers of Socrates are responsible, each in his own way, for the paradigm shift of the *metaphysical turn*, which redefined philosophical meditation—metaphysical thinking—as metaphysical philosophy.

For example, in contrast to the Socratic metaphysical thinking embedded in the world and history, Platonism and its doctrine of Ideas refers to the realm of otherworldly and eternal being. Moreover, being is not understood here as a transcendent nonbeing, which is not an entity, but as the highest being, meaning a higher-level entity.[14] Rather than the Socratic questioning of truth in the form of *alētheia*, the disclosure of being, Platonism imitates the ideal world and defines the absolute truth. Although Platonism preserves the distinction and limits rational reflection based on *logos*, and the eternal Ideas are never penetrated in their ultimate essence, the turn has been made and Socratic metaphysical interruptions are left behind in favor of Platonic metaphysical definitions.

Aristotle completes and radicalizes the turn from metaphysical thinking to metaphysical philosophy. As Patočka notes, "in Aristotle, transcendence is transformed, with a fatal inevitability, into a transcendent, supermundane reality, a transcendent deity."[15] For Patočka, Aristotelianism is thus a reinterpretation of the preceding tradition in terms of abstract logic. What Plato calls Ideas, Aristotle traces as forms. The highest being—or entity—is the condition and foundation of the intelligibility of reality.[16] Therefore, "with Aristotle, philosophy has become a science, raising a question concerning a second, or meta-physical level of being rather than the Socratic question concerning the meaning of the whole."[17] Aristotelianism immunizes metaphysical thinking, but the definition is not enough. From now on, the discourse is ruled by the syllogism.[18]

Despite its critical tenor, it would be a mistake to read Patočka's analysis of the nascent metaphysics, which resulted in the metaphysical turn, as a one-sided criticism that suggested everything went wrong after Socrates. Patočka makes it clear that "Plato would not be Plato if he were not also more than Plato,"[19] and he does not hesitate to speak of Aristotle's great mind.[20] The point is simply to spell out the difference between the Socratic moment of thinking and the philosophy of Platonism and Aristotelianism. The former involves the philosopher in questioning, thinking, and living. It all relates to Being (in-the-world), and so Socrates lives what he teaches. The latter does not suggest the complete opposite. Philosophy is still a way of life, and there is no doubt about the *ars vivendi* of Plato and Aristotle. But to understand Platonic and Aristotelian metaphysical writings, one does not have to live in truth—it is possible to comprehend them from a distance. Whereas Socrates's thinking is about living *in* truth—where "living" is the movement—Plato and Aristotle turn to the art of reasoning *about* truth—where the stress is on the object of truth. Patočka is therefore keen to point out an important distinction between metaphysical thinking and metaphysical philosophy.[21] He does not set a radical opposition between the two, but his reading of the history of philosophy suggests that a certain metaphysical philosophy slowly drowns out metaphysical thinking, which involved a constant reflection on the existential, that is, on the way of living in the world. This shift is crucial and highly problematic.

To sum up, the metaphysical turn is the shift from the task of thinking to the conception of the highest knowledge. Metaphysics becomes highly pretentious, almost arrogant, and marches in such manner through the ages. The self-critical theologian must admit, furthermore, that this all took place with no small amount of thanks to Christianity, as metaphysical philosophy has become an integral part of reflecting and presenting the faith of mainstream Christianity.

Theology elaborates on the metaphysical order of being as the foundation of the intelligibility of the whole and as the goal toward which everything is directed. Patočka remarks that medieval Scholasticism reads metaphysics, especially Aristotelianism, as the foundation of a "natural theology that is able to offer the rational grounding of the mystery of faith, although not to penetrate the last instance of being."[22] The distance between beings and the transcendent ultimate being is expressed in terms of two worlds of entities of different kinds. The object of theology—God—is conceived as the highest supernatural being—the *causa sui*—"not the dimension of the depth of Being but rather *a* being."[23] This means that theology based on metaphysical philosophy is concerned with the essence of beings and of the highest being that is rationally graspable.

For example, Scholastic theology draws from metaphysical philosophy the analogy of being. In this way it deduces the universal knowledge about the present order of being from the metaphysical otherworldly realm of being. In turn, the intelligibility and existence of this world is totally dependent on and conditioned by the eternal unchangeable metaphysical order. As Patočka appositely summarizes: "Being is ordered by God and every single being has its place, value, and aim within this order."[24] This is what is commonly called the ontotheological project:

> Metaphysics [is an] aspiration to a global understanding of the whole. Metaphysics, by its very nature, assumes going beyond all mundane being, but this going beyond is then taken to mean raising it to a new, "true" being and so to a "true science." Thus it becomes a doctrine of the true being, or, most frequently (on theological grounds), of a divine being. Metaphysics is the science of the divine.[25]

According to Patočka, this line of metaphysical philosophy is maintained almost uninterrupted until the Reformation, which presents itself as the emancipation from classical metaphysics—a move away from Athens. He nonetheless insists that despite this radical rhetoric, the break from metaphysics never happened.[26] Patočka takes note of occasional, haphazard attempts to develop a nonmetaphysical theology. For example, Pascal's orientation on human finitude and his emphasis on the nonpossibility of grasping the meaning of human existence by means of positive knowledge represents a singular development in early modern theological thinking.[27] Similarly, Nicholas of Cusa, Meister Eckhart, and Jan Amos Comenius, whom Patočka considers to be alternatives to the mainstream tradition of metaphysical philosophy, are from a historical point of view only marginal exceptions, mere parentheses.[28] What actually happens is the strengthening of the position of metaphysical philosophy and therefore the continuation of the ontotheological project.

Despite the fact that modernity eventually challenges metaphysics as the domain of theological rationality, ontotheology refuses to disappear. Patočka identifies two movements in this respect: Cartesianism and German Idealism.[29] Descartes, and after him Leibniz and Spinoza, propose a metaphysical rationalism of clear and distinct ideas. The foundation of Cartesianism is mathematical certitude, the ability to calculate, predict, and therefore to know. This fundamentally changes the modern understanding of reason and truth. The sense of the whole, still preserved in Scholastic metaphysics, becomes fragmented. Truth is no longer a statement about the whole but pertains to particulars or their sum.[30] Nonetheless, the highest being stands in the background and still provides the foundation of intelligibility. In the case of German Idealism—Patočka thinks of Fichte, Hegel, and Schelling—philosophy pretends to conceive the absolute and to elaborate a speculative system that grasps the totality.[31] Patočka's point is that despite these challenges, Christianity retains its monopoly on metaphysics and ontotheology.

Modernity nonetheless makes various attempts to overcome metaphysical philosophy. Patočka notes that the Enlightenment's battle with religion and theology is also a battle with metaphysics. Immanuel Kant is a key figure in this respect.[32] In fact, Kant invents the term *ontotheology*, which he uses for metaphysical proofs of the existence of God from "mere concepts, without the help of any experience whatsoever."[33] Kant also argues against classical metaphysical philosophy as the doctrine of the *Ding an sich*. For Kant, ontotheological metaphysics is impossible because a thinking subject is able to know only particulars (*phenomena*) and not things in themselves before they are encountered in a cognitive experience (*noumena*).[34] Every subsequent attempt by modernity to overcome metaphysics is marked by this position.

All modern attempts to overcome metaphysics—positivism, empiricism, humanism, Marxism, pragmatism, or any other *-ism* we may care to think of—share a common vision that rejects an absolute foundation for reality in favor of science, which unfolds causal relations, that is, things as they naturally are. Nothing more and nothing less. For Patočka, however, these philosophical projects—as well as other modern projects that recontextualize metaphysics, such as the philosophy of Bergson or Whitehead—are still part of the tradition of Western metaphysical philosophy after the metaphysical turn. It is not our task here to offer a detailed review of all these critical positions toward metaphysics.[35] What must be said, however, is that modern critiques and the many postmodern deaths of metaphysics often replace one metaphysical system with another that privileges positive, finite, and objective knowledge. Philosophers are interested in beings rather than Being. By the same token, Christian metaphysics, in its various expressions, seeks the knowledge of God as the highest being. When Patočka delves into the three principal Christian traditions of Orthodoxy, Catholicism, and Protestantism, he finds metaphysical foundationalism in all of them:[36] Platonic tendencies are present in Orthodoxy; Aristotelian Neo-Thomism takes the lead in (modern) Catholicism; and the Protestant radicalism of dialectical theology, which claims to accept nothing but the Word of God, appears to be some kind of metaphysical foundationalism of transcendent revelation.

Again, we would miss Patočka's point completely if we were to read his account of metaphysical philosophy as a simple turning away from those great thinkers who happened also to be metaphysicians. In fact, Patočka draws plenty of inspiration from them, especially for his own reflections on the meaning of metaphysics (as we will see later). Patočka's aim is to point out the ontotheological nature of most of metaphysical philosophy in contrast to metaphysical thinking. To be sure, Martin Heidegger's refocusing on the question of Being as one of philosophy's forgotten questions also inspires Patočka in this respect. Patočka ruminates upon why Heidegger asks his question when everything seems to be oriented to the being of beings, the question of entities. Medieval Scholasticism speculated on the being of beings and of the highest being. Modernity turned to the matter and asked the same question from an anthropological and scientific perspective. One way or another, Christian metaphysics, early modern metaphysical philosophy, and modern science share the same interest: "to extract being from a paragon of the highest being, like Aristotle's *theion* or Hegel's *absolute*."[37] As a result, the metaphysical turn identified by Patočka implies the inception of ontotheological philosophy.

Patočka's definition of metaphysics and Heidegger's understanding of the matter are uncannily alike. As the term *ontotheology* enters our discussion, it has become clear that Patočka is following Heidegger in his account of metaphysical philosophy. Bearing in mind the distinction

Patočka makes between metaphysical thinking and metaphysical philosophy, we will now turn to Heidegger's critique of metaphysics as ontotheology.

Heidegger's Critique of the Ontotheological Structure of Metaphysics

Heidegger is concerned with the question of Being (*Sein*), which is, as Aristotle reminds us, "said in many ways." For Heidegger, however, this multilayered question seems to have been inadequately formulated, forgotten even. The oblivion of Being is the reality of philosophy "in spite of all our interest in metaphysics."[38] Moreover, where the tradition of metaphysical philosophy considered Being to be given in beings, modernity focuses solely on beings. For this reason, beings become objects, and in this sense entities in knowledge. Despite metaphysical philosophy's obsession with explanations of being, genuine questioning of Being is somehow forgotten. Heidegger therefore suggests the deconstruction (*Destruktion*) of the metaphysical tradition in order to understand the question once again.

For Heidegger, metaphysics constitutes the frame of intelligibility and "determines the most basic presupposition of what *anything* is, including ourselves."[39] Metaphysics provides the basic sense of what it means to be, or, in Heidegger's own words, "metaphysics is the truth of the totality of entities as such."[40] Heidegger identifies five distinct metaphysical epochs in history, five different paradigms of *what* and *how* everything *is*. It is not necessary to review all these epochs. What is important is that they share the same principle, namely, their epistemological structure. Heidegger calls this unifying principle *ontotheology*.[41]

"The Onto-theo-logical Constitution of Metaphysics" involves, as the title of Heidegger's essay suggests, the intertwining of three aspects. First, the actuality of being is ontologically grounded in the first principle—an uncaused cause that causes the entire reality of beings. Second, being as a whole is theologically grounded in the highest, eternal being, that is, God as the source and the goal of all things. Finally, beings are ontically knowable because of their foundation in *logos*.[42] In Heidegger's scheme, ontotheologically constituted philosophy is concerned with three sets of double questions, each of which reflects both the ontological and the theological foundation against a background of postulating the meaningfulness—which modernity transforms into the "logical coherence"—of these questions: (1) What is an entity as such? How are entities as a whole? (2) What is the most basic entity? How are we to understand the highest entity that grounds all entities? (3) What is the essence—the *whatness*—of entities? What is the existence—the *thatness*—of entities? Heidegger argues that this metaphysical doubling can be detected through the entire tradition of metaphysics, from Thales and Anaximander to Nietzsche. Heidegger's point is presented succinctly in the following oft-quoted passage:

> When metaphysics thinks of beings with respect to the ground that is common to all beings as such, then it is logic as onto-logic. When metaphysics thinks of beings as such as a whole, that is, with respect to the highest being which accounts for everything, then it is logic as theo-logic.[43]

Therefore, metaphysics concerns not only the question of being as the totality of entities, that is, what an entity is in its essence (*ontology*), but also the being of entities as the question about their "thatness" and existence (*theology*).[44] The most important question, however, the question of Being, is put to one side.

Ontotheology thus occupies the center of Heidegger's critique of metaphysics in two senses. First, Heidegger criticizes the conception of the being of entities as the ground for intelligible order. Second, he argues against the conception of the highest entity as the source of all entities and the intelligible order of being itself. Heidegger objects to the presupposition of *analogia entis*, that philosophical reflection about the structure of the world and the phenomena in it can be deduced from reflection upon the divine.[45] Because ontotheological thought is interested solely in entities—in Heidegger's language, in objects present-at-hand that are penetrable by knowledge—ontotheology aims at the formulation of a total speculative system. God comprehended as the *self-caused cause* functions as the origin and the end in the chain of being qua entities.[46]

For Heidegger, the consequences of ontotheological metaphysics are quite serious. A static and ahistorical manner of philosophy forgets Being in favor of beings, meaning entities. This means that metaphysics prevents philosophy from asking the right question and theology is left with a conceptual understanding of God before whom "man can neither pray nor sacrifice . . . man can neither fall to his knees in awe nor can he play music and dance before this god."[47]

As has become clear, Heidegger is concerned with *thinking* the question of Being, which sank into oblivion because of the obsession of philosophy and theology with objectifying reasons. The problem therefore lies in the question. Heidegger does not appear to suggest that after reconsidering the question of Being there will be an answer; rather, that the question of Being leads us (back) to thinking, and to that which has been obscured by metaphysical philosophy.

Heidegger's alternative to metaphysics is "god-less thinking."[48] John Peacocke interprets this proposition as establishing the opposition between thinking and philosophy.[49] The former concerns serenity, whereas the latter privileges calculative reasoning. In this respect, metaphysical philosophy, as a positive account of the being of beings and the highest being (*causa sui*), is the science of being and the science of God. As such, philosophy prevents thinking. According to Peacocke, Heidegger's objections to theology—presented in his "Phenomenology and Theology"—should be read along these lines. Metaphysical theology prevents thinking God to the same extent that metaphysical philosophy obscures the question of Being. Only when metaphysical philosophy and the metaphysical God as the self-caused cause are abandoned can thinking make a reappearance. For Heidegger, thinking is still traceable in poetry, literature, and art (and, Peacocke adds, also in religion). In this sense, we should read in Heidegger's remark that his godless thinking "is thus perhaps closer to the divine God" and "more open to him than onto-theo-logic would like to admit."[50]

Heidegger's ideas are revived in the turn to religion in continental philosophy. Various authors adopt the critique of ontotheology as their own. Rather than adopting the notion of an absolute God—the highest object and the grounding principle of everything—they look for possibilities to name the divine from a new perspective while at the same time leaving a metaphysical model of God behind.[51]

Postmodern Overcoming of Ontotheology

Grand claims concerning the overcoming of metaphysics abound in postmodern accounts of religion and God. Heidegger's concern with Being and his critique of ontotheology provoke a particularly strong and widespread philosophical and theological reaction.[52] Janicaud goes as far as blaming Heidegger for the entire theological turn in continental philosophy.[53]

Indeed, Heidegger can be viewed as the dominant influence on the new wave of French phenomenology represented by Marion, Henry, Chrétien, and Lacoste, as well as on the Anglo-American movement of radical hermeneutics initiated by Caputo and succeeded by Westphal, Kearney, and Hart. As Wolfe succinctly summarizes, "[Postmodern theology after metaphysics] sees in Heideggerian philosophy the potential . . . for responding to the call of the divine without turning God into an idol by metaphysical speculations."[54]

Despite his critical attitude toward Christianity, Heidegger is taken as the redeemer from the logocentrism and oppression caused by metaphysics. Regardless of whether, ultimately, we find Heidegger incompatible with Christianity,[55] or attempt to reconcile his thinking with the Christian vision of the world and of God,[56] his philosophy remains the decisive element in every attempt to overcome metaphysics. Westphal offers a three-point summary of the shared vision of the thinkers who expound and expand on Heidegger: (1) Christianity is not ontotheology by definition; (2) Christianity is capable of resisting ontotheology and also capable of making Heidegger's critique its own; and (3) Christianity is always in danger of falling prey to ontotheology and, as history shows, often does.[57] By the same token, Vattimo points out what he sees as a tension within Christianity: he interprets the history of the last two thousand years as the gradual decline of a Christianity imprisoned in a metaphysical objectivism inherited from the Greeks, but he also identifies Christianity as the event that dissolves metaphysics through the principle of charity.[58]

In the following examples of the postmodern overcoming of metaphysics, I will first present Marion as a key figure of the New Phenomenology, and will then turn to Caputo as a founding figure of the American take on the continental philosophy of religion. Marion and Caputo both appropriate Heidegger's critique; both also criticize the metaphysical elements within Christianity while paradoxically using Christian argumentation for their respective reinterpretations of God and transcendence after metaphysics.

New Phenomenology: Jean-Luc Marion

The French phenomenologist Jean-Luc Marion gained renown as a thinker who occupies the nexus between philosophy and theology. Especially after the English translation of his early and theologically oriented *God without*

Being,[59] Marion received a great deal of attention and his ideas have been widely discussed. For this reason, he is also the prime target for Janicaud's attack on the theological turn in phenomenology, which, Janicaud insists, must remain free from theological aspirations.[60] Although Marion somewhat modified the standpoint he took in his inaugural lecture at the University of Chicago and rephrased his position as a "philosophy of religion" that mediates between philosophy and theology,[61] the question of God still appears on his agenda. In this sense, the critique of metaphysics and the necessity to overcome ontotheology play a notable role.

In Marion's view, the problem with metaphysics is that it reduced all thinking of God to a univocal language that completely obliterates the sense of God's radical difference from the world.[62] Marion's critical distance from metaphysics is indebted to two things: his expert knowledge of Descartes and his critical appropriation of Heidegger. For Marion, Descartes is, historically speaking, the first ontotheologian and his thinking thus fits Heidegger's definition of metaphysics. Marion therefore situates metaphysical philosophy in early modernity, as in his opinion the thinkers who went before, especially the giants of the Christian tradition such as Thomas Aquinas, do not in fact fall prey to ontotheology.[63]

Descartes's metaphysics is ontotheological in two ways. First, Cartesianism forgets the ontological difference between being as an entity and Being as such. For this reason, his system conceives the being of God in a similar way to the being of humans or of any other object. Second, Cartesianism grounds the *ego* of *cogito* in the highest being. God functions as the principle of intelligibility and as *causa sui*. Thus, when Marion sets out his program for overcoming metaphysics, he speaks of this Cartesian metaphysical ontotheology.[64]

When Marion moves to Heidegger, he makes use of his critique of ontotheology as a critique of the completion of metaphysics in techno-scientific culture. In other words, the problem of modernity is not so much that metaphysics has nothing to say, but that thinking is disallowed: "The principle of sufficient reason [is] a unique point of access to phenomenality."[65] In this sense, Marion interprets Heidegger's destruction (*Destruktion*) of metaphysics not as its dissolution but as the liberation from the bonds of the techno-scientific mentality that presents itself as the accomplishment of all the possibilities of metaphysics. In other words, ontotheological metaphysics is nihilistic, as according to its own logic, everything is accessible and can be turned into an object of knowledge. The ontotheological structure that needs to be overcome is therefore a synonym for representational thinking that claims to grasp "the non-representable, the non-orderable, the non-calculable Being."[66]

Marion also distances himself from Heidegger, however. In the first two chapters of *God without Being*, Marion elaborates on the thesis that if taken seriously and properly, God must be thought of in terms of "outside being." Or as Marion suggests: What if the question of the overcoming of metaphysics requires overcoming the question of being itself?[67]

Marion sheds light on this idea with his juxtaposition of the idol and the icon. The idol is a consequence of our way of looking at the divine. Interestingly, Marion does not consider the idol as a completely misguided image of God or the divine. The problem with idols is that our gaze freezes upon them and considers them to be complete images of the divine. One fails to realize that, instead of God, one is gazing at a projection—an invisible mirror.[68] But the idol is not necessarily an image, statuette, or material thing. For Marion, even ideas, thoughts, and concepts can become idolatrous.[69] In this sense, the conceptual approach of metaphysics is idolatrous in essence because it falls prey to the temptation to grasp God exhaustively. Marion therefore suggests that we must leave the language of being behind.

The icon, in turn, reverses the order of seeing: "The icon does not result from a vision but provokes one. The icon is not seen, but appears."[70] It is the divine that gazes at the viewer and establishes the relationship. The iconic naming of God, therefore, postulates the overcoming of metaphysics and its ontotheological structure.[71] From this perspective, Marion welcomes the death of God proclaimed by Nietzsche. For in his perspective, it is actually "god" between quotation marks, a "god" who does not deserve the name, who has died.[72] From now on, God with a capital *G* can truly live.

But how are we to understand this nonconceptual naming of the God beyond being? First, Marion introduces the "crossing out" of God. When he wants to speak about a real God, not the god of ontotheology, he writes "G⊗d."[73] This maneuver points to the impossibility of enclosing God in a concept. As Marion insists, this does not automatically mean that after the deconstruction of ontotheology, God as a concept is something forbidden. The point is to bear witness to the fact that the concept of God can never epistemologically exhaust the reality of God. In other words, the concept of God always contains the unthinkable.[74]

Second, Marion proposes to use the concept of love as the only concept capable of escaping idolatrous manipulation: "Love consists in the fact that it gives itself."[75] For Marion, this means that a genuine naming of God begins from God himself and from the very fact that he gives his love. In other words, to think about the unthinkable God presupposes that God gives himself as the gift.[76] In this respect, Marion differentiates theo*logy* and *theo*logy. The former is unable to speak of God and commits idolatry because it concerns a positive conceptual account of the divine and transcendence. Only the latter—*theo*logy—is *capax Dei*. For Marion, *theo*logy equals the language of prayer and mystical theology. This language is beyond both cataphatic and apophatic thinking. Its "content" is pure praise. Marion's alternative to metaphysical ontotheology is therefore the phenomenology of givenness.

RADICAL HERMENEUTICS: JOHN D. CAPUTO

Caputo is well known as a prominent popularizer of the continental philosophy of religion and a key figure—perhaps the key figure—of the theological turn in America. His long-term interest in the overlap between philosophy and theology is marked by his opposition to metaphysics. Simpson suggests that Caputo's entire work is an "exorcism of a faithless metaphysics."[77] Even in his earliest engagements with Heidegger, Caputo proclaims "the end of metaphysics" and defines his projects as "overcoming onto-theology." On this basis, he later develops a postmetaphysical project of "radical hermeneutics."

Caputo proposes a constructive deconstruction of metaphysical ontotheology using the metaphysical thinking of authors from the Middle Ages, especially Thomas Aquinas. According to Caputo, what we are engaging with here is something he calls *aletheiology*. But what does this mean? Medieval metaphysics contemplates the mystery of truth in terms of *union* rather than in terms of the *adequatio* more typical of modern metaphysical systems.[78] It appears from this perspective that Caputo is not ruling out all metaphysics but is leaving space for authentic metaphysical thinking, especially in the work of Aquinas. Nevertheless, he later corrects this possible interpretation of his thinking and makes it clear that overcoming metaphysics is an absolute necessity in the postmodern context. His point about Aquinas rather suggests that the problem of metaphysics is one of gradual decline. Caputo opposes the thesis that Aquinas escapes the ontotheological critique and makes it clear that the Angelic Doctor is part of the problem. For Caputo, Aquinas participates in the oblivion of the *difference* between Being and beings. In this respect, Caputo proposes an alternative interpretation of Heidegger's concern with the question of Being. The forgetfulness of Being is not primarily the concern for the ontological distinction between beings and Being, but the concern for that "which opens the distinction."[79]

Nonetheless, there is a "sphere of possibilities" for how to read Aquinas and bring him closer to Heidegger's aim of overcoming ontotheological modes of thinking.[80] To do so, we must bracket the modern point of view and read Aquinas within his context, that is, the context of contemplation and prayerfulness (*pietas*). In this respect, Caputo finds "a strong sense of the limits of reason" in Aquinas.[81] What Caputo means here is that reason as the metaphysical *ratio* needs to be guided and complemented by the mystical moment of thinking similar to Meister Eckhart's *Gelassenheit* (equanimity).[82] Aquinas, the champion of rationality and the greatest Christian metaphysician, is well aware of this. He thus serves as Caputo's main ally in setting limits to metaphysics and, ultimately, overcoming ontotheology just as Heidegger proposes it.

Caputo expands on his early work in his publications *Radical Hermeneutics* and *More Radical Hermeneutics*. Here, he elaborates on the idea of overcoming and relies heavily on Derrida, the thinker with whom Caputo seeks to overcome Heidegger's overcoming, which is why the word *radical* appears in the titles of his books. For Caputo, the problem is not simply the ontotheological structure of metaphysics but the whole idea of metaphysics. Following Derrida, Caputo opposes the metaphysics of presence, that is, the conceptual knowledge that determines being as present. Derrida calls this *logocentrism*: the presupposition that meaning gives itself—is present—in things themselves.[83] According to Caputo, this oppressive, negative power imposed on us by unlimited conceptual rationalism needs to be excised from our lives.[84] Simpson suggests that the four main points of Caputo's negative account of metaphysics are: (1) abstraction, (2) universalization, (3) unification, and (4) unfaithfulness.[85]

What does this mean exactly? For Caputo, metaphysics appears as disengaged and disinterested speculation that pretends to speak from a god's-eye viewpoint. Metaphysical abstraction withdraws from our historical existence and offers illusions of eternal truths and universal laws valid for eternity. Consequently, metaphysics creates universal systems and overarching hierarchical thought patterns. Metaphysics is the absolute static knowledge that protects us from any movement because everything is present.[86] In this sense, metaphysics proves itself unfaithful to life—historical life—because it ignores life's finitude. Questions play no role in the universal scope of metaphysics. Beginning with Plato's attempt to answer all Socrates's questions, metaphysics has offered a false illusion of direct access to the facticity of reality.[87] Nonetheless, Caputo claims that the human condition is much more complex than metaphysics would have us believe. The imposed truth covers a thorny doubt, a heretical idea (of radical hermeneutics): "the truth that there is no truth, no master name which holds things captive."[88]

Caputo's antimetaphysical radical hermeneutics can be summed up as a concern for a humility of thinking as against the metaphysical striving for absolute knowledge and a superior kind of rationalism; for a "hardness of life"[89] in place of the foundationalism of metaphysical claims;[90] for particularity rather than the metaphysical universalization of all instances; for alterity and plurality, otherness, open-ended thinking.

Caputo claims, nevertheless, that his suggestion of postmetaphysical rationality does not result in irrationalism or relativism. On the contrary, radical hermeneutics liberates reason from its metaphysical constraints and opens its true depths; under metaphysical oppression, reason has functioned as "the instrument of discipline, not [as] a mark of freedom."[91] However, the true vocation of reason is to "search everywhere, question everything."[92] Radical hermeneutics does not, therefore, represent a kind of hopeless indecision; rather, it is about hopeful "undecidability," the adventurous movement of life free from any kind of metaphysical determinism.[93] Theologically speaking, Caputo's critique of ontotheology and his deconstruction of metaphysics resemble an analogy of the liberating power of the Easter experience. Metaphysical rationalism must die and be buried so that reason may be resurrected in all its depth and richness. Or is that a little too . . . Hegelian? In any case, Caputo's proposal can be summed up as follows: rather than looking at things from above (*metaphysica*), we need to reconsider rationality as being on the way (*meta-hodos*).

OVERCOMING METAPHYSICS—WHERE TO?

The examples of Marion and Caputo confirm the opinion of Simmons and Benson in their *New Phenomenology* that the critique of ontotheology is not an opposition to theology as such. Rather, the overcoming of metaphysics liberates both philosophy and theology from their conceptual bonds.[94] The *causa sui*, the god of philosophers before whom there is neither dancing and rejoicing nor weeping and mourning, must be replaced with a living God, presumably the God of faith, under whose wings we find hope.

Marion and Caputo—and numerous others—propose to open the possibility of looking at the divine from a different perspective by overcoming epistemic arrogance and thus liberating both God and theology from the bonds of univocal metaphysical systems and reconstituting them as a critical reflection of faith. We are now living and thinking after metaphysics.

Indeed, it seems that what we have learned from Heidegger is *how* (not) to speak about God; the question remains whether it is still possible to say anything at all about God. We have reconsidered the question of Being and left metaphysics behind. But one question forgotten after the end of metaphysics is that of *what* we as theologians and philosophers can say about God herself. Although we have dispensed with speculative systems of metaphysics, we tend to forget about the metaphysical too. Wolfe, for example, argues against easy appropriations of Heidegger. It is one thing to apply Heidegger's critique to the conception of God as the highest being, thus claiming God to be uncontaminated by being (God without Being). Something else often left unaddressed in the current debate is *to respond* "to God as the self-giving being of the late Heidegger," says Wolfe.[95] In other words, the postmodern overcoming of ontotheology is preoccupied with our talk of transcendence as metaphysics, but it does not consider the transcendent realm itself. As a result, God, the Other, faith, love are all exempt from criticism. Schrijvers says of such fideistic overcoming of ontotheology that "here we have a bad theological response to a good philosophical question."[96] Marion and Caputo's overcoming of metaphysics is similarly questionable. Caputo's emphasis on the mystical element of faith consequently functions as an immunization against Heidegger's critique and, in fact, as a leap from problematic questions to the shelter of comfortable answers regarding hope. Marion's project seems to be more elaborate, but his concept of a pure giving and his naming of God as love is also, like motherhood and apple pie, beyond criticism. In general, although the postmodern overcoming of metaphysics makes us aware of the problem of ontotheology, it is possible to question whether it sets itself the right goal, namely, to spell out a nonmetaphysical kind of thinking, and, as a result, a theology beyond or without metaphysics.

Following Heidegger, Thomson claims that the critique of ontotheology is not a narrowly theological issue. The postmodern theological turns and their emancipation from metaphysics address only half of the problem. In fact, Heidegger presents ontotheology as a cultural problem of modernity and its metaphysics as the closure of and withdrawal from thinking. Heidegger's motivation is thus to step back, to break with onto-theology in order to unfold a genuine metaphysical thinking.[97] It seems now that the initial idea of overcoming metaphysics does not result in antimetaphysics. This is exactly the place where Patočka, who historically precedes the theological turn and is thus closer to Heidegger, is extremely helpful in searching for an alternative to the postmetaphysical endeavors of the theological turn.

Metaphysical Thinking Reconsidered

The main thesis of this concluding section is that Patočka understands the complexities surrounding metaphysics and elaborates upon its overcoming more productively than do the authors we have been discussing thus far. This argument is grounded in Kohák's claim that Patočka's critique of metaphysics can be read in the context of thinking God after onto-theology.[98] However, Rezek rightly points out that Patočka's contribution in this respect cannot be reduced to purely theological goals.[99] Rather, Patočka's critique of metaphysics must also be taken as a reflection upon the human condition while taking into account the "question mark" of human finitude. For Patočka, this is the task of phenomenological philosophy. It is important nonetheless to understand that this phenomenological endeavor "not only wants to analyze phenomena as such, but also wants to derive results from this; it wants to derive *results*, as is said, that are *metaphysical*."[100] Put another way, the critique of metaphysics is not merely a surpassing of conceptual knowledge but a reconsideration of human existence in the midst of the world of things.

To understand Patočka's alternative to metaphysical philosophy, we must set out his basic presuppositions. Instead of the traditional metaphysical approach, which looks at phenomena from the perspective of eternity, phenomenological philosophy raises the question from the perspective of finitude and of history. Patočka invokes the ancient maxim of "knowing thyself" in this respect:

> *Gnothi seauton* is the challenge to accept our own limits, the challenge of *sophrosynē* [reasonableness]. Is history not a challenge to reason to know itself and to recognize its limits? And is this challenge not simply awakening from the dogmatic slumber of a reason that is not aware of its own history?[101]

For Patočka, knowing thyself means "the awareness of being in the world,"[102] a Heideggerian motif that is a constant of Patočka's phenomenological philosophy. What is the meaning, however, of being-in-the-world? First, it refers to the historicity of an individual being and consequently to the consciousness of one's finitude. Second, it means being in the midst of things, that is, having neither clear ideas about their beginning (*archē*) nor exhaustive knowledge concerning their end (*telos*). Third, and above all, being-in-the-world means being with others. Any thinkable alternative to metaphysical philosophy therefore rejects the ideal of metahistorical being and the totality of knowledge grounded in eternal, extramundane principles, regardless of whether we call them God or Ideas. For Patočka, the problem of metaphysics—and its overcoming and sublimation (*Aufhebung*)—revolves around the ambiguity of the human condition as situated in world history, which is understood as an open horizon of those indeterminate possibilities that are open at any given moment.[103] In short, Patočka's movement beyond metaphysics is marked by a historical reason, or rather, is a philosophizing within history that is fascinated with the vibrant stream of life rather than the idol of facticity.

With this in mind, we recall the earlier division between metaphysical philosophy and metaphysical thinking. It could be argued that Patočka explicitly outlines something we call metaphysical thinking in his essay "Nonmetaphysical Philosophy and Science," which was never published and remained only in an unfinished draft. Despite the sketchy nature of the document, its main point is communicated clearly:

> Nonmetaphysical philosophy does not regard metaphysical problems as meaningless. On the contrary, this philosophy locates their meaning and function at a fundamentally different level from the level of what is purely, objectively, knowable and controllable. The attempt to completely eliminate metaphysical questions is, in fact, a manifestation of a certain metaphysics; that is, the attempt to propose definitive and exhaustive answers to the question of "what is," to obtain access to a nonschematized reality itself and thus grasp what we can know and how we must act.[104]

Two things are clear: for Patočka, overcoming metaphysical philosophy does not mean abandoning metaphysical problems; and his alternative, which he calls *the philosophy of distinction*, by no means prohibits interest in the sphere of the metaphysical but in fact asks the same questions as metaphysics, although from a different perspective. As I am not aware of any other place where Patočka consistently uses the notion of the philosophy of distinction, I will refer to this perspective as metaphysical thinking—which is the category I developed in contrast to metaphysical philosophy and which therefore fits the discourse adequately enough.

According to Patočka, we need a new perspective on fundamental metaphysical questions because metaphysics historically closes in on itself and falls prey to the idolatry of objectivity and what is objectively knowable and controllable. For Patočka, metaphysics betrays its own vocation and excludes questioning in favor of definitive answers and finite knowledge, which pretend to penetrate the whole, that is, objective reality in itself. Moreover, all these self-deceptive metaphysical presuppositions not only have an impact on thinking, which shifts from a contemplative *theória* to a scientific theory, they also change the way of handling things and consequently the way of acting in the midst of things.

Things are seen as objects present-at-hand, so that *technē*, originally understood as art, is replaced by technique. As a result, questions of truth, beauty, and the good—fundamental metaphysical questions—are not explored by means of internal questioning but are grounded in external objective knowledge that pretends to grasp truth, beauty, and the good in their totality as entities. The *ethos* reverts to myth (*mythos*), something that is already decided. Metaphysics closes the circle.

Nonetheless, Patočka does not see the solution in the total elimination of metaphysical concerns. Instead of *radical overcoming*, Patočka suggests the philosophy of *radical distinction* as a mode of metaphysical thinking that preserves metaphysical questions. The nature of the philosophy of distinction concerns the question of objectivity and nonobjectivity, in short, the question of knowledge. With this in mind, Patočka identifies three key aspects of metaphysical philosophy: (1) it is knowledge about beings; (2) it is a positive knowledge; and (3) it is knowledge about "what is" as well as about "what is good."[105] In each of these realms, metaphysical knowledge is considered to be objective. This means two things: first, metaphysics works with the idea that the object of knowledge is directly *present* before us, and second, that the object that is objectively present can be mastered completely. In other words, the desire for objective metaphysical knowledge does not reckon with the possibility of unknowing because everything is knowable. A lack of knowledge is temporary and fixable, for example, by means of calculations, predictions, and the manipulation of objects.

Although Patočka finds this conception of metaphysical objectivity to be false, dangerous, and geared toward decline, he does not dismiss objectivity completely. Just as he does not reject metaphysics *en bloc*, he attempts to liberate the core of the problem of objectivity from presuppositions that are, in his view, overly pretentious. For Patočka, the longing for objectivity is the natural desire of the human mind. What is needed, however, is to bring objectivity into a relationship with nonobjectivity and thus to rephrase metaphysical philosophy as metaphysical thinking.

Patočka holds that objectivity is not the final destination of knowledge where all answers are present but a philosophical problem that must be preserved. Objectivity is the ideal type and "unattainable anticipation."[106] Objective knowledge as dictated by metaphysics is impossible because the whole always escapes. Or as Patočka phrases the problem, "In objective terms, that is, in terms dictated by things themselves, the whole is never given completely, even though it is intended."[107] In this sense, Patočka's metaphysical thinking does not exclude the possibility of objectivity and objective knowledge as such but installs a distinction that designates objective knowledge as never exhaustive. In other words, objectivity is always to a certain extent interrupted by nonobjectivity.

Patočka illustrates his point in three ways. First, he uses the example of science: science is the indisputable driving force of objective knowledge, but scientific knowledge is *per definitionem* never complete, definitive, and closed. Second, the attempt to capture the objective whole, whether in science or philosophy, and the never-ending nature of this endeavor, refers to something that is outside objectivity. This presupposition regarding the intertwining of objectivity and nonobjectivity leads to Patočka's third point, which is that we are always dealing with a subject embedded in a concrete historical situation and therefore applying a particular perspective on what is deemed objective reality. In other words, objective reality is never given as such; reality is constructed or at least co-constituted by rational reflection.[108]

The philosophy of distinction suggests, therefore, that on the one hand objectivity is understood as the ideal type and as such distances us from a pure objectivity, but on the other it relies on nonobjectivity, or, better, always refers to overcoming objectivity, to something beyond. When we say that objectivity is the ideal type, we are not referring to the ideal goal of thinking. The notion of the ideal is deduced from the Platonic Idea, but Patočka reinterprets Platonism according to the rule of distance. The Idea is not a complete, eternal object to be reached but rather the manifestation of the gap between "our" limited knowledge and the open possibilities of intellectual insight. Patočka calls this *negative Platonism*, and we will examine the notion in the next chapter.

So the philosophy of distinction, Patočka's alternative to overcoming metaphysical philosophy, complements a rational moment with a "mystical" moment of thinking.[109] Patočka writes mystical between quotation marks to differentiate this moment from the common religious understanding of mysticism. For Patočka, the "mystical" does not refer to the soul's ecstasy or the experience of revelation. It is neither Marion's language of prayer nor Caputo's invitation to radical hermeneutics. Patočka is thinking of a philosophical mystical insight, a *theória*, in its original sense, that is, the contemplation of the whole through which the philosopher, the lover of wisdom, discovers problems and questions of a metaphysical nature. Instead of comfort, however, this "[shakes] the initial naive clarity about beings."[110]

The philosophy of distinction breaks with the firm metaphysical ground, leaves behind all naive foundations, and deconstructs hierarchical structures. Put positively, metaphysical thinking meditates and rationally reflects on the question of being, which always escapes ultimate possession.[111] Patočka draws an important conclusion from this:

> The philosophy of distinction empowers, for example, art and religion, instead of being just another form (of opinion and fantasy) of expressing objective facts . . . to retrieve the claim for their own veracity, not in the metaphysical, however, but in a strong sense of the word. Religion can talk about God again, and art can talk about nature and human being, that is, about that site which can never be objectively accessed and mastered.[112]

Religion, as Patočka writes, is a genuine manner of metaphysical thinking that by no means gives up the metaphysical questions of truth, meaning, and the good. Religion, like the philosophy of distinction, maintains the tension between the need for the systematization of these questions and their recourse to answers that appear present-at-hand. In contrast to the postmodern overcomings of ontotheology, which undo metaphysics because they claim that it is the only way to authentically name God, Patočka argues that only a reconsideration of the metaphysical via metaphysical thinking does justice to the truth of religion and consequently to the truth of theology. I will explore this in greater detail in the next chapter, which is dedicated to faith and metaphysical thinking.

To recap, Patočka's critical analysis of metaphysics points out the paradigm shift that he identifies with Plato and Aristotle, who provide answers to the questions of Socrates. Of course, Socrates and Plato—and Aristotle—figure as ideal types and philosophical metaphors for two connected yet different ways of thinking. Patočka's essay "Eternity and Historicity" explains the riddle. This essay associates nonproblematic eternity with Platonism and, in turn, the problematicity of historicity with Socratic questioning. Philosophy is in constant tension between these two positions. At a certain point, the science of being that seeks to confine knowledge of the whole is victorious over the alternative tradition of "thinking questioningly." This is what I call the metaphysical turn and is what distinguishes the metaphysical thinking of Socrates from the metaphysics of the later tradition.

Following Heidegger, Patočka identifies the metaphysical turn as the emergence of ontotheology, and, as we have seen, ontotheology becomes a key problem in the postmodern context. Although Patočka criticizes the ontotheological structure of metaphysical philosophy as finite exhaustive knowledge, it has become clear that he leaves room for something I call metaphysical thinking. For Patočka, this alternative thinking involves contemplating the whole by way of questioning and challenging all finite claims with regard to Being. The whole cannot be captured in totality, cannot be delineated as the sum of its parts, and cannot be scrutinized as if from God's viewpoint. For these reasons, the phenomenological philosopher cannot but be a metaphysician in search of genuine metaphysical thinking. Patočka's critique of metaphysics and its ontotheological structure is therefore directed against the metaphysical dogmatism framed by the tradition of metaphysical philosophy. Or as Findlay succinctly puts it:

> The reality is that Patočka is never so simplistic in his rejection of metaphysics. It is not the concept of the ground, the foundation in and of itself, with which he takes issue, but the concept of the unproblematic, solid ground that we artificially posit in our desire for a simple answer to our most difficult questions.[113]

For thinking questioningly, it is impossible to disperse the metaphysical domain of thinking completely. It even seems undesirable. To ask whether the overcoming of ontotheology and the critique of metaphysics leads to nonmetaphysics or even antimetaphysics is to pose the wrong question.

Patočka's metaphysical thinking clearly refers to questions and issues that suggest that the metaphysical field is still challenging and has by no means come to an end. In this sense, theology is called not to repeat the shortcuts of metaphysical philosophy but to take up the challenge of metaphysical thinking. In contrast to metaphysical philosophy—which Patočka summarizes as (1) the unification of knowledge, which is conceived as positive and finite, (2) the illusion of metahistorical ideas, and (3) the objectification of reality manipulating things that are present-at-hand—metaphysical thinking does not posit knowledge but rather questions and searches for meaning. What metaphysical thinking means concretely and what its consequences are, especially for theology, will be the key questions of the next chapter.

Chapter 4

Faith and/as Metaphysical Thinking

A Theological Reading of Patočka's Negative Platonism

The end of metaphysics has been heralded for many decades. In the early 1950s, Patočka published a significant volume devoted to the issue. In *Negative Platonism*, he presents an entire philosophical program for the age after metaphysics. The subtitle, *Reflections Concerning the Rise, the Scope, and the Demise of Metaphysics—and Whether Philosophy Can Survive It*, provides the context and reveals the main concern of this work. Two questions come immediately to mind: What kind of metaphysics has died? And what kind of philosophy can survive? These questions also suggest that in Patočka's opinion, philosophy and metaphysics are two distinct things (or to use Janicaud's phrase, *ils font deux*), which opens up a further question: What stands for the former, and what for the latter? Or as Kohák paraphrases the subtitle of Patočka's essay: "How can philosophy avoid the metaphysical turn and still have something to say?"[1]

In the wake of Nietzsche's critique, metaphysics is accused of introducing a dualism between the sensible material world and a second-level reality of higher being. Whether it be the Platonic Idea or the Christian God, the result is a hierarchical metaphysical system that secures the intelligible order. In contrast, philosophy would then mean an emancipation from metaphysics and a shift from propositional logic to thinking. For Patočka, however, the problem of metaphysics is not so simple. There is already more than simply metaphysics to be found in Plato, who for many was the first metaphysician. And Christianity—which its many critics would say has exercised the metaphysical hegemony for two thousand years—remains for Patočka the "unsurpassed élan" of human life.[2] We could therefore suggest that Platonism and Christianity share a certain ambiguity and leave us with the tension between a rigid system on the one hand and thinking on the other.

It seems that the proclaimed end of metaphysics is not in fact the end, at least not for Patočka. The concern of his reflections on "the origins, the problematics, and the end of metaphysics, and the question as to whether there is life for philosophy after metaphysics"[3] is best captured in his own words:

> The purpose of these reflections is not to show that unlike the older attempts this new way of overcoming metaphysics does not limit itself to mere negation and does not impoverish humans by taking away any essential theme, as the older anti-metaphysical tendencies claimed to do. For that very reason, this new way can understand even metaphysics itself, taking from it in a purified form its essential philosophical thrust and carrying it on.[4]

As we can see, the purpose of *Negative Platonism* is not to abolish metaphysics but to understand it aright. This is also the purpose of this chapter. I propose a close reading of the text as it relates to Patočka's overall project, which one can read as a critical and constructive engagement with the tradition of metaphysical philosophy.[5] My reading starts from a position of agreement with Rezek, who interprets *Negative Platonism* as Patočka's search for a positive approach to metaphysical thinking.[6] My aim is therefore to show that Patočka's project is not an apologia for philosophy, as Kohák suggests elsewhere,[7] but the possibility of *thinking* metaphysically in the postmodern context, that is, in the age after metaphysics. First, I will explain the core of metaphysical thinking. To illustrate Patočka's point, I will then analyze the conception of truth from the perspective of negative Platonism.[8] Finally, and most importantly, I will venture a claim concerning the relevance of all this for theology by introducing the figure of faith. This will reveal that in *Negative Platonism*, faith does not primarily refer to a confessional allegiance but can be reinterpreted as a movement of life close to metaphysical thinking. We will see that although Patočka does not advance a theological reading of his work, he leaves the door open to such a reading. The theologian is therefore invited to open the door and see what lies behind it.

Negative Platonism

Patočka writes *Negative Platonism* in the context of a general rejection of metaphysics, which seems to be an artifact from the past, an obscure caricature of science to be overcome by real—positive—science.[9] The key figures of modern philosophy (from Nietzsche, through Husserl and Heidegger, to Levinas) deal with metaphysics rather critically, and the current output in the field of the theological turn in continental philosophy suggests that nothing has changed with respect to this generally negative outlook. Nonetheless, if Patočka thinks and speaks about the end of metaphysics, we must realize that he is reacting to a problem that is phrased in a different way from the contemporary postmodern presentation of the overcoming of metaphysics.

Patočka distinguishes the classical metaphysics of Greek (Platonic) origin—and which informed the language of Christian theology—from the modern metaphysics of positivism and objectivist science. Despite its antimetaphysical proclamations, science creates a counterfeit of metaphysics. Patočka sometimes uses the terms *positive metaphysics* for the former and *negative metaphysics* for the latter.[10] These two metaphysical projects share the same goal—to systematize the totality of being and master the whole of beings—but employ different methodologies. Classical—positive—metaphysics postulates an ideal second-level reality that grounds the intelligibility of beings and contains the truth of beings. In modern—negative—metaphysics, the whole is purely immanent and present-at-hand. Humanity gains in knowledge and becomes more and more capable of mastering things in proportion to its techno-scientific development. There are nuances, of course. For example, classical metaphysics allows certain limits to its procedures. Saying *Deus semper maior*—God is always greater—illustrates this quite well. The ultimate truth is present but temporarily unreachable. The hope is that this will be resolved in the state of beatific vision. Modern metaphysics, however, tears down all limits. If there are limits, they are merely temporary obstacles caused by a lack of knowledge, but they will surely be overcome in the near future. Patočka's *Negative Platonism* therefore starts with an exposition of the impasse whereby attempts to overcome classical positive metaphysics still result in negative metaphysics.

Unfortunately, the current critical debate concerning metaphysics in the postmodern context blurs the distinction between the two metaphysical forms, the positive and the negative, and seems to suggest there is one metaphysics from which everyone is seeking to distance themselves. This tendency is apparent in contemporary theology and in the philosophy of religion, which is influenced by Heidegger's critique of ontotheology.[11] The theological turn in continental philosophy first and foremost formulates the problem as reflections on (the naming of) God after the demise of metaphysics and whether theology can survive it, but the imperative to leave metaphysical concepts and systems behind brings a serious threat to thinking. Fighting pretentious metaphysical answers prevents one from seeing the importance of metaphysical questions. We do not see, or are not willing to acknowledge, the original setting of the problem of metaphysics.

Patočka formulates two major objections regarding metaphysics.[12] First, he questions the metaphysical conception of a second-level objective reality, the realm of higher being. In this respect, he opposes positive metaphysics. Regardless of whether we are thinking of the Christian God or the classical interpretation of the Platonic Idea, we face the same problem. Classical metaphysics introduces a dualism between the sensible and the suprasensible, the latter being a true reality mirrored in the sensible world. However, the truth about this world is reachable only by means of participation in or imitation of the other world. For Patočka, any otherworldly reality is fiction. Second, Patočka laments the loss of doubts and questions in metaphysics, an objection primarily directed at negative metaphysics. The suprasensible realm is removed from the discourse and truth is placed into the sensible. As a result, objects become metaphysical facts and (scientific) language is taken as "a transparent mirror of objective realities."[13] For Patočka, this position is a fiction because it is based on the seduction of language, that is, on the presupposition that language penetrates the substance of objects. Against the use of language in negative metaphysics expressed in the mathematical and logical subject-predicate structure as a certain path to truth, Patočka formulates a thesis that language is inherently equivocal;[14] it is open and historical. This means that the thinking of things, which is impossible outside language, is creative and is oriented toward a deeper comprehension of the whole. Nevertheless, the whole as such, in Patočka's opinion, is incomprehensible in totality. Negative metaphysics erroneously postulates that the knowledge of particulars contributes to the comprehension of the whole and that language bears witness to the truth of the whole. For Patočka, language is a constant process of learning, asking questions, and living with doubts. In sum, positive and negative metaphysics introduce dualism, illusory metaphysical objectivity, and a passive experience of gaining knowledge. In addition, negative metaphysics aims to be the true science of the absolute object.[15]

The overcoming of these problems is the primary context of the question from the subtitle of Patočka's essay—whether philosophy can survive the death of metaphysics—and whether philosophy still has something to say.

Negative Platonism is a positive answer to the question, which may sound paradoxical or even contradictory. The explanation lies in the very title *Negative Platonism*. We should not be misguided by the term *negative*. It does not refer to the negative metaphysics described earlier as the positivist or techno-scientific attempt to abolish metaphysics. The juxtaposition of *negative* and *Platonism* is of crucial importance. One can interpret *Negative Platonism* as a return to Socrates in the metaphysical tradition.[16] By using the conjunction of two apparent antonyms, Patočka makes it clear that he intends to go beyond metaphysical philosophical systematization but without forgetting fundamental metaphysical questions. Kohák explains the title in a different way. *Platonism* refers to the philosopher's interest in the whole; *negative* expresses the philosopher's opinion that the whole cannot be grasped positively. The whole is explicable neither as a higher entity nor as the sum of particulars, but the metaphysical question of the whole is unavoidable.[17] In other words, the unusual collocation *Negative Platonism* shows that Patočka is engaging with the crisis of metaphysics by searching for what I call metaphysical thinking. The metaphysical is still operative in Patočka's project. To put it yet another way, Patočka withdraws from eternal ideal structures and subjective objectivism based on the sensible and turns our attention to history and to the world of the here and now. The metaphysical does not allude to the experience *we have* but to the experience *we are*.[18]

For Patočka, the elemental experience that "we are" is the experience of freedom. This explains the second context of Patočka's essay pointed out by Arnason.[19] Patočka's encounter with totalitarianism in 1950s Czechoslovakia, with the constraints placed on people's material and intellectual lives, motivated him to reflect on something solid and beyond the reach of hegemonic political powers. In this context, Patočka finds that freedom is not a quality we have but the reality that we are. This also explains why the initial subtitle of the essay read "The Concept of Freedom with Regard to Being." What is the meaning of freedom in the context of metaphysical thinking?

The Experience of Freedom

For Patočka, the experience of freedom stands at the beginning of metaphysical thinking.[20] Socrates explained this experience through his teaching on unknowing knowledge. He went no further, however, and remained in the anteroom of metaphysics. It was Plato, Patočka suggests, who was the first to set foot on the ground of metaphysics;[21] his decision influenced the entire philosophical tradition and marked the philosophical mainstream for thousands of years, right up to the present day.

According to Patočka, Plato is responsible for two things. First, he systematically articulated the experience of freedom. In this context, the experience of freedom is comprehended as the transition from the sensual to the transcendent realm.[22] Second, he opened the debate about metaphysics.[23] Figuratively speaking, Plato is both the first metaphysician and the first philosopher of the crisis of metaphysics. Patočka emphasizes the paradox in Plato, who finds the foundation of metaphysics in the experience of freedom but formulates metaphysics as a positive conceptual system and claims that his metaphysical philosophy is the true science of being. Patočka argues that the latter contradicts the former:[24] metaphysics cannot be a positive objective science if its foundation is in freedom. To understand this problem that Patočka diagnoses at the very dawn of metaphysical philosophy, we need to answer the question: What does it mean to be free?

As we have just noted, for Patočka, the experience of freedom is the fundamental experience of humans as historical beings. Instead of saying *we have* the experience of freedom, Patočka says *we are* free, we are experiencing our freedom, we live through freedom.[25] The distinction is an important one. Although freedom is the source of life, it is not automatically realized; it is experienced by a minority, although even in the darkest totalitarian oppression, and in what Patočka alludes to as a kind of dark night of the soul, the being of every human is being from freedom.

Patočka outlines six characteristics of the experience of freedom in *Negative Platonism*.[26] (1) The experience of freedom is not a sensual experience. It is not the experience of something objective. (2) On the contrary, the experience of freedom is dissatisfaction with sensual data because, as Patočka remarks, sensual data belong to particular objects. In this sense, freedom is a negative experience. (3) The experience of freedom is a holistic experience, an experience of the whole. (4) It is not a passive experience, accepting what is given. The experience of freedom is active acting and decision-making. (5) There is risk. Freedom can be rejected, and preference can be given to the posited given. This rejection can be either a fleeing to the second-level reality of the highest being or the immanent enclosure between empirically sensible objects. (6) Finally, in Patočka's own words, "for all these reasons, we can designate the experience of freedom as one of transcendence."[27]

The experience of freedom as transcendence is different from positive experiences that passively mediate objective beings. Patočka points out that we cannot ascribe any quality, quantity, substantiality, or relativity to freedom.[28] It is a negative experience because it possesses the nature of distance. The experience of freedom overcomes positive objectivity and transcends material limits. In other words, freedom is an open experience, without borders, because there is no ultimate point that can be grasped positively, as an entity. Patočka stresses that the distance from objectivity, the freedom from the sensible, makes objects accessible.[29] The positive and passive experience that participates in objective being, but which is not the totality of experience, is experienced because of a negative and active experience of transcendence. But where does freedom come from?

Landa, who reads *Negative Platonism* as "an attempt to formulate a post-metaphysical theory of freedom," argues that the origin of freedom is deduced from the peculiar situation of human beings in the world. Human being is in-the-world but is not explicable merely from the world.[30] Freedom is therefore a metaphysical distance from the empirical world and a fundamental indeterminacy, as Arnason claims, which defines human being-in-the-world.[31] As Patočka observes:

> The interpretation of our human experience, the experience of historical beings, is something different in principle from metaphysics. While metaphysics discovers a new universe, taking it as its starting point and transcending it, the interpretation of experience discovers, uncovers, sheds light on this our given lifeworld, uncovering what had been hidden in it, its concealed meaning, its intrinsic structure, its inner drama.[32]

It now becomes clear why Patočka turns to the interpretation of human experience in order to critically engage with metaphysical philosophy. Human experience, which for Patočka means being-in-the-world, is grounded in the experience of freedom. But freedom is always a new experience and as such is directed toward a deeper understanding of the whole. It is impossible, however, to positively define the content of the whole because it transcends objectivity. The whole is not the sum of objects so cannot be reduced to an entity. Experiencing the whole therefore means searching for the meaning of the whole. For Patočka, this means searching for the meaning of life as a historical existence in the midst of things and acting from this situation. But meaning is not an entity. It is not a thing. It is *nothing*. Hence, Patočka's overcoming of both classical positive metaphysics and modern negative metaphysics is phrased in terms of the negative interpretation of the Idea.

The Negative Idea

Patočka remarks that the history and development of positive metaphysics concerns the foundational moment of Platonism—the doctrine of Ideas—but offers a one-sided approach. Whether it is Christianity or Kant's theory of regulative ideas, metaphysical logic expands on the original intuition of Plato. This world relates to the other world of Idea(s) because, the supposition goes, the truth about this world is concealed in the ideal world. Consequently, the task of thinking is to make possible the transition from here to there. According to Patočka, this mainstream of metaphysical philosophy is extremely reductive. It misses an alternative interpretation of metaphysical thinking in general and of Platonism in particular. Patočka articulates his interpretation based on the crucial yet often neglected Platonic notion of *chorismos*:

> *Chorismos*, separation, isolation, is an important phenomenon that we cannot ignore and silence. . . . It is a gap that does not separate two realms coordinated or linked by a third something which would embrace them both and thus serve as the foundation of both their coordination and their separation. *Chorismos* is separateness, distinctness itself. It is the absolute separation, for itself. It does not entail the secret of another continent, somewhere beyond a separating ocean. Rather, its mystery must be read out of *chorismos* itself, found purely within it. In other words, the mystery of *chorismos* is identical with the experience of freedom, the experience of a distance with respect to real things, the experience of meaning independent of the objective and the sensory that we reach by inverting the original, "natural" orientation of life, an experience of a rebirth, of a second birth, intrinsic to all spiritual life, familiar to the religious man, to the initiate of the arts, and, not least, to the philosopher.[33]

For Patočka, this complex issue captures the ambiguity within the doctrine of Ideas. What is usually interpreted as a rigid system of eternal principles and the container of objective truths appears rather to be a force of separation, a gap. *Chorismos* reveals that there are not two objective realms of entities. Rather, as Evink comments, "it separates objectivity from that which can no longer be articulated in terms of objects."[34] *Chorismos*, in Patočka's interpretation, functions as a deobjectifying and derealizing force.[35] In contrast to traditional interpretations of Platonism as positive knowledge, Patočka suggests a return to the Socratic position of nonknowing knowledge.

Patočka wants to protect thinking from the dualism of the sensible and intelligible worlds and overcome the impasse of two metaphysical philosophies: positive metaphysics, which presents itself as the science of being, and negative metaphysics, which creates the illusion of the objective whole. Negative Platonism stands between two extremes: one where everything is claimed to be determined by absolute ideal structures and eternal laws, whether it be a classical reading of (positive) Platonism, Descartes's rational theology, the God of ontotheology, and so on; the other where empiricism pushes forward the opinion that there is nothing solid in being other than that which can be objectively observed.[36]

Instead, Patočka considers the Idea both negatively and metaphysically. The Idea is neither a suprasensible entity nor a general objectivity. As Ullmann summarizes, "The Idea expresses our ability to step back from the present and the given." And about its transcending power, he says that "it makes possible to see what is more and what is new as compared with the perceptually given."[37] In other words, the Idea is not an absolute object, a hierarchical system of substances, a thing *an sich* to be seen. Instead, the Idea opens the possibility of seeing. Patočka is thinking of a spiritual seeing, meaning the overcoming of the given presence. In this sense, the Idea is the call of transcendence; it is transcendence and freedom.[38]

Nevertheless, a negative conception of the Idea raises the question of the status of the Idea itself. If the Idea is not a being, and in fact stands in contrast to all beings, is it a nonexistent being? Or as Patočka puts it, "What remains when we exclude all that is, what other than sheer nothingness?"[39]

One way to avoid the problem is the reference to *nothingness* as a linguistically empty term. Absolute nothingness is unimaginable and unthinkable. Patočka deals with this problem in "Nothingness, the Absolute

Position and Negation," a draft document for another chapter of the unfinished project of *Negative Platonism*.[40] However, Patočka by no means evades the question of nothingness. Instead, he proposes an interpretation of the Idea not as nothing (an empty thing) but as a *no-thing*. In short, the Idea is nonobjectivity. But what does this mean?

For Patočka, the foundation of metaphysical thinking is the relation to the whole—the question of the whole.[41] Everyone is oriented toward the whole and no one and nothing are above the whole. In other words, the universe as such cannot be captured, exhausted, or fragmented as we find proposed in mainstream metaphysical philosophy. The whole is not an object, although it contains a certain objectivity. The Idea, then, makes possible the very relation to the whole because it introduces a distinction, a gap, between objectivity and nonobjectivity. Now, from the perspective of objectivity and metaphysical philosophy, the Idea appears as no-thing. However, Patočka reminds us that the revelatory potential of the experience of freedom is that we know that objects are not the totality of being. From the perspective of logical argumentation and the theory of truth as adequacy—in other words, after modernity—this makes little sense. Yet Patočka argues that there is something *metaxological*, that is, something in the midst of things and at the same time above things:[42] the Idea that is not a thing, no-thing. The Idea, as Patočka comprehends it, is nonreality that cannot be clarified from the world because it is not an object at all. The Idea cannot be contemplated. It is, however, essential for understanding historicity, freedom, human life as such. The Idea bears witness to transcendence.[43]

It seems that Plato interprets the Idea as the power of absolute objectification and, in this sense, as a challenge to human beings to master the universe. Patočka remarks that this tendency inherent in positive Platonism had never been fully realized either in antiquity or in Christian metaphysics. The ambiguity of the Idea and the call of transcendence challenge ultimate conceptualization of any kind. Modernity destroyed all limits and placed human being into the center with the task of ruling over the whole. Negative Platonism therefore shakes the presupposed meaning of the world and questions the very postulate that meaning and truth are discernible by means of objectivity, as proposed in classical metaphysical philosophy and radicalized in modern negative metaphysics. As Rodrigo aptly concludes, Patočka's reflections on the rise, the scope, and the demise of metaphysics do not overcome metaphysics as such. Rather, the negative conception of the Idea overcomes objectivity and representation.[44]

The key motivation behind negative Platonism is the dignity of the human being who discovers the task of thinking, which is to master and to serve, to know and to search, but not least to see "that there is something higher than man, something to which human existence is indissolubly bound, and without which the most basic wellsprings of our historical life dry up."[45] Using the Greek expression *to heteron*, Patočka calls this the *wholly other*.[46] This is something that is not a thing. The wholly other is outside positive knowledge. How, then, is it possible to know about the call of *to heteron*? For Patočka, this is the paradox of being in the world, a paradox illuminated by a negative conception of the Idea. The wholly other is something concealed in experience, but which transcends the experiential. In other words, one cannot *have* the experience of the wholly other; rather, one discerns the call of otherness in *experiencing* freedom and transcendence. In this sense, negative Platonism is both rich philosophy and poor philosophy. It is poor because it has nothing positive to say and it cannot provide access to the knowledge of the whole; it is rich because it liberates thinking from metaphysical constraints without losing key metaphysical questions. In fact, Patočka believes that his negative thinking enables a revealing of truth and, more importantly, the possibility of living in a truth that is neither objective nor relative.

Truth as In-Adequacy

"The Problem of Truth from the Perspective of Negative Platonism" is the title of a draft essay Patočka intended to include in his larger work on metaphysical thinking after the demise of metaphysics. It is clear that Patočka's understanding of the question of truth follows the argument of *Negative Platonism* and differs from the prevailing conceptions of classical metaphysics and modernity.

Patočka opens his argument with the thesis that the problem of truth has been a fundamental question from the very beginnings of philosophy.[47] He finds two elementary motifs that define the problem—the questions of *archē* and of *praxis*. Patočka suggests that the former is often wrongly interpreted as the search for the origin of being. In his opinion, however, *archē* concerns the question of the origin of the appearance of being. Similarly, the latter question should not be equated with pursuing objective rules and laws but with a (Socratic) quest for acting and making decisions based on the questioning of particular human situations.

After this twofold clarification, Patočka claims that the metaphysical turn fundamentally changed this perspective. In other words, positive Platonism—that is, metaphysical philosophy, later transposed into Christian theology—provides a foundation for what Patočka calls "classical European theories of truth."[48]

These theories consist of the intertwining of several philosophical motifs. Patočka lists three as basic: (1) logic—truth is a correct judgment; (2) material adequacy—truth is a correct reproduction of the objective relationship between the mind and things; and (3) ideal adequacy—truth is a correct reproduction of the intellectual archetype from a higher reality manifested in empirical reality.[49] Nonetheless, modernity adds a further decisive element, namely, the motif of the will to truth: "For classical metaphysics, the Idea sheds light on the world and thus on the essence of truth. Things and the human spirit participate in the Idea. According to the theological interpretation, the Idea is placed into God's mind."[50] As a result of the modern paradigm shift, God becomes the absolute will (*voluntas absoluta*) that leads to the idea of the absolute subordination of the human being. This tension is resolved in the modern subject's claim for autonomy and, indeed, in the very invention of the modern subject. How does this apply to the problem of truth? Instead of participating in the ideal realm containing truth, the modern subject owns its truth, that is, clear and distinct visions of being. Patočka stresses the importance of this shift from participation to clarity. Understanding truth is not derived from contemplation: truth is in the making; truth is the power of mastering being.

Patočka nonetheless reminds us that the modern shift is not a simplistic switch from one conception to another. In fact, the modern conception of *clare et distincte* knowledge absorbs the logical motif and material adequacy from the previous tradition while crossing out the ideal realm of being. The demand for absolute objectivity, which claims to oppose and finally overcome the old metaphysics, appears once again in this mixture of metaphysical elements but in modern guise: the problem of truth is framed by a confusion of positive and negative metaphysics. The crisis of truth can be defined as the loss of classical metaphysical philosophy—positive Platonism—and the disintegration of Christian theology but also as the rise of the modern techno-scientific mentality that displaced the question of truth. Patočka therefore extends the Heideggerian claim and argues that truth has become a forgotten question,[51] with the emphasis on the word *question*.

According to Patočka, the problem of truth is thereby reduced in an unprecedented way.[52] First, truth is phrased as a matter of correct judgment: the questioning of truth is reduced to the problem of truths, that is, particular truth claims concerning particular objects. Second, the question of truth is reduced to the problem of theory, in the modern sense of the word: having the truth is disconnected from being practically truthful. Finally, the opposite of truth is error, just as the opposite of a correct judgment is an incorrect one. The question of truth is thus disconnected from the human situation, from being-in-the-world and being in the midst of things. The problem of truth is grounded, in Patočka's opinion, on a groundless presupposition of the objective structure of truth.

The presumption of the objective structure of being operates on the level of logic and the theory of adequacy. In fact, material and ideal adequacy merge into a single theory of adequacy because the idea is actually an object, a thing. Here one seeks objective truths that mirror the truth. This is also true of the truth about human being. A human being is a thing among things. The truth of being human is not within but essentially outside human being because it must be eternal and objective. However, human being can objectively participate in the truth about itself without disclosing this truth within itself. As Patočka concludes, "Truth is a mere thing among things: it loses its function and the problem of truth vanishes."[53] The truth is in crisis. The question from the subtitle of *Negative Platonism* could now read: How can philosophy survive the demise of truth and still have something to say about it?

In his alternative conception of truth from the perspective of negative Platonism, Patočka proposes an answer based on his negative interpretation of the Idea. For Patočka, the truth is always the truth of human being, which is reflected in its finitude (being-toward-death). This peculiar situation opens us to a relation to the Idea as wholly other.

In Patočka, the Idea both grounds and challenges our relationship toward things. The Idea demonstrates that objectivity does not capture the totality of being; it establishes the distance from the whole that we desire to capture but find to be an inaccessible problem.[54] In other words, the Idea reveals both the whole and our "in-adequacy" regarding the whole. The Idea as the power of distance is therefore the cornerstone of Patočka's conception of truth. The Idea, however, is not an object—it is not something that can be formulated in positive terms. As such, Patočka replaces the adequacy theory of truth with the term *in-adequacy*.[55]

In-adequacy works on two levels. First, there exists a disproportion between the thinking of being and the whole of being. Second, there is a disproportion between objective beings and the thinking human being that participates in the call of the wholly other, the Idea.[56] As a result, articulated truths are only ever an approximation of the truth; truths are by definition inadequate. However, because the word *in-adequacy* is composed of the root *adequacy* and its negation, truth as in-adequacy contains a sense of provisional adequacy. Patočka does not of course deny the possibility of formulating objective truths. These are the truths of science, the truths of the natural world. He makes an important distinction, however.[57] A single objective truth is never the truth of the totality of objectivity. We are able to perceive this distinction through the Idea. The positive objectivity we adequately ascribe to beings is never the ultimate truth of the whole. Objectivity is an escape from the anxiety of truth. However, objectivity is never simply given; it is only construed. Objectivity is nothing given, present-at-hand, but rather a challenge, the task of thinking. In this respect, Patočka challenges metaphysical illusions of an objective structure of being that is discernible by means of clear and distinct knowledge, without completely losing the objective element. Truth as in-adequacy values objectivity as a provisional element in the search for truth. Yet the most important consequence of this conception of truth is the sensitivity to something I propose calling *meta-objectivity*.

Meta-objectivity is the presupposition of metaphysical thinking as against metaphysical philosophy as the science of objective suprasensory being. For Patočka, the privileged voices of the meta-objective side of the whole are art and religion, which he suggests are genuine authorities of truth because they use a language that goes beyond objectivity;[58] they are genuine agents of metaphysical thinking after the end of metaphysics. Art and religion do not withdraw from reality but return us to reality; their very essence is to throw us into this historical world and reveal its problematicity. Plato had already anticipated this dynamic by recuperating the Socratic position of being-in-the-world. Nonetheless, Patočka argues for a special role for Christianity in this respect: "From all the world religions, only Christianity is aware of the need to take a step back; that what is important for us (*in via*) is not to be found in some afterlife."[59] What does this paradoxical statement mean? Alas, Patočka does not expand on it but leaves us with an enigma. One thing is certain, however. Patočka links Christianity with truth as in-adequacy, with the truth that is not a thing, no-thing. In the same passage, he suggests that we touch upon the truth by means of a re-turn. But this return (*obrat*) can also be translated as a conversion.

I suggest that Patočka intuitively finds Christianity to be the spiritual power in the world that understands the conversion to history as the concealment of the truth. In this respect, Christianity is a historical religion, the only religion that is incarnated in history and therefore thinks historically.

Theology, Faith, and Metaphysical Thinking

Negative Platonism could be considered the *Aufhebung* of metaphysics.[60] Patočka's overcoming of metaphysical philosophy represents not a rejection but a positive reconsideration of the essential motifs of metaphysical thinking. We are now in a position to identify the key issues of negative Platonism as metaphysical thinking. I suggest focusing on three crucial points or moments that ground a genuine metaphysical thinking: (1) the wholly other, in Patočka's wording, *to heteron*; (2) in-adequacy; and (3) non-objectivity. The *meta* in metaphysical must, however, be understood in two senses: meta*physical* thinking thinks *above* objects and positively conceived objectivity; *meta*physical thinking thinks *from the midst of* objects, the world, and history. Metaphysical thinking is not, therefore, a passive philosophy that participates in the eternal ideas of truth, a higher reality of true being, but is the acting of historical, free beings that are capable of transcendence.

It is tempting, nonetheless, to develop a theological reading of Patočka's *Negative Platonism*, especially in the context of the passionate debates between the theological adversaries of metaphysics and its champions, who argue that one way or another theology needs metaphysics. Patočka's retrieval of metaphysical thinking can be understood as an alternative to the *either-or* approach that provides us rather with a *both-and* perspective. Furthermore, Patočka himself strengthens the argument for theologizing interpretations. Christianity is the only religion that understands what he is defining in *Negative Platonism*,[61] although this moment remains "un-thought" in Christianity itself.[62] Furthermore, Patočka opens *Negative Platonism* with an allusion to Nietzsche and to the aphorism about the madman who proclaims the death of God.[63] *Negative Platonism* can therefore be seen as a direct response to "the death of God."

Patočka's question as to whether philosophy can survive is answered positively by turning to the task of metaphysical thinking. It is perhaps legitimate to stretch the argument and raise the question of whether and how theology can survive the crisis of metaphysics. Can we draw inspiration from the metaphysical thinking of *Negative Platonism*? The fact that Patočka goes beyond objects while thinking from the situation between objects suggests that the answer might indeed be in the affirmative. Last but not least, Patočka says at one point, albeit somewhat rhetorically, that "there is something higher than man, something to which human existence is indissolubly bound, and without which the most basic wellsprings of our historical life dry up."[64]

However, before we enthusiastically adopt the possibility of a theological reading, we need to realize that bringing Patočka into the world of theology is highly problematic. First, we should be aware that the motivation behind writing *Negative Platonism* and consequently behind the retrieval of metaphysical thinking is not to provide theology with tools for its self-renewal. Although "the religious" returns in Patočka, and its intensity and importance even increase in his later works, it is not possible to talk about a theological turn. Patočka would surely protest loudly against any reduction of his metaphysical thinking to a quasi-theology. Only later in Patočka does metaphysics become distinguishable from theology as an original spiritual endeavor incorporated into theology.[65] In this sense, the author of *Negative Platonism* holds the same opinion that he presents in the early essay "Theology and Philosophy," in which he ardently opposes *philosophia ancilla theologiae* as the norm of theological thinking. Philosophy does not "help" theology as a mere handmaiden. For Patočka, theology and philosophy touch the same domain but from different perspectives.[66]

Second, to look for the foundation of theology in negative Platonism is already problematic in itself. The context of Patočka's metaphysical thinking is to reflect a situation with no foundation. For Patočka, the foundation cannot be a thing, an objective entity. Therefore, if we take Patočka's metaphysical thinking for granted, as a potentially given anchor of theology after the demise of metaphysical philosophy, we will be committing the same error as before.

Finally, for Patočka, the wellspring or source of life that theology calls God does not refer to an entity, the highest being, *causa sui*, or any other ontotheological (metaphysical) concept. Patočka is searching for the nonobjective. This no-thing is, however, different from absolute negativity, nothing. How can this work with the theological naming of God? Is it possible after all to think from a theological perspective about Patočka's philosophy in general and his metaphysical thinking in particular?

The obvious way to answer this last question positively is to adopt negative Platonism as a corrective to positive metaphysical-theological concepts. This is nothing new, however. Theology draws inspiration from many critical philosophical positions regarding ontotheology and metaphysics. Why should negative Platonism be any better in this respect? Do we really need another *via negativa*?

The reason I dare to propose a theological reading of Patočka's *Negative Platonism* lies precisely in the fact that Patočka's overcoming of metaphysical philosophy by way of metaphysical thinking does not represent a fall into negativity, even if the title of Patočka's essay would seem to suggest otherwise. As Jean-Yves Lacoste remarks in *From Theology to Theological Thinking*, "The task of thinking arises when the reign of metaphysics comes to an end."[67] My thesis is that Patočka's metaphysical thinking is first and foremost about *the task of thinking*, which to recall Lacoste once again begins by blurring the boundary between philosophy and theology. I propose that thinking metaphysically beyond metaphysics—as Patočka does—can provide genuine inspiration for theology in a postmodern context. This proposition is supported, for example, by Landa's suggestion that the metaphysical thinking of *Negative Platonism* concerns not only philosophy but religion and art, theology and aesthetics.[68] In what follows, we will examine the consequences for theological thinking from the perspective of negative Platonism.

Patočka stands between two extremes. He avoids falling into negativity (Heidegger) or even into nihilism (Sartre); he is no supporter, therefore, of antimetaphysical solutions to the problem of metaphysics. He also nonetheless refutes absolute philosophical positions such as mainstream metaphysical philosophy. The position of *Negative Platonism* can be defined by this in-betweenness. Patočka could not provide us with a positive statement because it would betray his philosophical goal and principal argument, which is to develop a metaphysical thinking that starts with a negative interpretation (of the Idea) while leaving room for some kind of positivity. Thinking from the between safeguards philosophy from pretentious absolute claims but at the same time allows the philosopher to formulate truth claims. In other words, Patočka's metaphysical thinking transcends the given objective knowledge—without denying its importance—and opens the sphere of disclosing otherness (*to heteron*).

Christianity finds itself in a similar position. Theological thinking rejects—or transcends—a purely objective and positive knowledge. As there is always a gap between dogmatic formulations and the truth to which any particular dogma refers, there is also a tension between "truth claims" and "the truth." Or to paraphrase Patočka's saying—originally stated about philosophy but which extends to theology and aesthetics—participation in the absolute is not possession of the absolute.[69] Theology is not primarily a content-related perception of objects and entities; rather, it concerns the more profound aspects of life. Theology concerns *the experience we are* rather than *the experience we have*. Augustine's *mihi questio factus sum*—I have become a question to myself—is a telling example of this theological dynamic. What is it that creates this tension between the objective and nonobjective? What is it that inserts the in-adequacy into a relationship to the absolute? What is it that drives us to the wholly other?

For Patočka, the answer is the Idea, interpreted through the notion of *chorismos*—the Idea as distance. The Idea is the deobjectifying power that opens up the field of transcendence. There is a theological parallel in the notion of faith.[70] Faith, which I suggest can be equated with the Idea, does not, however, exceed the critique of metaphysics. Current theological attempts to overcome metaphysics often succumb to this temptation and withdraw faith from the critique as something ametaphysical.[71] This is supposed to prove that Christianity is capable of escaping the clutches of metaphysics without losing anything. Nonetheless, I suggest that relating the conception of faith to Patočka's conception of the Idea cannot exempt it from critique because this faith is equivalent to metaphysical thinking.

Faith, as I understand it, contains all three metaphysical movements associated with negative Platonism: (1) the initiation into the wholly other; (2) in-adequacy regarding both the wholly other and the world; and (3) nonobjectivity, meaning that faith transcends the conception of things in merely positive manners, even being itself conceived as positively propositional (that is, faith in positive content, things, entities, and so on). Alternatively, faith can be defined as: (1) openness to the future as the other that is "to come"; (2) transcendence from the present, which establishes the in-adequacy between the given and the possibilities of the future; or (3) freedom from the past—freedom from conceiving what happened (*factum*) as objective facts that ineluctably determine the present and the future.

Having stated this pair of threefold correspondences between faith and the Idea in negative Platonism, I now propose to look more closely at them. The first of these triplets, concerning the notions of otherness, in-adequacy, and nonobjectivity, is referred to in other authors' interpretations of *Negative Platonism*. The second is to be found in Patočka's own work, mostly from essays that consider the question of time and were written as preparatory texts for *Negative Platonism* or at least in the same general period of Patočka's philosophical development.

Faith from the Perspective of Negative Platonism

According to Miroslav Petříček, philosophy in general, and Patočka's phenomenological thought in particular, can be defined as bringing *otherness* to light.[72] Against the background of Patočka's critique of metaphysical philosophy, the question of the other crystallizes as a static attempt to describe the world from the perspective of eternity. To resolve the problem, Patočka turns to historicity.[73] Petříček points out that in contrast to the search for eternal truths and principles, Patočka addresses the tension between continuity and discontinuity; otherness arises from the experience of these tensions.[74] How shall we understand this claim? Petříček recalls Patočka's conviction that human experience is capable of experiencing the distance between the given and the objective. This negative experience can be defined positively as a meta-experience of the other (*to heteron*) that cannot be reduced to an entity.[75] Here is an echo of Patočka's distinction between the experience *we have* and the experience *we are*. In fact, we are always more than we have. We experience more than just objects and entities, in short, beings. The appeal of the other and the relationship to otherness is a common experience of living (*Erlebnis*) in the world. Petříček summarizes Patočka's position as follows:

> Metaphysics attempts to define the mystery of the world in a definitive manner. It reduces the mystery to words, propositions, and being. . . . [Patočka's] philosophy is aware that its goal is not in defining objective propositions. [Patočka] knows that the words he uses must have an aura of mystery, the mythical background, and must be words that respect *the otherness of what-is-not*. Because it is impossible to say that *it is*.[76]

Petříček remarks that Patočka asks the question of the other, beyond the scope of metaphysics, in the same way as Emmanuel Levinas and Michel Foucault.[77] Interestingly, while Levinas is inspired by Jewish tradition and

Talmudic thinking, and Foucault draws inspiration from structuralism and Nietzsche, Patočka finds the cornerstone of his philosophy of otherness in antiquity—in Socrates's nonknowing knowledge. Evink suggests that Patočka's position is even more radical than that of Levinas, or of Derrida.[78] In their respective philosophies of otherness, Levinas and Derrida still reach overly positive answers to the metaphysical question of otherness. Levinas ends up with the absolute claim of a face-to-face encounter with the other. Derrida, for his part, "calls for abstracting from every concretely given phenomenon to the abstract other and singular as such."[79] In this sense, Derrida's plea for the messianic without messianism is a return to a metaphysical desire for the absolute.

Patočka's concern for the wholly other (*to heteron*) cannot be reduced to a singular (metaphysical) other, to the purity of otherness. In this respect, we need to return to the foundation of Patočka's negative Platonism, which is Socratic nonknowing knowledge. This philosophy of questioning, which is also the thinking of otherness, does not remain at the level of negativity that jumps into the discourse of *tout autre*. On the contrary, it contains the positive moment of a search for a solid, nonrelativistic meaning beyond metaphysical philosophy, although this meaning is nothing objective. Hence, as Petříček summarizes, Patočka's metaphysical thinking could be called *heterology*—a philosophy concerned with the other.[80]

The second metaphysical movement common to both faith and the Idea is in-adequacy (of meaning). We have seen that Patočka's conception of in-adequacy is not a radical opposition to adequacy as such. Two things must be said in this respect. First, Patočka cannot articulate the in-adequacy theory as an absolute statement as that would betray his endeavor. Second, he has no intention of doing that as there is a certain adequacy still operative in what he calls in-adequacy. He clarifies his position as follows: "The concept of in-adequacy does not suggest that no adequacy is possible, but rather that adequacy is never enough."[81]

In-adequacy holds a position between two extremes: Patočka's criticism of absolute objective claims regarding meaning and his intention to overcome nihilism and relativism, or meaninglessness. I see this in-betweenness as a further aspect common to both the Idea and faith. Edward Findlay links this middle position of in-adequacy with Patočka's concept of *problematicity*.[82] What is the meaning of this concept and what does it mean for any proposed theological reading of *Negative Platonism*?

Findlay explains that the concept of problematicity needs to be understood in light of Patočka's critique of metaphysical philosophy. We have already presented the problem, so we will not rehearse his entire critique. The aspect of most interest to us is Findlay's assertion that problematicity holds a liminal position between objectivity and subjectivity.[83] The former is associated with meaning as a thing, an entity that can be discerned merely by rational examination of the world, that is, by means of calculating, experimenting, and predicating; meaning is given objectively. The latter creates the impression that meaning is something subjective, individual, and random; the subject provides meaning. Both positions are profoundly modern and arise from various attempts to overcome classical metaphysical philosophy by means of techno-scientific rationality or the philosophy of humanism.

Findlay remarks that Patočka's point concerning problematicity turns our attention to a reality that cannot be adequately described solely in the mode of objectivity or subjectivity.[84] The basic situation of the human being is neither discerning the given meaning nor creating meaning. The essential experience of the human person is the loss of meaning. We could speak of interruptions, or, in Patočka, of *shaking*. For Findlay, problematicity is an awareness of shaking both naively received objective meaning and naively created subjective meaning. One way or another, it is a retrieval of Socratic "thinking questioningly."[85] The human situation of shaking meaning, as a negative moment, is incorporated as living in problematicity, as a positive moment of thinking. However, the theologian may say that shaking meaning, and thus the concept of problematicity, is also a retrieval of the tradition of *theological thinking*.[86]

Returning to in-adequacy and applying what we have just noted, we may conclude that the Idea and faith challenge naively received convictions and simply given knowledge, and are therefore, importantly, two analogous modes of *living in problematicity*. Interestingly, Findlay defines living in problematicity as the recognition that human beings are not divine but find the divine in themselves.[87] We find similar expressions regarding a certain theandric structure of human being in Patočka.[88] Unfortunately, neither Patočka nor Findlay elaborate on these statements. This lack of clarity can be viewed in two ways: either we accept that Patočka does not intend to open his philosophical thinking to a theological interpretation; or we take up the challenge of thinking with Patočka beyond the exclusively philosophical domain.

I suggest we take the second path. Faith and the Idea can be rephrased as living in problematicity, and as we have seen, living in problematicity is a mode of thinking. The Idea and faith are also, therefore, modes of thinking. First, they are modes of metaphysical thinking, which is the central point of this chapter. Second, they think the impossible possibility. As we have already stated, faith does not primarily concern propositional content. It is a mode of thinking about transcendence, that is, about something beyond thinking. To stretch Anselm's argument about the impossibility of thinking anything greater than God, faith is not so much about the impossibility of a *greater entity* as it is about the *impossibility* of thinking the greatest, God, mystery, whatever name we may find appropriate. In Patočka's vocabulary, we always think in-adequately. The reason this is so is the *chorismos*, the distance between us and the God about whom we think in faith. The same applies to both faith and the Idea. The distance exists not because God is somewhere in a different—higher—register of being. On the contrary, the divine appears from within us as historical beings who are confronted with the task of thinking. In this respect, although faith is always provisional and in-adequate, it can certainly bear witness to the real and the nonrelative.

Finally, we come to the third moment of negative Platonism, the nonobjectivity that I suggest represents a common ground for the Idea and faith. We have seen that one of the primary concerns of *Negative Platonism* is the critique of metaphysics as a philosophical approach to reality, the world, and the whole from the perspective of objectivism. In other words, metaphysical philosophy postulates that everything is reducible to or simply consists of beings, that is, entities. Patočka therefore introduces the distinction between objectivity and a nonobjective element of reality.[89] As we have seen, Patočka sometimes calls his alternative to metaphysics a "philosophy of distinction."[90] In his essay "Nothingness and Responsibility," Ladislav Hejdánek suggests that the search for nonobjective and nonobjectifying thinking is the hermeneutical key to Patočka's *Negative Platonism* and even to his critical engagement with metaphysics in general.[91]

In Hejdánek's interpretation, Patočka looks for that which transcends objective beings. However, the result of this endeavor can hardly be a higher or the highest being. The only way to exceed the dictate of objectivity present in most of the tradition of metaphysics is to develop a new understanding of *nothing* or *nothingness*. According to Hejdánek, this new understanding should avoid Sartre's nihilism of *Being and Nothingness* and radicalize Heidegger's treatment of negativity regarding Being.[92] In fact,

Patočka proposes a kind of negative reading of nothingness that contains a positive moment. This paradoxical statement needs to be unpacked.

For Patočka, nothingness represents the antithesis to the positive and the given. The notion of nothing is a necessary consequence of being-in-the-world and experiencing that positive objective beings by no means exhaust the whole of the world. Nothingness therefore functions as an appeal to transcendence, to going beyond things without negating them. Thus, what-is-not is not a being.[93] Nothing is the claim of that which is not given objectively. In other words, the notion of nothing leaves metaphysical problems open without denying the importance of metaphysical thinking (about the whole, truth, meaning, and so on).

In Patočka, the agent of metaphysical thinking is the Idea. The Idea is not an entity. It is not an object to be grasped. The Idea is the call of *no-thingness*. It becomes clear now what Patočka means when he says that the Idea is not present as a being to be seen and contemplated. The Idea allows us to see; the Idea is not an idol that can be fixed by sight; the Idea is iconic in character and directs sight beyond the given, to transcendence.

Likewise, faith does not gaze upon some-*thing* objective or ontotheological—an idol. Faith creates a distinction between the objective and the nonobjective. Faith is a distance and this distance generates a space for contemplation and insight into the mystery that exceeds the objective register of being. Faith teaches that, first, we must wonder in the face of what we see, then understand what we see, and only then, if possible, formulate propositions regarding what we see. The distance remains, however. This all bears a striking resemblance to Thomas Aquinas's three levels of being regarding God: the ipseity of what one sees (*modus essendi*), the knowledge of what one sees (*modus intelligendi*), and the proposition articulated about what one sees (*modus significandi*).[94] The nonobjective moment of faith appears to follow the traditional path of three ways that are, again, associated with Thomas Aquinas. Although faith is articulated in propositional claims (positive moment), it always negates them to show that there is more than mere objectivity (negative moment). Finally, faith refers to that which is not-being, according to the ontotheological conception, and to that which is not nonbeing as a sheer nothing. Faith does not correspond to "metaphysics [in which] *a* vision of a thing becomes *the* vision of things."[95] Faith is a form of metaphysical thinking—thinking *no-thing* meta-objectively.

We can now clearly see that Patočka's critical engagement with metaphysical philosophy is not antimetaphysical. Rather, Patočka develops a metaphysical thinking, and, as in previous centuries, theology can benefit from borrowing the language of metaphysical thinking in order to name the one who transcends the objective.

Faith from the Perspective of Time

Our argument now moves to the second triplet of ideas associated with the notion of faith as we find it in Patočka. As noted earlier, Patočka addresses the problematic in essays that originated around the time of *Negative Platonism*, or that he intended should become part of the corpus itself. It is no surprise, therefore, that he deals with problems corresponding to our question about (a theological) reading of the Idea through the lens of faith in various works, even if the primary focus changes slightly from one text to another. Here, I will focus on the texts dedicated to the problem of time: *Eternity and Historicity*; *Time, Myth, Faith*; and *Treatise on Time I* and *Treatise on Time II*. Patočka's primary goal is to shed light on the problem of a historical and creative time as against a static concept of metaphysical eternity. I will not follow him in detail in this respect, but as the title of one of the essays suggests, the concept of faith turns out to be crucial for Patočka's argument.

As we have already noted, this second triplet of ideas reflects on three basic modalities of time—the past, the present, and the future—and Patočka associates a different mode of thinking with each of them: the orientation to the past is typical of myth, the present is the domain of metaphysics, the future pertains to faith.

In myth, everything has already been decided: the present is merely an alteration of what is already here, and the future is set in stone from the beginning.[96] Whether through the original event, fate, or the decision of the gods, the individual being is completely hamstrung. There is no escape from the order of things. Nothing can be done to change the flow of life. One can only participate in it and wait to see whether the predictions turn out to be good or bad.

Myth appears to be objective, but according to Patočka this is not the case.[97] Rather, myth perceives the past as solid ground, the fact—*factum*—that cannot be revoked but must be narrated again and again. In other words, myth has a form of objectivity, but its main character is nonobjective. We see this in the mythical blurring of the boundary between past and present. The past affects the present and determines the future by narration. In this respect, myth "has all the answers before the questions."[98] Myth is full of mysteries, or rather secrets. Secrets are everywhere, which means they are not taken seriously. In the end, the gods, fate, or another force decides. Myth therefore knows all about the other (*to heteron*) of life, but in myth life participates in otherness only passively; it is a bare life without freedom.

Elsewhere, Patočka offers a more complex understanding of myth. In fact, the problem of myth can be traced from his earliest essays to his later works,[99] but it is not necessary to continue this line of thought now.[100] Suffice it here to illustrate the nature of myth's orientation to the past in preparation for a comparison with faith.

For Patočka, an orientation to the present is the rule of objectivity: "For the metaphysical conception, it is typical that being must contain all its possibilities in the given present state. Nothing new can occur. The world is entirely objective and contains nothing foreign. Everything is manageable by means of our categories."[101] This is no more or less than a critique of the metaphysics of presence, a term that belongs of course to Derrida. The point, however, is the same. Patočka is referring here to a sense of being as presence and to the present (time) as the determination of our intelligible order. In this respect, metaphysics pretends to be the science of being. What are the consequences of this manner of reasoning? First, the metaphysics of presence is founded on the supposition that beings are objectively present. Objects are therefore present-at-hand and manageable by knowledge. Second, objects are present as completely transparent entities with no secrets. There may be certain unknowns with regard to an object, but nothing unknowable in essence. Third, objects are re-presented in knowledge. Everything happens now. In consequence, metaphysics embraces all its possibilities. In other words, the orientation to the present knows no genuine transcendence because metaphysical philosophy participates in a static now.

We have already dealt with Patočka's critique of metaphysical philosophy. The lesson we will take here is that Patočka favors neither myth nor metaphysics. We therefore move swiftly on to the orientation to the future, which for Patočka is faith. Faith is openness to the future.[102] Faith is based on freedom—freedom with respect to the past and the present. The past does not predetermine the necessary development of things. Although past events influence the present and even suggest what the future will be like, the regimen of faith leaves open all kinds of possibilities for how to deal with a situation. The absolute claim of the past is not valid for the life of faith because in faith humans are co-creators of their situations.

In other words, faith is the school of responsibility, and responsibility means responding to the situation as well as to the otherness (*to heteron*) that reveals itself through the situation. Faith is therefore freedom from external powers that falsely claim the right to decide on behalf of human beings. Faith is not fate.

Regarding freedom from the present, faith emancipates itself from the given; it does not subscribe to a naive belief in the objective presence. Faith is an appeal to transcendence. Human beings are not in the absolute center; they do not possess the keys to total knowledge as modern metaphysics and science suggest. Faith is an open possibility regarding transcendence; it has no need to prescribe what the highest being is like or to abolish anything higher, deeper, the other of human life as such. Faith is not objective knowledge. Patočka uses rather enigmatic language when he unfolds his understanding of faith: "Faith believes that no decision is yet final and irrevocable. Faith is essentially a faith in life. And this faith in life is essentially a faith in the life eternal."[103] These words offer a summary of what was noted earlier. First, the reference to decisions that are never ultimate alludes to freedom from the bonds of myth in which everything has already been decided. Second, the presentation of faith as a faith in life breaks with the objective world of the metaphysics of presence where there is no real life, no possibility of going anywhere because everything is given in the here and now. A riddle remains, however, regarding Patočka's expression "a faith in the life eternal." Patočka uses other theological-sounding expressions. Faith is "preparation for the true time . . . the fulfilment of time";[104] faith is directed toward "the redemption of man" and "the cooperation between God and man in the work of redemption."[105] This is unusual vocabulary for Patočka. He continues as follows:

> Faith—the orientation to the future—believes in the importance and necessity of the interrupting of what *is*, in its shaking by what *is not*. In this context, faith is a faith in the life eternal and a faith in what (from the perspective of the presence) *is not*.[106]

It seems clear that Patočka does not mean any kind of afterlife as the continuation of this life according to the logic of *do ut des*. What is faith then for? I suggest that the faith of Patočka can be described in three ways: faith is the sense of transcendence and thus establishes a relationship to what is beyond objectivity; faith refers to the source of life, which is (objectively) inexplicable; and faith gives meaning to the whole, even though the whole of meaning is unattainable. In other words, faith is a solid experience of being shaken, of being in the world and living historically.

Patočka evaluates myth and faith more positively than he evaluates the orientation to the present in science and metaphysics. Both myth and faith contain a sense of historicity but only faith is truly historical. It seems legitimate, however, even though the word itself is not mentioned in the text of *Negative Platonism*, to consider faith as the lens through which to read the Idea theologically.

Lessons for Theology

We must conclude this bold attempt at a theological reading of *Negative Platonism* through the notion of faith by answering the objections, already raised, to interweaving theology with Patočka's thinking: (1) Patočka's criticism of *philosophia ancilla theologiae*, (2) the tension between the nonfoundationalist perspective of Patočka's metaphysical thinking and the search for a solid ground for theology from the perspective of negative Platonism, and (3) problems with the nonobjective thinking of God in theology.

Patočka vehemently protests against reducing philosophical thinking to being simply the handmaiden of theology. I tend to agree with him in this respect. Theology is sometimes quite impertinent in its use of philosophical concepts and does not pay sufficient attention to the original context of philosophical disputes. For example, the concept of transubstantiation is based on a theological reconfiguration of the Aristotelian doctrine of substance, but the result of this reinterpretation—that substance is transformed while accidents remain the same—is quite far from Aristotle's original point. I am not saying that theology should not be allowed to stretch philosophical arguments, but it should not forget the original question of the philosopher and should bear witness to it. If theology pays no heed to the source of its inspiration, it becomes a self-proclaimed master of knowledge—the science of God/transcendence, a parody of metaphysics as the science of being. In such cases, theology succumbs to the triumphalist principle of *philosophia ancilla theologiae*.

The question remains as to whether this is a necessary state of affairs. I suggest that it is not. The border between theology and philosophy is not an impermeable wall; it is porous. Theology can be understood as a form of *vita philosophica*, the unity of intellectual insight and faith. The result of this providential encounter is known in tradition as *fides quaerens intellectum*. The engagement with Patočka from a theological point of view makes sense from this perspective. Moreover, Patočka's metaphysical thinking and theological thinking are concerned with the same issue: the other (*to heteron*) of thinking itself. However, thinking about otherness presupposes that the task of thinking is taken seriously. In my opinion, both theology and Patočka's metaphysical thinking are capable of heeding this call.

The objection concerning foundationalism must be approached from Patočka's point regarding the notion of questioning. In fact, Patočka never speaks about foundationalism. He prefers to use expressions such as "living without an anchor" yet "standing on solid ground." How should we disentangle his enigmatic language? I suggest that the key to this, and to Patočka's metaphysical thinking in general, is to be found in the first of his *Heretical Essays*. The subtitle of the first essay, in Patočka's own German translation, reads: "Die Frage der natürlichen Welt und die Welt ohne Fraglichkeit." Questioning is the final point of this essay, but what does it mean for our problem? For Patočka, living with an anchor is a life without questions. The world without questions is the world of myth and the world of modern science and metaphysics. However, living as if there were no anchors—living in problematicity—would imply metaphysical thinking. For Patočka, questioning and shaking meaning are the solid ground on which we stand. Questioning and shaking are a metaphysical stance, an active position that allows and welcomes answers, provided those answers never close off the stream of questions. Hence, questioning and shaking open the very possibility of meaning, truth, freedom, and the experience of transcendence. The other name for this position is faith. Faith is a solid ground, although a life lived in faith involves a profound and unending shaking. Faith is the world of questions. Because it understands this dynamic, Christianity is *the* religion in Patočka's thought. (The next three chapters will explore the possibilities of Christianity in Patočka in detail.)

Finally, we come to the most difficult question. How should we name God from the perspective of negative Platonism? Patočka proposes a nonobjective thinking. Is it acceptable for the theologian to follow the philosopher in this respect? We have seen that in his metaphysical thinking, Patočka does not reject objectivity as such but protests against the dictates of objectivity as presented in metaphysical philosophy and modern science.

Rather than using the negative term *nonobjective thinking*, it would perhaps be better, therefore, to call Patočka's proposal *meta-objective thinking*.

Meta-objective thinking transcends objectivity and claims that there is something beyond mere things, entities. This might sound heretical to modern minds. But does it sound heretical to the mind of theologians? The God of modernity appears to be the highest object, the object of rational reflection, the guarantor of reason itself. This God requires proofs of existence and rational justification according to the standards of logical argumentation. The question is whether a meta-objective thinking of God is not the original way in which the task of thinking—from a theological perspective—is realized. Is not a God who is almost nonexistent, a God who is no-thing, closer to reality than a God who is? It is not my intention to label anyone guilty of instigating the shift from the God of mystery to the God of mastery. My point is that Patočka's negative Platonism can lend a language and structure of thought to theology in order to think about God meta-objectively and at the same time metaphysically.

Although Patočka cautiously protects his thinking from explicit theologizing, he opens much space for theological interpretations. In the case of negative Platonism, the notion of faith is the most obvious intersection between theological interests and Patočka's articulation of metaphysical thinking. It is unfortunate that Patočka does not develop his work in a similar fashion to, for example, Karl Jaspers, but although he is reluctant to say it explicitly, I am convinced that Patočka invites us to think about a certain vision of *philosophical faith*. It is known that Patočka read Jaspers and that he approached him with sympathy and evaluated him positively.[107] It is my conviction that the theological potential of Patočka can be further expanded in dialogue with thinkers such as Jaspers regarding the notion of faith, Lacoste regarding theology as a form of *vita philosophica*, and many others who challenge metaphysical philosophy from a phenomenological perspective—Henry, for example, or from the postmodern postphenomenological point of view, Derrida or Nancy.

Chapter 5

Deconstruction or Heresy

Reconsidering the Un-thought of Christianity

The deconstruction of Christianity is one of the principal motifs of the so-called theological turn in contemporary philosophy of religion. Although the term itself appears explicitly only in the work of Jean-Luc Nancy, as a concept it reaches much wider. Philosophically, the idea of deconstruction draws on the work of Jacques Derrida, who developed the notion for the purpose of rethinking the scope of rationality and reconsidering the limits of Enlightenment reason, by no means as a ban on rationality itself, as some critiques have unjustly pointed out.[1] Authors from different backgrounds follow on from the French *enfant terrible* and introduce various deconstructive projects regarding Christianity. Caputo proposes "religion without religion," Vattimo writes *After Christianity*, and the aforementioned Nancy initiates the whole project of deconstructing Christianity. None of this is about the renewal of religion, the development of a new theology, or even the re-Christianization of culture. The message is that religion is still with us, but in different ways from times past.

Before Caputo, Vattimo, Nancy, and even before Derrida, and preceding the turn to religion, Jan Patočka formulated similar questions and suggested that we are living in a post-Christian age. Christendom has disintegrated. The world is disenchanted. But does this mean that Christianity has ceased to be important? Although Patočka did not announce the project of deconstructing Christianity, he constantly circles around the notion of a Christianity that comes after the end of Christianity. In this respect, a significant number of philosophical studies have appeared and have interpreted Patočka's project variously as a heretical Christianity (Chvatík), a radically demythologized Christianity (Hagedorn, Veselý), and the reconsideration of Christianity as a central philosophical theme (de Warren). But a thoroughgoing theological engagement with Patočka's inspiring work is still notable by its absence. The figures of the theological turn are widely discussed in the current debate on the future of Christianity, but Patočka still awaits discovery. Given limited space, this chapter will not pretend to remedy such a lacuna. I will nonetheless argue that Patočka's reconsideration of Christianity opens new horizons for understanding Christianity after the end of Christianity, even from a theological perspective.

Like the authors of the deconstructive projects within the theological turn, Patočka is not interested in projecting a new future *for* religion; his work lacks any desire to reconstitute Christendom. Rather, he proposes that our future is *in* reconsidering religion. The future as such seems to overlap with a Christianity (re)interpreted as "the greatest, unsurpassed, but also un-thought-through élan that enables humans to struggle against decadence."[2]

What we will explore is the meaning of Patočka's "future Christianity," and the leading motif will be an inquiry into "the un-thought of Christianity." Although Patočka says only once that Christianity has not yet been thought to its end, I will argue that the idea is of immense importance for him.[3] More specifically, I suggest that Patočka's thesis on the un-thought of Christianity is open to theological retrievals. In what sense? As the title of *Heretical Essays in the Philosophy of History* suggests, Patočka's vision of Christianity will most likely differ from what in theological circles is considered orthodox Christianity. First of all, therefore, the chapter will analyze Patočka's starting point, that is, the situation after the end of Christianity, in which any reflection on Christianity is embedded. From the midst of this context, Patočka recognizes the double sense of deconstruction: the need to deconstruct Christianity, and the self-deconstruction of Christianity or Christianity as deconstruction. Second, I will argue that according to Patočka, Christianity after the end of Christianity provides an exit from myth and enhances the deconstruction of a timeless metaphysical religion. Finally, I will turn to the figure of the un-thought. Drawing from Patočka's insights, I will propose a fundamental theological interpretation of his philosophical reconsideration of Christianity and enhance the line of argument on the un-thought element of Christianity after Christianity.

Before we enter the problematic through the prism of Patočka's writings, the use of a somewhat provocative notion of heresy requires clarification. Heresy can be understood as alienation from orthodoxy. Heresy damages right and true opinions and provokes division. A different meaning is possible, however. Miroslav Petříček interprets Patočka's entire oeuvre as a stream of heretical thinking motivated by his passionate commitment to the most important questions:

> Heresy is the same "act" as the original creative interpretation which carries on, taking a thought further. It is—perhaps—a sort of "over-interpretation," but never a misinterpretation, since this mode of [Patočka's] heretical thinking implies a reflection on the very limits of the thought to be understood and implies such an extension of these limits that it is able to transform even the basic definitions and fundamental concepts while preserving the core of the thought in question.[4]

In this sense, it would be misleading to consider heresy to be a lie, which is merely a false statement. Each heresy venerates the truth. Heresy transgresses borders, pushes ideas beyond the limits, and opens new horizons of understanding. Suddenly, we realize that heresy has a value as it indicates different perspectives. In short, heresy reveals something that for whatever reason remains unthought.

Phenomenology and Deconstruction

Contemporary thinking moves around the (re)turn to religion. Common sense suggests that this turn is a reaction to modernity and its tragic outworkings. Patočka is a thinker of the crisis of modernity. One could say that his entire philosophical work moves around the dialectic of light and dark opened by the Enlightenment.[5] He shows how the crisis of modernity, the crisis of human identity, the loss of meaning, the rise of nihilism, and the tragic inhuman consequences of the proclaimed modern humanism are affected by the displacement of Christianity and the disenchantment of the world. Our question, however, turns our attention from the external by-products of a post-Christian age back to the internal core, the heart of Christianity, from the effects of modernity to the sources of Christian existence.

Patočka's essay "Christianity and the Natural World"[6] raises the question of the possibilities of openness to the divine—God—in the context of a fundamentally reshaped post-Christian epoch. What are the conditions of thinking the divine, of thinking and understanding Christianity? Before heading into the argument, it is necessary to issue a warning against enthusiastic theological recuperations of the matter. True, Patočka's query explicitly involves the divine, or the God of Christian faith. But his interest is not the content of theological questions and the consequent proposition of positive answers to them. The essay referred to shows, rather, an inquisitiveness concerning the very possibility of raising such questions in a context after the end of Christianity and the death of God. Patočka asks, "Is there something in the natural world like an original approach to the divine? Is there something like an original human understanding of what is sacred and divine?"[7]

First, we must clarify Patočka's understanding of the natural world—*Lebenswelt*—the world of human life. Husserl formulates the problem of the natural world in opposition to the objectivism of modern scientific rationalism. Expanding on this note, Heidegger interprets modern techno-scientific rationality as the height of metaphysics, as "an inverted understanding of being which makes a mere object, a mere thing, out of the essential non-objectivity."[8] In this respect, Patočka says that the natural world is a crucial philosophical problem of the twentieth century as a reaction to the crisis of modernity:[9]

> The natural world is simply the world in which we live, the one that comes to us, whose things we meet, and to whose issues we relate as soon as we open our eyes and start to come into contact with things and others . . . [the world] that is familiar to us and where we must be at home whenever we start to pose problems, to elaborate theories, and to think. This is the world we live in, the one we are talking about when we talk about the position of man in the world.[10]

It is not our task here to address the detail of this complex philosophical problem. Patočka himself dedicated hundreds of pages to such reflections, leaving much space for a variety of interpretations. For our question, two points are important. First, for Patočka, the world is history. And second, being-in-the-world means being placed in a particular situation. The natural world is not an unmoving entity, the world in the original *status nascendi* before its reflection, and nothing like an ahistorical metaphysical concept. On the contrary, the natural world is in constant motion. For Patočka, therefore, the natural world is what defines the way something appears to us. Human beings as active agents of history, conscious of their own historicity, also co-constitute the world and its history. The world of our life—the situation we are thrown into—shapes our openness to the world, and the way we are open to the world—while reflecting on it—shapes the world around us. According to Patočka, "The world in this sense is a set of possibilities opened in front of the human being in a concrete moment. These possibilities frame his living space, and human actions constantly refer to them."[11] The idea of openness, whether with reference to the divine or to any other phenomena, has a bearing on a specific historical epoch and its particular forms. In other words, all historical epochs manifest openness of a certain kind. That said, the answer to the initial question of Patočka's "Christianity and the Natural World" is negative. Phenomenological philosophy challenges all timeless constitutions of the world.[12] There is no such thing, therefore, as an original—natural in a metaphysical sense—openness to the divine. This does not mean the disappearance of the question, however. From the perspective of phenomenological philosophy, the question is simply rephrased to read: What is the situation from which we ask for openness to the divine?

Patočka uses the words "We modern people . . ." to describe the contemporary situation. For him, the prevailing mode of thinking operates in objective terms, mathematical logic, techno-scientific rationality, and so on. This modus operandi devours all sides of being. It includes, for example, the use of language that seeks clear and distinct terms and prefers syllogisms to poetry. The modern mentality embraces human society and its organization. The polis is not a community of those who care for the Good, but a unit to be governed and mastered. Finally, the inner aspect of human being—that which used to be called the soul—becomes one entity among others. As a result, the conception of phenomena, the way things appear and can be seen, is completely changed. Together with Heidegger, Patočka defined "modern people" as those who forget the question of being.[13] The same applies to the possibility of openness to the divine. Gods are strangers in the world of modern objectivism and techno-scientific civilization. In this sense, the purported progress of enlightened rationality ends in the decline of human being because a deeper transcendent aspect of our being in the world is laid aside as a redundant hypothesis or a postulate beyond reason.

Nevertheless, Patočka is never simplistic. Modernity is not merely the obscurantism of reason. Looking from this perspective, Patočka stresses that the phenomenon of the divine is not easily understandable, is perhaps even incomprehensible, because "we modern people" have reached a point of no return. Modernity advances critical thinking. The darkness of the Enlightenment is redeemed by the light of philosophical reflection that challenges all kinds of precritical statements:

> This means that modern man, even where he answers the call of one who is higher, has an entirely different relation to the divine and the divinity. His attitude is definitely not the permanent *tremendum*, the constant questioning and worry with which the man of antiquity lived in the face of the divine.[14]

In Patočka's opinion, our situation cannot be satisfied with a return to any preceding conception of the divine and religion. Gods are not unquestioned rulers. The divine is not the answer. The divine suffers a question mark. Again, the question is not to be seen as the search for the original—natural—openness to the divine. The situation calls for questioning the divine and religion in the *Lebenswelt* of the day.

Finally, the story does not only concern modernity, the disenchantment of the world, and the loss of a sense of the divine caused by techno-scientific rationality or critical thinking. Patočka reminds us that the key role in this development is played by Christianity itself. Indeed, Christianity advances a thorough criticism regarding what is not the divine appearance in this world. From the beginning, and throughout its history, Christianity calls for conversion. The Christian existence can never be satisfied with an image of the divine and is constantly challenged to remain open to new forms of the appearance of the divine. This does not cease to be true even in a context based on the objectification of being, including of the divine.

To sum up, we are left in a peculiar situation. Openness to the divine is a standing challenge, but the content that used to be given to it is no longer acceptable. The world is changing. And as Patočka clarifies, the world is "our" understanding.[15] The understanding of phenomena is changing. Nature is understood as the sum of objects, and the understanding and self-understanding of the human as a part of nature changes accordingly. Ultimately, this affects the understanding of the divine and human self-understanding in relation to the divine. Patočka describes it in terms of analogy: Greek philosophy influenced Christian theology and opened new ways of thinking the divine; modernity sets its own path.

To be sure, like any analogy, this one contains more dissimilarities than similarities. The important point with regard to our question is that the opening of new horizons always implies the closing of others. The movement of history therefore provokes movement within Christianity, but this movement is not necessarily caught between the polar opposites of adaptation to, or resistance to, the given historical context. Patočka notes that the Christian experience of history is different from the Greek and the modern experiences, and he asks a crucial question:

> Does this conception, which encompasses the understanding of both change and permanence, enable us to find in our present time, in our present understanding of being, in the natural world of ours, a possibility that remains? Is it able to make us understand that the closing and the withdrawal of the old possibilities during the movement, the becoming that is the human understanding, do not mean the loss of something essential, but only a successive transformation of the fundamental experiences from our openness to what is?[16]

The key idea here is the openness that remains a movement that cannot be taken for granted. In fact, Patočka places before us the hiddenness of the openness. The hidden—the un-thought—is apparent in the aftermath of modernity. In *Heretical Essays*, this is phrased as follows: "To uncover what is hidden in manifestation entails questioning, it means discovering the problematic character not of this or that but of the whole as such."[17] This is what I call the sense of deconstruction in Patočka. Of course, Patočka never actually used the term *deconstruction*. Nonetheless, the conception of understanding as movement is highly reminiscent of the Derridean motif of the reevaluation of all Western values, not in order to destroy them but to reach deeper into their meaning in changing historical circumstances.[18] Ludger Hagedorn expresses a similar idea in his interpretation of Patočka's relationship to Christianity:

> De-construction is an attempt to stay within the tradition, but to loosen its structural ties; to make them move and to dare to play the game of establishing new references and interventions.
>
> De-construction is a *move* for the contemporary reassessment of a tradition that cannot simply be refuted or declared as

invalid, because every attempt to do so already starts off from its very ground.[19]

Why does Christianity need to be deconstructed? The answer is twofold. Patočka wants to demonstrate a certain continuity in the history of the understanding of being, which in his opinion enables humans to fight against the modern abstract rationalism that results in nihilism. However, deconstruction is necessary if we are to see that our understanding is being transformed according to the context, that understanding is a movement. In this sense, the Christianity that survives modernity is Christianity after (the end of) Christianity. Patočka pleads for the possibility of such a Christianity that would reactivate openness to the divine in the context of its present-day hiddenness.

One preliminary conclusion we can draw from this way of reasoning is that Patočka's notion of deconstruction is fully embedded in phenomenological philosophy. It is not deconstruction for the sake of destruction; it is re-creation. The ultimate goal of this movement is an openness to the divine in line with our historical possibilities of understanding. The deconstruction proposed by Patočka is not a search for original essence. In contrast to some postmodern authors of the theological turn, for Patočka, there is no pure Christianity understood as religion without (the obscurity of) religion (Caputo), or a community of charity without hierarchical elements (Vattimo). Patočka rather searches for an understanding of Christianity in the world we are thrown into and against the contemporary critical consciousness that is engaged with the crisis of modernity, the disintegration of metaphysics, and the end of religion. Only from such a place does openness to the divine make sense and perhaps, in unexpected ways, allow for a reconsideration. Only from this situation does the un-thought of Christianity begin to appear.

Christianity Demythologized and Deconstructed

What is the un-thought of Christianity? We have seen that the issue can be raised only by way of deconstruction. Although Patočka never uses the term *deconstruction*, in the essay "The Dangers of Technicization in Science" written in 1973, he explicitly mentions the need for a "demythologized Christianity."[20] In fact, Patočka's interest in the possibilities of a demythologized Christianity began much earlier. In the early 1950s, Patočka read Rudolf Bultmann, whom he found groundbreaking and did not hesitate to define as a genuine theologian.[21] Around the same time, Patočka turns his attention to the critique of myth. He considers myth the polar opposite of religion and expresses the opposition in terms of closure versus openness. It is beyond doubt that Bultmann inspired Patočka's thought in this respect. Nevertheless, Patočka does not simply follow the German biblical scholar, whose ultimate goal is to retrieve the Old Testament—Jewish—element within Christianity and to contrast the Hebrew motif of absolute dependence on God with the Hellenistic aspect of the universal harmonious whole. If the former is attributed to Bultmann, the latter clearly refers to the Hegelian metaphysical system. In his own thinking, Patočka seeks to transcend both:

> It is a challenge to philosophy to situate itself between these poles, which refers to Hegel's *Phenomenology of Spirit*, on the one hand, and to Bultmann's *Urchristentum* on the other, and to draw conclusions from the open space between them in order to prepare a solution to the problem.[22]

Patočka's central question can thus be rephrased as thinking beyond myth and enlightenment,[23] and for Patočka, such a mode of thinking would be Christianity. However, to avoid both the alternatives we have just mentioned, we must turn from the past toward the future. In other words, Patočka searches for a Christianity after Christianity, for a Christianity that is to come.

The call for "after" nevertheless begs the question: After what? The answer lies in Patočka's formulation of the problem. Christianity after Christianity is a Christianity beyond myth and rationalism. But we should not forget one crucial thing. It is still *Christianity* after Christianity. Patočka sets out not to find an exit from Christianity but *to think* Christianity in our particular epoch. In this sense, Patočka proposes much more than a simple demythologization. He deconstructs certain forms of Christianity in order to reconsider Christianity's unthought potential.

Beyond Myth

The problem of myth held a lifelong fascination for Patočka. Given the length of his career, Patočka's position naturally develops and assumes various contours, but in general terms, Patočka conceives myth as a counterweight to philosophy. Myth is understood as a mode of thinking that contrasts with philosophical reasoning: myth represents a precritical narrative perspective; philosophy stands for criticism that sheds light on the obscurity that myth produces. This schematic "black-and-white" perspective does not of course do justice to the complex notion of myth in Patočka. It is neither possible nor desirable to review Patočka's argument in its entirety.[24] Our interest here is how myth relates to Christianity. In this respect, in addition to presenting it as a mode of thinking, Patočka primarily considered myth (a) in its relation to history and human historicity, and consequently, (b) as a way of being in the world.

As the title of the essay "Time, Myth, Faith" suggests, there are two ways of relating to time and history. One is myth, the other is faith, but both belong in some way to the domain of religion.

The mythical world is governed by god(s) and other unquestioned forces beyond our control, such as the fate to which everything is unconditionally tied. This state of affairs is grounded in the narration of the originary event(s): the past legitimizes the present and projects the future. Myth has its answer before anyone asks the question. It represents an archetype. It is usually portrayed as the original state of bliss and the subsequent fall. Myth is the event that is over. It can only be, and must be, represented. Otherwise, new catastrophes might come. In other words, myth is the consciousness that everything has already been decided and nothing can be changed. Myth is the "ontological safety of the past."[25]

Patočka describes three elementary characteristics of myth: (1) Myth does not know questions because answers precede every possibility of asking, challenging, and problematizing. (2) Myth does not differentiate between the imaginary and the real. Everything that is narrated is real, and it is real because it is narrated. And (3), in mythical representation, human beings are thrown into passive participation.[26] Nothing can be challenged unless one particularly wishes to invoke the wrath of the gods. Everything must be accepted. The meaning of the world is imposed; there is no way to challenge it. Myths contain the deposit of meaning, and human life is a life of passive subscription to this meaning. The gods want it this way, and so be it. As Patočka would say, "Myth ignores human freedom."[27] And he continues elsewhere:

> Myth is a grand passive fantasy—a fantasy that is not aware that it is fantasy and that answers to certain deep affective needs of man. . . . Religion on the other hand is something which requires a personal act of faith; it is something actively carried out by us.[28]

Clearly, myth is contrasted with religion, which for Patočka means Christianity. In contrast to the passive nature of myth, Christianity stands for a personal act of faith. Moreover, "only in the case of Christianity can one speak of faith."[29] In this sense, Christianity is something unique and extraordinary, perhaps even the "greatest and unsurpassed"[30] moment in history.

We would nevertheless be mistaken to read these lines as Patočka's apology for Christian faith in its traditional garb. As we have just seen, Patočka deals with myth as something that does not know history as a creative flow of time. In contrast to prehistorical myth, faith therefore stands as the exemplar of historicity and genuine historical consciousness. For Patočka, faith is openness to the future, and Christianity as the religion of faith is a way of opening to the future. In other words, life in faith is a life that possesses a future, whereas myth is locked in the past. Faith breaks with the logic determined by the past and provides an exit from fate. The breakthrough provided by Christianity is "the belief that no decision is ultimate and irrevocable."[31]

In sum, Patočka contrasts myth—where everything depends on the gods, where the fate of human beings is out of their hands—with a form of Christianity that is understood as a personal drama in which "man freely co-determines his existence."[32] Faith as openness to the future and an affirmation of the "undecidability" of history functions as the principle of differentiation. I propose to call this Patočka's discovery of the sense of deconstruction within Christianity.

Later, Patočka elaborates on myth as a mode of being in the world and on the answer to the question of the meaning of human existence. Patočka differentiates three movements of existence: (1) the movement of anchoring, (2) the movement of self-prolongation or self-preservation, and (3) the movement of breakthrough, sometimes called the movement of truth and transcendence.[33] In the first movement, one accepts the situation one is thrown into. It is the passive adoption of existing forms of life (traditions, opinions, practices), and the recognition of being-in-the-world, an awareness that the situation is contingent and in many ways beyond control. The first movement represents accommodation to *es ist so*. This anchoring, or establishing roots, makes one feel at home in the world and provides one with the ground for living. One may be inclined to hear an echo of Heidegger in Patočka, but the conception of the first movement is also an attempt to emancipate the discussion from

Heidegger's concept of our being thrown into the world. In contrast to Heidegger's formalism, Patočka emphasizes that the movement of existence is always in relation to something other, including things and persons.[34] In other words, whereas Heidegger focuses on a single individual being that seems isolated in the world, and thus alone in its thrownness into being, Patočka's first movement of existence aims to analyze the concrete world of every person, and in this sense existence in intersubjectivity and openness to the world.

The second movement shifts from setting roots in the world to a confrontation with the world, which manifests itself as an active life, but still within the framework of assumed practices, traditions, and opinions. Every action is constrained by the way the world is given in the moment of acceptance. For this reason and despite a concern for an active life in the present, the second movement, like the first, is caught up in what already exists and is thus determined by the past.[35] It therefore seems as though the combination of the first and second movements fits perfectly into the picture of the mythical world. Furthermore, "Humanity [in myth] lives only in order to live, not to seek deeper, more authentic forms of life. Precisely because human beings are focused on the movement of acceptance and preservation, this entire life remains something of an ontological metaphor."[36] Everything is in the hands of the gods. There is nothing to be done but to work, procreate, venerate deities, keep feasts, and, of course, represent the past inscribed in myths. These are the only ways of securing life in isolation from the third movement.

The third movement of existence introduces the breakthrough, the breakaway from this rule. All presuppositions imposed by myth are shaken. Everything previously taken for granted ceases to have a decisive effect on the horizon of possibilities. One is able to leave myth behind and to live in history. But how? What has changed?

At some point, Patočka associates the movement of breakthrough with philosophy.[37] "The world has become mysterious, our existence uncertain, and our ideas . . . questionable."[38] The third movement equals critical thinking, the awareness of problematicity, and openness to the hidden element of the world rather than to the obvious.[39] It would be a misunderstanding, however, to take the three movements of existence as a progressive development of human being. Patočka is not suggesting here that we must all climb from ignorance to learned unknowing. All three movements are interrelated in concrete human existence. What is needed is not so much the suppression of the first and second movements in favor of the third, but the groundbreaking conversion of human existence. At this moment, we finally return to religion.

One could object that we entered the field of religion some time ago. Does not myth first and foremost concern the religious? Have we not already encountered ever-present gods, the unquestioned forces that govern the world, and a bare human life enclosed in mythical representations of the past? We could certainly claim that one of the pillars of the mythical world is cultic religion, mysteries, and rituals. The sacred swallows up the entire human being, who has no choice but to accept the given state of affairs, to surrender to the almighty gods, and to live a life of hard work with no end in sight. However, it is precisely the religious aspect of myth that, in Patočka's opinion, seeks to transcend everydayness and the struggle of a bare and accepted life. Myth somehow anticipates all that becomes explicit in the third movement, even though "it remains thematically subordinated to the movements of acceptance and defense."[40] In its religious aspect, myth manifests a certain openness. Alternatively, we could say that religion can take the form of myth by obscuring its potential for openness.

Opening up, the turn from the determinate to the undecided, the turn from the thought to the un-thought, the ability to see the world from a new perspective—this is precisely what Patočka calls *conversion*.[41] As with the notion of faith—which Patočka associates exclusively with Christianity, arguing that we overcome ahistorical myths by a historical faith—it is no coincidence that Patočka picks up a specifically Christian term with regard to myth as a way of being in the world.[42] He notes, "[The world of myth is] the world prior to the discovery of its problematic character. And the world without problematicity is one in which the hiddenness as such is not experienced."[43] The gods, divine forces, and liturgical cults, rites, and secrets—the religious—manifest openness to being in a particular way. Nonetheless, myth does not experience the hiddenness of openness, the nonapparent character of being, the problematicity that energizes questioning and challenges everything, including the gods. For Patočka, it is Christian conversion that opens itself to the mystery of the world. This mystery remains hidden but in a fundamentally different way from the secrets of *religio*. Whereas ancient mysteries included only those who were initiated, Christianity appeals to everyone, calls everyone to turn from a closed life to a life lived in openness. Christianity is a turn from the life of the everyday, a life ruled by the past and by endless routine, to an openness toward the future. In this sense, Christian conversion is openness to hiddenness. God, despite his revelation, remains hidden. Christianity does not remain locked in the past because its conception of God is inherently historical.[44] At the same time, one can never be sure what exactly is to come. The cross of Christ is the example par excellence of a break from the inevitability of myths. We will return to this later. Here, I will simply note two lessons to be learned from the contrast between myth and religion. First, Christianity is the deconstruction of myth by a turn (*metanoia*) to the hidden God. In this respect, Christianity provides an alternative to the cultic religion of Rome and the philosophical endeavor of Athens. Put simply, Athens and Rome need to be counterbalanced by Golgotha in Jerusalem. Second, the Christianity that makes sense in the present-day context is a demythologized Christianity. This means that Christianity is called to incorporate the truth of myth but not to become the religion of myth. Despite its initial radicalness, it is tempting for Christianity to reconvert and become a mythical religion. But rather than recapitulate the myths of ancient times, Christianity opts for the rationalization of its own myths. Certainties have greater currency.

Beyond Rational Theology and a Moral God

In *Heretical Essays*, Patočka invokes the authority of Saint Paul and holds on to one particular sentence from the first letter to Corinthians: "Has not God made foolish the wisdom of the world?"[45] Patočka interprets this proclamation as Christianity's break with the logic of pure rationalism.[46] Of course, Paul is referring here to Greek metaphysics and the eidetic method of theoretical insight. He intends to challenge the metaphysical belief that the soul, to use the Greek notion proper to this case, is in direct contact with the order of being. Instead of participating in the world of ideas or in the essences of entities, one has to depend on God. Patočka obviously does not follow Paul's zeal for the supreme being of God. His point is simply to state that the Christian tradition stands fundamentally as a revolt against metaphysics. Furthermore, Christianity introduces a fruitful tension between philosophical and theological perspectives on the world and brings them into mutual dialogue. In this sense, Paul's voice represents Christianity's moment of deconstruction of rationalism.

Nonetheless, this tension disappears in the aftermath of early modernity. The agenda of the day is to develop rational proofs of the Christian doctrine. The effect is a purely rational form of theology. Like the mathematical image of the world provided by modern science, God must be conceived with mathematical certainty: "We [modern people] have grown accustomed to considering the mathematical project of nature as the evident basis for all interpretations of nature and spirit," says Patočka in his essay "On Masaryk's Philosophy of Religion."[47] The title is somewhat misleading, however, as Patočka's main topic in his final piece of writing (completed in 1977) is the question of meaning in the aftermath of the crisis of religion and metaphysics. In this respect, Patočka's main interlocutors are Kant and Dostoevsky; Masaryk comes only third in line. Interpretations in secondary literature therefore generally follow the point concerning the question of meaning and the juxtaposition of Kant and Dostoevsky or seek to interconnect these topics.[48] I, however, suggest looking at the problem from the other side and concentrating rather on the consequences of Patočka's treatment of these authors for the deconstruction of the pretentious rationalism of a timeless religion.

For Patočka, the longing of the Christian to be certain about his or her soul's salvation became transposed into the need to possess certain truth.[49] It could be argued that Cartesianism and modern rational theology forget about the foolishness against which the Apostle Paul warns his brothers and sisters. At this point, Kant enters the scene: "Kant substitutes for an absolute onto-theology a moral theology relative to human life. His concern is to replace the ancient divine objective order with a new order on a human foundation, but one that will be no less viable, persuasive, and supra-objective."[50] As Patočka explains, Kant breaks with the rational conception of God as an entity understood as the *ens maximum* and *necessarium*. In Kant's alternative, God cannot be thought of as an object of pure reason. Rather, God—together with the notions of immortality and freedom—is a necessary postulate of practical reason. This means that religion has nothing to do with positive knowledge. Rather, faith is a necessity that finds itself outside speculative reasoning. On this basis, according to Patočka, Kant construes a new moral theology. This theology presupposes that the ultimate purpose and meaning of the world is phrased in moral terms. God is not conceived as an independent transcendent being that grounds the intelligibility of the whole: God is conceived in relation to human beings. Following the postulates of practical reason, one is able to realize the good and thus to act in accordance with the moral law of the world. In this way, one discovers the meaning of life and also discovers God as the guarantor of the moral order. For Kantian moral theology, without God, without reward for the good and retribution for the bad, there would be only *skepsis* and meaninglessness. This reasoning is obviously not based on any kind of transcendent revelation. Patočka makes it clear that moral theology is deduced from reason. The foolishness of worldly wisdom seems to repeat itself.

"Yet is it necessary for the world to have a moral meaning?"[51] Patočka challenges Kant's moral theology and its concept of a God who rewards and punishes and that the postulates of practical reason are valid only under the condition that one accepts the moral meaning of the world as given. Kant's moral theology presupposes a particular metaphysical order. Like the Platonic world of ideas, Kant postulates the metaphysics of values. Although the Kantian God relates to human beings, the meaning of being in the world has already been decided.

Drawing on Dostoevsky's *Brothers Karamazov*, Patočka formulates his alternative. Patočka reads Dostoevsky as a critic of Western rationalism—a rationalism that overlaps with Kantian moral theology. Patočka does not subscribe, however, to the traditional opinion that Dostoevsky is an advocate of Orthodox Christianity in opposition to modern rationalism. Meditating on the argument of Ivan Karamazov against the moral God, Patočka formulates the following challenge:

> Is it not necessary now to conceive God other than from the perspective of moral conflict? Is this conflict itself not proof that we have believed in God in the wrong way, that we have implicated him in our antinomies and contradictions? Is all of this not the concrete way of saying: (the moral) God is dead?[52]

We got it wrong, says Patočka. Both rational and moral theology abuse God. The former needs him as the guarantee of intelligibility and correct calculations; the latter drags him into a perverse construction of an otherworldly transcendental accounting office with a desk for receiving complaints. Perhaps Nietzsche has it right. God is dead. The other world does not exist. Nothing like eternal ideas, the postulates of practical reason, or absolute unshakeable meaning exists to provide us shelter. It seems that the destiny of human beings after the death of God is nihilism. But is this the one and only ineluctable result?

Patočka proclaims the death of the moral God, an overrationalized God whom we do not understand. From a theological point of view, the lesson of Patočka is not a flight from God but rather a restating of the question of God. Patočka concludes his essay on the philosophy of religion with a clear reference to the theology of his day, which left modern rationalist tendencies behind.[53] As previously noted, the theology at stake probably refers to Bultmann's demythologization.[54] Nonetheless, one does not have to stop here. A closer engagement with Patočka's ideas opens new ways for Christian thinking. Demythologization does not necessarily refer to a simple updating of the language of ancient Christian concepts thereby enabling their understanding in the current mind-set, or a hermeneutical attitude to sacred texts that separates the form of the message—historical, cosmological, scientific claims—from the meaning—theological, ethical, sapiential claims. Patočka's reflections on Christianity should be read rather as the deconstruction of a timeless metaphysical religion, the religion of postulatory rationalism.

Heresy, or: What Is Patočka's Christianity?

What kind of Christianity after Christianity can be derived from Patočka's thought? What kind of Christianity will rise after leaving myth and rationalism behind? After the death of God, resurrection—one believes—will come. Patočka's interpreters remain somewhat skeptical, however. Ivan Chvatík, for example, emphasizes the discontinuity between Patočka's reconsideration of Christianity and the prevailing theological tradition.[55] He is convinced that the term *heretical* in the title of Patočka's most famous philosophical work is not a coincidence but a deliberate rebellion against the doctrinal orthodoxy. According to Chvatík, Patočka starts his philosophical career as a believer looking for support in Christianity. Later, although Patočka draws inspiration from Christianity for thinking through questions of meaning, truth, and human existence, he ultimately moves beyond the religious.[56] After leaving myth behind, after the disintegration of both rational and moral theology, there is no transcendent referent outside this world. The resolution is crude. God has forsaken us.

Ludger Hagedorn proposes a more nuanced account. In place of heresy, he proposes a figure of demythologized Christianity.[57] Hagedorn suggests that Patočka considers Christianity from the perspective of human being-in-the-world without direct access to the transcendent realm of being, if such exists. In addition to the deconstruction of the deities of natural religion and the deconstruction of rational constructions of the divine, Hagedorn argues that Patočka's Christianity does not reckon with (1) individual immortality, (2) a revealed transcendent God, or (3) God as a postulate of reason.[58] Because of this, Jindřich Veselý criticizes Patočka for developing a tragic Christianity that contains neither transcendence nor hope.[59] Interestingly, in contrast to Chvatík, Veselý argues that in this respect Patočka's position is consistent throughout his philosophical career. Rather than Christianity *after* Christianity, Patočka leaves us the challenge of an almost unbearable Christianity *without* Christianity.

It would be disappointing to end on this pessimistic note. Hagedorn, by far the most active interpreter of the meaning of "a Christian message after the end of Christianity" in Patočka, does not give up, therefore, but tries to make sense of it. He agrees with Karfík that Patočka's references to Christianity are more than contingent historical examples and that they have their purpose.[60] As Hagedorn explains, we are not here considering the relationship to Christianity of a believer or unbeliever but rather of a philosopher,[61] but Patočka intends to use Christianity not as a figure subordinated to philosophy but as a challenge to philosophical thinking itself.[62] Christianity is both the other of reason and the other of religion. Hagedorn explains that for Patočka, Christianity possesses "the most radical potential to articulate some kind of *protest*, a protest that is directed against the merely anthropocentric world of individual and social self-affirmation."[63] Here we hear an echo of the third movement of existence, the movement of breakthrough from the movements of anchoring and defense enforced in myth. Christianity stands as the principal source of the third movement. The radical message of the New Testament is not about blind obedience to the pantheon of deities as required in mythical cultic religiosity, or about accumulating knowledge as proposed in Greek metaphysical philosophy. For Patočka, Christianity turns our eyes inward and calls for a care for being. The message is "the abysmal deepening of the soul," which results in "thus far the greatest, unsurpassed, but also un-thought-through élan that enabled humans to struggle against decadence."[64] Drawing on these statements, Hagedorn concludes that Patočka associates Christianity with the sense of living in problematicity.[65] It is this that could be called "deconstruction" in his writings. Christianity therefore represents a challenge to philosophy as a thought-provoking endeavor. Christianity is thinking beyond myth and enlightenment, but it remains, as Patočka notes, un-thought through. In his recent publication, Hagedorn assesses this aspect of Patočka's Christianity on the fringes of heresy:

> Christianity unthought would then indicate the maintenance of some core of Christianity even after its suspension, and through its suspension . . . in the sense of metaphorically reclaiming

some resurrection after the Cross. . . . It is the signal for an investigation into what is left of the Christian spirit without being confessional or credulous.[66]

For Hagedorn, the un-thought of Christianity does not refer to its doctrinal deposit. The un-thought is not something to be thought in the sense of being mastered by knowledge. But if the matter at stake is not confessional content, what is it?

The answer is disclosed in *Heretical Essays*. The kernel of Patočka's vision of Christianity, which is valid even after the end of Christianity as religion, is the soul.[67] Miroslav Petříček explains that the soul in Patočka's conception comes close to what one might consider critical thinking.[68] The soul is the achievement of certain knowledge (*epistēmē*) but also the ability to maintain a critical distance from knowledge. In Petříček's words, "[The soul is] aware of the impossibility of grasping or embracing the whole."[69] The soul is the openness of human being; the openness to questions and to being questioned.

Although the notion of the soul is indisputably of Greek origin, it is transformed and radicalized by Christianity. Hagedorn calls this the shift from "being subjected to history" to the "realization of history."[70] In other words, Christianity advances a form of being-in-the-world that is not merely participatory but in fact reminds every person of their historicity, which includes co-creativity and co-responsibility for the world. The un-thought therefore stands in contrast to propositional beliefs and ventures the formulation of faith as openness to the future: "Care for the soul was and is the principle for this Christianity to come."[71]

So, what is Patočka's Christianity? We can summarize it as follows. In addition to the demythologization and deconstruction of rationalism, Christianity after Christianity must be interpreted as a kind of deconstructive movement in itself. Patočka's Christianity is the breakthrough of deconstructive critical consciousness, in his own words, "caring for the soul." The major issue at stake is a thinking that is impossible to grasp positively via definitions, logical arguments, and propositions. In this sense, it seems right to speak of the un-thought rather than of heresy.

All this makes perfect sense from a philosophical perspective. Christianity reveals the depth of being. One may even call it the ontological revelation that discloses the difference between being and beings, the difference between human beings and entities.[72] Paradoxically, if there is heretical thinking in Patočka, it is a heresy committed against Heidegger's conception of Christianity as a positive revelation. In this sense, Patočka returns Christianity to the center of the philosophical agenda.

Christianity is a historical religion that resists mythical simplifications and rational mastery. Naturally, it is in constant danger of falling prey to idolatries of irrational fideism and rational (moral) theology, but Patočka proposes a way of overcoming these shortcomings. For him, Christianity is a mode of thinking and being. This point already offers inspiration for a theological reading of Patočka's reconsideration of Christianity. But is this enough? Is it not too little? Patočka does not exceed the competence of the philosopher. What will the theologian say? In the final section of this chapter, I will propose the thesis that Patočka's enigmatic idea of Christianity after Christianity contains far more theological significance than might first appear. The center of gravity is the figure of the un-thought.

The Un-thought of Christianity

By its very definition, the concept of the un-thought refers to something that has not yet been thought. The un-thought is something forgotten, omitted, something that through ignorance has not been considered; it might even have been intentionally erased. Or, the un-thought is perhaps something that cannot be thought because of a particular historical situation that prevents it from appearing. This would mean that our situation, the situation of "modern people," denies any possibility of the un-thought being thought. In one way or another, we have either lost the openness or are waiting for the openness to come.

However, the un-thought can also be considered something partially thought, a thought that is not yet finalized and perhaps never can be. This notion of the un-thought would fit the Christian conception of dogma. A typical way of seeing dogmatic statements is their identification with closing declarations, rigid definitions, irreversible propositions, and the expression of metaphysical truth. However, this perspective fails to think of dogma as a new opening and a call for further thinking and questioning, as a pointer or a sign that something has been thought. Dogmas are open to the un-thought, albeit only within certain limits and in the direction delineated by dogmatic definitions. In comparison to other religions, the dogmatic teaching of Christianity is unique. Dogmas are a means of critical reflection, or, expressed more poetically, *fides quaerens intellectum*. In contrast to dogmatism, dogmas bear witness to the equivocality of thoughts on a given matter. In theology, the solemn codification of a dogmatic statement is the result of continual questioning and ongoing debate and by no means the end of the conversation. In this sense, the un-thought is operative in the dogmatic structure of Christianity as a constant reminder of freedom and a warning against the slavery of fundamentalism and dogmatism.

Although these interpretations seem plausible, we can always argue that Patočka's enigmatic statement concerning the un-thought of Christianity promises more. The previous cases are unsatisfactory because they consider the un-thought to be a provisional state of affairs that awaits eventual completion. The un-thought is a lack to be remedied, a question to be answered, and a limited perspective in need of broadening. The un-thought looks for a thought. One possible alternative to this is the un-thought that remains unthought, resists all attempts to finalize it, and becomes the absolute nonthought.

The un-thought of Christianity as the nonthought makes sense in the context of the contemporary theological turn in continental philosophy. Negative theology, apophatic thinking, *via negationis*, and mystical riddles are currently enjoying a revival. The un-thought is neither sensible nor intelligible. It is placed between existence and nonexistence. The unthought is present in our language, but all we say is that "there is"—*il y a*—the un-thought. In this respect, Patočka's concept resembles certain deconstructionist attempts to develop a radical hermeneutics of religion. For example, Jacques Derrida and John D. Caputo play with the Platonic notion of *khôra* as a third kind of being, the desert of negativity, the place where everyone is confronted with the limits of conceptual thinking.[73]

This seems like a promising way to read Patočka. Indeed, what if the un-thought bears witness to the impossibility of thought? The question is raised again and again but always hits a wall. Christians find themselves in a Kierkegaardian *fear and trembling* without an exit. Moreover, it seems that no exit indeed exists. In this sense, the un-thought is a contemporary synonym for mysticism after the end of Christianity.

Although his scheme appears to contain a contradiction, Nicolas de Warren rightly states that Patočka's Christianity can be read either as the un-thought to be completed, or as the absolute nonthought.[74] Even *Heretical Essays* supports both points of view. At one point, Patočka says: "Religious conversions . . . do not have the fundamental importance of the *ontological* experience of philosophy. Perhaps for that reason, too, it may turn out that religion is subject to temporary obscurity until its problems have been resolved philosophically."[75] Later in this same essay, Patočka changes tone and describes Christianity as a *mysterium tremendum* that is ultimately incomprehensible by means of reason alone. For Patočka, Christianity is an "inscrutable relation to the absolute highest being in whose hands we are not externally, but internally."[76] Which of these alternatives is closer to Patočka's heart? And which represents a more viable option for Christianity after Christianity? It is an almost Hamletian dilemma. To be thought or not to be thought? That is the question.

Perhaps still another reading is possible—a reading between the two alternatives that takes seriously the un-thought as unthought. I suggest that the key to such an understanding is the notion of the soul, or, more concretely, the movement of caring for the soul described earlier. We have seen that the notion of the soul refers to a particular way of being-in-the-world based on critical reflection and self-examination. In contrast to the static reasoning of ontotheological metaphysics and the unquestioned world of myth, the soul is a movement from the present toward the future. It is the present continuous. Put another way, care for the soul is *thinking*.

In thinking, the un-thought of Christianity is further elaborated and "thought through" again and again. And since for Patočka philosophy is a systematic method of reflection, it makes perfect sense to use it for reflecting on the un-thought. In this respect, thinking the un-thought bears certain elements of the first alternative suggested in *Heretical Essays*. The un-thought is not, however, an object in front of us. It is not a content to be dragged down to Earth. The un-thought of Christianity is beyond positive definitions and confessional propositions. In this sense, Patočka is closer to negative thinking. Nonetheless, if following Patočka leads us to the edge of a cliff called heresy, it is heretical in the alleged sense proposed in the introduction, that is, in reinterpreting and perhaps even overinterpreting—building on paradoxes—but never misinterpreting. Patočka never sought to dispel fears about his (un)orthodoxy. This simply was not his aim. He had no reason to defend his position. He could not accept any orders from God because the philosopher must stand firmly on the Earth. This does not prevent us from gazing up at the sky, however.

I propose that a deeper meaning of Patočka's thoughts on the un-thought, and one with possible theological implications, is pronounced by Jean-Luc Nancy. Nancy never refers to Patočka. Nevertheless, alluding to a Patočkian note, he explains his project of a deconstructed Christianity in terms of the un-thought. For Nancy, the un-thought of Christianity can be understood only in its coming.[77] It is the movement of a continuous opening up of the possibility of reconsidering Christianity in a nonrestorative and nonapologetic sense.[78] Jacques Derrida, who in contrast to Nancy draws much inspiration for his own reflections on Christianity from reading Patočka's *Heretical Essays*,[79] expresses something similar. The unthought breaks with metaphysical logic because it is not an entity to be thought and realized at some point. Neither is it an impenetrable negative theology. The un-thought is the distance between the present and the future. This distance is impossible to bridge and master rationally, yet it is a distance that calls for constant reflection.

In the context of Patočka's work, the figure of the un-thought serves a similar purpose in the field of religion to the notions of Idea and *chorismos* in the reconsidered conception of metaphysical thinking called *negative Platonism*.[80] The un-thought is a gap that actually makes room for something new to come. In this sense, Patočka's un-thought of Christianity comes close to Derrida's notion of the undeconstructible.[81] The un-thought is the undeconstructible condition that makes the deconstruction of Christianity possible. Deconstruction sets the tension between the "already" and the "not yet." This is why the un-thought cannot acquire a finite meaning, even though the un-thought is a challenge to be thought through again and again. Theologically speaking, the un-thought of Christianity is the enhancement of negative thinking with regard to the present. It always questions "already," but this questioning is not merely for the sake of questioning itself. The point is an openness toward the future that will come. Patočka has a special name for this position: faith. It is clear, however, that Patočka does not propose to remain in the desert of the *khôra*, even though his thought also acknowledges this side of human being in its relationship to the divine. Rather, Patočka's position would coincide with that of Richard Kearney, who argues for a possible God and for *khôra* as a space where openness to the divine is possible in experience.[82] This openness is not tied to metaphysics or rational theology. In Patočka's wording, Christianity after Christianity is coming as unthought. The meaning of the un-thought is faith beyond myth and rational-moral theology: faith that is openness.

Conclusion: Toward Christianity after Christianity

Christianity after Christianity does not therefore refer to the current state of religion in a post-Christian age. The "after" is not a relation to the past but an opening to the future. The "after" does not propose that a concrete future will come and fulfill the lack of the un-thought. The un-thought of Christianity after Christianity lies in its coming. The un-thought is not a secret to be revealed to the faithful at the end of history. It will never be grasped in possession. This does not mean, however, that it cannot become operative and active. In other words, the un-thought is not the impossible. On the contrary, the un-thought is openness to the possible, the ultimate—and everyday—possibility of overcoming the attempt by myth and metaphysical rationalism to reduce openness to the divine either to an irrational fideism or an overrationalized system.

Although we must resign ourselves to giving up on positive answers regarding the content of Patočka's Christianity after Christianity, it seems to me that this vision offers fresh insight into the recent reconsiderations, by means of deconstruction, of Christianity formulated from the perspective of the theological turn in continental philosophy. In the wake of Nietzsche and Heidegger, it has become fashionable to speak of Christianity as nihilism and as a community of charity (Vattimo). Following Derrida, others argue for religion without religion, the passion for the Impossible, truth without knowledge (Caputo). Although Patočka's negation of objective content with regard to the un-thought of Christianity seems to participate in the same debate, it is clear that in comparison to the perhaps overly negative theologies mentioned earlier it is possible to disclose in Patočka's idea of Christianity something we could call a content beyond positive content. This can be sketched out in three points.

First, Patočka reintroduces the centrality of Christianity as a new "religiosity" of thinking. In thinking, Christianity overcomes both *mythos* and *logos*. This shift seems to propose more Christianity rather than less of it. In contrast to the disenchantment of the world, the outcome of Patočka's reconsideration of Christianity is a reenchantment. Of course, this is not a return to anything from the past. Nonetheless, something is coming, and this something is related to Christianity, even though we may be standing on the edge of a cliff called heresy.

Second, Christianity after Christianity escapes the sociological-anthropological and becomes an existential category whose basic expression is faith as openness to the future. Patočka helps us to see clearly that the Christian *proprium* lies precisely in the movement of faith that is a radicalized, philosophical notion—the care for the soul. This is the depth of Christianity. This is the outcome of demythologization and deconstruction. Thus, with Patočka, we certainly do not find ourselves in Christianity without Christianity but in its enforced core, namely, faith and/as critical thinking.

Third, and finally, Christianity as existential thinking is not only a theoretical concept. Faith testifies to itself in acting and living. Patočka speaks of its double meaning. In everyday existence, one is called to live in responsibility, being questioned by the un-thought. Patočka does not, as one may suppose, associate this life with an exclusive group of philosophers (thinkers). Rather, he decontextualizes Christian universalism and proposes to speak of spiritual persons. Such persons are "those who are capable of understanding what life and death are all about, and so what history is about."[83] Nevertheless, there is also the extraordinary and ultimate expression that lies in how his form of Christianity bears witness to the world concerning its authenticity. For Patočka, this is sacrifice, the responsibility for living that is able to surrender its own existence in the name of a truth beyond positive contents, outside the logic of reward and punishment, and, in a certain sense, for nothing. I will explore each topic in some detail in the chapters that follow.

Chapter 6

The Call to Responsibility

Derrida's Reading of Patočka's Christian Thinking

This chapter focuses on the complex relationship between Jan Patočka and Jacques Derrida. They are indeed two very different thinkers, and although they neither met nor corresponded, they are related very closely through books. We know from the archive register that Patočka had a copy of Derrida's *De la grammatologie* in his personal library. Whether he also read it and how it might have inspired him remains open to question. Derrida certainly read Patočka's *Heretical Essays in the Philosophy of History*. In 1992, the Institut für die Wissenschaften vom Menschen in Vienna invited Derrida to deliver the sixth Jan Patočka Memorial Lecture,[1] for which he chose the theme of responsibility, later adapting his talk into the book *Donner la mort* (The gift of death). Here, Derrida enters a dialogue with Patočka and proposes a novel and provocative interpretation of his thought, although he focuses only on the fifth and sixth heretical essays, "Is Technological Civilization a Civilization in Decline, and If So Why?" and "The Wars of the Twentieth Century and the Twentieth Century as War." The revolutionary aspect of Derrida's reading of Patočka is in his interpretation of *Heretical Essays* as an unfolding of the complexities of thinking Christianity after modernity. So here, the *enfant terrible* of postmodern philosophy, who claims to "quite rightly pass for an atheist,"[2] provides a theological reading of Patočka, a thinker who can hardly be described as a philosopher of religion and whose phenomenology is absolutely not that of confessional Christianity.

The response to Derrida's book, especially the English translation in 1995, was dramatic. Existing scholars of Patočka were deeply shocked and began to argue fiercely with Derrida, but Patočka's thought also attracted fresh waves of attention in the international debate and was brought to a much broader audience. Although Derrida did Patočka something of a service in this respect, the overall feeling regarding Derrida's contribution was one of disappointment. Patočka specialists had something to discuss and a few other scholars joined the club and started to read Patočka's philosophy, but the majority of those who read Derrida's book probably felt that chapters 1 and 2 spoke about a philosopher whose name was difficult to pronounce and hard to remember, and quickly jumped to chapters 3 and 4, which presented the much more familiar character of Søren Kierkegaard. In short, although Derrida's book is based on Patočka's later ideas, most interpretations sadly ignore this major influence on Derrida, which according to the argument presented later in this chapter, did not end with the completion of the manuscript of *The Gift of Death* but continued to grow in Derrida's reflections on religion.

Here, however, I propose to take Derrida's reading of Patočka seriously and perhaps even move it forward somewhat. First, I will outline what Patočka and Derrida have to say regarding responsibility, as it is this issue that leads Derrida to his surprising conclusion about the *essential Christianity* of Patočka's thought. Second, I will review the debate that emerged following the publication of *The Gift of Death*. I will present both sides: the critics of Derrida's reading and the sympathizers. This section will also include a curious argument from the pen of John D. Caputo, who joined the debate not to evaluate Derrida's appropriation of Patočka but to deal critically with Patočka himself. Despite the shining reputation of this renowned American scholar, his contribution here is seriously flawed. I will argue against him and show that Derrida, even in his later works, was deeply influenced by Patočka. Finally, I will present my own interpretation of the lesson to be learned from Derrida's reading of Patočka. This will not tell us much about Derrida himself but rather about the possibility inscribed within Patočka's thought, namely, the openness to that which I propose to call *Christian thinking*.

Patočka and Derrida on Responsibility

Derrida approaches *Heretical Essays* as an inquiry into "the origin and essence of the religious."[3] In this respect, the idea and genealogy of responsibility appears crucial, as the field of "responsible life" provides a meeting point for philosophical and theological interests. For Patočka, responsibility emerged in the Greek polis and is what made "Athens" distinct from other traditions of thinking.[4] It has two interrelated meanings: it is the capacity to make free decisions in concrete historical situations based on rational-intellectual reflection; more importantly, however, it means the capacity to question the status quo when necessary and thus represents the possibility of the creative treatment of a world that is not accepted as simply given but perceived as essentially problematic. In other words, for responsible life, responsible thinking, and responsible acting, no question is off-limits. For this reason, Patočka considers Greek philosophy to be a decisive breaking point and the beginning of history.

The ancients did not of course use this same notion of responsibility. They spoke rather of "caring for the soul." Patočka devoted hundreds of pages to the Platonic concept of *epimeleia tēs psychēs*.[5] Rather than reiterate his argument in its entirety, it will suffice to say that for Patočka, care for the soul is at the heart of a European culture that begins with Socrates and Plato and is later transformed and carried forward in Christianity. To clarify what is meant by the soul, it is perhaps best to go directly to Patočka:

> When thinking begins, the most it is possible to say is that on one side there stands the world, like a collection of everything that is; on the other side stands the philosophizing man with his ability to understand that which is the world. In the Greek conception, this ability to understand is called the soul. This is the original understanding, on the basis of which man has the ability for truth and individual truths.[6]

Thus, the soul is the fundamental human capacity for (self-)transcendence. The soul is not an object, an (im)material thing, "but the locus of our relationship to our own being."[7] However, to attain this very heart of being presupposes a certain care for the soul, or responsibility. In *Heretical Essays*, Patočka narrates care for the soul in terms of two conversions: the turn from myth to philosophy and the turn from philosophy to Christianity.

The first conversion concerns the turn from the world of myths, expressed in orgiastic mysteries and religious cults, to philosophy, that is, to the philosophy of Platonism:

> The Platonic "conversion" makes a vision of the Good itself possible. This view is as unchanging and eternal as the Good

itself. The journey after the Good, which is the new *mystery* of the soul, takes the form of the soul's internal dialogue. Immortality, inseparably linked with this dialogue, is thus different from the immortality of the mysteries. For the first time, it is individual immortality, individual because inner, inseparably bound up with its own achievement.[8]

As mentioned in the previous chapter, myths are oriented toward the past and create the impression of a finite world where everything is already established, given. Hence, the only possibility for myth and its orgiastic cults is to recall the initial state that withdraws human beings from the problematic world and leaves no space for responsibility. The only concern at stake is the preservation of life, the submission to social duty, and the possession of mystery.[9] In contrast, Platonism opens a new mystery of the soul and in this sense allows the individual subject to appear. The guarantee of the free and individual soul derives from a relationship to the transcendent Good. From now on, it is not the blueprint presented in myths, the total construction of the world revived in mysterious religious cults again and again, but the internal dialogue within the soul that comes to be a decisive element of life, a truly historical life.[10] In other words, the Good can be discovered by means of theoretical knowledge. Of course, the idea of the Good is transcendent and in this sense inexhaustible; no one can capture this idea in its totality. But the Good in its totality is also present in the sphere of eternal ideas, the true reality that is only mirrored in this apparent world. Naturally, it is tempting to focus all efforts on penetrating the essence of the Good and thereby gaining as much insight into it as possible. This, in short, offers the basis of personal responsibility and personal subjectivity. The result of the first conversion is therefore a free individual soul, the call to care for the soul, and the absolute principle of the transcendent Good as the ground and telos of the soul as an immortal being.

The problem with Platonism, at least the problem Patočka uncovers in his analysis, is that the idea of the Good remains an abstract principle. How can it be that the personal-individual aspect of the soul is deduced from its relation to something impersonal? The Good is an object, albeit the highest one. This means there is a finite version of the Good. Somewhere in the world of ideas, full knowledge is present, and, through theoretical knowledge—insight—is discoverable. Hence, in Patočka's opinion, a new myth is created—the mythology of the soul that acquires knowledge and thus ascends the ladder of being.¹¹ The Platonic belief that the soul is in direct theoretical contact with the highest being is nonetheless interrupted by Christianity and its radical challenge:

> [In Christianity] responsible life was itself presented as a gift from something which ultimately, even though it has the character of the Good, also has traits of the inaccessible and forever superior to humans—the traits of the *mysterium* that always has the final word. Christianity, after all, understands the Good differently from Plato—as a self-forgetting goodness and a self-denying (not orgiastic) love.¹²

If Platonism incorporates the mythical world into a universal philosophy of the Good, Christianity suppresses the Platonic metaphysical Ideas and introduces the idea of a personal God. In place of the supremacy of the highest object over individual souls, Christianity comes with the mutual relationship between a personal transcendence and an individual human person.¹³ Chvatík is therefore able to summarize the essence of Christian conversion as follows: "In relation to the personal God, the human being becomes a person."¹⁴ The consequences of this turn are obvious.

Whereas Platonism subordinates responsibility to objective knowledge, the Christian idea of responsibility is deduced from the personal transcendence of the Other that exceeds rationalization and can never be fully grasped through human knowledge. In comparison to Platonic (eternal) Ideas, the idea of Christianity is historical. "Yet the problem of history," Patočka says, "cannot be resolved, it must be preserved as a problem."¹⁵ In other words, while Platonism provides us with answers concerning the Good and responsible life, Christianity provides us with the capacity to live in questions. This is what Derrida finds so appealing and original in Patočka's work, condensing it into a single succinct sentence: "Religion is responsibility, or it is nothing at all."¹⁶

Before moving on to a detailed exploration of Christianity as the call to responsibility, I want to emphasize Patočka's use of the concept of *conversion-metanoia*. It is almost certain that Patočka's use of this explicitly religious and even specifically Christian term is no accident.¹⁷ For Patočka, turn (*obrat*) and conversion (*obrácení*) allude to a certain experience—the movement of existence—that shakes and interrupts presupposed meaning. Conversion is not an exchange of one opinion for another, a switch from one community or church to another. Conversion begins with the shock of doubts and questions and in this sense is more of a loss than a gain, but a loss that nonetheless motivates movement rather than stagnation. What is usually assumed to exist on the personal-individual level, Patočka also finds on the broader historical level. In fact, history itself begins with a conversion: the turn from the solid, predetermined meaning of myths to the search for meaning by way of philosophical questioning. After the birth of philosophy, Christianity represents the second epoch-making conversion in history. Conversion involves a radical change, and we must have this in mind when we consider the Christian conversion to responsibility in Patočka and Derrida.

In *Heretical Essays*, Patočka opens his reflections on the uniqueness of Christianity by recalling Nietzsche: "Nietzsche coined the saying that Christianity is Platonism for the people, and there is much truth in this, in that the Christian God took over the transcendence of the onto-theological conception as a matter of course."[18] Insofar as Christianity imitates the metaphysical structure of Platonism and situates God above all beings as the highest being, it is surely Platonism's twin and, in this sense, brings nothing new. Nevertheless, Nietzsche is only partially right. For Patočka, the essence of Christianity, its inner core, is better expressed by Saint Paul and his great cry: "Has not God made foolish the wisdom of the world?" (1 Cor 1:20) Patočka suggests that this early Christian position, canonized in the sacred text, has a double meaning. First, and somewhat obviously, the apostle rejects the Greek conception of *sophia tou kosmou*; the wisdom of metaphysics. Christians deduce their wisdom from Revelation and in this sense from Jesus Christ, who is the personified Wisdom of God. No wonder Pauline theology has attracted so much attention in recent postmetaphysical discourse.[19]

However, Patočka assigns a second and in his opinion far more important meaning to Saint Paul's viewpoint. Yes, Christianity distances itself from the metaphysical method of eidetic intuition and theoretical rationalism, but "the chief difference appears to be that it is only now that the innermost content of the soul is revealed."[20] In other words, Christianity deconstructs fundamental beliefs: first, the philosophical belief that human beings are in direct rational contact with the order of being as it is; second, the belief that the imitation of eternal reality makes them responsible agents who participate in the truth of being. Christianity in fact throws the human person into history. Or, better, standing before a personal God who gives himself freely to the human being, the person realizes the inescapable situation of being-in-the-world. The opening of this abyss between the divine and the human, Patočka argues, reveals that the soul is called to discover not objective truth but "the truth of its own destiny, bound up with eternal responsibility."[21]

For Patočka, the Christian point of view implies that the soul is the other of objective beings.[22] The soul is not an entity. Caring for the soul is therefore much more than the adoption of a certain technique (*technē*). The aim is not to put the soul into some predefined shape. Rather, it is *responding* to others and to the Other. Moreover, it is always a personal responsibility—*my* responsibility—and it is always a concrete person who finds him- or herself in the midst of an undecided situation. In other words, to adopt theological language, care for the soul is giving "myself" instead of "giving something," because God first gave himself. Here we touch the very nerve of Patočka's interpretation of Christianity: "By virtue of this foundation in the abysmal deepening of the soul, Christianity remains the greatest, unsurpassed but also un-thought-through élan that enabled humans to struggle against decadence."[23] In Derrida's reading, the uniqueness Patočka ascribes to Christianity concerns the innermost mystery of human being. What I described earlier as the two conversions on the journey toward responsibility, Derrida captures as the shift from the sacred of the mythical world to the mystery of Platonism, which is later converted in the Christian mystery—*mysterium tremendum*.[24] On this journey, this way, the mystery (myth) that possesses human beings and the possession of mystery by means of theoretical insight (philosophy) is transformed into a relationship with mystery (religion). According to Derrida, Patočka is correct in his evaluation of Christianity as a radical challenge.[25]

The novelty of Christianity is that God gives himself completely and ultimately as an act of infinite love.[26] In turn, the finite human person experiences her own singularity and irreplaceability but at the same time faces the call to responsibility. Christianity establishes a mysterious relationship of love between the infinite Other and finite beings. Although Christianity means a genuine personification of human beings, this situation is terrifying and the relationship itself quite asymmetrical. For Derrida, this means that guilt and a sense of sinfulness are deduced "from the situation of the responsible individual."[27] As we will see, this interpretation of Patočka's conception of responsibility is highly questionable. But before making a critical evaluation of Derrida's reading of Patočka, we should consider the point of Derrida's argument: "It seems necessary to reinforce the coherence of a way of thinking that takes into account the event of Christian mystery as an absolute singularity, a religion par excellence, and an irreducible condition of a combined history of the subject, responsibility, and Europe."[28] Derrida suggests that Patočka's genealogy of responsibility, which finds its deepest realization in Christianity, should not be confused with Christianity as it is traditionally understood. In fact, *Heretical Essays* proposes a nondogmatic couplet of Christianity.[29] Derrida explains that what Patočka has in mind when he praises Christianity for its deepening of the soul is an intrinsic possibility within Christianity regardless of whether this possibility has ever been historically realized. In other words, Christianity is most powerful as a particular mode of thinking: "a thinking that repeats the possibility of religion without religion."[30] Derrida therefore associates Patočka with the concept of a Christianity emancipated from Athens and Rome.[31] I read this as the search for a Christianity that leaves behind the metaphysical heritage of Greek philosophy and breaks with the *religio* characteristic of cultic religions. Derrida's reading of Patočka suggests that Christianity should be understood as *philosophia vera*—true thinking.

On this basis, although *Heretical Essays* is not necessarily an example of Christian philosophy, Derrida finds a Christian thinker in Patočka.[32] It is this claim concerning Patočka's Christianity—which Derrida sees as differentiating him from, for example, Heidegger, Levinas, and other philosophers with an interest in religious issues[33]—that sparked the debate among scholars of Patočka and drew unprecedented levels of attention to his thought.

An Assessment of Derrida's Reading

Maria Sá Cavalcante Schuback sheds some welcome light on what lay behind Derrida's reading of Patočka's *Heretical Essays*. In her opinion, Derrida finds in Patočka a correction of Heidegger, and even to some extent the completion of Heidegger.[34] In other words, Derrida listens to Patočka as to someone who proposes an alternative answer to Heidegger's question as to how one becomes an authentic self. For Derrida—although he is troubled, for many reasons, with Heidegger's conclusions, partly because of Heidegger's antireligious background, which Derrida associates with his Nazi past—this question is paramount.[35] In contrast to Heidegger's narrative, religion plays and important role in the story narrated by Patočka, who "re-ontologizes the historic themes of Christianity."[36] Ludger

Hagedorn summarizes Derrida's interest in Patočka in three key words: *responsibility*, *mystery*, and *heresy*.[37] Indeed, this captures the main point of Derrida's *Gift of Death* and, according to Hagedorn, also aptly describes how "Patočka has laid out his world, his history, his Europe, and also his religion, that is, his Christianity."[38] So Derrida approaches Patočka from the right angle, but is his interpretation correct? This is something of a complex question.

Derrida against Patočka

Rodolphe Gasché claims that Derrida "provides an exemplary reading of Patočka's conception of Europe and responsibility, of its intricacies and ambiguities."[39] Gasché focuses mostly on what Derrida calls Patočka's *essential Christianity*[40] and emphasizes both the step by which Patočka moves beyond Heidegger and also the importance of Christianity for the emergence of authenticity, that is, of responsibility. It is not necessary to revisit the argument regarding the two turns—from myth to Platonism and from Platonism to Christianity—that Gasché repeats verbatim. What is worth noting, however, is that Gasché explores the work of Patočka beyond *Heretical Essays* in order to test Derrida's claim concerning Patočka's essential Christianity. Gasché refers to Patočka's lectures that preceded *Heretical Essays* but were edited and published only later under the title *Plato and Europe*. Here, Patočka states that only Christianity is a religion in the proper sense.[41] We do not know whether Derrida read these lectures; it is certainly possible, as the French translation was published in 1983.[42] In any case, Derrida reads Patočka as the thinker of essential Christianity, so it seems that Gasché strengthens Derrida's point and proves it correct.

Nevertheless, Gasché reminds us that the Christianity that Derrida associates with Patočka is by no means a traditional ecclesial-orthodox religion but rather a heretical one.[43] What is the nature of Patočka's heresy? Derrida observes that Patočka does not criticize a particular historical form of Christianity and replace it with his own. The heresy is not therefore a matter of a heretical opinion versus an orthodox one. The point Derrida is making is that the entire conception of Christianity in Patočka is heretical: Patočka suggests that Christianity has never been completed, that it is still on its way to becoming a real Christianity. In other words, Christianity contains something that is unthought and this un-thought resists, for example, proposing an ultimate definition of responsibility.[44]

It is precisely this incompleteness of Christianity that appeals to Derrida. The openness of Christianity is thus contrasted with the closedness of Platonism. Whereas in Christianity the truth of responsibility is always ahead of us and never complete, Platonism pushes us to disclose the ultimate truth of responsibility by way of an inquiry into the eternal world of Ideas. Interestingly, Gasché argues that this opposition, and consequently the emphasis on mystery in Patočka's Christianity, is what actually troubles Derrida,[45] who uses the rhetoric of the gift to present his critique. Christianity concerns "the gift of something that remains inaccessible, unpresentable, and as a consequence secret."[46] Gasché claims that Derrida finds this radical mystery to be something "tremendous" because it establishes an asymmetrical relationship between the person and mystery (God). The essence of Derrida's argument is therefore that the turn from Platonism to Christianity cannot be absolute. The inheritance of Platonic responsibility is incorporated in Christianity, but suppressed. In other words, Platonism can still be found in Christianity. For Gasché, Derrida acts as the protector of a European memory rooted in both Platonism and Christianity, whereas Patočka emphasized only the Christian element. This is how Gasché interprets Derrida's comment concerning the emancipation of Christianity from Athens and Rome in Patočka.[47]

Gasché therefore appears to propose that Derrida simultaneously identifies Patočka as a Christian thinker and criticizes him for being one. In fact, each element is open to dispute and we will address them both in the course of this chapter. Now, however, it is important to say a few words about Gasché's reading of Derrida against Patočka. We have already noted that Gasché supports Derrida's view that Patočka represents a heretical approach to an essential Christianity. This should mean that Patočka's Christianity is totally separated from Platonism. Gasché provides us with this conclusion on the basis of Derrida's *Gift of Death* and a few references to Patočka's *Plato and Europe*. One point of note is that Gasché's conclusion contradicts the evidence of Patočka's text. On the same page that Gasché refers to in order to present Patočka's view that Christianity is religion in an eminent sense (which might indeed be true from Patočka's perspective), Patočka clearly associates Christianity with its Greek heritage—Christianity owes to Greek philosophy the entire structure of a faith expressed in dogmas.[48] For Patočka, this is a unique development in the history of religion and precisely the point that makes Christianity "the greatest and unsurpassed" force of history.[49] Patočka does not hesitate to claim that "Europe stands on one pillar,"[50] and that pillar is Greek.

Reading Derrida's account of Patočka's Christian responsibility, Gasché suggests that Derrida deconstructs Patočka's conception of Christianity by reference to the Platonism still present within it. As we have seen, Patočka never advocated such a separation: he points out the historical succession of Christianity, but succession is not displacement. Unfortunately, Gasché takes Derrida's text as the authoritative interpretation of Patočka's thought, and Derrida suggests that Platonism and Christianity seem to be separated. For Gasché, Derrida is thus the hero who safeguards the whole of European memory, whereas Patočka privileges the Christian element. Interestingly, however, another reading seems to suggest quite a different picture.

Patočka against Derrida

Eddo Evink is critical of Derrida's interpretation of Patočka, which he sees as confusing the Christian responsibility described in *Heretical Essays* with Patočka's own concept of responsibility.[51] We should not, however, read this as an unambiguous opposition to Derrida's claim concerning Patočka's essential Christianity, as is the case, for example, with Lubica Učník.[52] Evink does not close the door on such an interpretation. Quite the contrary. But what troubles Evink is that Derrida's *Gift of Death* stretches Patočka beyond the limits of legitimate interpretation. Derrida seems to be aware of his hyperbole, however, and concludes his discussion of Patočka by saying, "Patočka does not say that in so many words, and I am stretching things a little further than he or the letter of his text would allow."[53] How exactly does Derrida cross the line?

Evink charges Derrida with an illegitimate universalizing of Patočka's perspective. For example, Patočka always speaks of a concrete historical Christianity. Derrida suggests that Patočka does not need "the event of a revelation,"[54] which might perhaps be true from the confessional perspective, but what is important is that Patočka understands Christianity not only as something that takes place within history but even more as something that, as Hagedorn puts it, "leads into history."[55] Derrida fails to see this and prefers to describe a universal structure of religion without religion. For Evink, this is why in Derrida's perspective the relationship between the person and a personal God who becomes a man resembles the relationship between the subject and the absolute gift of infinite love.[56] As a consequence, Derrida finds the emergence of responsibility as the absolute responsibility.[57] But this is much more Derrida than Patočka. The difference will appear after a brief exploration of the major problem with Derrida's absolute responsibility.

First, Derrida transforms the gift of infinite love—presented by Patočka as the key element of the second conversion, from Platonism to Christianity—into an absolute gift.[58] But the concept of a pure and absolute gift could easily become a metaphysical foundation, which is something Patočka criticizes when he speaks of Platonism as objective knowledge and of its overcoming by (Pauline) Christianity. Second, Derrida suggests that a pure gift calls for absolute responsibility on the part of human beings. Such responsibility, Derrida argues, is unreachable and inherently impossible. This is not, however, what Patočka means by responsibility, and it is doubtful whether this would be a proper description of Christian responsibility at all. We have seen that for Patočka the result of the second—Christian—conversion is not an absolute call to responsibility but a vocation to responsibility in concrete situations. Christianity is not about the absolute gift (of death); it is a message concerning the personification of human beings and their essential historicity.

Evink continues this discussion in "The Gift of Life: Jan Patočka and the Christian Heritage." As the title and subtitle suggest, Evink reads Patočka against Derrida, but this reading does not entirely reject Derrida's conclusion concerning Patočka's Christianity. The bottom line of Evink's argument is that the notion of care for the soul in Patočka's understanding is in fact a Christian concept. That is to say, Patočka reads the original Greek concept through a Christian lens. In Evink's own words: "The idea of the care for the soul needs to be interpreted as a religious way of life beyond religion, that is, beyond Christianity, but still characterized by many Christian notions."[59]

To unlock the meaning of Patočka's Christianity, Evink turns to the doctrine of the three movements of existence—perhaps Patočka's most significant contribution to phenomenology. We have described Patočka's phenomenological kinesiology elsewhere;[60] for the sake of Evink's argument, it is primarily the third movement—the movement of truth/transcendence/breakthrough—that requires our attention. Here the human subject finds itself thrown into the world: nothing is certain in life, the world is problematic, every given meaning—of both life and the world—must be constantly questioned. The only certainty in the third movement of existence is one's own finitude. But being finite and fundamentally shaken opens a space for becoming a responsible person, a free person. This task of becoming both responsible and free is what Patočka calls caring for the soul.[61]

Like Derrida, Evink turns to *Heretical Essays* to support his interpretation. There is no need to detail Evink's explanation of the two conversions from myth to the deepest foundation of caring for the soul in Christianity. What interests us is the meaning Evink attributes to this process. Unlike Derrida, who reads the process as a gradual development, the replacement of one entity with another, Evink contends that Patočka presents it as a mutual complementing. Christianity transcends the purely rational search for the truth (Platonism) and complements it with the element of faith. Against Derrida's suggestion that (Patočka's) Christianity represses the Platonic heritage,[62] Evink insists that Patočka interprets Christianity as something that provides balance:[63] "Reason as the natural organ for the understanding of truth loses its place of pride in life, but we might claim that this loss is at the same time a gain."[64]

The deepening of the soul in Christianity does not mean the end of rational reflection through the dictate of some transcendent mystery that Derrida interprets as *mysterium tremendum*.[65] In fact, what trembles and is shaken is blind belief in reason and its ability to pin down truth in its totality. Christianity does not, however, introduce irrationalism. The conversion from philosophy to Christianity brings faith in mystery, but this faith is rationally comprehensible, although never rationally exhaustible. In other words, the Christian conversion means the beginning of a relationship between philosophy and theology, because reason and faith are mutually dependent. What does this allegiance mean for the care for the soul—for responsibility? Evink argues that care for the soul means openness, that it transcends the one-sided theoretical intellectualism of the Greeks by being incorporated into the Christian search for the truth of a person. Or, as Martin Cajthaml would say, care for the soul means a readiness to change convictions and in this sense represents an opposition to both dogmatism and blind rationalism.[66] In other words, the Christian conversion complements the Platonic turn to responsibility and this is why Patočka speaks of the "greatest and unsurpassed" achievement of Christianity.

Evink finds another sense of caring for the soul in Patočka, and that is the readiness to "give-oneself-away" for truth.[67] Caring for the soul is not simply an inner, spiritual-intellectual activity—it has practical consequences. Evink suggests that Patočka has in mind the story of Jesus of Nazareth—the myth of the God-man—who gives up everything for truth. Without explicitly naming Christ, Patočka thematizes this issue at the end of his "*The Natural World* Remeditated Thirty-Three Years Later."[68]

When we speak about truth in this respect, we should understand it not as a truth in our possession but as the very truth of being human. In the self-surrender of Jesus Christ, as Evink explains, "the truth of Being stands over against the power of beings."[69] Caring for the soul therefore means giving "what we are" in order truly to become what we are meant to be. Caring for the soul is the gift of life, even if attaining it may necessitate a journey through the darkness of death.

Evink claims that this reference to sacrifice is more than simply a metaphor. In fact, Patočka develops a fascinating interpretation of the theological idea of kenotic sacrifice in his later works, of which we will say more in the next chapter. Here, it will suffice to follow Evink in concluding that "Patočka's existential phenomenology . . . demonstrates the essential Christian character of [the care for the soul]."[70] Indeed, Patočka turns out to be a proponent of Christian thinking but in a different way from that suggested by Derrida. According to Evink, the Christian heritage in Patočka can be traced in his doctrine of the three movements of existence, especially the third of these, which equates to the vocation of caring for the soul.

There is one more thing to say, however. We should not read Patočka as an advocate of traditional Christianity in its various ecclesial-dogmatic manifestations. Rather, Patočka construes something that Paul Ricoeur called the "hyperbolic Christianity" of *Heretical Essays*.[71] As we will now show, this point is easily missed.

Derrida against (pseudo) Patočka

John D. Caputo renarrates Derrida's reflections on Patočka in his *Prayers and Tears of Jacques Derrida*,[72] a work that may appear to strengthen our argument: a prominent advocate of the continental philosophical tradition in America concerns himself with Patočka, whom we are seeking to read in the context of the recent theological turns within the same tradition that Caputo himself defends and admires. The reality is somewhat different, however.

Caputo repeats Derrida's assertion that Patočka is a Christian thinker but stretches the point further and charges Patočka with Hegelian Christian triumphalism: "Patŏcka [*sic!*] illustrates the unnerving alliance of Hegel and the Pope, of which Derrida elsewhere complains, which embodies the dangers that inhere in concrete, determinable messianisms."[73] According to Caputo, Patočka proposes a typical dialectical move. The turn from the mysteries of myth to Platonism—a world without mystery[74]—and then to the *mysterium tremendum* of Christianity follow the logic of thesis-antithesis-synthesis. Christianity thus appears to be the climax of history and the only legitimate framework for Europe.

Caputo acknowledges that Derrida draws inspiration from Patočka for a "religion without religion" based on Patočka's attempt to think the Christianity that is still to come. But he reads this as a proposal for the "Christian Hegelian philosophy of history" and thus the ultimate solution for all sorts of questions.[75] For Caputo, Patočka and Christocentrism thus seem to present the same image of a Christian Europe as that pushed through by another Christian triumphalist, John Paul II.[76] If none of the previous claims have set off alarm bells concerning Caputo's reading, the strange alliance he establishes between Patočka and the Pope certainly does.

It is clear that Caputo, a careful reader of Derrida, misses the point completely when he talks about Patočka. Caputo is correct to confirm that Patočka provides us with Christian thinking, but it is wholly incorrect to conclude from Derrida's *Gift of Death* that Patočka is seeking the restoration of Christendom. Regardless of what Derrida claims, Patočka's Christianity may be questionable, but it is certainly not triumphalist. As Evink has shown, Patočka's Christianity is rather an openness to something new, something that is to come, and by no means the overwhelming *Geist*. In fact, Patočka opposes the master narrative of Christianity that Caputo seeks to attribute to him.

The problem with Caputo is that he reads Patočka—whom he sees as a typical representative of the continental European school of thought—through his American lens and this brings about a fatal misunderstanding. Caputo takes the claim for a Christian Europe—a claim that is in fact more Derrida's than Patočka's[77]—as equivalent to the claim for a Christian America, which in Caputo's eyes rightly evokes the threat of fundamentalism (as expressed, for example, in opposing contraception, or dismissing the theory of evolution and advancing creationism). But this is simply a misguided American perspective on the European problem with which Patočka and Derrida concern themselves.

Ludger Hagedorn's elucidating essay "Beyond Myth and Enlightenment" makes it very clear that Patočka's thought cannot be interpreted as an instance of Hegelianism.[78] For Patočka, there is nothing like a sense of history coming to its end. On the contrary, for Patočka, history knows no ultimate solution. The example of responsibility, which in its Christian manifestation is stretched between faith and knowledge, is a clear illustration of this essential openness of Patočka's thought.

In summary, Caputo takes Derrida's reading as a harsh criticism of Patočka's Christian thinking as Eurocentric, triumphalist, and Hegelian. In what follows, I will argue that in fact Derrida reads Patočka constructively, and that ultimately Patočka's work had a strong influence on Derrida's own thinking concerning religion.

Patočka and Derrida

Perhaps Derrida's best-known work on "the return to religion" is his essay "Faith and Knowledge."[79] Like *The Gift of Death*, the essay has its origins in a lecture Derrida delivered, in this case on the island of Capri in 1994. Gil Anidjar, who edited the English translation, says of the essay that it "can be read as Derrida's own introduction to the question of religion in his work."[80] In my hypothesis, Derrida's "Faith and knowledge" in fact elaborates on the line of thought introduced in *The Gift of Death*: Derrida continues his discussion on Patočka, but without mentioning the Czech phenomenologist by name.

Christian Sternad suggests that to understand the link between Patočka and these works by Derrida, we must take account of what we could consider to be Patočka's definition of religion:[81]

> Religion is not the sacred, nor does it arise directly from the experience of sacral orgies and rites; rather, it is where the sacred *qua* demonic is being explicitly overcome. Sacral experiences pass over religious as soon as there is an attempt to introduce responsibility into the sacred or to regulate the sacred thereby.[82]

This quotation from *Heretical Essays* contains enigmatic terms—"the sacred," "the demonic"—which call for clarification. This experience of the sacred, or its extreme form in the demonic, is not yet religion. In fact, the demonic refers to an overwhelming experience of the sacred that we associated in the previous chapter with myths. For Patočka, therefore, religion begins where the experience of the sacred is related to responsibility. In other words, religion maintains a certain inner tension.[83] This extract from Patočka appears to be decisive for Derrida's own account, and he renarrates Patočka's point as follows:

> [Patočka] warns against an experience of the sacred as an enthusiasm or fever for fusion, cautioning in particular against a form of demonic rapture that has as its effect, and often as its first intention, the removal of responsibility. At the same time, Patočka wants to distinguish religion from the demonic form of sacralization. What is religion? Religion presumes access to the responsibility of a free self.[84]

According to Hagedorn, Derrida maintains the tension introduced by Patočka and expands on it in "Faith and Knowledge."[85] Derrida claims that religion has two sources: the unscathed (the sacred, the holy) and the fiduciary (faith).[86] For Sternad, too, this internal tension between the two sources indicates that Derrida is following the structure of thinking offered by Patočka.[87] Moreover, the tension Derrida sets between the two notions can be translated into the title of his essay. Knowledge, which stands for the revelation received from the sacred sphere, constantly intertwines with faith, which is not simply blind acceptance but a faithful thinking about and reflecting on what has been received in revelation. Responsibility is therefore another name for holding a tension—rather than a dichotomy—between the traditional rivals of faith and knowledge. It is in this sense that we must read Derrida's remark from *The Gift of Death* that Patočka's Christianity—the authentic religion that maintains the tension—emancipates itself from both Rome and Athens.[88] Or, as Hagedorn puts it, the possibility of Christianity envisioned by Patočka is to go beyond myth and enlightenment,[89] which means to overcome the opposition between reason and revelation, to overcome cultic religiosity and metaphysics. This Christianity has yet to come, however, and this opinion is shared by Patočka and Derrida.

Returning to the standard considerations of Derrida's account of religion, what immediately strikes us is that the inspiration Derrida took from Patočka is completely neglected. Even Michael Naas, the great exegete of Derrida's work, fails to trace the origin of Derrida's thought back to Patočka.[90] Christian Sternad is right, I believe, to want to read "justly or unjustly, the first part of *The Gift of Death* as a pretext to 'Faith and knowledge.'"[91]

In an interview with Richard Kearney, Derrida insists that he considers his thinking neither Jewish nor Greek. It is rather a non-site beyond both the Jewish and the Greek.[92] It seems to me that Patočka is among those who point the way to this "non-site beyond" that Derrida adopts as his own. I do not mean to say that the concept of Jew-Greek, which Derrida had already developed in *Violence and Metaphysics*, is drawn from Patočka. My point is that Patočka's thought is one of the most important sources for Derrida's reflections on religion. For example, Derrida's conception of "religion without religion" is very close to what he calls Patočka's essential Christianity, that is, the possibility of a Christianity that is still to come.

It has become clear, therefore, that the point of this discussion is not about whether Derrida understood Patočka rightly or wrongly. Opinions on this matter differ significantly, but for simplicity's sake, we can summarize them into two camps: the first approaches Derrida's reading as more or less critical of Patočka; the other protects Patočka from Derrida's misreading. However, despite the interesting discussion generated by these mutually competing claims, it makes more sense to read Patočka and Derrida together: although Derrida appears to misread certain parts of Patočka's *Heretical Essays*, I argue that he is suggesting something very important when he considers Patočka to be a Christian thinker.

It is advisable, nonetheless, to exercise caution before calling Patočka a "Christian thinker." The reason for such vigilance is of course Patočka's own resistance to being labeled as such. Nowhere in Patočka do we find any hint of his describing himself as a Christian thinker. The notion is both too bold and too superficial: too bold because it gives the impression that Patočka's phenomenology is seeking to contribute to the restoration of Christendom (Caputo's reading); too superficial because almost all Western philosophy is somehow related to the Christian heritage. I therefore propose not to accept or suggest that Patočka is a Christian thinker, but to explore the latent Christian thinking that I deem to be present in his work. Derrida's interpretation offers a degree of inspiration in this respect.

Christian Thinking

The debate over whether Derrida's appropriation of Patočka is plausible or problematic focuses predominantly on the theme of responsibility. In this respect, critics of Derrida may be correct, as Patočka constructs his own project of a responsible and free life in terms of existential phenomenology—specifically his teaching on the three movements of existence—rather than in relation to Christianity. However, the point of interest for us, and therefore for the argument I am proposing, concerns a different issue. In one of his *Heretical Essays*, Patočka says that Christianity remains "the greatest, unsurpassed but un-thought-through human élan," which with Derrida I propose to read as offering the possibility of thinking Christianity beyond or after Christianity, and therefore as claiming that Patočka's thought is open to thinking a new allegiance between theology and philosophy. Derrida's greatness lies precisely in that he senses and detects the possible consequences of Patočka's profound analysis, for which he calls him a Christian thinker.

I therefore argue against Evink, who claims that "Patočka's work can very well be interpreted as a *non-Christian thinking-through* of the Christian tradition,"[93] and suggest approaching Patočka's work from exactly the opposite angle: as the opening of a very particular kind of *Christian thinking* that sets itself in opposition to the predominant Christian tradition.

Indeed, it is no accident that Patočka chose the title *Heretical Essays* for his magnum opus. Although the text contains numerous heresies—with regard to Marxism, the "official" philosophical doctrine of the context in which Patočka lived and worked; with regard to Husserl, especially his attempts to lay a rigorous foundation for scientific knowledge; with regard to Heidegger, by taking his "ontological difference" back to the context of Christianity—the clearest and most enigmatic is Patočka's reinterpretation of the role of Christianity in a post-Christian world, something Derrida calls the search for Christianity beyond Rome and Athens.[94] I propose to speak of the shift from Christianity to *Christian thinking*.

Now let us return to the words "the greatest," "the unsurpassed," and "the un-thought" (or "un-thought-through") from the enigmatic quotation that occupies center stage in our argument. To say that Christianity is the greatest and unsurpassed seems to suggest a highly positive appraisal, triumphalism even. Christianity has it right. Christianity is the ideal. Christianity is the pinnacle of history. If this were true, Caputo would be correct to associate this kind of reasoning with Hegelianism, which considers Christianity to be the only true monotheism. But Patočka does not understand Christianity in Hegelian terms and is far from situating Christianity on top of the religious tree. Neither does Patočka understand Christianity in Kantian terms as the highest moral call. For Patočka, Christianity is not "better" than other religions. I see the "unsurpassed" nature of Christianity as referring to a recontextualization of the soul advanced by Christianity.

Patočka introduces his appraisal of Christianity like this: "by virtue of this foundation in the abysmal deepening of the soul, Christianity remains . . ."[95] This means Christianity redeems the soul from reductionist objectivistic conceptions. The soul is neither a material nor an immaterial entity. The soul is the organ of being. In Christianity, the soul is the locus of our engagement with problematicity; it is where we experience the upheaval of being-in-the-world. The soul is the organ of reflection upon the concrete historical situation into which we are thrown; it is the flexibility to think, to question, to challenge given meaning in order to search for a deeper meaning, time and again. The soul is what leads us into thinking.

I therefore agree with Hagedorn that care for the soul generates something we might call "after-thinking."[96] So, when we propose the existence of a Christianity after (the end of) Christianity, this does not primarily refer to the need to accommodate Christianity within the new context of postmodernity because such a concrete historical situation urges us to do so; Christianity is not challenged to become a post-Christianity by its postmodern context. The issue at stake is rather that Christianity is intrinsically the moving factor of after-thinking; Christianity is the openness to think outside predetermined frameworks, or at least the readiness to interrupt what are deemed to be the traditional modes of reasoning. Why is this so? And is it legitimate to consider Christianity to be a type of constantly renewable after-thinking?

When we consider the central theological ideas—the incarnation, the crucifixion, the resurrection—we are engaging in each instance with something that breaks with the logic of what ought to be. God becomes a human being. This is nonsense in Jewish thinking. But Christianity forces us to think differently. The crucifixion of the savior and redeemer of the world is a scandal, blasphemy. But in Christianity, God is not like the heroes of myths and fables. God is dead, yet he breaks the chains of death and rises again. Once more, Christianity provokes a search for a deeper meaning concerning the finitude of being-in-the-world. Christianity cannot claim any privilege as a religion among other religions; it is the greatest and unsurpassed mode of thinking—it is *philosophia vera*.

Nonetheless, to do justice to Patočka's reconsideration of Christianity, it is necessary to move to the end of the sentence: "Christianity is the . . . élan that enabled humans to struggle against decadence."[97] The struggle against decadence is of great importance here. Although Patočka's thought sheds new light on the possibilities of Christian thinking, his prime concern is not to help theology but to think about the meaning of being-in-the-world. Decadence ignores the question of meaning and is left with everydayness and boredom.[98] Patočka is not referring here to feelings of any kind. The issue at stake is the ontological state of being human, the state he considers to be decadent. The reason for this predicament is the reign of (modern) rationalism, the supremacy of knowing over being, whereby the responsibility for human life and action is subordinated to the (modern) endeavor to master things. As Patočka expresses it: "Humans are thus destroyed externally and impoverished internally, deprived of their 'own-ness,' of that irreplaceable 'I.' "[99] Christianity, with its emphasis on the personhood of human beings, restores to history the search for meaning and understanding.

We must not, however, forget that Christianity's greatness is always accompanied by its un-thought-through-ness: Christianity is unsurpassed, but at the same time a grand failure. There are many forms of Christian decadence, such as the submission to metaphysical conceptions of the soul, and later to the modern mathematization and geometrization of theology, which resulted in the search for proofs (of God) rather than for meaning; God himself became an unmoving mover, the grounding principle and the highest object. Last but not least, the entire ontotheological project, rightly criticized by Heidegger and more recently by New Phenomenology, fails to do justice to Patočka's high appreciation of Christianity. The possibility intrinsically embedded within Christianity can never be adequately thought through. Derrida's summary of this point is quite challenging: "Something has not yet arrived, neither at Christianity nor by means of Christianity. What has not arrived at, or happened to, Christianity is Christianity. Christianity has not yet come to Christianity."[100] The idea of the un-thought is a fascinating proposal concerning how to think about the essence of Christianity after Christianity. To illustrate the logic behind it, Patočka turns to an element of Christianity we may not expect to appear in this regard: dogma.

For Patočka, Christian dogmas are not doctrines to be accepted blindly. On the contrary, dogmas are something the human mind can never comprehend in their ultimate profundity. But a dogma creates a space where it is possible to understand what is right and what is wrong: "Dogmata have meaning, they are meaningful." And as Patočka emphasizes, "In this, there is something that no other spiritual domain [than

Christianity] has. Again, the Greek is reflected here."[101] In fact, dogmatic structure does not contradict the un-thought foundation of Christianity. In fact, dogmas promote this very mode of thinking and conceiving Christianity because they acknowledge, in Derrida's words, that there is still something that is yet to come.

This is extremely important and has multiple connotations. First, Patočka makes it clear that Christianity engages with Platonism (Greek philosophy) in a creative way. Second, it seems that Patočka has in mind here a different kind of Platonism from the one he criticizes as promoting objective knowledge deduced from the realm of eternal Ideas. Third, and consequently, Christianity's Greek heritage provides it with the apparatus to reflect on what is right and wrong, and Christianity reciprocates with its emphasis on the transcendent truth that can never be grasped in its totality. Plato and Saint Paul seem to meet each other here. How should we deal with this tension?

I suggest it is possible to read Patočka as follows: Greek philosophy in general and Platonism in particular influenced Christianity in such a way that it became a mode of thinking—*philosophia vera* as the Church Fathers would have it—that leads to a certain mode of life—the practice of *vita theologica*. The core of Christianity is not cult, therefore, or orgiastic mystery, or rituality, but faith—thinking. Christianity also, however, gives back to Platonism and metaphysical philosophy an emphasis on the *distance* from absolute truth. This distance, which we could translate as a kind of negative turn, provides the engine for thinking further because it reveals the truth as comprehensible but by no means exhaustible. Ultimately, I argue that Patočka's negative Platonism—where the Idea is not an object to be grasped but a sign of transcendence—is in all likelihood influenced by this understanding of Christianity as openness.[102]

This very much resembles Ratzinger's famous claim concerning the providential marriage between the Greek and the Christian.[103] Patočka finds the intertwining of the two a truly great achievement. However, this reading of Patočka reveals that it is really a mutual relationship, a marriage in which each party gives of its best to the other. What we have here is not, therefore, a matter of the Hellenization of Christianity but a reflection of the Greek in Christianity and a reflection on the Greek from the perspective of Christianity. In this sense, Ratzinger's thesis is correct.

This leads to the final idea in my interpretation, and that is seeing a link between the un-thought of Christianity and the concept of conversion in Patočka. Here, I draw inspiration from Ivan Chvatík, who suggests that the course of Patočka's reasoning calls for a third conversion.[104] Chvatík interprets the third conversion as the experience of being shaken, that is, as the loss of faith after the death of God and the end of metaphysics. Chvatík then associates the passage to the third conversion with kenotic sacrifice.[105] I will return to this fascinating and thought-provoking topic in the following chapter. Here I want stress that even according to Chvatík, the third conversion pertains in some way to Christianity. In Ricoeur's words, Patočka's Christianity is hyperbolic. In this sense, we can understand the call for the third conversion as the challenge of something that, as Derrida notes, has not yet come to Christianity. The un-thought would therefore mean a turn to faith as openness to the future.[106]

The problem with Caputo's reading of Patočka—to make one final reference to one of the more prominent representatives of the theological turn—is that it looks to the past, as if Patočka were seeking to revisit a Christianity that is dead. But Derrida rightly understands that Patočka is looking to the future. If Caputo had read Patočka more carefully, he would have found Derrida to be correct on this point. In fact, it seems that Caputo never read Patočka at all. Caputo thus misses the point of Derrida's fascination with Patočka, which Cavalcante Schuback aptly summarizes: "Heresy as the un-thought or the un-thought as heresy is what seems to seduce Derrida to Patočka's *Heretical Essays*."[107]

But returning to the third conversion, Patočka's concern with the un-thought of Christianity could, taken to its extreme, be translated as a theological turn in phenomenology. This is not to say that Patočka is calling for what we recently described as the theological turn in continental philosophy. In the first chapter, I clearly showed that Patočka's position is rather complex in this respect. What I am arguing is simply that Patočka's search for the un-thought raises the same question as our age of various theological turns also aims to address. To paraphrase Sternad's point of view on reading Patočka together with Derrida, I am seeking—justly or unjustly—to read Patočka's thought as a pretext to the theological turn in contemporary phenomenology.

To summarize, Derrida goes out on a limb when he calls Patočka a Christian thinker. Such a label causes numerous problems. Scholars of Patočka reject it and point to the broader context of Patočka's thought in order to protect their hero. Caputo completely misunderstands it because of his anxiety that his own hero—Derrida—may be seen as a promoter of a Christianity that he, Caputo, does not like. Nevertheless, the vigorous rejection and Caputo's caricature both miss the point. Derrida's consideration of Patočka as a Christian thinker does not necessarily lead to the conclusion that the Czech philosopher formulates a Christian philosophy. The meaning—and genius—of Derrida's reading is the revealing of the possibilities, the potential, of Patočka's thought, that is, its inspiration for *thinking* Christianity after the end of Christendom; for *thinking* faith after Christianity; for *Christian thinking*.

Chapter 7

Sacrifice for Nothing

The Movement of Kenosis in Patočka's Thought

How, if at all, can Patočka be read as an interlocutor of theology in the context of the theological turn in contemporary philosophy? That is the central question of this book. When Patočka died in 1977, the notion of the theological turn—the intertwining of phenomenology and theology—was yet to become a regular feature of the debate surrounding phenomenology and religion. My hypothesis, however, is that Patočka's conclusions are comparable to and sometimes even more radical than those of some prominent present-day authors who enjoy a good deal more attention in theological circles. The theme of kenotic sacrifice—an issue of great theological significance—illustrates this very clearly.

The biblical idea of kenotic sacrifice has recently inspired the so-called death of God theologies that draw on Nietzsche and see secularization as the natural outcome of Christianity. Thomas Altizer and Mark C. Taylor frequently employ the metaphor of kenosis to indicate God's withdrawal from the world. However, continental philosophy's engagement with the theological turn provides us with a much more interesting and thought-provoking debate. Jean-Luc Marion, for example, breaks away from the classical religious-ritual understanding of sacrifice by developing a phenomenological concept of sacrifice in the context of the phenomenology of the gift; Jean-Luc Nancy associates his project of the deconstruction of Christianity with the "kenosis of thought," an idea inspired by Gérard Granel; Gianni Vattimo places kenosis at the center of his "Christianity without transcendence" in the form of "the community of pure charity" on Earth; an exploration of Jacques Derrida's kenosis of discourse would require a chapter of its own. This list is by no means exhaustive but is sufficient to suggest the idea that kenotic—theological—sacrifice is a popular concept that resonates in many a postmodern ear.

In this chapter, I will show that Patočka's reflections on kenotic sacrifice—mostly in his later writings, after 1968—are more concrete, paradoxical, and thought-provoking than the modern and postmodern lines of thought that have appeared recently in much of the discussion on the theological turn.

More concrete because Patočka goes beyond the phenomenologically reduced conceptualization of the phenomenon of sacrifice to inquire into the experience of sacrifice—as suggested by his engagement with Sakharov and Solzhenitsyn.[1] More paradoxical because although Patočka can be counted neither as a philosopher of religion nor a representative of the theological turn, he somehow precedes this debate. Although many studies have demonstrated Patočka's lifelong interest in religious issues (Hagedorn, Evink)[2] and his reconsideration of Christianity as a central theme within philosophy (de Warren),[3] it is still challenging to counter the mainstream interpretation (Chvatík)[4] and suggest that Patočka is in some ways a precursor of the theological turn. All of this makes his thought still more thought-provoking.

Patočka was not afraid of heresy. On the contrary, he frequently transgressed the limits to point out forgotten questions. His (re)interpretation of the Czech national narrative is a case in point.[5] His views on sacrifice are doubly heretical: regarding phenomenology, he re-ontologizes this crucial Christian notion as a manifestation of the central phenomenological theme of the ontological difference between beings and being, and he does not respect the traditional Christian meaning of kenotic sacrifice but develops his own way of thinking. This makes him an inspiring but still underestimated source for theology.

Despite all this—or perhaps precisely because of it—I am convinced that it is possible to read Patočka through a theological lens. To be even more "heretical," I suggest that Patočka's expositions are open to theological appropriations in the tradition of *fides quaerens intellectum*. My argument will proceed as follows. First, I will introduce Patočka's concept of "sacrifice for *nothing*." Beginning with a critique of sacrifice as an economic exchange, Patočka develops, as we have just noted, a phenomenological concept of sacrifice which re-ontologizes kenosis as a manifestation of the ontological difference between beings and being and thus sketches a *heretical* way of

(Christian) thinking about sacrifice that does not respect the traditional interpretation. Second, I will briefly present the phenomenological concept of sacrifice developed by Jean-Luc Marion, an author who resonates strongly in the present-day theological discourse.[6] I single out Marion not only because of the attention he attracts among theologians but also, and especially, because of the role Patočka plays in his phenomenological concept of sacrifice. As we will see, Marion refers to Patočka in support of his argument, but I will challenge the impression that Patočka's argument is the same as Marion's and ask whether Patočka might not merit more serious consideration from a theological perspective than that which is awarded to Marion. Third, I will show how Patočka's reflections on kenotic sacrifice challenge theological discourse on biblical loci such as Matthew 27:46 and Philippians 2:6–8 and open the way to a reinterpretation of this significant theological issue. To investigate a possible source of Patočka's inspiration, I will explore a juxtaposition of the biblical narrative and the image of sacrifice in *Phaedo*. Is Patočka's treatment of sacrifice closer to Socrates? Or does "sacrifice for *nothing*" correlate rather with the idea of God's kenosis manifested in the cross of Christ? Finally, on the basis of Patočka's reconsideration of sacrifice, I will attempt to show how he can be read as an interlocutor of theology and how his thought can influence our understanding of Christianity.

Sacrifice for Nothing

Patočka's interest in the experience of sacrifice arose in the final decade of his philosophical life. One of the most coherent outlines of the theme can be found in the "Varna lecture" prepared for the 15th World Congress of Philosophy in 1973, later published under the title *The Dangers of Technicization in Science according to E. Husserl and the Essence of Technology as Danger according to M. Heidegger*.[7] As this lengthy title suggests, the context of Patočka's reflection is the state of advanced modernity understood in terms of crisis and endangerment. Patočka finds danger in a technologically framed world that has lost sight of the truth of being.[8] For Patočka, both Husserl and Heidegger are aware of the ambiguous nature of modernity, where everything becomes manageable and presentable as a thing among other things. Both philosophers look for ways out of the impasse. Husserl proposes a new rationalization, that is, a reconfiguration of philosophy as the real science that rules over all other sciences. For Heidegger, the redemption (*das Rettende*) comes from Art as a sphere outside the technical understanding of the world. For Patočka, it is the notion of sacrifice that sheds light on the impasse of modernity and its dangers:

> The experience of sacrifice, however, is now one of the most powerful experiences of our epoch, so powerful and definitive that humankind for the most part has not managed to come to terms with it and flees from it precisely into a technical understanding of being that promises to exclude this experience and for which there exists nothing like a sacrifice, only the utilization of resources.[9]

Modernity develops a fascination with sacrifice, but one that is profoundly ambiguous. Although with cold calculation "our epoch" sacrifices myriad people for *something* (the two world wars and the totalitarian regimes of the twentieth century are the most striking examples of this modern readiness to sacrifice), sacrifice is also something that breaks away from the ordered and well-managed modern world of technology. Sacrifice is essentially the refutation of calculation. To push the internal ambiguity still further, one needs to understand the original Czech word Patočka uses to speak about the experience of sacrifice. Like the German word *Opfer*, the Czech notion of *oběť* carries the double meaning of both sacrifice and victim. Patočka thus adroitly reveals the confusion brought about by modernity: many victims sacrificed for *something* understand their victimization in terms of a sacrificial act. Against this background, Patočka raises the question of "authentic sacrifice" and what it might be. What is the experience of sacrifice truly about? What is the deepest meaning of this radical and irreversible act of self-surrender and self-abandonment?

For Patočka, the original context of sacrifice is myth and religion.[10] Sacrifice is any act of intentional deprivation that strengthens a relationship to something or someone superior—the divine. The logic behind a sacrificial act is the economy of exchange: a gain arises through renunciation. In other words, what we possess is given up to ultimately increase what we possess, whether materially or spiritually. It is this economic conception of sacrifice that Patočka intends to break with. In pursuing this goal, Patočka does not dismiss religious experience completely. Its value, later lost and obscured in modernity, is that sacrifice in religion manifests the difference within the order of being between being as such and beings as manageable entities.[11]

At this point, Patočka moves from the religious to the phenomenological concept of sacrifice and contrasts the experience of sacrifice with the technological world of modernity, in which everything is manageable within the logic of calculation: "Sacrifice means precisely drawing back from the realm of what can be managed and ordered, and an explicit relation to that which, not being anything actual itself, serves as the ground of the appearing of all that is active and in that sense rules over all."[12] Following Heidegger, Patočka argues that the experience of sacrifice renews the thinking of being in contrast to the counting and manipulation of beings. Sacrifice is irreducible to anything objective and quantifiable and for that reason opens a new horizon of the understanding of being. The key notion used by Patočka in this respect is *difference* (*rozdíl*), by which he clearly means ontological difference. However, he stretches Heidegger's point further and argues that the difference between being and beings should be understood in terms of conflict (*polemos*).[13] In concrete sacrifice, being appears as appearing from itself.[14] Sacrifice therefore serves the function of ontological revelation. In giving oneself away, one learns that being only "is" as giving itself away. As Cavalcante Schuback notes, Patočka's phenomenological concept of sacrifice "refers to a metamorphosis within Being, whereby the difference between Being and beings appears as a real transformative force."[15] Thus, sacrifice transgresses all limits of beings and, to invoke Heidegger and his vocabulary once more, breaks with the forgetfulness of being.

Against this background, Patočka distinguishes authentic sacrifice—or sacrifice in a proper sense—from improper sacrifice.[16] The latter involves the economy of exchange. Something is sacrificed and something else is expected in return. For example, modern warfare demands sacrifice for the country in order to create a better world of peace, progress, and so on.[17] One entity is exchanged for another.

Patočka is not saying that to sacrifice something valuable—even the highest value of human life—for *something* is inferior or unworthy. The problem is the logic of exchange that focuses on beings, things, and entities while forgetting being as such. For this reason, Patočka opts for an authentic sacrifice as a protest against the reduction of being to a thing. He proposes the following definition: "In giving themselves for something, they dedicate themselves to that of which it cannot be said that it 'is' something, or something objective."[18] From this perspective, authentic sacrifice is an experience that is no longer concerned with any positive content: it is "sacrifice for *nothing*."[19] This is a troublesome term, however. If *nothing* stands against any positive content, what does this imply? Patočka himself has difficulty explaining sacrifice for *nothing*, which is perhaps why he constantly refers back to the counter-pole of inauthentic sacrifice. Taken to its extreme, the sacrifice for *something* ceases in a certain sense to be a sacrifice at all; to give something and to expect something else in return is simply a logical calculation.[20] Hence Patočka presents his idea of sacrifice for *nothing*, for no-thing.[21] The prerequisite for this way of seeing sacrifice is an understanding of the difference between beings as entities and being as such. Sacrifice for *nothing* is an emancipation from the exchange of beings and is the locus of the appearing of Being.

Although this all sounds rather abstract, Patočka finds concrete examples that bear witness to such authentic sacrifice. He mentions Andrei Sakharov and Aleksandr Solzhenitsyn as authentic persons who are willing if necessary to go to the threshold of negativity;[22] they are ready to engage with their own finitude. And they are not doing this for *something*, such as material gain in this world or some kind of reward in the next. We will see, however, that it is especially those about whom Patočka is silent who reveal the meaning of authentic sacrifice for nothing.

Interestingly, a confrontation with negativity can reveal something positive. This positivity of negativity can clearly not be delineated in terms of objective content. It is perhaps better to speak of a constructive aspect of negativity that is, paradoxically, a deconstruction of the "thinghood" of the human being.[23] In other words, the experience of sacrifice is not nothing—*nihil*—or evaporation into nothingness. Rather, sacrifice for *nothing* reveals something higher, beyond beings. Patočka calls this "something divine."[24] I will leave this enigmatic notion aside for a moment and continue with Patočka's own words: "It is not a sacrifice for something or for someone, although in a certain sense it is a sacrifice for everything and for all. In a certain essential sense, it is a sacrifice for nothing, if by that we mean that which is no existing particular."[25] Patočka shifts, therefore, from a phenomenological to an existential meaning of sacrifice that stands as a challenge before every human being. To strengthen his point, Patočka presents it as inherently Christian.[26] Even more radically, sacrifice for *nothing* is the singular element of Christianity that distinguishes it from other religions: "Christianity remains thus far the greatest and unsurpassed"[27] force of the human spirit against decadence and "the maturity of human being."[28] Christianity is unique among religions, and sacrifice is the ultimate manifestation of this uniqueness.

Such an interpretation is not accepted by all scholars of Patočka. Lubica Učník argues that Patočka is completely uninterested in the Christian aspect of sacrifice, that despite a temptation to trace the notion of sacrifice to Christianity, the bottom line of Patočka's argument is only a phenomenological interest concerning the modern context of technology while using the concept of sacrifice.[29] *Plato and Europe*, in which Patočka addresses the relationship between philosophy and religion and argues for the emergence of religion from Platonism, seems to confirm this point of view and to suggest that Christianity is but one example of Patočka's phenomenological explorations. From that perspective, based on Patočka's reading of *Phaedo*, the logic of sacrifice appears not to be of the economy of exchange, criticized earlier, but of sublation (*Aufhebung*).[30] Sacrifice in Platonism (based on the story of Socrates) and in Christianity (Jesus of Nazareth) would then be no more than examples of the sacrifice found in myths. In other words, there is little difference between the philosophical and the theological-Christian notion of sacrifice. However, Patočka complicates the relationship between philosophy and religion in his *Heretical Essays* by pointing out two groundbreaking historical conversions or shifts: first from myth to philosophy (Platonism) and second from Platonism to Christianity,[31] thus suggesting that with respect to sacrifice, Christianity and Platonism are not "just" two instances of the same vision. Ivan Chvatík argues that in fact Patočka seeks a third conversion. And although this conversion-*metanoia* takes place in an age after the death of God, the achievements of Christianity remain valid.[32] Following this intuition that Christianity has something unique to say, and expanding on Patočka's allusions to the Christian discourse in his discussions on sacrifice, I will suggest that Patočka's sacrifice for *nothing* represents the opening of a new horizon of theological interpretation and theological appropriations. This will become clear in a comparison with the voice of the French phenomenologist Jean-Luc Marion, who unlike Patočka enjoys a healthy reputation among theologians.

Sacrifice as the Moment of Gift

In *Negative Certainties*, Marion refers to Patočka in his discussion of a phenomenological conception of sacrifice. He cites a substantial passage from the Varna lecture, where Patočka relates the experience of sacrifice to Heidegger's notion of *es gibt* and therefore appears to follow Heidegger's interpretation of sacrifice as an experience of the modality of disclosure with regard to being.[33] Marion sets Patočka in the context of other authors such as Levinas and Bataille, but also Thomas Aquinas and Augustine.[34] If reference to Levinas and Bataille seems perfectly justifiable—Levinas shares a background in phenomenology with Patočka and Bataille an interest in sacrifice—mention of Aquinas and Augustine comes as something of a surprise. It is as if Patočka confirmed the tradition of thinking that had recently enjoyed fresh waves of attention from the authors belonging to the theological turn in contemporary phenomenology, among whom Marion was a leading light. In other words, Marion seems to suggest that Patočka's reflections on sacrifice correspond to his phenomenological concept of sacrifice as the moment of the gift. Does Marion do justice to Patočka by transposing his argument into the context of the theological turn?

Marion opens his phenomenological sketch of sacrifice by pointing out its origin, which he finds in the act of "making sacred" (*sacrum facere*), that is, in removing something from the profane realm. However, as Marion suggests, it is doubtful whether the disenchanted world, where no clear line exists between the sacred and the profane, allows for such an understanding of sacrifice. On the contrary, sacrifice according to the terms of exchange remains a widely acknowledged concept even today. For Marion, this includes giving up *something* for *something* else.[35] Whether I sacrifice a sheep for rain or my very life for eternal salvation, the difference is one not of essence but of degree. Something is destroyed, dispossessed, lost, immolated, or given up in return for something else. The problem with this logic of exchange is that sacrifice involves only objects. For Marion, this "most current explanation of sacrifice," predominant in the history of Christianity, creates "the illusion of a contractual agreement."[36] I give up something and someone else ought to give something back. Marion suggests that this point of view obscures the real meaning of sacrifice and, worse, proves the opposite of sacrifice—"a construction of the self."[37] The economy of reciprocity conflates the notions of "exchange" and "gift" as if they were one and the same reality,[38] whereas the aim of Marion's argument is to maintain the distinction.

To break with the common conception of sacrifice, Marion introduces the notion of the other: "Sacrifice always assumes the other as its horizon of possibility."[39] This reveals an important aporia in sacrifice. To sacrifice indeed means to give something up, out of one's possession, as the reciprocal conception of exchange suggests. But to give something up also means to make it visible and available for the other so it can be acknowledged, accepted, appropriated, or simply rejected. Marion's point is to turn the spotlight on the dynamic within sacrifice between the subject sacrificing something and the other who validates that which has been sacrificed. This is the dynamic of the gift.

For Marion, the phenomenon of the gift transcends the logic of exchange because it takes into consideration the act of giving up, of abandonment.[40] Using his third phenomenological reduction in givenness, Marion argues that the gift can undo all the components of the sacrifice according to terms of exchange, namely, the giver, the recipient, and even the thing that is given. Marion therefore suggests reconsidering sacrifice as the moment of giving and giving up unconditionally.[41] To break with the metaphysical rules of exchange, reciprocity, causality, and objectivity, the giver, the recipient, and the object of the gift itself must be suspended. In suspending these conditions, the gift may authentically appear as emerging from givenness alone.[42] Sacrifice is then the locus where the gift appears genuinely as givenness,[43] the event that "enables a gift to appear in visibility."[44] According to Marion:

> Sacrifice gives the gift back to the givenness from which it proceeds, by returning it to the very return that originally constitutes it. Sacrifice does not separate itself from the gift but dwells in it totally: it maintains the gift in its status as given, by reproducing it in an abandon. Sacrifice, this abandon, manifests itself by returning to the gift its givenness because it repeats the gift on the basis of its origin.[45]

What is at stake in Marion's phenomenological conception of sacrifice is therefore not giving up a possession for the purpose of receiving anything beneficial in return but taking cognizance of the gift and thus making visible givenness as such. Marion uses the example of Abraham's sacrifice of Isaac to illustrate his point.

For Marion, the story of Genesis 22 is not a narrative that legitimizes ritual sacrificial action but a story about the suspension of sacrificial violence and the interruption of the common concept of sacrifice—the reconstitution of sacrifice without claim to possession and thus its reconsideration, paradoxically, as *non*sacrifice. Marion argues that such an interpretation follows from his phenomenological reduction of the gift to givenness.[46]

The main message of the biblical narrative, in Marion's phenomenological interpretation, is the rediscovery of the givenness of Isaac. God gives Isaac as a gift to the aged and supposedly infertile Abraham and Sarah (Gen 18:11). But Abraham forgets that his son was a gift and starts to treat him as his possession. The givenness is objectified and the gift becomes something that is present-at-hand. This violates God's claim on Isaac in two senses. First, it ignores God's claim on all firstborns and their nature as a gift in Israel (Ex 22:29–30). Second, God gives the son to a couple for whom all available evidence suggests that having a child is impossible. Yet nothing is impossible for God who gives (Gen 18:14). Therefore, from the beginning, Isaac belongs to God, from whom he comes as a gift. Marion argues that when God demands the sacrifice of Isaac from Abraham, he is not asking for a return of his possession but for the return of Isaac to the status of a gift.[47] The fact that Isaac is ultimately not sacrificed provides a crucial insight into the true meaning of sacrifice as the manifestation of givenness.

To sum up Marion's account, sacrifice is not the exchange of gifts. Rather, in the dynamic of regiving the gift in the giving up (*abandonment*), sacrifice makes givenness visible. In this sense, sacrifice functions as a privilege but still as an example that reveals the order of givenness.[48] Or, according to Marion, "the function" of sacrifice is "to make appear . . . a phenomenology of the gift."[49]

It is clear that Marion plays with theological motifs. It is not surprising, therefore, that he inspires others to draw theological implications from his thought. For example, his reading of the sacrifice of Isaac on Mount Moriah seems to be applicable to the passion of Christ on Golgotha.[50] If a genuine sacrifice manifests givenness, the sacrifice of Jesus Christ does the same. Jesus's sacrifice undoes the exchange of possession and reveals God as the originator of the gift. Marion's statement that "Christ appears as an absolute phenomenon"[51] suggests that God is pure givenness, the ultimate giver, and also the goal of the gift. This fundamental supposition of Marion's project becomes apparent, for example, in his treatment of the sacraments as the supreme gift that is paramount for the phenomenality of givenness as such.[52] In other words, the sacrifice of Christ and its repetition in the Eucharistic celebration are the moments of the gift given. Everything that appears is a gift.[53] From Marion's perspective, therefore, sacrifice manifests givenness and reveals God, based on his interpretation of Genesis 22, as the ultimate giver. The gift from God is given back to become regiven and thus to manifest givenness.

To support his argument about a sacrifice free from the terms of exchange, Marion complements his argument with a discussion about forgiveness. To regive a gift that has been unjustly turned into a possession is what it means to forgive. Interestingly, Marion concludes his account of forgiveness with a quasi-theological argument that because for God everything has the status of a gift, God is the only one who can forgive everything. God, the creator of everything in the mode of givenness, has given everything.[54] Marion's conclusion that sacrifice is, to quote Thomas Aquinas, "every virtuous deed . . . in so far as it is done out of reverence of God,"[55] must therefore be read in this context. A phenomenological concept becomes a theological one. It is striking that the vocabulary of "the gift coming from elsewhere" is suddenly replaced by a reference to "every work" that strengthens the relationship to the divine. At this point, Patočka would differ from Marion, although they would agree on the critique of sacrifice according to the terms of exchange. In what follows, I will first show that Patočka cannot simply be aligned with the traditional interpretation as presented by Marion. Second, I will suggest that Patočka proposes a much more engaged concept of sacrifice than reduction to the gift is able to offer and in this sense challenges theology to reconsider sacrifice not only as free from the logic of economic exchange but also as a sacrifice for nothing.

Kenosis in Patočka's Perspective

In the *Four Seminars on Europe* that followed the Varna lecture, Patočka once again discussed the matter of sacrifice with his students in detail. Although the students were interested mostly in the Heideggerian line and constantly forced Patočka to comment on the ontological difference and the problem of being, at one point Patočka makes an emancipatory move away from the giant of modern philosophy and presents a revelatory experience of sacrifice beyond phenomenological terms. Patočka complements the understanding of sacrifice as the "appearing of Being" with the existential perspective of the "emptying of life" to the absolute limit.[56] What is this emptying of life? Patočka gives a radical answer. The emptying is not simply a break with the content of life—a sort of spiritual conversion to become independent of material things. It is the overcoming of all the bonds and attachments one has with regard to life as such. For Patočka, this self-surrender, which can hardly be interpreted as anything other than absolute loss, means the triumph of life.[57] Reading this, it is impossible not to recall one particular passage from the New Testament:

> Who, though he was in the form of God, did not regard equality with God something to be grasped. Rather, he emptied himself,

taking the form of a slave, coming in human likeness; and found human in appearance, he humbled himself, becoming obedient to death, even death on a cross. (Phil 2:6–8)

Patočka generally avoided quoting from the Bible in his philosophical writings. To my knowledge, he does not quote this hymn to Christ's kenosis at any point. Ludger Hagedorn suggests, however, that the central leitmotif of Patočka's interpretation of Christianity, indeed the axis of his entire philosophical oeuvre, is captured in these words from Paul's letter to the Philippians.[58] I will be following two particular places in Patočka where the idea of kenosis forms the backdrop to his analysis. The first is Patočka's striking reflection on the crucifixion, and in particular on Christ's words noted in Matthew 27:46: "Why have you forsaken me?" Second, after thirty years Patočka dedicates the final part of the postscript to his republished *Habilitationsschrift* to the "myth of the God-man." But before we enter a discussion with Patočka, a short note on kenosis from a theological perspective seems appropriate.

The doctrine of a God who becomes a man, accepts the destiny of the ultimate slave, and dies on a cross is peculiar and ambivalent. How is it possible that an almighty and eternal God should enter history and accept every consequence, including death? For Saint Paul it is "foolishness"; for (ancient) metaphysics, Judaic religion, and mythical cults it is incomprehensible; for Judaism kenosis is a scandal, blasphemy. The history of theology can be interpreted metaphorically as the tension between attempts both to make kenosis rationality accessible—councils, dogmas, theological disputations—and to protect it from rationalization—mysticism, the critique of metaphysics. The story is not limited to theology, of course. From Hegel's elaboration on *Entäußerung*—the translation of kenosis in Luther's Bible—to the recent philosophical appropriations of Saint Paul—Badiou, Žižek—and postmetaphysical ventures—Vattimo, Caputo, among others—the idea of kenosis and a kenotic God has provoked a good deal of profound thinking.[59] Nevertheless, I do not wish to simply argue that Patočka's contribution is one part of this wave of interest. Although it may be a logical explanation, Patočka's turn to kenosis is somehow deeper and harks back to the very meaning of the Greek words *kēneô* and *heauton ekenôsen*—to empty, to empty oneself, to make oneself nothing.

Theologically, the hymn from Philippians speaks of Christ's annihilation.[60] He became *nothing*. Kenosis is an engagement with negativity in which a person experiences his or her own finitude in self-surrender. There is also a second layer, however. Kenosis is a revelatory event that reveals the mystery of *nothing* not only in a moral sense—the person humbled and hanged on the cross—but in an ontological sense. To use a concrete example, the one on the cross is nothing—not a thing (*Zeug*)—nothing manageable. He unties his bonds with life and frees himself completely. He has totally emptied himself. From a phenomenological perspective, the same passage alludes to the manifestation of the ontological difference between being (*Sein*) and beings (*Seiende*). Now the link between Patočka's phenomenological approach and that of theology becomes apparent. The sacrifice for *nothing* is a kenotic sacrifice—a unique Christian contribution to the history of ideas—and Patočka's philosophical thought elaborates upon this crucial theological idea in novel ways, as will become clear in the following discussion.

Why Have You Forsaken Me?

In the *Four Seminars on Europe*, Patočka explicitly recalls the passion narrative.[61] Regardless of classical interpretations of this passage that suggest that Christ was quoting Psalm 22, Patočka focuses solely on the single sentence mentioned in Matthew's gospel. Interestingly, Patočka does not even name Christ explicitly, though it is clear that he is referring to him:

> Why have you forsaken me? The answer lies in the question. What would have happened if you had not forsaken me? Nothing would have happened. Something happens only when you forsake me. The sacrifice must be carried to the very end. He has forsaken me so that there would be nothing, no thing that I could still hold on to.[62]

For Patočka, the question says it all. Both the essence and the effects of sacrifice appear in these words of total abandonment. Sacrifice therefore reveals the difference within the order of being. This is Patočka's answer to Heidegger. Sacrifice is remembering the forgotten question, the question of being. It is not a passive participation in art but an active movement of self-surrender. In this sense, sacrifice is not *for* something, rather it manifests something. What appears is "something divine," something that is no-thing, not an object, nothing manipulable, but something that rules over everything.[63] This reveals some crucial insights. First, the event of sacrifice provides the person with a new understanding of being because he or she realizes that being is nothing like a thing. To use Heideggerian wording, the person sees the ontological difference. Second, and perhaps much more important, is the insight revealed to those who witness the event of sacrifice. To keep with our example of Christ's crucifixion, those who witnessed, experienced, the sacrifice of the one held to be the Messiah—his kenosis—were fundamentally challenged in their self-understanding, were confronted with a question they had not expected, and this question turned their lives and their perspective on the world upside down. Only later traditions reconceived sacrifice as the ultimate response to human sinfulness. The very moment of witnessing the kenotic sacrifice, however, raises a question rather than an answer.

Although Patočka is anxious not to succumb to theological discourse, he makes the link with the central message of the New Testament himself. Filip Karfík calls this Patočka's endeavor toward a retheologization of Heideggerian ontology.[64] Patočka even recalls "some modern theologians" who would be in favor of his interpretation that rejects the metaphysical happy ending of sacrificing for some kind of afterlife in the next world. And as his next reference is to a secular context of Christianity, he is no doubt referring to the theologians of the demythologization movement whom Patočka read and discussed with his friend, the Czech Protestant theologian Josef Souček. Absolute kenotic sacrifice does not call for reward but reveals a question, that is, the question concerning the meaning of being human.

However, some recent interpretations have questioned the absoluteness of sacrifice in the way Patočka demands it. Martin Ritter, for example, finds Patočka's radical kenosis a traumatic and overly heavy burden that breaks with any kind of transcendence: "Authentic sacrifice is of little importance if *nothing* stands there as a higher transcendence above the human."[65] Jindřich Veselý is even more skeptical and argues that Patočka's kenosis unfolds the mystery of the loss of faith. From the perspective of the Easter mystery, Veselý argues, Patočka bears witness to the descent into hell.[66] A more moderate position is suggested by Riccardo Paparusso, who seeks to reconcile the classical view of sacrifice in Christianity—Christ sacrificed himself for *something*—with Patočka's thoughts on authentic sacrifice for *nothing*.

Paparusso's argument is simple: the sacrifice for something—the economic exchange typical of religious sacrifices—is a genuine sacrifice because everything is given away in an ultimate and irreversible way.[67]

The cause is irrelevant. Be it atonement for sin or the restoration of communion with the divine, the breakthrough of nothing (nonbeing) comes forth. There is no way to avoid it. From this perspective, it is possible both to suggest that Christ sacrificed himself for the forgiveness of sins and to claim that the event of Christ was about genuine and absolute sacrifice. What can we say in response to these critiques?

We would be wrong to place too much emphasis on the *for* of sacrifice in Patočka. It is not true that Patočka deems a sacrifice for something as meaningless. The center of gravity is not the tension between sacrifice for objective and nonobjective purposes. The point is the very experience of sacrifice and its performative character. For Patočka, the moment of sacrifice is completely outside economic calculation because what is at stake is not beings (*Seienden*) but Being (*Sein*). Sacrifice reveals the openness to Being and transmits this openness to others. Of course, this can happen on the battlefield where soldiers die for their country as well as on the cross where God's only Son gives his life for many. The point is, once again, that authentic sacrifice is not performed with economics in mind but rather for nothing. Or as Patočka says in his enigmatic dictum: "No thing—but this does not mean that this *nothing* does not contain *das All*, as the poet said."[68] In Patočka's thought, the act of sacrifice is not apocalyptic but prophetic. It is an act of love. And love is not a thing, although it may be coerced and objectified, as it was in the totalitarian regimes that Patočka experienced firsthand.[69] The movement of love is what makes sacrifice possible, but this love transcends ethical and moral meanings.[70] For Patočka, love is the transubstantiation of life, the moment of breakthrough in which the depth of being appears. But what is this love?

Love is not a sentimental emotional posture but a manifestation of the ontological difference. In other words, love is giving oneself away, but this giving does not appear as giving something (for something else), but as the appearing of being itself. Now we see the meaning of Patočka's extrapolation of *nothing* and *das All—everything*. From the perspective of human finitude, human life has already been decided. It will end at some point. Yet for Patočka, sacrifice as yielding itself unconditionally to others—kenosis—overcomes finitude because it reveals to all that this life is not everything but nothing, and that there is a greater no-thing that rules over everything. For ears trained in theology, this sounds very appealing. However, before drawing conclusions, let us turn to the second instance where the words of Philippians underline Patočka's argument.

The Myth of the God-Man

At the very end of "The Natural World Remeditated Thirty-Three Years Later," Patočka provides a short note on the "inexhaustible" idea of a perfect—divine—man who lives in truth and who because of his commitment must die and later be resurrected.[71] Patočka thinks of the God-man as the one who lives in self-surrender, that is, kenotically. Again, the reference to the Bible is beyond doubt. According to Patočka:

> Truth—the word—has become flesh: the event of being, which has chosen man as the locus of its appearing, has found its fullness in a fully "true" man, living entirely in devotion, beyond concern for his own interest, not like the creatures of the field and the birds of the air, on the ground of instinct which binds only one existent to another, but rather in the light of being. If the event of being is conceived as that with which divinity is inseparably associated, then it can be said that such a fully true man is rightly called the God-man.[72]

For Patočka, the event of being is inherently linked with the divine. The God-man is essentially a threat to the forces of the world, which Patočka understands as the dictatorship of beings. Although he does not pretend to become a new king, he must be destroyed and expelled from sight because he reveals the truth. The God-man reveals what is truly important in the world, and he reveals this through his openness, self-surrender, and kenotic posture: "The God-man will, therefore, inevitably be made to perish," because he reveals that ruling over everything is not the force of the existent "but rather the truth of being."[73]

Hagedorn interprets this thought as a philosophical exercise that disregards the historical fact—or fiction—of the life-story of Jesus of Nazareth.[74] It does not matter whether the event of Christ happened or did not happen. What counts is the force of this central Christian idea that continually provokes thinking about the depth of human being in the world. Similarly, Chvatík argues that Patočka does not develop a philosophical Christology but uses the example of Christ's self-surrender—kenosis—as the proper expression of the internal conflict experienced by every human being.[75] Christianity, which Patočka considers to be the greatest and unsurpassed agent of human history, makes sense in the context of these interpretations. The conceptualization of the most intimate yet most critical question of human being is Christianity's unrivaled contribution. Unlike Marion, for example, who postulates an external objective order of givenness, and kenosis as participation in this order, Patočka's understanding of kenosis is directed at the inner element of every person. Moreover, in Patočka, Christianity succeeded in expressing this inner struggle in the depth of the soul in a universally comprehensible manner. Although Nietzsche would detest it as a Platonism for the masses, humanity as a whole is now invited to think of, reflect on, and remember this conflict within being. Christ's kenosis reveals what the truth of history is truly about. The idea of God's renunciation is a scandalous provocation to shift from a simple life and its preservation to *thinking* about human being. It seems that herein lies the motivation behind Patočka's plea for fighting for the Christian legacy, albeit in a deconstructed and demythologized manner, for the post-Christian world.

Toward a Theological Appropriation of Patočka's Concept of Sacrifice

It is clear that Patočka is at great pains to avoid sounding theological in his formulations. It is not his intention to develop a "crypto-theology." He repeatedly insists, furthermore, that there is nothing mystical about his conception of sacrifice.[76] Nonetheless, two questions must be asked in this respect. Why does Patočka maintain a polite distance from theology? And, more importantly, does his thought really exclude the theological and the mystical? Answering these questions involves a consideration of three different but interrelated contexts: the contexts of Patočka, of the theological turn, and of theology itself.

Arguably, any resolute opposition to theological discourse can be explained by taking into account Patočka's historical context. First, the 1970s predate the theological turn in (French) phenomenology. Marion's *Dieu sans l'être*, a milestone in creating a porous boundary between theology and philosophy/phenomenology, is not published until 1982, five years after Patočka's death. Although it is possible to discern the same intuition in Patočka as in Marion—that phenomenology can serve as a philosophical background to theology after the end of metaphysics—Patočka himself does not transgress the boundaries of his discipline. Second, and perhaps more importantly, Patočka reacts to particular historical events. True, he never refers to it explicitly, but it seems difficult to disconnect

Patočka's reflection on sacrifice from the act of Jan Palach, the university student who immolated himself in protest against the Soviet occupation of Czechoslovakia following the Prague Spring of 1968. Without going into historical details and without resolving the question of the motivation behind Patočka's tacit acknowledgment of the absolute sacrifice committed by Palach, it seems clear that Patočka has a message for his contemporaries. In this context, references to theology and attempts to interpret biblical material explicitly could obscure the main point, which is to question the (self-)understanding of concrete human beings in particular situations. In short, Patočka has good reason to distance himself from theological discourse. Whether he would change his standpoint if he had lived to see the theological turn in its first (French) wave remains unanswerable.

The turn to the religious, or the theological turn, provoked a lively debate among phenomenologists and theologians. Regardless of which side of the conflict we choose, one thing is clear: the way of thought developed by Patočka in the last years of his life is very close to that which would become the mainstream of phenomenological-theological discussion from the 1980s onward. Authors of the theological turn in phenomenology considered theological issues and certain traditions of Christian thinking, mysticism for example, as viable alternatives and responses to the crisis of modernity. From the revived philosophical interest in such questions, a number of theological appropriations have been developed, and Patočka's lifelong interest in Christianity and its interpretations and reinterpretations is a prelude to these later engagements. It would be no exaggeration to claim that if Patočka were better known in the Anglo-American context—the main locus of the debate surrounding the theological turn—his phenomenological philosophy would play a much more important role, a claim confirmed by some recent philosophical interpretations of Patočka. Hagedorn, de Warren, Evink, and Derrida propose a reading that takes into account the Christian background and suggest that to read Patočka in this context makes sense. Interestingly, all these authors are from "abroad" and go somewhat against domestic—Czech—interpretations of Patočka, which generally present him as a pure-blooded phenomenologist with no interest in theology. The interpretation proposed in the present volume elaborates on these "foreign" thinkers and reaches still further into the realm of theology.

Unlike other figures of the theological turn, Patočka does not pretend that his philosophy is there to serve theology. Patočka would surely reject any such language of servitude: "*Philosophia ancilla theologiae* has never been and will never be true."⁷⁷ How do we understand theology? If it is understood in the metaphysical sense, Patočka's opposition makes sense. If it is taken outside metaphysics, however, Patočka's conception of sacrifice suddenly acquires—as do many other ideas of his—a theological potential and can be read as an open call to theological thinking. For example, after analyzing all the works of Patočka that contain an allusion to the idea of kenosis, Evink concludes that many of Patočka's concepts that appear to be of a purely philosophical—Greek—origin are, in fact, already influenced by their respective Christian reinterpretations.⁷⁸ So, is Patočka thinking about Socrates or about Christ in his reflections on sacrifice?

The Experience of Sacrifice: Christ or Socrates?

Krzysztof Michalski, a young friend of Patočka's,⁷⁹ elaborates on this question in his essay "The Death of God."⁸⁰ The essay strays beyond the borders of theology and philosophy, and although Patočka is not mentioned explicitly, his shadow is certainly detectable in the argument. Michalski addresses the experience of sacrifice in both Socrates—Patočka's great hero—and Christ—about whom Patočka is mostly silent. At least, Patočka does not name Christ when he speaks of the "God-man" or when he interprets the cry of the crucified, "Why have you forsaken me?" Michalski's text thus reveals the tension between the figure of Socrates and the person of Christ, a tension internalized in the history of theology.

Patočka says of Socrates that his constant questioning had a fatal end: "the fate of sacrifice."⁸¹ In this sense, the Christian narrative seems to bear many similarities to "the myth of Socrates."⁸² How are we to understand the relation between these two eminent models of sacrifice? What is the relative weighting between the philosophical and the theological? Whose sacrifice is the principal source of inspiration for Patočka's reflections?

Michalski challenges the claim that the acts of Socrates and Christ bear an essential similarity. Plato's dialogue *Phaedo* presents a Socrates who is reconciled with his death. Socrates welcomes his death and even rejoices over it. As Michalski explains, for Socrates, death means entering knowledge, contemplation, the ultimate insight into the truth. Philosophy is, after all, the care for death and a preparation for the moment when everything obscure will become clear.⁸³ Michalski reminds us that Socrates's companions were very unsettled by his point of view: "What about the fear of the child in each of us?" asked Socrates's friends when they realized he seemed strangely indifferent to his fate. Perhaps he was capable of rationally grasping the mystery of death and finding inner peace. The argument about the immortality of the soul may be convincing, but death is still the riddle of all riddles. A child, Michalski says, needs consolation. Rational arguments are meaningless.[84] For Socrates, things are quite different. It is impossible to convince children. The point is to become a mature person and leave childhood behind. A rational person has nothing to fear because death is no loss at all; death is a gain.

From the perspective proposed by Michalski, Socrates's sacrifice seems to function according to the logic of exchange. According to Patočka's analysis of such an exchange, Socrates sacrifices himself *for something* and thus understands his punishment as reward. Death brings him peace. Socrates's last moments seem to provide affirmation of his indifference to death. His final words need no explanation: "Crito, I owe a cock to Asclepius; will you remember to pay the debt?" Moreover, Michalski reminds us that Plato, the author of the dialogue, was not there to say goodbye to his dear friend and teacher because of an illness.[85]

How different, then, do the words of the gospel sound: *Eli, Eli lama sabachthani?* Christ appears to experience despair, uncertainty, and abandonment on the cross. Where is God? There is no God on Golgotha but fear. What is Christ, the Messiah, afraid of? Does he fear death? Michalski reflects:

> Death is not a *something* that one can understand. Death is the annihilation of all conditions for understanding, of all the conditions by which we think something, ourselves included. In the same way, the prospect of death pulls the ground out from under us, it subverts all possible support, it takes away our chance for a place to sit, for certainty, for peace. Death exposes the limit of all concepts, and so death itself is incomprehensible.[86]

Death is not a *something*. In death, a person comes face to face with nothingness, which is why Michalski argues that death is incomprehensible. Facing finitude, the engagement with nothingness, is not a mathematical problem. Reason is too small. Fear is simply larger. Not even God can calculate this enigmatic "equation," and Christ is unable to do away with the thorny riddle. In short, death does not open the gate of knowledge, it is the breakthrough of the un-thought.

Death requires that everything known should be left behind. Preparation is impossible. The possibility of nothing is too strong. However, this nothing may open a new beginning: "The prospect of death demonstrates that the world and thus also I myself contain more than we can hold," says Michalski.[87] To recall Patočka, the possibility of nothing is also the possibility of a new horizon of no-thing and thus "a new continent of meaning."[88] In this sense, we understand Patočka when he says that *nothing* would have happened if God had not forsaken Christ. To realize what the experience of sacrifice is truly about, it must be performed as a total abandonment and for *nothing*.

Which figure of sacrifice is closer to Patočka's conception of a kenotic sacrifice for nothing? Because of their commitment to live in truth, both Socrates and Christ actively risk everything. They are ready to go to the threshold of negativity and accept every consequence of their disruptive way of life. For Patočka, then, the fate of Socrates and the sacrifice of Christ are on the same level. But their experience is quite different. Socrates steps away undisturbed and fearless in the face of death. Christ is terrified and undergoes an emptying—a kenosis—until the very end. Michalski interprets this as a tension between the power of ideas and the mystery of the un-thought. Importantly, this tension is not necessarily the opposition between truth and falsehood. Perhaps, Michalski concludes, the tension represented by Christ and Socrates is a constitutive human condition.[89]

Patočka explicitly acknowledges the fact that he draws inspiration from Socrates on many occasions. Nevertheless, as his reflections on sacrifice progress, his fascination with Christ's kenosis becomes increasingly apparent.[90] It is as if a calm philosophical mind would not suffice in addressing this ambiguous question. Eddo Evink brings the provocative idea that Patočka projects the Christian kenotic sacrifice into the figure of Socrates as described in *Phaedo*.[91] God's self-surrender and total emptying manifests the experience of sacrifice in the most radical and absolute way. Does this mean Patočka follows the Christian path in his thought? I propose that his ideas are without doubt open to a theological interpretation. I also see his ambivalent shuffling around Socrates and Christ as intentional, which is why references to Socrates sometimes better resemble the image of Christ, and why clear scenes from the life of Christ fail to name the protagonist. Patočka's message is existential. It is a challenge to everyone, including the philosopher himself. What are the consequences for the theologian and the Christian?

Kenotic Christianity after Christianity

We have shown that Patočka's concept of sacrifice can be associated with a certain kind of *Christian thinking*. The intention is not to oppose the phenomenological—mainstream—reading of Patočka. For example, Cavalcante Schuback and Učník rightly argue for the importance of the ontological difference to Patočka's reflections. The difference between beings and being is crucial for understanding the notion of sacrifice in Patočka. This is the challenge of sacrifice in the proper sense; it has revelatory power and shows that something greater, something deeper, "something divine" "rules over everything."[92] Nevertheless, the very language Patočka uses impels us to go further.

Ludger Hagedorn is among the first to accept the challenge and to interpret Patočka's reflections on sacrifice as part of the larger project of a philosophical (re)interpretation of Christianity after (the end of) Christianity.[93] In other words, Hagedorn argues that Patočka's point is to transpose the truth of the biblical message for our context. This is why Patočka does not focus on the person of Christ but on the meaning of kenosis for every human being, and why the incarnation is not linked to the descent of the transcendent God to the world but is presented as *Seinsereignis*—the event of Being. The notion of transcendence does not therefore refer to the division between "here" and "there" but to the ontological difference.[94] Kenotic Christianity breaks with metaphysics, and Christ's divinity must be understood accordingly. Hagedorn summarizes Patočka as follows:

> God is with human beings, but this relationship is very different from the traditional idea and nothing like the theological wasteland. He is with us in an essentially problematic world. . . . He will be experienced as the questionable-ness of this world, as the ability to transcend this world in the task of the renunciation of all singular interests and attachments. God is in history and is "the living hope for world reversal."[95]

From a theological perspective, although Hagedorn's interpretation remains faithful to the philosophical discourse, it is certainly inspiring. Hagedorn discusses Christianity in Patočka as a cultural phenomenon, and since we no longer live in a Christian age, it makes perfect sense to speak of a Christianity that comes "after Christianity." Rather than approaching

Patočka's Christianity after Christianity on the basis of a historical-sociological analysis, I suggest appropriating Patočka's thought as a challenge to theology itself. This means that Patočka reveals something about the inherent dynamism of a Christianity that is constantly transcending itself and that becomes a Christianity after Christianity again and again.

We therefore return to our initial question: How, if at all, can Patočka be read as the interlocutor of theology? First, Patočka can be placed in the tradition of Bonhoeffer's religionless Christianity, Bultmann's demythologized Christianity, and, more recently, Vattimo's nonreligious Christianity, or Derrida and Caputo's religion without religion. Space does not permit a detailed comparison between Patočka's intuition and these other facets of theological-philosophical reasoning. Instead, we will concern ourselves with the question of how this kenotic form of Christianity after Christianity, drawn from Patočka's reflections on sacrifice, would appear.

As the previous discussion has shown, Patočka is critical of the reciprocal conception of sacrifice as found in myth and metaphysics. His vision of Christianity after Christianity is free from calculative behavior and the logic of *do ut des*. There is no need to act in a certain way in order to receive a reward or avoid punishment. The development of Christianity after Christianity has no set course. On the contrary, it contains a moment of surprise perceptible both internally and externally. Internally, Christianity is a self-critique—*thinking*—that has not been decided from the beginning. This thinking means living in questions and problematicity; these are seen not as obstacles but as thought-provoking engines and paths toward realizing the depth of the entirety of life in history and in the world, yet beyond the world. Externally, then, this form of Christianity is open to the future; it is free from the fear of what the future may bring or take away. Nobody knows what the future will be like, but what can be known, on the basis of this critical Christian consciousness, is that history does not follow any predetermined pattern of development.

Second, for Patočka, sacrifice in its kenotic conception is what distinguishes Christianity from other religions and their conception of the divine as the omnipotent power, and also from the modes of thinking that would suggest that sacrifice is an unavoidable consequence of a certain way of being in the world.[96] In this sense, Christianity after Christianity goes beyond cultic sacrificial religions but also beyond a certain philosophical existence, as illustrated by the story of Socrates's tranquility in the face of death. Patočka praises the radicalness of sacrifice in Christianity, which breaks with the ordinary and the everyday manifested in the story of

Christ. From a theological perspective, therefore, sacrifice manifests an existential conflict that pertains to every human being, and Christianity after Christianity bears witness to this conception of sacrifice that is for nothing—no-thing—that contains everything.

This brings us to a comparison between Patočka and Marion. First, it has to be said that Marion is used theologically and is frequently commented upon from that perspective, whereas Patočka is rather more neglected by theologians. The reason I juxtapose Patočka and Marion is not simply to repudiate one philosophical approach and replace it with another, supposedly better approach. In fact, it is Marion who invokes Patočka's authority and brings it into his argument. Marion provides us with the phenomenological reduction of sacrifice and recuperates crucial biblical narratives from this point of view. In short, for Marion, sacrifice is the revelation of givenness, that is, something that functions within the framework of the present-day debate on the frontiers of philosophy and theology as the apology for the gift of God's presence.[97] Nevertheless, Patočka can hardly be associated with this debate or with theological consequences drawn from the argument that God is the ultimate giver and the creator of everything in the mode of givenness.[98] The importance for theology of Patočka's reflections on sacrifice lies in redirecting attention from a phenomenological concept to an existential one.

For Patočka, sacrifice manifests the existential conflict within each human being. Sacrifice appears, therefore, first and foremost, as an individual experience. This experience is repeatable but, when the situation calls for it, irreplaceable. This says two things. First, as with Marion, Patočka's intention is to overcome the logic of exchange by pointing to the irreversible act of sacrificial self-abandonment. Second, unlike Marion, Patočka points out that sacrifice—the gift—is decisive. Marion presents sacrifice as a privilege but nonetheless as an example of a given gift, as though sacrifice is a natural, logical consequence of the order of givenness, or, as Joeri Schrijvers summarizes, "the given phenomenon gives itself . . . of itself and as its self."[99] For Patočka, however, to give, and thus to sacrifice, is not self-evident at all. The difference will become visible when we revisit the story of Genesis 22 as a prefiguring of the passion narrative.

Marion interprets this passage as the manifestation of givenness by the regiving of the gift (of Isaac). This leads him to conclude that sacrifice "shows being given." From the perspective of Patočka's conception of sacrifice for nothing, Marion's position seems to leave those who are actually involved in sacrifice in some way as passive bystanders. More specifically,

Isaac appears as an object ready-to-hand in the moment of the gift. We accept Marion's critique of the economy of exchange, according to which Isaac is not a possession given up in exchange for something else, but Isaac's role is nonetheless completely passive. He does not sacrifice; he is "used" to allow givenness to appear through sacrifice. Although Patočka does not discuss this particular scene, his allusions to biblical narratives offer a different picture. First, Patočka makes it clear that sacrifice is painful. Isaac and Jesus of Nazareth clash with the nothing. This engagement with no-thing is something existential, something that touches the very core of being human, something traumatic that can perhaps contain everything, as Patočka enigmatically points out. Second, sacrifice is not, then, a moment of the gift but a decisive act, an event that is nothing, but which says everything at the same time. Neither Isaac nor Christ is the same after their experience of sacrifice.

It is possible to say the following, therefore. Marion is absolutely right to recall Patočka in the context of the theological turn. Although Patočka died before the notion emerged, Marion justly senses that his contribution regarding sacrifice should not be neglected. But it should be made clear that despite sharing the same point of departure as Marion, Patočka comes to a different conclusion about sacrifice. Patočka does not keep to the phenomenological reduction of sacrifice—be it Husserl's *epochē*, Heidegger's reduction to being, or Marion's third reduction to givenness—but shifts from a phenomenological moment to an existential movement.

The notion of kenotic sacrifice for nothing is not without perils, however. The narrative of nothing is disturbing and unsettling; it contains a greater element of despair than of comfort. Is it possible or desirable to dwell in such horror, in such a night, without answers? Does sacrifice for nothing leave us with anything other than the hopelessness of the desert? This dramatic concept seems to be drawing closer to postmodern attempts to use kenosis—emptying God—as a grounding principle for purifying Christianity of all traces of transcendence, of the religious-cultic, of doctrine, and so on.[100] In this sense, kenosis would function as a metaphor for a weak God, the God of human experience, and for a future form of the religion that provides an exit from religion. Such a Christianity would be *nothing* more than the immanent community of pure love, whatever that may mean, with no hierarchical, doctrinal element. The kenotic sacrifice for nothing then appears as a powerful concept that affects Christianity by radically reconstituting its self-understanding. In other words, kenosis and the nothing seem to be new metaphysical principles that ground the claim that postmodern Christianity is longing for the impossible. However, such a Christianity can turn out to be a Christianity without content, that is, a Christianity of nothing. By contrast, Marion's attempt to recover Christianity is rather modest and more convincing. Drawing on the notion of sacrifice, which has a revelatory meaning and thus bears witness to being given, Marion reconsiders Christianity as a testimony to the phenomenology of givenness and, from a theological perspective, the manifestation of the divine self-giving.

Nevertheless, both Marion's suggestion and the risks of the nothing conceive sacrifice as a principle that affects Christianity externally. But, in fact, Patočka aims to point out that kenotic sacrifice for nothing pertains, like the truth of Christianity, to the internal on both the personal and the interpersonal level. Apart from the revelatory aspect of sacrifice with regard to the ontological difference, which Patočka does not diminish, sacrifice is first and foremost a challenge to the individual understanding of human being, rather than an argument for a revolution within the system or a representation of Christianity according to a particular phenomenological order. In other words, sacrifice for nothing manifests the conflict within being (within each of us). This conflict also, however, has the potential to transform community and thus reconstitute Christianity after (the end of) Christianity. What does this mean?

It appears from Patočka's reflections that sacrifice is something more than an individual act—that the confrontation with the nothing has an important *interpersonal* effect. Put another way, sacrifice is a performative deed that involves the one who sacrifices, surrenders everything, but also those who witness the event of sacrifice or hear the testimony about it later. Whereas sacrificial actors break with the terms of exchange, giving themselves for nothing, that is, outside the order of *do ut des*, witnesses are withdrawn from the everydayness of ordinary life because they do not see sacrifice—and the death involved—merely as the deed of some third party. Their experience is that the engagement with no-thing concerns them too. As Patočka puts it, authentic sacrifice for nothing causes them to be fundamentally shaken; any sense of a blind faith that things ought to be this way or that way is interrupted. Instead of subscribing to a presupposed meaning, an openness to a new understanding of everything that "is" breaks through.

Patočka does not leave us, therefore, with a sense of hopeless despair at the meaninglessness of history. Rather he seems to suggest a radical—spiritual—way of being-in-the-world. He calls for courage to live and to strive for meaning while risking everything for that which is greater than any kind of thing, that is, for *nothing*. The material effect of this radical spirituality, of this positive content beyond possession, is the community of those who have experienced the meaning of being shaken. Sacrifice creates the possibility of realizing *the solidarity of the shaken*. And, as Patočka remarks, "the solidarity of the shaken is the solidarity of those who understand" the conflict between the slavery of finiteness and the freedom of transcendence. That is, the freedom of transcending the world not for something but rather for no-thing.[101] Applied theologically, the negativity of sacrifice can give rise to something positive in the sense that it can be seen as a challenge for the reconsideration of (Christian) community. Thus, what we describe as Christianity after Christianity appears as the community that guards being from its reduction to some*thing*. It is the space of sharing the question of God in relation to human being-in-the-world. Patočka challenges theology to apply itself not to seeking knowledge of God but to thinking about the God whose sacrifice challenged us to engage with a problematic, shaken meaning (*sinnerschütterte*) of the world. This radical historicization of theological thinking does not necessarily cross out transcendence, but it manifests God's sacrifice as nothing—not a thing—to be dragged down to earth and portrayed accurately; it is nothing that can be seen but rather everything we are called to witness in our Christian being-in-the-world.

Conclusion

Thinking Transcendence, Living Transcendence

Having said so much about the open-ended nature of theological thinking, the idea of presenting anything like a "conclusion" seems ambitious, dubious, implausible even. Perhaps we could begin with an indisputable fact. The life of Jan Patočka came to an end on March 13, 1977. After being interrogated at length by the StB—the Communist secret police—Patočka's health deteriorated. He was taken to hospital but died the following week of a brain hemorrhage. Because of his public activities in the human rights movement Charter 77, Patočka was considered an enemy of the state. His utter commitment to endless questioning, to challenging presupposed meanings, and to searching for truth was deemed to pose an unacceptable threat to the corrupt Czechoslovak Communist regime. I have devoted little space to a description of the sociopolitical context of Patočka's thought, preferring rather to explore the content of his philosophy and raise the question of its relevance for theological thinking. So why mention his death now? The answer may sound somewhat provocative: as the Socrates of the twentieth century, Patočka had to die for his truth.[1] More radically, for many, Patočka was a martyr who sacrificed himself.[2] I held back this narrative because I wanted to present Patočka as a thinker, not as a hero. I mention the events of 1977 now because I am convinced that in Patočka's case, death represents not the final word but the opening of a new perspective on his work and helps us to understand him as a genuine seeker of the truth of being. His death—his sacrifice—does not put an end to Patočka. Rather, it offers a call to thinking with him.

We have shown that Patočka cannot be recuperated as a theologian, nor, despite his interest in religion, as a philosopher of religion. Patočka is a phenomenologist, a thinker of being-in-the-world, who questions the meaning of history and of human existence. Many of his philosophical intuitions are nonetheless open to theological readings and can even stimulate theological reasoning itself. I would suggest that the challenge Patočka provides, together with Jean-Yves Lacoste, is the task of shifting from theology to theological thinking.

My intention has been to demonstrate that Patočka's phenomenological thinking offers a source of inspiration for theological thinking. The reconsideration of Christianity, a constantly recurring theme in Patočka, provokes us to think differently about crucial issues such as the relationship between philosophy and theology, the union between faith and metaphysics, and the meaning of sacrifice. Moreover, Patočka's interpretation of Christianity provides us with an alternative but complementary perspective on the theological turn in contemporary continental philosophy. It would be inappropriate to include Patočka among the authors of the theological turn. He died in 1977 and thus before the emergence of the main discussions concerning philosophical recuperations of theological issues. True, Patočka's contemporaries, such as Jacques Derrida and Emmanuel Levinas, did the preparatory work for the later theological turn, and Martin Heidegger, whom Patočka followed in many respects, is deemed responsible for the whole movement. But I situate the breaking point that blurred the boundary between philosophical questioning and theological thinking to the 1980s, that is, after the publication of Marion's *God without Being*. Patočka therefore precedes the theological turn. This nonetheless makes an engagement with Patočka's work, which in many ways is more than sensitive to theological themes, even more important and certainly no less interesting. Patočka's reluctance to cross the border between philosophy and theology, and his repeated insistence that he was, and always remained, a phenomenologist, should be attributed to the times, the context, of Patočka's work as a philosopher. In other words, although he does not explicitly invite theological explorations, Patočka's reconsideration of the Christian tradition is as relevant to theological discussion as much of the work of current authors such as Marion, Henry, Chrétien, Lacoste, Nancy, Kearney, Caputo, Westphal, and Vattimo.

Patočka shares three fundamental premises with the current proponents of the theological turn. First, Patočka exercised a lifelong interest in the question of the relationship between philosophy and theology. Chapter 1 mapped this rather neglected facet of Patočka's thought and its development and filled something of a lacuna in current scholarship. Second, like

Conclusion 229

many postmodern authors, Patočka's thought, including his reflections on religion, is framed by the crisis of modernity. Elaborating upon Husserl's *Krisis* is a constantly recurring pattern and an ever-present motivation in Patočka (chapter 2). In fact, the failures of modernity and its objective rationalism led Patočka to reconsider religion as an alternative thought pattern and as a means of going beyond modernity and its shortcuts. Like the "new phenomenologists" of the theological turn, Patočka does not intend to reconstitute an institutionalized religion. He does not serve the Church or Christendom. His aim is to reconsider an understanding of our being, and in this respect, Christianity plays an irreplaceable role. Finally, Patočka follows Heidegger and his critique of the ontotheological constitution of metaphysics (chapter 3). The adagio of overcoming metaphysics can be heard in almost all contemporary philosophical reconsiderations of theology. Nevertheless, unlike many authors who yearn for a postmetaphysical or even antimetaphysical theology, Patočka expands on a particular form of metaphysical thinking that is not about overcoming the finite but about transcending it (chapter 4).

Patočka's thought bears witness to the idea that finitude is not the final word. Even his death is not an end but a point of transcendence, a sign that there is something more, something above us, something that may be called "divine" and that challenges us to open ourselves and to surrender everything.[3] At the same time, as we have repeatedly emphasized in these pages, this "divine" is nothing objective. It cannot be mastered, penetrated, and grasped conceptually. The "divine" is no-thing; it is the un-thought; it is the task for thinking (chapters 5, 6, and 7).

It is clear that the question of transcendence is crucial for a theological appropriation of any philosophical reasoning. Although never stated explicitly, this question runs like a golden thread through each chapter. Patočka's conception of both philosophy and theology points beyond finite, positive thinking (chapter 1). For Patočka, the crisis of modernity is caused by the loss of vertical thinking (chapter 2), and the scheme of ontotheological metaphysics is enclosed in too narrow a comprehension of reality as the sum of entities with a clearly localizable ground and aim (chapter 3). In place of this forgetfulness concerning the depth of being, Patočka develops a metaphysical thinking that transcends knowledge and reconsiders the sphere of faith (chapter 4). In Patočka's engagement with Christianity and his attempts to go beyond "myth and enlightenment," and thus in his discovery of the un-thought of Christianity, we hear a clear echo of his search for transcendence (chapter 5). Finally, Patočka's interest in the idea of kenosis and his meditation on sacrifice (chapter 7), later confirmed by his willingness to risk his life in defense of truth, proves that the bottom line of his life's work is nothing less than a transcending of the boundaries of the finite.

Arguably, Patočka's thought can be summarized as a constant revisiting of problematicity in opposition to finiteness and fullness. To use theological vocabulary, Patočka promotes the promise and criticizes the present; the future and its un-thought is yet to come (chapter 5); faith is a basic modality capable of turning our gaze toward the future (chapter 4). It seems legitimate, however, to claim that Patočka leads us to an open eschatology.[4] The question remains whether it is Christianity that inspires Patočka to such claims, or Patočka who inspires Christian theology to recontextualize some of its central doctrines. What does Patočka have to say to theologians, and based on their engagements with Patočka, what can theologians think?

The former question concerns a point of departure whereas the latter points to the horizon before us. In a preparatory draft to the *Heretical Essays*, Patočka writes: "The absence of God is our experience and it is also our theology."[5] Indeed, God is absent from much of this present volume. This is because the context of Patočka's work is God's silence. Or, as he expresses it in his very first publication, "Theology and Philosophy," the philosopher is forbidden to listen to God; the philosopher must obey the appearances in the world. Although Patočka softens his youthful, apologetic enthusiasm for philosophy and becomes gradually more open and explicit concerning his theological interests, he still hesitates to name Jesus Christ as the prime example in his reflections on the idea of kenotic sacrifice (chapter 7). Reticence does not necessarily mean ignorance, however. On the contrary, we are often silent about "things" we revere. As Wittgenstein says: "Wovon man nicht sprechen kann, darüber muß man schweigen" (Whereof one cannot speak, thereof one must be silent). But what cannot be said can perhaps be thought.

The evidence that Patočka thinks a great deal about the One who is difficult to grasp in words is to be found in the preparatory drafts of *Heretical Essays*. Patočka entitled the last of these manuscripts "The Understanding of the Higher, the Holy, and the Divine (*Göttlichen*)."[6] If Patočka's prewar writings are critical of any possibility of locating transcendence outside the human person, the later Patočka understands transcendence as "something" (for want of a better word, as transcendence is not a thing, of course) that is in relationship with the human person. Conversely, for the Patočka of *Heretical Essays*, the idea that human being relates to "something" higher, holy, and the divine is acceptable.[7] However, for Patočka, God cannot be situated in otherworldliness. God reveals himself, dies, and is resurrected: "This God must live *with us* in this world."[8] This sounds like pure immanentism; the closure of genuine transcendence. So where is the proclaimed openness?

I argue that openness is to be found securely in Patočka's statement that "God must live with us in this world." Why must God live in our world? The answer, another paradox, is that God is not the ultimate answer. God is not the solution to all questions. God *is* the question. And questioning, as we have seen throughout, is a serious matter. For Patočka, questioning transcends the passive resignation that says very little but shores up its "argument" simply by invoking the magic word, *mystery*. Questioning takes the mystery (of God) seriously and engages with its problematicity: "Contemporary theology needs the world without meaning or, at least, with a problematic, shaken meaning (*sinnerschütterte*). Its God can reveal himself only as a paradoxical-turning solution, as the one who gives courage to live and serve in such a [problematic] world."[9] How should we interpret these enigmatic words, which perhaps represent the only explicit and straightforward advice Patočka offers to theologians? What is Patočka trying to say? Where is he leading us? In my view, the key lies in the words with which we opened this book: faith is thinking. Theology is called to be a way of understanding. It is not called to be scientific knowledge. Understanding the world as problematic and essentially unsolved opens the space for understanding God as the un-thought. Because if God is conceived as the final thought, the solution, and the highest object—which is the way of positive, modern metaphysics—then God has forsaken us.

Patočka does not want to conclude in this manner. The Christian God—the only true God—is both close to and distant from human beings: "God is with us in history."[10] Patočka aligns himself with Meister Eckhart and those mystics whose works, in his opinion, represent variations on this simple yet challenging truth: God and man are interrelated and cannot be divided; one is meaningless without the other.

This is the voice of Patočka, the voice I have sought to hear and to understand in the course of this exploration, the voice I find both an inspiration and a motivation for my own—theological—thinking. The question is, how are we to think about Patočka's attempt to, as Filip Karfík once put it, humanize transcendence?[11]

Reflecting on the essence of transcendence, our first thoughts lead in the direction of something/someone above us. In this respect, Patočka's words about the higher, the holy, and the divine make sense. However, if transcendence is to be meaningful and understandable, it cannot be absolute. Transcendence outside ourselves transcends nothing because such transcendence would lack the relational dimension.[12] In other words, transcendence is *per definitionem* relational, and Patočka's thoughts can be read as emphasizing this point. It is also the meaning of Patočka's provocative suggestion that "man stands in a closer and more intimate relation to God than is either safe or pleasant."[13] This statement can also, however, be interpreted as a critique of certain kinds of religion. It is intended to contradict: (1) myth, in which the divine powers are totally distant and have absolute control over human beings; (2) metaphysical conceptions of the divine as the grounding principle and highest object; (3) Enlightenment deism, which regards the divine as an impersonal power, a precise "watchmaker" who backs up our calculations. Such a criticism is already a useful lesson for theology, but Patočka's provocative statement can also be taken as a challenge. To situate transcendence within ourselves does not necessarily have to be a sign of immanentism; it could describe a way in which it is possible to think about the incarnation of transcendence—although as a phenomenologist, Patočka would probably use the term embodiment.

As this work has shown in several places, movement is a crucial notion for Patočka and the best description of human existence. In fact, existence is a movement. This point of view should be taken not as a fact but as a task assigned to every human being. According to the theory of the three movements of existence—the movements of anchoring, of defense, and of transcendence—only the third represents the full realization of the meaning of being-in-the-world. It is important to note that "the full realization of meaning" does not refer to an epistemological operation that would provide us with total knowledge concerning human existence. On the contrary, the realization Patočka has in mind concerns the understanding of life as a movement, as an existence on the way, and thus as a continual struggle (*polemos*) of questioning and problematicity. But let us return to the question concerning the incarnation of transcendence.

In light of Patočka's reflections on the movement of human existence, I argue that the incarnation of transcendence can be reconsidered along the following lines. Incarnation is traditionally viewed as presence. God became human and lived among us. The Word (*logos*) became flesh, and we have beheld the fullness of glory and truth (Jn 1:14). In this sense, the fact of the incarnation signifies a full presence of meaning. The meaning of transcendence is accessible; everyone can discover it. It is only a matter of the right approach, the matter of seeing the truth. The meaning of human being—its essence and its aim—is communicated in clear signs. One is called to adopt it and imitate the model that has been given. Nevertheless, the idea of movement offers an alternative perspective. Rather than emphasizing presence, the incarnation of transcendence in this world should be taken as a promise of the future. It is perhaps more fruitful to think about the incarnation not as a fact that happened and thus once and for all time determined everything meaningful, but as an ongoing movement and a task to be embodied in our finite existence. In other words, the incarnation is not only a particular moment in the past, but also the movement of transcendence that opens the possibility of understanding human existence as being (which differs significantly from the being of entities). To use the language of a previous chapter, the incarnation includes something un-thought. And since the un-thought is nothing that can be ultimately thought through, but remains unthought, the incarnation would thus not point to the ultimate truth that has become present but rather to the distance from a full, "clear and distinct" signification of meaning. A theology inspired by Patočka does not therefore seek absolute meaning in transcendence but searches for meaning—the meaningful life of the human being—through engagement with transcendence.

Human existence understood as movement can be transposed as the experience of transcendence within us. This movement entails going beyond mere objectivity, beyond seeing our being as an entity among other entities. On this basis, Patočka's fascination with sacrifice makes perfect sense. Self-surrender is not a loss but a gain. This gain, however, is not a measurable profit. There is no place here for the economy of exchange. To understand what is at stake, we need to hear Patočka:

> The movement of self-gaining through self-surrender and self-giving away becomes a relationship to the world as a whole. This relationship does not tear the veil of mystery from the world, as strict objectification seeks to do. On the contrary, this movement maintains the mystery; confides in the mystery; and brightens and deepens itself, without losing or diffusing itself, through self-givenness to the mystery. For in this movement, a man becomes a part and a participant of this last mystery;

the mystery of the world as a whole, the mystery of the spirit, of Earth and Heaven and their mysterious encounter.[14]

If Patočka had not warned us that his words had nothing to do with mysticism, it would be easy to think a mystic had just spoken. But Patočka is not a mystic. He is a philosopher. His philosophy nonetheless has something to teach theology. The emphasis on a mystery that is within us and also somehow above our heads leads to a perspective that does not contradict what theology calls God. In fact, we can read Patočka's words as a reminder that we are capable of God (*capax Dei*) but are able to find him only within ourselves. In other words, Patočka's tireless concern with reductionist objectification tells us that transcendence is not an object outside ourselves. Human beings already partake in the movement of transcendence, although it is impossible to understand this movement fully. It even seems that a theology inspired by Patočka must hold that the nature of transcendence will never become completely clear. Once again, the un-thought remains. In this sense, such a theology should develop a negative eschatology, that is, should replace the traditional doctrine of beatific vision (gazing at a static image of a deity) with an insightful seeing without end. From the perspective of negative eschatology, and in line with the concept of negative Platonism (chapter 4), to see means to understand distance as the iconic expression of transcendence. This is where the invocation of Meister Eckhart—the one who in Patočka's opinion has an authentic understanding of the divine—seems to fit our narrative.

When Eckhart and mystics enter the frame, the theologian must exercise caution as heresy may be floating in the air. It is now no surprise to us that Patočka entitled his most famous work, his philosophical testament, *Heretical Essays*. Indeed, Patočka commits a number of heresies. First, he breaks with Husserlian orthodox phenomenology. Although he shares the point of departure, namely, the crisis of modernity and its rationality, for Patočka, phenomenology does not mean the search for the absolute meaning of transcendental subjectivity. Rather, phenomenology is thinking transcendence from within the world.[15] Second, Patočka is heretical with regard to his Heideggerian inspiration. We have seen that Patočka does not hesitate to revisit certain patterns of ancient Greek philosophy (Platonism, for example), something that Heidegger deemed undesirable. More importantly, Patočka pulls Heidegger's thought back into Christianity. Instead of passively waiting for redemption from the world of art, Patočka explores the possibilities of an active relationship to transcendence-in-the-world. Third, Patočka goes beyond classical phenomenology, which concerns phenomena, to develop an existential phenomenology that concerns both the truth of individual being and "something divine," that is, something that rules over everything but is not a thing. This does admittedly sound metaphysical. The last and most interesting heresy in Patočka is perhaps that regarding Christianity. Although this work has argued for the possibility of reading Patočka's thought as an inspiration for *Christian thinking*, Patočka remains a phenomenologist insofar as he does not accept "any orders from God," meaning he refuses to ground his reasoning in revelation. But is this really an unbridgeable gap? Theology cannot but accept transcendent revelation that is not from this world. Nonetheless, theology can only receive this revelation in the situation of being-in-the-world. What is revealed appears as a phenomenon, and understanding revelation is the interpretation of such phenomena. So, when we suggest that Patočka's thought to a certain extent understands Christianity as *philosophia vera*, we should not appropriate this insight across the theological board but rather consider it as a piece of advice and as an inspiration for a particular theological domain, namely, fundamental theology.

I understand fundamental theology as a conversation between three partners: academia, the Church, and the world.[16] The task of a fundamental theologian is to think reasonably about transcendence in all three fields. In academia, fundamental theology explores, together with philosophers and other scientists, the possibilities of thinking transcendence. In the Church, the main task is to challenge ready-made answers concerning transcendence and to problematize the discourse in order to promote thinking about the meaning of transcendence, instead of repeating learned statements without exploring their meaning. Finally, fundamental theology challenges the world in its simplistic overlooking of an overseeing transcendence. Understood in traditional terms, fundamental theology was an apologetic. In our time, its mission is perhaps to promote reasonable and understandable thinking—which is fundamentally different from offering evidence for faith in God—regarding the possibility of transcending everydayness, objectivity, and a modern rationalism that is based on efficacy. In short, I argue that fundamental theology can draw inspiration from Patočka and understand itself as Christian thinking that arises from academic discourse, is based in the world, and is for the good of the Church.

Despite such an impressive list of heresies in Patočka's thought, we must go on to answer the question concerning the status of a proposed theological appropriation of this Czech phenomenologist. The problem with heresies is not that they are completely wrong, but that they are one-sided. For example, the heresy of modalism emphasizes a single Godhead and is thus blind to the Trinitarian nature of God; modalism proposes three modes of one God, instead of three persons, while firmly confessing monotheism. Applying this discussion about heresies to our overall investigation, Christianity certainly appears to contain the aspect Patočka emphasizes—and can further elaborate on these points—but these philosophical-theological views must be complemented by the theological-doctrinal perspective. I have already highlighted, for example, the reconsideration of the doctrine of the last things in terms of an open and negative eschatology, and the incarnation as the continuous embodiment of transcendence. In other words, if our exploration has opened certain possibilities for fundamental theology, it should also be taken as an invitation to dogmatic theology to contribute to theology's present-day, postmodern context.

Drawing inspiration from Patočka, I argue that Christianity after Christianity—that is, a Christianity in search of its own revival after the end of traditional Christendom, as announced by modernity, and after the collapse of metaphysics in postmodernity—is both contextually plausible and theologically valid. Recent scholarship seems to confirm this theological intuition. Let us remind ourselves of some examples. Filip Karfík concludes his study *Unendlichwerden durch die Endlichkeit* by stating that that traditional Christian motifs lie behind Patočka's reflections on transcendence.[17] By the same token, Eddo Evink argues that the teaching concerning the three movements of existence, in which the notion of transcendence plays a crucial role, draws inspiration from the Christian heritage.[18] Nicolas de Warren claims that the golden thread of Patočka's thought is his reconsideration of eternity: that the experience of finitude is not the final word and that human beings are able to transcend it.[19] Ludger Hagedorn suggests that Patočka holds Christianity to be the driving force behind transcending finite perspectives. Christianity is called, moreover, to continually transcend itself by its attentiveness to the un-thought.[20] Each of these philosophical interpretations invites a theological reading of Patočka's work. The idea of Christianity after Christianity is indebted to these authors as well as to other interpreters who confirm the intuition that Patočka's fascination with Christianity can be read in the context of the theological turn and thus as a source of inspiration for theology.

We have seen that Patočka's thought leads to a reconsideration of the boundary between philosophy and theology; that it presents an alternative perspective on the overcoming of ontotheology without completely discarding metaphysical thinking. In fact, on the basis of Patočka's thought, we have understood faith as a particular version of metaphysical thinking. The notion of Christianity after Christianity can be explained using the three categories we thought through in chapters 5, 6, and 7: the unthought, responsibility, and sacrifice. This reasoning begins with Patočka, but rather than aspiring to present Patočka's position alone, we have explored the possibility of using his thought to inspire a revival of the Christian theological tradition.

What, then, do these reflections on Christianity after Christianity suggest? The basis of my argument is that Christianity *shakes* presuppositions concerning the meaning of life and of God. Although (religious) life may be somewhat easier with a known God above our heads and solid ground beneath our feet—and certain brands of Christianity indeed propose this—Patočka provokes us into thinking about a single important idea: what if Christianity's main task, its vocation, is to transcend Christianity? What if the main message of two thousand years of tradition is to go beyond itself and to become open—again and again—to that which is yet to come?

The perspective of Christianity after Christianity cannot be absolutized, however, or it would simply create another idol out of never-ending seeking. And for what? For better questions? If that were the case, how would this differ from the negative theologies of postmodernism? Where would be the alternative I promised at the outset?

It is not possible to live without any certainties whatsoever. But how are we to reconcile an emphasis on shaken meaning and life in problematicity—to which Christianity, according to our interpretation, bears witness—with something positive that we need to rely on in our lives? How can we live without firm ground beneath us and not fall prey to absolute negativity, skepticism, and nihilism?[21] These are all serious questions that must be critically admitted and addressed to Patočka. The final point of this "conclusion" is therefore dedicated to the problem of dealing with the (perhaps) overly negative transcendence that seems to be the result of a theological engagement with Patočka.

The lesson we learn from Patočka is not a little shocking: it is not that the time of upheaval (modernity, postmodernity) shakes the meaning of things, but that shaking meaning is the kernel of Christianity (after Christianity) itself. We could call it the death of God, the dissolution of metaphysics, or the loss of faith, but despite these dark elements of

Patočka's reflections, we have seen that his thought opens the possibility that Christianity is the hallmark of responsible living and even represents an authentic call to sacrifice. It is as if our journey through negativity has guided us toward something positive. I argue, therefore, that a theological appropriation of Patočka's philosophical thought is more than a useful theoretical exercise or an inspiration for theological method—*thinking*. In what Patočka calls the solidarity of the shaken, we find the possibility of a concrete historical incarnation of *living* Christianity after Christianity.

Christianity after Christianity offers an insight into the problematicity of being-in-the-world. It calls us to live in *un-anchoredness*. But the main point is not problematicity or shaken meaning, but an invitation to those who are shaken—Patočka calls them spiritual persons—to share this experience with one another. The emphasis is not on the shakenness, but on the solidarity. And solidarity creates community. In other words, the Christianity drawn from a fundamental theological engagement with Patočka is not meant for intellectuals living high up in their ivory towers. Wise philosophers can certainly be among the shaken Christians, but their knowledge is not above the wisdom of others. The community of the shaken comprises those who are committed to struggling against decadence—to showing that human life is more than an object among other entities, to transcending finitude—and to fighting for (*polemos*) a meaning in history that is neither absolute nor relative. The community of spiritual persons searches for what is right in a particular situation and acts accordingly, even if it means surrendering everything. In this sense, the sought-for meaning is both absolute and problematic.

Patočka sometimes pleaded the need for a third conversion—the first being from myths to philosophy, the second from philosophy to Christianity.[22] I propose that Christianity after Christianity is this third conversion. Although it represents a shaken life, there is hope for the future and there is faith in the meaningfulness of living.

We began with the suggestion that faith must be not only lived but thought. We now see that after much thinking, we have come back to the issue of living. The call to thinking transcendence and living transcendence-in-this-world is perhaps the most appropriate conclusion for something that cannot be summed up in a single word, because thinking and living in this respect may include nobody less than God.

Notes

Introduction

1. "Pojem evidence a jeho význam pro noetiku." The manuscript of the thesis remained unpublished during Patočka's lifetime but is included in his collected writings, *Sebranné spisy Jana Patočky*. SS 6, 13–125.

2. Jan Patočka, *The Natural World as a Philosophical Problem*, trans. E. Abrams (Evanston: Northwestern University Press, 2016); hereafter abbreviated to NW.

3. Jan Patočka, *Andere Wege in die Moderne: Studien zur europäischen Ideengeschichte von der Renaissance bis zur Romantik*, ed. L. Hagedorn (Würzburg: Königshausen & Neumann, 2006). It is worth noting that some of the chapters included in *Andere Wege* were published as separate studies and articles during Patočka's lifetime.

4. This set of texts is included in SS 1, 139–336 and 443–488. In chapter 4, I will explore the essay "Negative Platonism: Reflections Concerning the Rise, the Scope, and the Demise of Metaphysics."

5. Jan Patočka, *Europa und Nach-Europa: Zur Phänomenologie einer Idee*, ed. L. Hagedorn and K. Nellen (Freiburg: Verlag Karl Alber, 2017); *Heretical Essays in the Philosophy of History*, trans. E. Kohák (La Salle: Open Court, 1996); hereafter abbreviated to HE.

6. Petr Rezek, "Třetí životní pohyb u Jana Patočky jako problém intersubjektivity," *Filosofická reflexe* 4 (1990): 5.1–5.13; here 5.1. If not stated otherwise, all translations throughout the book are mine.

7. Interestingly, the only two English monographs on Patočka focus precisely on the care for the soul. Edward F. Findlay, *Caring for the Soul in a Postmodern Age: Politics and Phenomenology in the Thought of Jan Patočka* (Albany: State University of New York Press, 2002); Martin Cajthaml, *Europe and the Care for the Soul: Jan Patočka's Conception of the Spiritual Foundations of Europe* (Nordhausen: Traugott Bautz, 2014).

8. See, for example, Renaud Barbaras, *L'ouverture du monde: Lecture de Jan Patočka* (Chatou: Éditions de la Transparence, 2011).

9. A comprehensive exposition of Patočka's potential for political philosophy is Francesco Tava and Darian Meacham, eds., *Thinking after Europe: Jan Patočka and Politics* (London: Rowman & Littlefield, 2016).

10. Erazim Kohák, "Jak číst Patočku: Bibliografický úvod," *Proměny* 24 (1987): 24–33.

11. Edmund Husserl, *The Crisis of European Sciences and Transcendental Phenomenology: An Introduction to Phenomenological Philosophy*, trans. E. Carr (Evanston, IL: Northwestern University Press, 1970).

12. Paul Ricoeur, "Jan Patočka: De la philosophie du monde naturel à la philosophie de l'histoire," *Studia Phaenomenologica* 7 (2007): 193–200.

13. Jan Patočka, "Phénomenologie et ontologie du movement," in *Papier phénoménologique*, trans. E. Abrams (Grenoble: J. Millon, 1995), 31.

14. "Le mouvement en tant qu'actualisation en route n'est pas plus subjectif qu'objectif. L'être en mouvement se passe." Ricoeur, "Jan Patočka: De la philosophie du monde naturel," 198.

15. See, for example, Václav Havel, "Politics and Consciousness," trans. E. Kohák and R. Scruton, *Salisbury Review* 2 (1985): 31–38. Havel's famous essay "The Power of the Powerless" is arguably inspired by Patočka's idea of "the shaken." See Václav Havel et al., *The Power of the Powerless: Citizens against the State*, ed. J. Kane (London: Routledge, 2009), 23–94.

16. Ivan Chvatík, "The Responsibility of the 'Shaken': Jan Patočka and His 'Care for the Soul' in the 'Post-European' World," in *Jan Patočka and the Heritage of Phenomenology: Centenary Papers*, ed. A. Abrams and I. Chvatík (Dordrecht: Springer, 2011), 263–279; here 275.

17. In this work, I refer to the English edition: Jean-Luc Marion, *God without Being: Hors-Text*, trans. T. Carlson (Chicago: University of Chicago Press, 1991).

18. Jack Reynolds, "The Implicit and Presupposed Theological Turn in Phenomenology," *Sophia* 47 (2008): 261–263.

19. Ludger Hagedorn, "Religion and the Crisis of Modernity," *IWM Post* (Winter 2014/15): 20.

20. Patočka contributed to the German translation of the novel *Boží duha* (God's rainbow) by the Czech Catholic author Jaroslav Durych: *Gottes Regenbogen*, trans. J. Patočka and F. Boldt (Bremen: Verlag K-Presse, 1975).

21. Both interpretations are possible and will be discussed later.

22. HE, 108.

23. Chvatík, "The Responsibility of the 'Shaken,'" 266.

24. *Essai hérétique sur la philosophie de l'historie*, trans. E. Abrams (Lagrasse: Verdier, 1988); *Ketzerische Essais zur Philosophie der Geschichte*, trans. J. Bruss and P. Sacher (Stuttgart: Klett-Cotta, 1988).

25. Ivan Chvatík, "Jan Patočka," in *A Companion to the Philosophy of History and Historiography*, ed. A. Tucker (Malden: Blackwell, 2009), 518–528.

26. Hereafter, I will modify Kohák's translation accordingly. All translations of Patočka from Czech to English are therefore my own unless indicated otherwise.

27. For the Czech edition of *Heretical Essays*, I use Jan Patočka, *Kacířské eseje o filosofii dějin* (Praha: Oikoymenh, 2007); here 95.

28. Jindřich Veselý, "Jan Patočka a křesťanství," *Studia Philosophica* 60 (2013): 63–84.

29. Ibid., 73–76.

30. Jan Patočka, "Le christianisme et le monde naturel," trans. E. Abrams, *Istina* 38 (1993): 16–22.

31. Jan Patočka, "Some Comments Concerning the Extramundane and Mundane Position of Philosophy," in *Living in Problematicity*, ed. Eric Manton (Praha: Oikoymenh, 2007), 26.

32. See, for example, Zuzana Svobodová, "Česká tradice křesťanské víry v Patočkově reflexi," in *Jan Patočka, české dějiny a Evropa* (Semily: Státní okresní archiv Semily, 2007), 59–68.

33. Jean-Yves Lacoste, *From Theology to Theological Thinking* (Charlottesville: University of Virginia Press, 2014).

34. I will come later to the interpretations of Patočka proposed by these authors. It will suffice here to mention a few important essays from Ludger Hagedorn and James Dodd, eds., *The New Yearbook for Phenomenology and Phenomenological Philosophy XIV. Religion, War and the Crisis of Modernity: A Special Issue Dedicated to the Philosophy of Jan Patočka* (London: Routledge, 2015): Ludger Hagedorn, "Christianity Unthought: A Reconsideration of Myth, Faith, and Historicity," 31–46; Eddo Evink, "The Gift of Life: Jan Patočka and the Christian Heritage," 47–63; Nicolas de Warren, "The Gift of Eternity," 161–180.

35. I discuss the problem of the lack of actual themes in Czech theology in "Ein unbekannter Gott: Herausforderungen für die Systematische Theologie in einer postchristlichen und posttotalitären Gesellschaft," in *Diaspora als Ort der Theologie: Perspektiven aus Tschechien und Ostdeutschland*, ed. B. Kranemann and P. Štica (Würzburg: Echter Verlag, 2016), 169–187.

36. A critical appraisal of attempts to see Patočka as a Christian thinker is presented, for example, by Ivan Chvatík, "Jan Patočka: Christian or Platonist?" (Unpublished manuscript of a conference paper presented at the conference The Reasons of Europe, Rome, December 2013).

37. An introduction to this recent theological endeavor is provided by Lieven Boeve and Christophe Brabant, eds., *Between Philosophy and Theology: Contemporary Interpretations of Christianity* (Farnham: Ashgate, 2010).

38. See, for example, the collection of essays in Ilse N. Bulhof and Laurens ten Kate, eds., *Flight of the Gods: Philosophical Perspectives on Negative Theology* (New York: Fordham University Press, 2000).

39. I will deal with Janicaud's critique of the theological turn in the context of Patočka's thought in chapter 1.

Chapter 1

1. Edmund Husserl, *Ideen zu einer reinen Phänomenologie und phänomenologischen Philosophie* (The Hague: Martinus Nijhoff, 1976), 124–125.
2. Martin Heidegger, "Nur noch ein Gott kann uns retten," *Der Spiegel* 30 (May 1976): 193–219.
3. László Tengelyi, "On the Border of Phenomenology and Theology," in *Phenomenology and Religion: New Frontiers*, ed. J. Bornemark and H. Ruin (Stockholm: Södertörn University Publishers, 2010), 21.
4. Dominique Janicaud, *La phénomneologie éclatée* (Paris: Éditions de l'Eclat, 1998), 43.
5. Jan Patočka, "Theologie a filosofie," in SS 1, 15–21; here 19.
6. "Phenomenology is a mode of philosophizing that does not take ready-made theses for its premises but rather keeps all premises at arm's length. . . . Phenomenology examines the experiential content of such theses; in every abstract thought it seeks to uncover what is hidden in it, how we arrive at it, and what seen and lived reality underlines it. We are uncovering something that has been here all along, something we had sensed, glimpsed out of the corner of our eye, but did not fully know, something that 'had not been brought to conception.' Phenomenon—that which presents itself; *logos*—meaningful discourse." Jan Patočka, *Body, Community, Language, World*, trans. E. Kohák (Chicago: Open Court, 1998), 3.
7. Jeffrey Bloechl, "Eschatology, Liturgy, and the Task of Thinking," in Lacoste, *From Theology to Theological Thinking*, vi–xxviii; here vii.
8. See, for example, Jan Patočka, "Some Comments Concerning the Extramundane and Mundane Position of Philosophy," 18–28; "O dvojím pojetí smyslu filosofie," in SS 1, 68–84.
9. SS 1, 15–21.
10. SS 1, 17.
11. SS 1, 18.
12. SS 1, 18.
13. SS 1, 19.
14. Martin Heidegger, "Phenomenology and Theology," in *Pathmarks*, ed. W. McNeill (Cambridge: Cambridge University Press, 1998), 39–62. Interestingly, both lectures were presented in Protestant theological faculties.
15. Ibid., 41.
16. Ibid.
17. Ibid., 45.
18. Ibid., 50.
19. Ibid., 48–49.
20. Ibid., 53.

21. Ibid.
22. Ibid., 52.
23. Matheson Russell, "Phenomenology and Theology: Situating Heidegger's Philosophy of Religion," *Sophia* 50 (2011): 641–655.
24. Ibid., 642–643.
25. Martin Heidegger, "The Onto-theo-logical Structure of Metaphysics," in *Identity and Difference*, trans. J. Stambaugh (New York: Harper & Row, 1969), 42–74.
26. Russell, "Phenomenology and Theology," 652.
27. Heidegger, "Phenomenology and Theology," 46.
28. Judith Wolfe, *Heidegger and Theology* (London: Bloomsbury, 2014), 61ff.
29. Benjamin Crowe, *Heidegger's Religious Origins: Destruction and Authenticity* (Bloomington: Indiana University Press, 2006), 37–43.
30. Martin Heidegger, *Unterwegs zur Sprache* (Pfüllingen: Gunther Neske, 1959), 96; translation taken from Crowe, *Heidegger's Religious Origins*, 15.
31. The historical background concerning the (non)publication of Heidegger's essay can be found in Adrian Peperzak, "A Re-reading of Heidegger's 'Phenomenology and Theology,' " in *The Multidimensionality of Hermeneutic Phenomenology*, ed. B. Babich and D. Ginev (Heidelberg: Springer, 2014), 317–338; here 317–318.
32. I refer to the English edition: Dominique Janicaud, "The Theological Turn of French Phenomenology," trans. B. G. Prusak, in *Phenomenology and the "Theological Turn": The French Debate* (New York: Fordham University Press, 2000), 16–104.
33. Ibid., 26.
34. Ibid., 22.
35. Ibid., 24–25.
36. Ibid., 27.
37. "The evocation of Heidegger's enigmatic path might seem to lead us away from the question of the theological turn. But, on the contrary, it places us at the crux of the matter where everything is decided: at the point of rupture between a positive phenomenological project and the displacement of its 'possibility' toward the originary." Ibid., 30–31.
38. Ibid., 52–53.
39. Ibid., 55.
40. Ibid., 55–56. Interestingly, Patočka would agree with this statement about Husserl's relationship to metaphysics. He evaluates this inclination rather critically, however: "The so-called phenomenological metaphysics which Husserl puts forth as the result and the basis of his analytic description of the 'natural' world is in the end disappointing." Jan Patočka, "Edmund Husserl's Philosophy of the Crisis of Science and His Conception of a Phenomenology of the 'Life-World,' " in PSW, 223–238; here 233.
41. Janicaud, "The Theological Turn," 86.

42. Edmund Husserl, "Philosophie als strenge Wissenschaft," in *Aufsätze und Vorträge* (1911–1921), ed. H.-R. Sepp and T. Nenn (Dordrecht: Kluwer, 1986), 3–62.

43. "The polemical part of this little book is not at all directed against the theological as such." Janicaud, "The Theological Turn," 34.

44. Ibid., 100.

45. Ibid., 103.

46. SS 1, 20.

47. John Caputo, *Philosophy and Theology* (Nashville: Abingdon Press, 2006), 33.

48. Jean-Yves Lacoste, "Philosophy," in *Encyclopedia of Christian Theology*, vol. 3, ed. J.-Y. Lacoste (New York: Routledge, 2005), 1234–1242.

49. Patočka, "Some Comments Concerning the Extramundane and Mundane Position of Philosophy," 22.

50. Ibid., 22.

51. Ibid., 23.

52. Jan Patočka, "Kapitoly ze současné filosofie," in SS 1, 85–100; here 87.

53. SS 1, 96.

54. SS 1, 90.

55. SS 1, 88.

56. Friedrich Nietzsche, *On the Genealogy of Morals* (New York: Vintage Books, 1967), 119.

57. Friedrich Nietzsche, *The Will to Power* (New York: Random House, 1968), 905.

58. SS 1, 93–94.

59. SS 1, 92.

60. Jan Patočka, "K dopisu Timotheovu," in SS 1, 126–130.

61. SS 1, 128.

62. Josef Lukl Hromádka (1889–1969), one of only a handful of Czech scholars to be recognized internationally, was a pupil of Karl Barth and the most prominent Protestant theologian of his time.

63. Jan Patočka, "J. L. Hromádka a filosofie," in SS 12, 127–135; here 130.

64. SS 12, 129.

65. SS 12, 131.

66. SS 12, 134.

67. Rocco Gangle and Jason Smick, "Political Phenomenology: Radical Democracy and Truth," *Political Theology* 10 (2009): 342–363.

68. Ibid., 346.

69. Ibid., 353.

70. Ibid., 355.

71. Ibid., 357.

72. HE, 98–100.

73. Gangle and Smick, "Political Phenomenology," 356.

74. Gangle and Smick see this as Patočka's reinterpretation of the phenomenological epoché. Ibid., 358.

75. Jan Patočka, "Význam pojmu pravdy pro Rádlovu diskusi s pozitivismem," SS 12, 34–51; here 39.

76. See, for example, Petr Rezek, *Jan Patočka a věc fenomenologie* (Praha: Oikoymenh, 1993), 62.

77. See, for example, Ivan Chvatík, "Patočka's Philosophy of Meaning in Human Life and History," in *Asubjective Phenomenology*, ed. L. Učník, I. Chvatík, and A. Williams (Nordhausen: Traugott Bautz, 2015), 213–226.

78. Evink, "The Gift of Life"; Ludger Hagedorn, "Beyond Myth and Enlightenment: On Religion in Patočka's Thought," in *Jan Patočka and the Heritage of Phenomenology: Centenary Papers*, ed. E. Abrams and I. Chvatík (Dordrecht: Springer, 2011), 245–262.

79. Veselý, "Jan Patočka a křesťanství," 63.

80. Lacoste, *From Theology to Theological Thinking*, 68.

81. Ibid., 70.

82. SS 1, 92.

83. SS 1, 100.

84. Filip Karfík, *Unendlichwerden durch die Endlichkeit* (Würzburg: Königshausen & Neumann, 2008).

85. Lacoste, *From Theology to Theological Thinking*, 78.

86. Ibid., 80.

87. HE, 108.

88. Lacoste, *From Theology to Theological Thinking*, 82ff.

89. Ibid., 85.

90. Ibid., 3–10.

91. Letter to Josef B. Souček dated August 8, 1944 (Vienna: Patočka Archive).

92. "Thomistic philosophy tends to follow one unchanging pattern: it lays out problems, points out aporias, and then looks for proofs that the solution is to be found in Thomas Aquinas." Despite this harsh evaluation, Patočka respects Aquinas and respects the philosophical system of Thomism if it is presented adequately. For example, after meeting with Erich Przywara at the Thomistic congress in Prague (1932), Patočka praises the Jesuit for bright thinking and his engagement with philosophical questions of the day, even though Patočka obviously does not share most of his conclusions. The main reason Patočka enters the polemic with certain Catholic philosophers and theologians is his suspicion that they are not honest thinkers. They disregard the complexities of philosophical questioning and the potential equivocities of philosophical answers. It is almost certain that these polemics with Thomism—and the criticism he received from Thomists—forced Patočka to distance himself from much of the Catholic tradition and the theological issues in his thought. Jan Patočka, "Mezinárodní filosofická konference tomistická," in SS 12, 463–467; citation 463.

93. Emmanuel Falque, *Crossing the Rubicon: Exploring the Borderlands of Philosophy and Theology* (New York: Fordham University Press, 2016); see especially 121–136.

94. Falque, *Crossing the Rubicon*, 122.

95. Lacoste, *From Theology to Theological Thinking*, 83.

Chapter 2

1. Paul Hazard, *La crise de la conscience européene 1680–1715* (Paris: Boivin, 1935). Willem Schinkel argues that the terminology of crisis in relation to modernity is a common feature of philosophers from Nietzsche onward. Some take the notion of crisis affirmatively, others polemically, but all use it. "The Image of Crisis: Walter Benjamin and the Interpretation of 'Crisis' in Modernity," *Thesis Eleven* 127 (2015): 36–51.

2. Paul Valéry, *La crise de l'esprit* (Paris: Éditions Manucius, 2016).

3. Radim Palouš, "Patočkovo KRINEIN," in *Jan Patočka, české dějiny a Evropa* (Semily: Státní okresní archiv Semily, 2007), 90–94.

4. See, for example, Jan Patočka, "The Spiritual Person and the Intellectual," in *Living in Problematicity*, ed. Eric Manton (Praha: Oikoymenh, 2007), 51–69.

5. Jan Patočka, "Humanismus, pozitivismus, nihilismus a jejich překonání," in SS 3, 714–731.

6. Patočka, *Andere Wege in die Moderne*, 95ff.

7. SS 1, 247.

8. Husserl, *The Crisis*, 5–10.

9. Martin Heidegger, *What Is a Thing?* (New York: Lanham, 1985).

10. Jan Patočka, "Two Senses of Reason and Nature in the German Enlightenment: A Herderian Study," in PSW, 157–174; here 160.

11. Ibid., 162.

12. Patočka, *Andere Wege in die Moderne*, 273–280.

13. Jan Patočka, "Cartesianism and Phenomenology," in PSW, 285–326.

14. Patočka, "Edmund Husserl's Philosophy of the Crisis," in PSW, 224.

15. Martin Heidegger, "Modern Science, Metaphysics, and Mathematics," in *Basic Writings*, ed. D. F. Krell (San Francisco: HarperCollins, 1993), 271–273.

16. SS 1, 154.

17. Lubica Učník, "*Esse* or *Habere*. To Be or to Have: Patočka's Critique of Husserl and Heidegger," *Journal of the British Society for Phenomenology* 38 (2007): 297–317; here 304.

18. Patočka, "Two Senses of Reason," in PSW, 161.

19. Husserl, *The Crisis*, 37.

20. Jan Patočka, "Husserlova idea evropské racionality," in SS 3, 161–185.

21. For a detailed account of the mathematical in Husserl, Heidegger, and Patočka, see Anita Williams, "The Meaning of Mathematical," in *Asubjective Phenomenology*, ed. L. Učník, I. Chvatík, and A. Williams (Nordhausen: Traugott Bautz, 2015), 227–251.

22. Heidegger, "Modern Science, Metaphysics, and Mathematics," 278.

23. Učník, "*Esse* or *Habere*," 298.

24. Heidegger, "Modern Science, Metaphysics, and Mathematics," 293.

25. Patočka, "Cartesianism and Phenomenology," in PSW, 286.

26. Ibid., 286–287.

27. Ibid., 291.

28. Patočka, "Two Senses of Reason," in PSW, 158.

29. Erazim Kohák, *Jan Patočka: Philosophy and Selected Writings* (Chicago: University of Chicago Press, 1989), 37.

30. Patočka, "Cartesianism and Phenomenology," in PSW, 292.

31. Patočka, "Two Senses of Reason," in PSW, 164.

32. Ibid., 170.

33. Ibid., 167.

34. Martin Heidegger, *Being and Time*, trans. J. Macquarrie and E. Robinson (Oxford: Blackwell, 2001), 59ff.

35. Kohák, *Jan Patočka*, xi–xii.

36. Patočka, "The Dangers of Technicization in Science according to E. Husserl and the Essence of Technology as Danger according to M. Heidegger (Varna Lecture)," in *The New Yearbook for Phenomenology and Phenomenological Philosophy XIV. Religion, War and the Crisis of Modernity: A Special Issue Dedicated to the Philosophy of Jan Patočka*, ed. L. Hagedorn and J. Dodd (London: Routledge, 2015), 13–22; here 14.

37. Věra Schifferová, "Jan Amos Komenský—portrét filozofa," in *Patočka a novoveká filozofia*, ed. V. Leško, V Schifferová, et al. (Košice: Acta Facultatis Philosophicae Universitatis Šafarikinae, 2014), 105–128.

38. Jan Patočka, "Komenský a otevřená duše," in SS 10, 337–351.

39. SS 10, 350.

40. *Sapientia* from the Latin *sapere*, to relish, to taste, even to smell, to come to know, to find out. In sum, a dynamic wisdom that involves the whole human being.

41. Jan Vítek, "Patočkovo pojetí krize moderní doby a člověka: Duševní krize evropského lidstva," in *Jan Patočka, české dějiny a Evropa* (Semily: Státní okresní archiv Semily, 2007), 175–181.

42. Tomáš G. Masaryk, *The Making of a State: Memories and Observations (1914–18)* (London: Allen & Unwin, 1927). This book is not merely a description of the historical events that led to the creation of Czechoslovakia. The author presents a profound, if highly questionable, philosophical reflection on historical

questions concerning the Czech people in order to argue for their unique place in the geopolitical and intellectual map of Europe.

43. Jan Patočka, "Masaryk's and Husserl's Conception of the Spiritual Crisis," in PSW, 145–156.

44. Masaryk was criticized mainly by Catholics, who did not share his theological opinions but often attacked him with ad hominem arguments for his Protestant confession. Masaryk's Catholic critics were concentrated in the Dominican journal *Filosofická revue* (Philosophical review). Patočka responded to some of the invective in *Česká mysl* (The Czech mind), the major Czech periodical of the time. See, for example, "Ještě k Masarykově filosofii náboženství," in SS 12, 527–529. In this sense, Patočka's controversy with the Czech Neo-Thomists, mentioned in chapter 1, continues in his interpretation of Masaryk.

45. Kohák, *Jan Patočka*, 109.

46. Masaryk, *V boji o náboženství* (Praha: 1904), 22; cited in SS 12, 402.

47. Patočka, "Masaryk's and Husserl's Crisis," in PSW 149–150.

48. Ibid., 150.

49. *Der Selbstmort als soziale Massenercheinung der Gegenwart.* First published in German in 1881, later in Czech in 1904.

50. Jan Patočka, "On Masaryk's Philosophy of Religion," in NYP, 120–121.

51. Ibid., 116.

52. Ibid., 99.

53. Jan Patočka, "Edmund Husserl," in SS 6, 366–378; here 376.

54. SS 1, 193.

55. François Dastur, "L'Europe et ses philosophes: Nietzsche, Husserl, Heidegger, Patocka," *Revue Philosophique de Louvain* 104 (2006): 1–22.

56. HE, 59.

57. Friedrich Nietzsche, *Thus Spoke Zarathustra: A Book for All and None* (Cambridge: Cambridge University Press, 2006), 8.

58. HE, 93.

59. Patočka, "Spiritual Person," 61–62.

60. This tendency to caricature postmodernism as relativism is criticized by Kevin Hart in *Postmodernism: A Beginner's Guide* (Oxford: Oneworld Publications, 2004).

61. Nietzsche, quoted in SS 3, 164.

62. Friedrich Nietzsche, *The Gay Science: With a Prelude in German Rhymes and an Appendix of Songs* (Cambridge: Cambridge University Press, 2001), 119–120.

63. Patočka, "Masaryk's and Husserl's Crisis," in PSW, 149.

64. Dermot Moran, *Husserl's Crisis of the European Sciences and Transcendental Phenomenology: An Introduction* (Cambridge: Cambridge University Press, 2012), 7.

65. Patočka, "Edmund Husserl's Philosophy of the Crisis," in PSW, 223.

66. Husserl, *The Crisis*, 21–100.

67. SS 6, 371.
68. Robert Hanna, "Husserl's Crisis and Our Crisis," *International Journal of Philosophical Studies* 22 (2014): 752–770; here 756.
69. Jan Patočka, *An Introduction to Husserl's Phenomenology*, trans. E. Kohák (Chicago: Open Court, 1996), 13.
70. Hanna, "Husserl's Crisis," 765–767.
71. SS 6, 370.
72. Karl Marx, "Theses on Feuerbach," in K. Marx and F. Engels, *The German Ideology*, ed. C. J. Arthur (New York: International Publishers, 2004), 121–123; here 123 (thesis 11).
73. Hanna, "Husserl's Crisis," 755.
74. Patočka, "Edmund Husserl's Philosophy of the Crisis," in PSW, 227.
75. Moran explains that Husserl "is a critic of narrow rationalism that has been pursued since the Enlightenment. The main problem facing the renewal of reason is that in the modern period, reason has become construed in a one-sided manner, due to the successes of the mathematical sciences." Moran, *Husserl's Crisis*, 300.
76. Patočka, "Edmund Husserl's Philosophy of the Crisis," in PSW, 226.
77. Patočka, "Masaryk's and Husserl's Conception of Crisis," in PSW, 145–156.
78. Patočka, "Edmund Husserl's Philosophy of the Crisis," in PSW, 226.
79. Ibid., 232.
80. Ibid., 233.
81. See chapter 2.
82. Patočka, "Edmund Husserl's Philosophy of the Crisis," in PSW, 227–228.
83. Ibid., 233.
84. Patočka, "Masaryk's and Husserl's Conception of Crisis," in PSW, 148.
85. "The question of the meaning of things was substituted by the question of the purpose of things." Vítek, "Patočkovo pojetí krize," 178.
86. Krzysztof Sroda, "Patočka, Platón a nesmrtelnost duše," *Filosofický časopis* 39 (1991): 357–362; here 359.
87. Martin Heidegger, "The Question Concerning Technology," in *Basic Writings*, ed. D. F. Krell (San Francisco: HarperCollins, 1993), 307–342; here 319; hereafter abbreviated to QCT.
88. QCT, 322.
89. QCT, 321.
90. Patočka, "The Dangers of Technicization," 17 (translation modified).
91. Ibid., 16.
92. QCT, 322–328.
93. Jan Patočka, "Čtyři semináře k problému Evropy," in SS 3, 374–423; here 388–389.
94. SS 3, 390.
95. QCT, 339–341.

96. SS 1, 243–302. For a general introduction and interpretation, see Jakub Homolka, *Koncept racionální civilizace: Patočkovo pojetí modernity ve světle civilizační analýzy* (Praha: Togga, 2016).

97. Johann Arnason, "Myšlenkové a politické pozadí Patočkovy konfrontace s modernitou," in *Dějinnost, nadcivilizace a modernita: Studie k Patočkově konceptu nadciviliace*, ed. J. Arnason, L. Benyovszky, and M. Skovajsa (Praha: Togga, 2010), 9–19; here 10–12.

98. Marek Skovajsa, "'Moderantní' nadcivilizace: nekonečná krize liberalismu a možnost jejího překonání," in *Dějinnost*, 81–122; here 83–84.

99. Johann Arnason, "Nadcivilizace a její různé podoby: Patočkova koncepce modernity ve světle dnešních diskusí," in *Dějinnost*, 23–56; here 55.

100. SS 1, 245.

101. Skovajsa, "Moderantní nadcivilizace," 87–88.

102. SS 1, 250–251.

103. Golfo Maggini, "Europe's Janus Head: Jan Patočka's Phenomenological Elucidation of the Crisis of Modern European Civilization," *Epoché* 19 (2014): 103–125; here 107.

104. SS 1, 250–251.

105. SS 1, 251.

106. Skovajsa, "Modernatní nadcivilizace," 99.

107. SS 1, 260.

108. SS 1, 260.

109. Arnason, "Nadcivilizace," 42.

110. SS 1, 255–257.

111. SS 1, 257.

112. SS 1, 263.

113. SS 1, 271.

114. SS 1, 271.

115. SS 1, 286–288.

116. SS 1, 273.

117. Maggini, "Europe's Janus Head," 114–115.

118. SS 1, 278.

119. SS 1, 287.

120. SS 1, 291.

121. In this respect, see Ilja Šrubař, "Jsou dějiny morální? K Patočkově dialektice úpadku," in *Dějinnost*, 57–80; here 71–75.

122. SS 1, 283.

123. SS 1, 289.

124. Šrubař, "Jsou dějiny morální?," 74–75.

125. Milan Hanyš, "Radikální nadcivilizace a ortodoxie: O některých nezamýšlených důsledcích teologie Pavla z Tarsu," in *Dějinnost*, 271–287.

126. Havel, "The Power of the Powerless," 13ff.

127. Václav Bělohradský, "Absolutno uprostřed všedního dne: Nad několika motivy Patočkova fragmentu," in *Dějinnost*, 173–200; here 192.
128. Ibid., 194.
129. Kohák, *Jan Patočka*, 6.
130. Ibid., xii.
131. Jan Patočka, "Evropský rozum," SS 1, 116–118; here 116 (italics not in original).
132. Vlastimil Hála, "Duchovní člověka a 'majitelé rozumu,'" *Filozofia* 62 (2007): 487–496; here 490.
133. Werner Heisenberg, *Physics and Beyond: Encounters and Conversations*, trans. A. Pomerans (New York: Harper & Row, 1971), 117–124. Interestingly, Patočka must have been deeply interested in Heisenberg. He contributed to the volume dedicated to this German scientist: H. Pfeiffer, ed., "Vom Ursprung und Sinn des Unsterblichkeitsgedankens bei Plato," in *Denken und Umdenken: Zu Werk und Wirkung von W. Heisenberg* (München: Piper, 1977), 102–115.
134. Jan Patočka, *Plato and Europe*, trans. P. Lom (Stanford: Stanford University Press, 2002), 136; hereafter abbreviated to PE.
135. Palouš, "Patočkovo Krinein," 90.
136. Patočka, *L'Europe après l'Europe*.
137. SS 1, 117.
138. James Mensch, *From Being to Knowing: A Postmodern Reversal* (University Park: Pennsylvania State University Press, 1996).
139. SS 6, 377.
140. Jan Patočka, "Symbol země u K. H. Máchy," in SS 4, 104–124; here 106.

Chapter 3

1. Jan Patočka, "Negative Platonism: Reflections Concerning the Rise, the Scope, and the Demise of Metaphysics" (hereafter abbreviated to NP) in PSW, 175–206.
2. See, for example, Mark Wrathall, ed., *Religion after Metaphysics* (Cambridge: Cambridge University Press, 2003).
3. Gianni Vattimo, "Nihilism as Postmodern Christianity," in *Transcendence and Beyond: A Postmodern Inquiry*, ed. J. D. Caputo and M. J. Scanlon (Bloomington: Indiana University Press, 2007), 44–48; here 47.
4. Richard Kearney, *The God Who May Be: A Hermeneutics of Religion* (Bloomington: Indiana University Press, 2001), 20–38.
5. John D. Caputo, "Introduction: Who Comes after the God of Metaphysics?," in *The Religious*, ed. J. D. Caputo (Oxford: Blackwell, 2001), 1–19.
6. Jan Patočka, "Metafyzika ve XX. století," in SS 6, 265–289; here 265.

7. Jan Patočka, "Démokritos a Platón jako zakladatelé metafyziky," in SS 2, 356–369; here 366.
8. SS 2, 367.
9. NP, 180.
10. NP, 180–181.
11. Kohák, *Jan Patočka*, 54–55.
12. NP, 180–181.
13. NP, 181.
14. NP, 181–182.
15. NP, 182.
16. SS 2, 368.
17. Kohák, *Jan Patočka*, 57.
18. NP, 181.
19. NP, 182.
20. See, for example, Jan Patočka, *Aristote, ses devanciers, ses successeurs*, trans. E. Abrams (Paris: J. Vrin, 2011), 23–35.
21. Jean-Yves Lacoste, a protagonist of the theological turn in French phenomenology, recently formulated a similar point concerning the difference between Socrates and Plato-Aristotle: "Socrates is a practitioner of *theória* . . . the contemplation of the whole of being or the being that we are. . . . Plato and Aristotle . . . recourse to an a priori and geometric construction of the cosmos (Plato) or to its description grounded on rudimentary experimentation tied to some a priori schemes (Aristotle), in such a way that philosophy can then be practiced without being ipso facto a form of moral knowledge. Thus we must accept that there was a transition from *theória* to theory. . . . In this movement, what must be seen, on the one hand, is the annexation of all knowledge by philosophy and, on the other hand, the quasi bracketing of the 'philosophical life' in favor of a 'wise' life defined as access to the highest knowledge." Lacoste, *From Theology to Theological Thinking*, 3–5. From this turn, Lacoste deduces serious consequences for theology. Assuming Heidegger's critique of metaphysics, Lacoste suggests that Christianity must appropriate the task of thinking and preserve what we call here a metaphysical thinking.
22. SS 6, 265.
23. Kohák, *Jan Patočka*, 57.
24. SS 1, 153.
25. NP, 188 (translation modified).
26. SS 1, 153–154.
27. NP, 184.
28. Jan Patočka, "Mezihra na prahu moderní vědy: Cusanus a Komenský," in SS 10, 134–148.
29. SS 6, 265.
30. NP, 183–184.

31. SS 6, 265.

32. "Kant banned metaphysics." SS 6, 266. Patočka discusses Kant's critique of metaphysics in detail in his essay "On Masaryk's Philosophy of Religion."

33. Immanuel Kant, *Critique of Pure Reason*, trans. N. K. Smith (New York: St Martin's Press, 1965), 525.

34. "Kant substitutes for an absolute onto-theology a moral theology relative to human life. His concern is to replace the ancient divine objective order with a new order on a human foundation, but one that will be no less viable, persuasive, and supra-subjective." Patočka, "On Masaryk's Philosophy of Religion," 99.

35. Patočka elaborates on the modern development of metaphysical philosophy in great detail but there is no need to renarrate his elucidating work. SS 6, 265–289.

36. SS 6, 284–286.

37. SS 1, 190.

38. Heidegger, *Being and Time*, 43. The following analysis focuses mostly on Heidegger's essay "The Onto-theo-logical Structure of Metaphysics." Other important texts on metaphysics include: "What Is Metaphysics?," in *Pathmarks*, ed. W. McNeill (Cambridge: Cambridge University Press, 1998), 82–96; *Introduction to Metaphysics*, trans. G. Fried and R. Polt (New Haven: Yale University Press, 2000); *The Fundamental Concepts of Metaphysics: World, Finitude, Solitude*, trans. W. McNeill and N. Walker (Bloomington: Indiana University Press, 1996).

39. Iain D. Thomson, *Heidegger on Ontotheology: Technology and the Politics of Education* (Cambridge: Cambridge University Press, 2005), 8.

40. Martin Heidegger, *Nietzsche: The Will to Power as Knowledge and as Metaphysics*, trans. D. F. Krell (New York: Harper & Row, 1987), 179.

41. Iain D. Thomson, *Heidegger, Art, and Postmodernity* (Cambridge: Cambridge University Press, 2011), 8–11.

42. Václav Umlauf, "Tractate on God Almost Non-existing," *AUC Theologica* 3 (2013): 9–35; here 30.

43. Heidegger, "The Onto-theo-logical Constitution of Metaphysics," 70–71.

44. Thomson, *Heidegger on Ontotheology*, 11–13.

45. Peter Jonkers, "God in France: Heidegger's Legacy," in *God in France: Eight Contemporary French Thinkers on God*, ed. P. Jonkers and R. Welten (Leuven: Peeters, 2005), 1–42.

46. Joeri Schrijvers, *Ontotheological Turnings: The Decentering of the Modern Subject in Recent French Phenomenology* (Albany: State University of New York Press, 2011), 5–9.

47. Heidegger, "The Onto-theo-logical Constitution of Metaphysics," 72.

48. Ibid.

49. John Peacocke, "Heidegger and the Problem of Onto-theology," in *Post-Secular Philosophy: Between Philosophy and Theology*, ed. P. Blond (London: Routledge, 1998), 93–102.

50. Heidegger, "The Onto-theo-logical Constitution of Metaphysics," 72.

51. J. Aaron Simmons and Bruce E. Benson, *The New Phenomenology: A Philosophical Introduction* (New York: Bloomsbury, 2013), 96.

52. The Heideggerian inspiration behind recent debates concerning the theological turn is pointed out, for example, in Hent de Vries, *Philosophy and the Turn to Religion* (Baltimore: Johns Hopkins University Press, 1999); Christina M. Gschwandtner, *Postmodern Apologetics? Arguments for God in Contemporary Philosophy* (New York: Fordham University Press, 2013), 19–38.

53. Janicaud, "The Theological Turn," 28–34.

54. Wolfe, *Heidegger and Theology*, 193–194.

55. Richard Kearney, *Strangers, Gods and Monsters* (London: Routledge, 2003), 213–228.

56. Duane Armitage, "Heidegger's God: Against Caputo, Kearney, and Marion," *Philosophy and Theology* 26 (2014): 279–294.

57. Merold Westphal, *Overcoming Onto-theology: Toward a Postmodern Christian Faith* (New York: Fordham University Press), xvi.

58. Gianni Vattimo, "The Christian Message and the Dissolution of Metaphysics," in *The Blackwell Companion to Postmodern Theology*, ed. G. Ward (Malden: Blackwell, 2005), 458–466.

59. Marion, *God without Being*.

60. Janicaud suggests Marion as one of the key representatives of the theological turn ("The Theological Turn," 50–69). In his second book on the theological turn, Janicaud focuses almost exclusively on Marion's philosophy, which he intends to criticize for violating phenomenology. See his *Phenomenology Wide Open*, trans. C. N. Cabral (New York: Fordham University Press, 2005).

61. Jean-Luc Marion, "*Mihi magna questio factum sum:* The privilege of unknowing," *Journal of Religion* 85 (2005): 1–24.

62. Jean-Luc Marion, "Metaphysics and Phenomenology: A Summary for Theologians," in *The Postmodern God: A Theological Reader*, ed. G. Ward (Malden: Wiley, 1998), 279–296.

63. Jean-Luc Marion, *In Excess: Studies of Saturated Phenomena*, trans. R. Horner and V. Berraud (New York: Fordham University Press, 2002), 128–134.

64. Gschwandtner, *Postmodern Apologetics?*, 106–109.

65. Jean-Luc Marion, "The 'End of Metaphysics' as a Possibility," in *Religion after Metaphysics*, ed. M. A. Wrathall (Cambridge: Cambridge University Press, 2003), 166–189; here 169.

66. Ibid., 174.

67. Marion, *God without Being*, 2–3.

68. Ibid., 12–13.

69. Ibid., 16–17.

70. Ibid., 17.

71. Ibid., 44–45.

72. Ibid., 30.
73. Ibid., 46–47.
74. Ibid., 46.
75. Ibid., 47.
76. Ibid., 49.
77. Christopher B. Simpson, *Religion, Metaphysics, and the Postmodern: William Desmond and John D. Caputo* (Bloomington: Indiana University Press, 2009), 7.
78. John D. Caputo, *Heidegger and Aquinas: An Essay on Overcoming Metaphysics* (New York: Fordham University Press, 1982), 8–12.
79. Ibid., 3.
80. Ibid., 274.
81. Ibid., 251.
82. John D. Caputo, *The Mystical Element in Heidegger's Thought* (New York: Fordham University Press, 1986), 118–127.
83. "Logocentrism would thus support the determination of the being of the entity as presence." Jacques Derrida, *Of Grammatology*, trans. G. C. Spivak (Baltimore: Johns Hopkins University Press, 1997), 12; Maria Margaroni, "Metaphysics of Presence," in *Encyclopedia of Postmodernism*, ed. V. E. Taylor and C. E. Winquist (London: Routledge, 2001), 245–246.
84. John D. Caputo, *Radical Hermeneutics: Repetition, Deconstruction, and the Hermeneutic Project* (Bloomington: Indiana University Press, 1987), 3–6.
85. Simpson, *Religion, Metaphysics, and the Postmodern*, 49–54.
86. Caputo, *Radical Hermeneutics*, 34.
87. Ibid., 6.
88. Ibid., 192.
89. Ibid., 1.
90. Ibid., 258.
91. Ibid., 221.
92. Ibid., 212.
93. John D. Caputo, "Richard Kearney's Enthusiasm," *Modern Theology* 18 (2002): 87–94; here 93.
94. Simmons and Benson, *The New Phenomenology*, 91.
95. Wolfe, *Heidegger and Theology*, 195.
96. Schrijvers, *Ontotheological Turnings*, 23.
97. Thomson, *Heidegger, Art, and Postmodernity*, 33–39.
98. Kohák, *Jan Patočka*, 59.
99. Rezek, *Jan Patočka a věc fenomenologie*, 55–62.
100. PE, 33.
101. Jan Patočka, "Několik poznámek k pojmům dějin a dějepisu," SS 1, 35–45; here 36.
102. SS 1, 41.

103. Jan Patočka, "Několim poznámek k pojmu světových dějin," SS 1, 46–57; here 53.
104. Jan Patočka, "Nemetafyzická filosofie a věda," in SS 3, 604–611; here 604.
105. SS 3, 609.
106. SS 3, 605.
107. SS 3, 607.
108. SS 3, 606–608.
109. SS 3, 605.
110. SS 3, 610.
111. SS 3, 611.
112. SS 3, 605.
113. Findlay, *Caring for the Soul*, 196.

Chapter 4

1. Kohák, *Jan Patočka*, 58.
2. HE, 108.
3. This is an alternative translation of the subtitle to *Negative Platonism* provided by Johann P. Arnason. "The Idea of Negative Platonism: Jan Patočka's Critique and Recovery of Metaphysics," *Thesis Eleven* 90 (2007): 6–26; here 8.
4. NP, 188. Here I use the English translation of *Negative Platonism* (trans. Kohák) in PSW. Occasionally, I modify the translation based on my understanding of the original text of "Negativní platonismus" in SS 1, 303–336. All such modifications are noted in the following notes.
5. Arnason, "The Idea of Negative Platonism," 21.
6. Rezek, *Jan Patočka a věc fenomenologie*, 63–67.
7. Kohák, "Jak číst Jana Patočku."
8. *Negative Platonism*—in italics and with an uppercase *N*—refers to Patočka's text; negative Platonism—in roman and with a lowercase *n*—refers to the concept in general.
9. NP, 175.
10. NP, 189. The project of negative Platonism obviously contrasts with any form of *positive metaphysics* (be it Platonism, Aristotelianism, or medieval Scholasticism). The term *negative metaphysics* as the designation of science as a new metaphysics is also used in the essay "Supercivilization and Its Inner Conflict," SS 1, 299–302.
11. A detailed account of this problem is provided in chapter 3.
12. NP, 179 and 189–190.
13. Arnason, "The Idea of Negative Platonism," 15.
14. NP, 191.

15. NP, 189.
16. Pavel Sladký, "Negativní Platonismus jako případ sokratismu," *Filosofický časopis* 58 (2010): 753–756.
17. Kohák, *Jan Patočka*, 58.
18. NP, 192.
19. Arnason, "The Idea of Negative Platonism," 8.
20. NP, 195.
21. NP, 180.
22. NP, 195.
23. NP, 182.
24. NP, 195–196.
25. NP, 192.
26. NP, 193–195.
27. NP, 193.
28. NP, 195.
29. NP, 196.
30. Ivan Landa, "Patočka a negativní platonismus," in *Jan Patočka, české dějiny a Evropa* (Semily: Státní okresní archiv Semily, 2007), 40–49; here 40.
31. Johann P. Arnason, "Negative Platonism: Between the History of Philosophy and the Philosophy of History," in *Jan Patočka and the Heritage of Phenomenology*, ed. E. Abrams and I. Chvatík (Dordrecht: Springer, 2011), 215–228.
32. NP, 197 (translation modified).
33. NP, 198–199 (translation modified).
34. Eddo Evink, "The Relevance of Patočka's 'Negative Platonism,'" in *Jan Patočka and the Heritage of Phenomenology: Centenary Papers*, ed. E. Abrams, and I. Chvatík (Dordrecht: Springer, 2011), 57–70; here 66.
35. Arnason, "The Idea of Negative Platonism," 18–19.
36. Tamás Ullmann, "Negative Platonism and the Appearance-Problem," in *Jan Patočka and the Heritage of Phenomenology: Centenary Papers*, ed. E. Abrams, and I. Chvatík (Dordrecht: Springer, 2011), 71–86; here 74.
37. Ibid., 74.
38. NP, 200.
39. NP, 201.
40. Jan Patočka, "Nicota, absolutní pozice a zápor," in SS 3, 652–668.
41. Rezek, *Jan Patočka a věc fenomenologie*, 64.
42. Patočka does not use the term *metaxological* himself. In this respect, I am indebted to William Desmond and his metaxological metaphysics. Although beyond the scope of the present analysis, a detailed comparison of Patočka's metaphysical thinking and Desmond's metaxology would undoubtedly be very helpful. See, for example, William Desmond, *God and the Between* (Malden: Blackwell, 2008).
43. NP, 204.

44. Pierre Rodrigo, "Negative Platonism and Maximal Existence in the Thought of Jan Patočka," in *Jan Patočka and the Heritage of Phenomenology: Centenary Papers*, ed. E. Abrams, and I. Chvatík (Dordrecht: Springer, 2011), 87–97; here 97.
45. NP, 205.
46. Jan Patočka, "Time, Myth, Faith," in NYP, 3–12; here 6.
47. Jan Patočka, "Problém pravdy z hlediska negativního platonismu," in SS 1, 447–480; here 447.
48. SS 1, 447.
49. SS 1, 448.
50. SS 1, 448.
51. SS 1, 457.
52. SS 1, 450–451.
53. SS 1, 452.
54. SS 1, 458.
55. SS 1, 459.
56. SS 1, 459–461.
57. SS 1, 460.
58. SS 1, 460.
59. SS 1, 465.
60. Rezek, *Jan Patočka a věc fenomenologie*, 67.
61. SS 1, 465.
62. HE, 108.
63. Nietzsche, *The Gay Science*, 49.
64. NP, 205.
65. NP, 178.
66. For a detailed account of the relationship between theology and philosophy, see chapter 1.
67. Lacoste, *From Theology to Theological Thinking*, 78.
68. Landa, "Patočka a negativní platonismus," 40–41.
69. SS 1, 92.
70. Regarding the conjunction between the idea of Patočka's negative Platonism and the Christian notion of faith, I am indebted to the revealing intuition of Filip Härtel's unpublished thesis "The Problem of Self-Fulfillment in the Philosophy of Jan Patočka" (unpublished thesis, Faculty of Arts, Charles University, Prague, 2012).
71. For example, Westphal, *Over-coming Ontotheology*, 1–28; Simmons and Benson, *The New Phenomenology*, 111–145.
72. Miroslav Petříček, "Mýtus v Patočkově filosofii," *Reflexe* 5–6 (1992): 6.1–6.15. Translation of quotations from this source are mine.
73. The title of Patočka's essay *Eternity and Historicity* ("Věčnost a dějinnost," in SS 1, 139–242) grasps the tension between metaphysical philosophy and historical thinking.
74. Petříček, "Mýtus," 6.5.

75. Ibid., 6.6.
76. Ibid., 6.15 (emphasis mine).
77. Ibid., 6.5.
78. Evink, "The Relevance of Patočka's Negative Platonism," 67-70.
79. Ibid., 69.
80. Petříček, "Mýtus," 6.13.
81. SS 1, 466.
82. Findlay, *Caring for the Soul*, 161-162.
83. Ibid., 167ff.
84. Ibid., 168.
85. Ibid., 66.
86. See, for example, Lacoste, *From Theology to Theological Thinking*.
87. Findlay, *Caring for the Soul*, 60-61.
88. See, for example, Jan Patočka, "The 'Natural' World and Phenomenology," in PSW, 239-273; here 267.
89. SS 1, 460.
90. SS 3, 604.
91. Ladislav Hejdánek, "Nicota a odpovědnost," *Filosofický časopis* 39 (1991): 32-37.
92. Ibid., 34.
93. Ibid., 35-36.
94. Umlauf, "Tractate on God Almost Non-existing," 11 and 18-19.
95. Joeri Schrijvers, "Thinking Despite Everything? On Unknowing God, and the Common Concerns of Philosophy and Theology," *Modern Theology* 31 (2015): 666-675; here 672.
96. Patočka, "Time, Myth, Faith," 5-6.
97. Jan Patočka, "Studie o času II," in SS 3, 644-651; here 645-646.
98. SS 3, 645.
99. A detailed analysis of the theme of myth in Patočka is offered by Jindřich Veselý, "Mýtus v myšlení Jana Patočky" (unpublished doctoral dissertation, Protestant Theological Faculty, Charles University, Prague, 2014).
100. We will return to the matter of myth in relation to Patočka's conception of Christianity in chapter 5.
101. SS 3, 644.
102. SS 3, 647.
103. SS 3, 647.
104. Patočka, "Time, Myth, Faith," 4-5.
105. SS 3, 649.
106. SS 3, 647.
107. "I recently came upon Jasper's beautiful book *Der philosophische Glaube*, which gave me great insights and helped me to clarify the whole concept underlying philosophy, its relationship to science, and to other disciplines of the spirit." Jan Patočka to Václav Richter, June 9, 1951, SS 20, 36.

Chapter 5

1. Maria Margaroni, "Jacques Derrida," in *Encyclopedia of Postmodernism*, ed. V. E. Taylor and C. E. Winquist (London: Routledge, 2001), 92–94.

2. HE, 108. I point out the difficulties concerning the English translation of this sentence in the introduction.

3. A note about the translation of this enigmatic place in *Heretical Essays*: the literal translation would read "Christianity unthought." Unfortunately, Kohák's translation adds, in my opinion too hastily, unthought-through, which suddenly defines the concept as temporary, as if Patočka were thinking about some point in the future by which Christianity would be completed. My position agrees rather with Ludger Hagedorn, who opened the debate on Christianity unthought in all its complexity. Hagedorn, "Christianity Unthought," 31–46.

4. Miroslav Petříček, "Jan Patočka and Phenomenological Philosophy Today," in *Jan Patočka and the Heritage of Phenomenology: Centenary Papers*, ed. E. Abrams and I. Chvatík (Dordrecht: Springer, 2011), 3–6; here 6.

5. James Dodd, "Philosophy in Dark Times: An Essay on Jan Patočka's Philosophy of History," in NYP, 64–91.

6. Originally a lecture entitled "Christian Faith and Thinking" delivered to a group of philosophers and theologians in 1972, transcribed and published in samizdat three years later. On the historical background of Patočka's lecture, see Chvatík, "The Responsibility of the 'Shaken,'" 266. We refer here to the French translation, Patočka, "Le christianisme et le monde naturel," hereafter abbreviated to CN.

7. CN, 18.

8. Jan Patočka, "The Natural World and Phenomenology," in PSW, 242.

9. Jan Patočka, "Přirozený svět v meditaci po 30. Letech," SS 7, 265–278.

10. CN, 17.

11. SS 1, 53.

12. Jan Patočka, "Co je fenomenologie?," in SS 7, 497–523; here 497–501.

13. CN, 17–18.

14. CN, 19.

15. Patočka says this explicitly in the discussion that followed his lecture. This discussion is noted and transcribed in the Czech version of the text. The French translation omits it.

16. CN, 22.

17. HE, 25.

18. Jacques Derrida, "Et cetera," in *Deconstructions: A User's Guide*, ed. N. Royle (London: Palgrave Macmillan, 2000), 282–305; here 300.

19. Hagedorn, "Christianity Unthought," 42 (emphasis mine).

20. NYP, 13–22.

21. Jan Patočka, review of *Das Urchristentum im Rahmen der antiken Religionen* by Rudolf Bultmann, *Křesťanská revue* 19 (1952): 311–315.

22. Ibid., 315.

23. Hagedorn, "Beyond Myth and Enlightenment," 245–262.

24. All the more because others have already done this job. The problem of myth in Patočka is thoroughly mapped out by, for example, Veselý, "Mýtus v myšlení Jana Patočky." This unpublished dissertation provides a detailed renarration of Patočka's understanding of myth. Veselý's work does not read quite like a doctoral thesis but more as a detailed "book report" and an anthology of Patočka's arguments relating to the idea of myth in literature, art, philosophy, and, of course, religion.

25. Patočka, "Time, Myth, Faith," 7.

26. Ibid., 8.

27. Ibid., 8.

28. PE, 122.

29. This sentence is also recorded in the samizdat transcription of the discussion that followed the lecture on Christianity and the natural world.

30. HE, 108.

31. Patočka, "Time, Myth, Faith," 9.

32. Ibid., 10.

33. Patočka treats the movements of existence exhaustively in various places. The most elaborate treatments can be found in SS 7, 314–334; *Body, Community, Language, World*, 147–161. The teaching on the movements of existence is considered Patočka's most original contribution to phenomenological philosophy. See, for example, Ludger Hagedorn, "*Bewegung* als Leitmotiv von Patočkas Ideengeschichte," in *Andere Wege in die Moderne: Forschungsbeiträge zu Patočkas Genealogie der Neuzeit*, ed. L. Hagedorn and R.-M. Sepp (Würzburg: Königshausen & Neumann, 2006), 10–25.

34. Miloslav Bednář, "Jan Patočka a Martin Heidegger," *Reflexe* 14 (1995): 1–18. Another important aspect of Patočka's critique of Heidegger concerns the issue of the body, which seems, in the eyes of Patočka, neglected. For Patočka, the body is the condition of the possibility that any existential movement has existential relevance. Precisely in this sense, Heidegger's approach, closely related to the question of consciousness, appears too formalist.

35. SS 7, 318.

36. HE, 29.

37. Jan Patočka, "Autorův doslov k francouzskému vydání díla *Přirozený svět jako filosofický problém*," in SS 7, 367–378.

38. Evink, "The Gift of Life," 50.

39. "[The third movement] concerns nothing already existent, but on the contrary, that which fundamentally differs from all that exists, and which makes

any encounter possible: the possibility par excellence, the world. Being as the link between all meaning and the key to all understanding." Jan Patočka, "Co je existence," in SS 7, 335-366; here 354 (translation taken from Chvatík, "Jan Patočka's Studies on Masaryk," in NYP, 136-160; here 151).

40. HE, 33.
41. HE, 75.
42. Chvatík, "The Responsibility of the 'Shaken,'" 267.
43. HE, 12 (translation modified).
44. CN, 22.
45. 1 Cor 1:20.
46. HE, 107.
47. Patočka, "On Masaryk's Philosophy of Religion," 96.
48. Chvatík, "Patočka's Studies on Masaryk," 136-160; De Warren, "The gift of eternity," 161-180; Ludger Hagedorn, "Fatigue of Reason: Patočka's Reading of *The Brothers Karamazov*," 181-198; all in NYP; Tomáš Hejduk, "K Patočkově filosofii náboženství," in *Jan Patočka, české dějiny a Evropa* (Semily: Státní okresní archiv Semily, 2007), 50-58.
49. Patočka, "On Masaryk's Philosophy of Religion," 132.
50. Ibid., 99.
51. Ibid., 101.
52. Ibid., 102.
53. Ibid., 130.
54. Rudolf Bultmann, *New Testament and Mythology and Other Basic Writings*, trans. S. M. Ogden (London: SCM, 1985).
55. Ivan Chvatík, "Religion oder Politik? Zu Patočkas Begriff des politischen Handelns," in *Lebenswelt und Politik: Perspektiven der Phänomenologie nach Husserl*, ed. G. Leghissa and M. Staudigl (Würzburg: Königshausen & Neumann, 2007), 147-158.
56. Chvatík, "Patočka's Studies on Masaryk," 154-155.
57. Hagedorn, "Beyond Myth and Enlightenment," 252ff.
58. Ibid., 257.
59. Veselý, "Patočka a křesťanství," 82-84.
60. Karfík, *Unendlichwerden durch die Endlichkeit*, 81.
61. Hagedorn and Dodd, "Editor's Introduction," in NYP, xv-xvi.
62. Ludger Hagedorn, "Auto-immunity and Transcendence: A Phenomenological Re-consideration of Religion with Derrida and Patočka," in *Phenomenology and Religion: New Frontiers*, ed. J. Bornemark and H. Ruin (Stockholm: Södertörn University Publishers, 2010), 131-148; here 140.
63. Ibid., 136.
64. HE, 108.
65. Hagedorn, "Auto-immunity and Transcendence," 144-145.
66. Hagedorn, "Christianity Unthought," 43.

67. HE, 107–108.
68. Petříček, "Phenomenological Philosophy Today," 6.
69. Ibid., 6.
70. Hagedorn, "Christianity Unthought," 39.
71. Ibid., 43.
72. De Warren, "The Gift of Eternity," 166.
73. "*Khôra* is neither present nor absent, active nor passive, the Good nor evil, living nor nonliving . . . but rather atheological and nonhuman—*khôra* is not even a receptacle. . . . *khôra* is *tout autre*, very." John D. Caputo, *The Prayers and Tears of Jacques Derrida* (Bloomington: Indiana University Press, 1997), 35–36.
74. De Warren, "The Gift of Eternity," 161–162.
75. HE, 101–102.
76. HE, 106.
77. Jean-Luc Nancy, "Entzug der Göttlichkeit: Zur Rekonstruktion und Selbstüberschreibung des Christentum," *Lettre International* 76 (2002): 76–80; here 76.
78. Laurens ten Kate, "Intimate Distance: Rethinking the Unthought God in Christianity," *Sophia* 47 (2008): 327–343.
79. Christian Sternad, "Spectres of the Sacred: Jan Patočka, or: The Hidden Source of Jacques Derrida's 'Phenomenology of Religion,' " in NYP, 287–299.
80. See chapter 4.
81. Derrida makes reference to the undeconstructible in *The Spectres of Marx: The State of the Debt, the Work of Mourning, and the New International*, trans. P. Kamuff (New York: Routledge, 2006), 33, 74, and 112.
82. Kearney, *Strangers, Gods and Monsters*, 191–212.
83. HE, 134.

Chapter 6

1. Another possible version traces Derrida's relationship to Patočka's thought back to the early 1980s when he visited Prague and lectured at the "underground university" organized by the Jan Hus Foundation—the international organization that supported Czech intellectual dissent during the Communist era. Derrida was even a cofounder of the French branch of the Jan Hus Foundation. It is worth noting that in 1981, on one of his trips to Prague, Derrida was arrested by the Czech Communist officials, accused of smuggling drugs, and imprisoned. He was released only after the intervention of President Mitterrand and protests from French intellectuals. A humorous coincidence is that at the time of his incarceration, Derrida was working on Kafka's "Before the Law." In Kafka's hometown, Derrida had a truly Kafkaesque experience. Jason Powell, *Jacques Derrida: A Biography* (New York: Continuum, 2006), 151.

2. The citation in full reads as follows: "My religion about which nobody knows anything, any more than does my mother who asked other people a while ago, not daring to talk to me about it, if I still believed in God . . . but she must have known that the constancy of God in my life is called by other names, so that I quite rightly pass for an atheist, the omnipresence to me of what I call God in my absolved absolutely private language being neither that of an eyewitness nor that of a voice doing anything other than talking to me without saying anything." Jacques Derrida, "Circumfession," in G. Bennington and J. Derrida, *Jacques Derrida* (Chicago: University of Chicago Press, 1993), 154–155.

3. Jacques Derrida, *The Gift of Death*, trans. D. Wills (Chicago: University of Chicago Press, 1995), 2; hereafter abbreviated to GD.

4. HE, 103.

5. Perhaps the most concise exposition of the matter is offered in PE, 87–137.

6. SS 3, 398 (translation modified from Findlay, *Caring for the Soul*, 63).

7. Findlay, *Caring for the Soul*, 63.

8. HE, 105.

9. HE, 97.

10. HE, 105.

11. HE, 106.

12. HE, 106.

13. HE, 106–107.

14. Chvatík, "The Responsibility of the 'Shaken,'" 271.

15. HE, 118 (translation modified).

16. GD, 2.

17. Chvatík, "The Responsibility of the 'Shaken,'" 267 and 276.

18. HE, 107.

19. A growing interest in Saint Paul is mapped in John D. Caputo and Linda Martin Alcoff, eds., *St. Paul among the Philosophers* (Bloomington: Indiana University Press, 2009).

20. HE, 107.

21. HE, 107. On the following page, Patočka continues: "The intrinsic life of the soul, its essential content, comes not from seeing ideas and so from its bond to the being which agelessly, eternally is, but rather in an openness to the abyss in the divine and the human, to the wholly unique and so definitively self-determining bond of divinity and humanity, the unique drama to which the fundamental content of the soul relates throughout."

22. HE, 108. This place contains a fundamental mistake in Kohák's translation of *Heretical Essays*. It is obvious that the translator confuses two very similar words that have completely different meanings. The original text states *věcné* (material, objective) whereas the translation assumes the word is *věčné* (eternal). To say that "the soul is by nature wholly incommensurate with all objective beings" (as

the original has it), and to say that the soul is incommensurate will all "eternal being" (as Kohák's translation suggests), are two quite different things.

23. HE, 108.
24. GD, 8–9.
25. GD, 10ff.
26. GD, 30–31.
27. GD, 52.
28. GD, 2.
29. GD, 49–51.
30. GD, 49.
31. GD, 29.
32. GD, 48.
33. GD, 22.
34. Marcia Sá Cavalcante Schuback, "Negative Responsibility," *The Journal for Cultural and Religious Theory* (JCRT) 15 (2015): 39–50.
35. GD, 22.
36. GD, 23.
37. Hagedorn, "Beyond Myth and Enlightenment," 250.
38. Ibid., 247.
39. Rodolphe Gasché, "European Memories: Jan Patočka and Jacques Derrida on Responsibility," *Critical Inquiry* 33 (2007): 291–311; here 293.
40. GD, 22.
41. Gasché, "European Memories," 295.
42. Jan Patočka, *Platon et l'Europe*, trans. E. Abrams (Lagrasse: Verdier, 1983).
43. Gasché, "European Memories," 296–297.
44. Ibid., 297.
45. Ibid., 303.
46. GD, 29.
47. Gasché, "European Memories," 308.
48. PE, 139.
49. HE, 108.
50. PE, 89.
51. Eddo Evink, "Patočka and Derrida on Responsibility," in *Analecta Husserliana LXXXIX*, ed. A.-T. Tymieniecka (Dordrecht: Springer, 2006), 307–321; here 311.
52. Lubica Učník, "Patočka on Techno-power and the Sacrificial Victim (*Oběť*)," in *Jan Patočka and the Heritage of Phenomenology: Centenary Papers*, ed E. Abrams and I. Chvatík (Dordrecht: Springer, 2011), 187–202; here 188.
53. GD, 51–52.
54. GD, 49.
55. Hagedorn, "Beyond Myth and Enlightenment," 247.

56. Evink, "Patočka and Derrida," 313.
57. Ibid., 317.
58. Ibid., 313.
59. Evink, "The Gift of Life," 48.
60. See chapter 5.
61. Evink, "The Gift of Life," 50.
62. GD, 7.
63. Evink, "The Gift of Life," 52–53.
64. HE, 69.
65. GD, 27.
66. Cajthaml, *Europe and the Care for the Soul*, 87–94.
67. Evink, "The Gift of Life," 53.
68. SS 7, 265–278.
69. Evink, "The Gift of Life," 54.
70. Ibid., 59.
71. Paul Ricoeur, "Preface to the French Edition," in HE, vii–xvi; here ix.
72. Caputo, *The Prayers and Tears*, 191–196.
73. Ibid., 192. Note the misspelling of Patočka's name in Caputo. Even this small detail suggests that the American philosopher offers us a dubious reading.
74. GD, 33.
75. Caputo, *The Prayers and Tears*, 195.
76. Ibid., 127.
77. GD, 29.
78. Hagedorn, "Beyond Myth and Enlightenment," 250.
79. Derrida mentions the return to religion or the return of the religious several times in his "Faith and Knowledge: Two Sources of 'Religion' at the Limits of Reason Alone," in *Acts of Religion*, ed. G. Anidjar (New York: Routledge, 2002), 42–101; here 43, 45, 65, 77, 78–79, and 81.
80. Gil Anidjar, "A Note on 'Faith and Knowledge,'" in *Acts of Religion*, ed. G. Anidjar (New York: Routledge, 2002), 40–41; here 41.
81. Christian Sternad, "Spectres of the Sacred: Jan Patočka, or: The Hidden Source of Jacques Derrida's 'Phenomenology of Religion,'" in NYP, 287–299.
82. HE, 101.
83. Sternad, "Spectres of the Sacred," 292.
84. GD, 1–2.
85. Hagedorn, "Beyond Myth and Enlightenment," 254.
86. Derrida, "Faith and Knowledge," 70.
87. Sternad, "Spectres of the Sacred," 294.
88. GD, 29.
89. Hagedorn, "Beyond Myth and Enlightenment," 254–255.
90. Michael Naas, *Miracle and Machine: Jacques Derrida and the Two Sources of Religion, Science, and the Media* (New York: Fordham University Press, 2012).

Similarly, Gil Anidjar, the editor of the English edition of "Faith and Knowledge" (Anidjar, "A Note on 'Faith and Knowledge,'" 40–41), mentions among the main interlocutors of Derrida only Kant, Hegel, Bergson, and Heidegger (41). Carl Raschke ("Derrida and the Return of Religion: Religious Theory after Postmodernism," *JCRT* 6 [2005]: 1–16) is also silent.

91. Sternad, "Spectres of the Sacred," 292.

92. Richard Kearney, *Dialogues with Contemporary Continental Thinkers* (Manchester: Manchester University Press, 1984), 107.

93. Evink, "Patočka and Derrida," 311.

94. GD, 31.

95. HE, 108.

96. Hagedorn, "Beyond Myth and Enlightenment," 251–252.

97. HE, 108.

98. HE, 114–115.

99. HE, 117.

100. GD, 28.

101. PE, 129.

102. For a detailed discussion of Patočka's *Negative Platonism* and its intertwining with theological issues, namely, the notion of faith, see chapter 4.

103. Joseph Ratzinger, *Truth and Tolerance: Christian Belief and World Religions* (San Francisco: Ignatius, 2004), 95.

104. Chvatík, "The Responsibility of the 'Shaken,'" 277.

105. Ibid., 272–273.

106. In chapter 4, I show that this understanding of faith is proper to Patočka.

107. Cavalcante Schuback, "Negative Responsibility," 39.

Chapter 7

1. Jan Patočka, "Hrdinové naší doby," in SS 3, 186–190.

2. Hagedorn, "Beyond Myth and Enlightenment" and "Christianity Unthought"; Evink, "The Gift of Life."

3. De Warren, "The Gift of Eternity."

4. Chvatík, "Religion oder Politik?" and "The Responsibility of the 'Shaken.'"

5. Jan Patočka, "Co jsou Češi?," in SS 13, 253–324.

6. Christina M. Gschwandtner, *Marion and Theology* (London: Bloomsbury T & T Clark, 2016).

7. Patočka, "The Dangers of Technicization," in NYP, 13–22.

8. Jan Patočka, "Čtyři semináře k problému Evropy," in SS 3, 374–423; here 388.

9. Patočka, "The Dangers of Technicization," 20.

10. Ibid., 20.

11. Ibid., 20.
12. Ibid., 17.
13. Patočka, "Čtyři semináře," 392. In fact, the idea of conflict—*polemos*—also comes from Heidegger, *Introduction to Metaphysics*, 64–65.
14. Marcia Sá Cavalcante Schuback, "Sacrifice and Salvation: Jan Patočka's Reading of Heidegger on the Question of Technology," in *Jan Patočka and the Heritage of Phenomenology: Centenary Papers*, ed. E. Abrams and I. Chvatík (Dordrecht: Springer, 2011), 23–38; here 29–30.
15. Ibid., 31.
16. Patočka, "Čtyři semináře," 421.
17. HE, 119.
18. Patočka, "The Dangers of Technicization," 21.
19. Ibid., 22.
20. Patočka, "Čtyři semináře," 411.
21. Patočka, "The Dangers of Technicization," 20–22.
22. Patočka, "Čtyři semináře," 186–190.
23. Ibid., 402.
24. Ibid., 403.
25. Patočka, "The Dangers of Technicization," 22.
26. Ibid., 22.
27. HE, 108.
28. Patočka, "The Dangers of Technicization," 22.
29. Učník, "Patočka on Techno-power," 187.
30. Patočka, *Plato and Europe*, 126.
31. HE, 105–106.
32. Chvatík, "The Responsibility of the 'Shaken,'" 277–278.
33. Jean-Luc Marion, *Negative Certainties* (Chicago: University of Chicago Press, 2015), 132.
34. In an earlier version, published as "Sketch of a Phenomenological Concept of Sacrifice," in *The Reason of the Gift* (Charlottesville: University of Virginia Press, 2011), Marion concludes with a reference to Augustine's definition of sacrifice. In the revised version of *Negative Certainties*, Marion cites Thomas Aquinas and his definition; Augustine is moved to a footnote but remains part of the argument.
35. Marion, *Negative Certainties*, 116–117.
36. Ibid., 120.
37. Ibid., 117.
38. Ibid., 119.
39. Ibid., 117–118.
40. Ibid., 121.
41. Ibid., 123.

42. Christina M. Gschwandtner, *Degrees of Givenness: On Saturation in Jean-Luc Marion* (Bloomington: Indiana University Press, 2014), 126ff.
43. Ibid., 132.
44. Gschwandtner, *Postmodern Apologetics?*, 120.
45. Marion, *Negative Certainties*, 126–127.
46. Ibid., 128.
47. Ibid., 130.
48. Gschwandtner, *Degrees of Givenness*, 137.
49. Marion, *Negative Certainties*, 128.
50. Dan Arbib, "Donner la mort? Phénomenologie et sacrifice: Note sur une interprétation de Derrida," *Studia Phaenomenologica* 12 (2012): 383–397; here 396.
51. Jean-Luc Marion, *Being Given: Toward a Phenomenology of Givenness* (Stanford: Stanford University Press, 2002), 238.
52. Jean-Luc Marion, "The Phenomenality of the Sacrament," in *Words of Life: New Theological Turns in French Phenomenology*, ed. B. E. Benson and N. Wirzba (New York: Fordham University Press, 2010), 89–102.
53. Marion, *Being Given*, 53–61.
54. Marion, *Negative Certainties*, 146.
55. Ibid., 132.
56. Patočka, "Čtyři semináře," 392.
57. Ibid., 393.
58. Hagedorn, "Beyond Myth and Enlightenment," 258.
59. *The Enigma of Gift and Sacrifice* illustrates the recent fascination with sacrifice and kenosis in philosophy and beyond. Edith Wyschogrod, Jean-Joseph Goux, and Eric Boynton, eds., *The Enigma of Gift and Sacrifice* (New York: Fordham University Press, 2002).
60. Emilio Brito, "Kenosis," in *Encyclopedia of Christian Theology*, Vol. 2, ed. Jean-Yves Lacoste (New York: Routledge, 2005), 853–856.
61. Patočka, "Čtyři semináře," 403–404 and 412–413.
62. Ibid., 413.
63. Ibid., 403.
64. Karfík, *Unendlichwerden durch die Endlichkeit*, 31.
65. Martin Ritter, "Transcendence u Jana Patočky a problém oběti," in *Dějinnost, nadcivilizace a modernita: Studie k Patočkově konceptu nadciviliace*, ed. Johann P. Arnason, Ladislav Benyovszky, and Marek Skovajsa (Praha: Togga, 2010), 201–215.
66. Veselý, "Patočka a křesťanství," 83.
67. Ricardo Paparusso, "Life, Technology, Christianity: Patočka's Sacrifice for Nothing and Its Economic-mythical Roots," in *Asubjective Phenomenology*, ed. Lubica Učník, Ivan Chvatík, and Anita Williams (Nordhausen: Traugott Bautz, 2015), 187–198; here 194.

68. Patočka, "Čtyři semináře," 413.

69. It is no coincidence that the theme of one of the most penetrating literary critiques of totalitarian regimes is love and its counterfeits. See George Orwell, *1984* (New York: New American Library, 1981).

70. Hagedorn, "Fatigue of Reason," 195.

71. Jan Patočka, "*The Natural World* Remeditated Thirty-Three Years Later," in *The Natural World as a Philosophical Problem* (Evanston: Northwestern University Press, 2016), 115–180.

72. Ibid., 178–179.

73. Ibid., 179.

74. Hagedorn, "Beyond Myth and Enlightenment," 259.

75. "[Patočka] interprets the myth of Christ as a parable of the crisis wherein everyone is involved and where what is at stake is whether human life shall be ruled by that which is or by the 'truth of being.'" Chvatík, "Jan Patočka's Studies on Masaryk," 152.

76. Patočka, "*The Natural World*," 180; "Čtyři semináře," 393.

77. Jan Patočka, "Theologie a filosofie," in SS 1, 15–21; here 20.

78. Evink, "The Gift of Life," 59–60. In *Europe and the Care for the Soul*, 87–94, Martin Cajthaml argues for the opposite and claims that Patočka's interpretations are indebted to his understanding of Greek philosophy.

79. The correspondence between the Czech and Polish philosophers was recently published in "Letters between Krzysztof Michalski and Jan Patočka," trans. N. de Warren, P. Eldridge, and V. Tylzanowski, in NYP, 223–269.

80. Krzysztof Michalski, *The Flame of Eternity: An Interpretation of Nietzsche's Thought* (Princeton: Princeton University Press, 2007), 75–89.

81. Patočka, *Plato and Europe*, 50.

82. Ibid., 149.

83. Michalski, *The Flame of Eternity*, 75–77.

84. Ibid., 78.

85. Ibid., 80.

86. Ibid., 81 (italics mine).

87. Ibid., 86.

88. Patočka, "On Masaryk's Philosophy of Religion," 95–135; here 113.

89. Michalski, *The Flame of Eternity*, 89.

90. Patočka, *Plato and Europe*, 128.

91. Evink, "The Gift of Life," 59.

92. Patočka, "Čtyři semináře," 415.

93. Ludger Hagedorn, "Kenosis: Die philosophische Anverwandlung eines christlichen Motivs bei Jan Patočka," in *Figuren der Transzendenz: Transformationen eines phänomenologischen Grundbegriffs*, ed. Michael Staudigl and Christian Sternad (Würzburg: Königshausen & Neumann, 2014), 349–366.

94. Ibid., 358–359.
95. Ibid., 363. The text in quotation marks is from Patočka, "Čtyři semináře," 452.
96. Patočka, "The Dangers of Technicization," 22.
97. Gschwandtner, *Postmodern Apologetics*, 121.
98. Marion, *Negative Certainties*, 146.
99. Schrijvers, *Ontotheological Turnings*, 55.
100. I think, for example, of Gianni Vattimo's project presented in *After Christianity*, trans. L. D'Isanto (New York: Columbia University Press, 2002); "Toward a Non-religious Christianity," in *After the Death of God*, ed. J. W. Robbins (New York: Columbia University Press, 2007), 27–46.
101. HE, 135.

Conclusion

1. See Patočka's obituaries. For example, Ludwig Landgrebe, "Jan Patočka," *Philosophy and Phenomenological Research* 38 (1977): 287–290.
2. Marci Shore, *The Taste of Ashes: The Afterlife of Totalitarianism in Eastern Europe* (New York: Broadway Books, 2013), 26.
3. Texts Patočka wrote as a spokesperson for Charter 77 bear witness to the philosopher's appeal. See, for example, Jan Patočka, "Čím je a čím není Charta 77," in SS 12, 428–430.
4. Eddo Evink, "Horizons of Expectation: Ricoeur, Derrida, Patočka," *Studia Phaenomenologica* 13 (2013): 297–323; here 319–320.
5. Jan Patočka, "Deset náčrtů ke *Kacířským esejům*," SS 3, 439–452; here 449.
6. Patočka wrote these preparatory drafts in German. SS 3, 450–452.
7. On Patočka's development of the question of transcendence, see Ritter, "Transcendence u Jana Patočky," 203–211.
8. SS 3, 450.
9. SS 3, 451.
10. SS 3, 452.
11. Karfík, *Unendlichwerden durch die Endlichkeit*, 42–43.
12. Ritter, "Transcendence u Jana Patočky," 201.
13. Patočka, "Some Comments Concerning the Extramundane and Mundane Position of Philosophy," 26.
14. Jan Patočka, "K prehistorii vědy o pohybu: svět, země, nebe a pohyb lidského života," in SS 7, 192–201; here 200.
15. Michael Gubser, "Jan Patočka's Transcendence to the World," in *Asubjective Phenomenology*, ed. L. Učník, I. Chvatík, and A. Williams (Nordhausen: Traugott Bautz, 2015), 71–95.

16. In this respect, I draw inspiration from Lieven Boeve, *Theology at the Crossroads of University, Church, and Society* (New York: Bloomsbury, 2016).
17. Karfík, *Unendlichwerden durch die Endlichkeit*, 80–81.
18. Evink, "The Gift of Life," 59–60.
19. De Warren, "The Gift of Eternity," 177–178.
20. Hagedorn, "Christianity Unthought," 43.
21. Patočka, "The Spiritual Person," 61.
22. Chvatík, "The Responsibility of the 'Shaken,'" 275.

Bibliography

Anidjar, Gil. "A Note on 'Faith and Knowledge.'" In *Acts of Religion*, edited by G. Anidjar, 40–41. New York: Routledge, 2002.

Arbib, Dan. "Donner la mort? Phénoménologie et sacrifice: Note sur une interprétation de Derrida." *Studia Phaenomenologica* 12 (2012): 383–397.

Armitage, Duane. "Heidegger's God: Against Caputo, Kearney, and Marion." *Philosophy and Theology* 26 (2014): 279–294.

Arnason, Johann P. "The Idea of Negative Platonism: Jan Patočka's Critique and Recovery of Metaphysics." *Thesis Eleven* 90 (2007): 6–26.

———. "Myšlenkové a politické pozadí Patočkovy konfrontace s modernitou." In *Dějinnost, nadcivilizace a modernita: Studie k Patočkově konceptu nadciviliace*, edited by J. P. Arnason, L. Benyovszky, and M. Skovajsa, 9–19. Praha: Togga, 2010.

———. "Nadcivilizace a její různé podoby: Patočkova koncepce modernity ve světle dnešních diskusí" In *Dějinnost, nadcivilizace a modernita: Studie k Patočkově konceptu nadciviliace*, edited by J. P. Arnason, L. Benyovszky, and M. Skovajsa, 23–56. Praha: Togga, 2010.

———. "Negative Platonism: Between the History of Philosophy and the Philosophy of History." In *Jan Patočka and the Heritage of Phenomenology*, edited by E. Abrams and I. Chvatík, 215–228. Dordrecht: Springer, 2011.

Augustine. *The City of God*. Translated by M. Dods. Peabody: Hendrickson, 2009.

Barbaras, Renaud. *L'ouverture du monde: Lecture de Jan Patočka*. Chatou: Éditions de la Transparence, 2011.

Bednář, Miloslav. "Jan Patočka a Martin Heidegger." *Reflexe* 14 (1995): 1–18.

Bělohradský, Václav. "Absolutno uprostřed všedního dne: Nad několika motivy Patočkova fragmentu." In *Dějinnost, nadcivilizace a modernita: Studie k Patočkově konceptu nadciviliace*, edited by J. P. Arnason, L. Benyovszky, and M. Skovajsa, 173–200. Praha: Togga, 2010.

Bloechl, Jeffrey. "Eschatology, Liturgy, and the Task of Thinking." In J.-Y. Lacoste, *From Theology to Theological Thinking*, vi–xxviii. Charlottesville: University of Virginia Press, 2014.

Boeve, Lieven. *Interrupting Tradition: An Essay on Christian Faith in a Postmodern Context*. Louvain: Peeters, 2003.

———. *Theology at the Crossroads of University, Church, and Society*. New York: Bloomsbury, 2016.

Boeve, Lieven, and Christophe Brabant, eds. *Between Philosophy and Theology: Contemporary Interpretations of Christianity*. Farnham: Ashgate, 2010.

Brito, Emilio. "Kenosis." In *Encyclopedia of Christian Theology, Vol. 2*, edited by J.-Y. Lacoste, 853–856. New York: Routledge, 2005.

Bulhof, Ilse N., and Laurens ten Kate, eds. *Flight of the Gods: Philosophical Perspectives on Negative Theology*. New York: Fordham University Press, 2000.

Bultmann, Rudolf. *New Testament and Mythology and Other Basic Writings*. Translated by S. M. Ogden. London: SCM, 1985.

Cajthaml, Martin. *Europe and the Care for the Soul: Jan Patočka's Conception of the Spiritual Foundations of Europe*. Nordhausen: Traugott Bautz, 2014.

Caputo, John D. *Heidegger and Aquinas: An Essay on Overcoming Metaphysics*. New York Fordham University Press, 1982.

———. *The Mystical Element in Heidegger's Thought*. New York: Fordham University Press, 1986.

———. *Radical Hermeneutics: Repetition, Deconstruction, and the Hermeneutic Project*. Bloomington: Indiana University Press, 1987.

———. *The Prayers and Tears of Jacques Derrida*. Bloomington: Indiana University Press, 1997.

———. "Introduction: Who Comes after the God of Metaphysics?" In *The Religious*, edited by J. D. Caputo, 1–19. Oxford: Blackwell, 2001.

———. "Richard Kearney's Enthusiasm." *Modern Theology* 18 (2002): 87–94.

———. *Philosophy and Theology*. Nashville: Abingdon Press, 2006.

Caputo, John D., and Linda Martín Alcoff, eds. *St. Paul among the Philosophers*. Bloomington: Indiana University Press, 2009.

Cavalcante Schuback, Marcia Sá. "Sacrifice and Salvation: Jan Patočka's Reading of Heidegger on the Question of Technology." In *Jan Patočka and the Heritage of Phenomenology: Centenary Papers*, edited by E. Abrams and I. Chvatík, 23–38. Dordrecht: Springer, 2011.

———. "Negative Responsibility." *The Journal for Cultural and Religious Theory* 15 (2015): 39–50.

Chvatík, Ivan. "Religion oder Politik? Zu Patočkas Begriff des politischen Handelns." In *Lebenswelt und Politik: Perspektiven der Phänomenologie nach Husserl*, edited by G. Leghissa and M. Staudigl, 147–158. Würzburg: Königshausen & Neumann, 2007.

———. "Jan Patočka." In *A Companion to the Philosophy of History and Historiography*, edited by A. Tucker, 518–528. Malden: Blackwell, 2009.

———. "The Responsibility of the 'Shaken': Jan Patočka and His 'Care for the Soul' in the 'Post-European' World." In *Jan Patočka and the Heritage of*

Phenomenology, edited by A. Abrams and I. Chvatík, 263–279. Dordrecht: Springer, 2011.

———. "Patočka's Philosophy of Meaning in Human Life and History." In *Asubjective Phenomenology*, edited by L. Učník, I. Chvatík, and A. Williams, 213–226. Nordhausen: Traugott Bautz, 2015.

———. "Jan Patočka's Studies on Masaryk." In *The New Yearbook for Phenomenology and Phenomenological Philosophy XIV. Religion, War and the Crisis of Modernity: A Special Issue Dedicated to the Philosophy of Jan Patočka*, edited by L. Hagedorn and J. Dodd, 136–160. London: Routledge, 2015.

Crépon, Marc. "Fear, Courage, Anger: The Socratic Lesson." In *Jan Patočka and the Heritage of Phenomenology: Centenary Papers*, edited by E. Abrams and I. Chvatík, 175–186. Dordrecht: Springer, 2011.

Crowe, Benjamin D. *Heidegger's Religious Origins: Destruction and Authenticity*. Bloomington: Indiana University Press, 2006.

Dastur, Françoise. "L'Europe et ses philosophes: Nietzsche, Husserl, Heidegger, Patocka." *Revue Philosophique de Louvain* 104 (2006): 1–22.

Derrida, Jacques. "Circumfession." In G. Bennington and J. Derrida, *Jacques Derrida*. Chicago: University of Chicago Press, 1993.

———. *The Gift of Death*. Translated by D. Wills. Chicago: University of Chicago Press, 1995.

———. *Of Grammatology*. Translated by G. C. Spivak. Baltimore: Johns Hopkins University Press, 1997.

———. "Et cetera." In *Deconstructions: A User's Guide*, edited by N. Royle, 282–305. London: Palgrave Macmillan, 2000.

———. "Faith and Knowledge: Two Sources of 'Religion' at the Limits of Reason Alone." In *Acts of Religion*, edited by G. Anidjar, 42–101. New York: Routledge, 2002.

———. *The Spectres of Marx: The State of the Debt, the Work of Mourning, and the New International*. Translated by P. Kamuff. New York: Routledge, 2006.

Desmond, William. *God and the Between*. Malden: Blackwell, 2008.

De Vries, Hent. *Philosophy and the Turn to Religion*. Baltimore: Johns Hopkins University Press, 1999.

De Warren, Nicolas. "The Gift of Eternity." In *The New Yearbook for Phenomenology and Phenomenological Philosophy XIV. Religion, War and the Crisis of Modernity: A Special Issue Dedicated to the Philosophy of Jan Patočka*, edited by L. Hagedorn and J. Dodd, 161–180. London: Routledge, 2015.

Dodd, James. "Philosophy in Dark Times: An Essay on Jan Patočka's Hhilosophy of history." In *The New Yearbook for Phenomenology and Phenomenological Philosophy XIV. Religion, War and the Crisis of Modernity: A Special Issue Dedicated to the Philosophy of Jan Patočka*, edited by L. Hagedorn and J. Dodd, 64–91. London: Routledge, 2015.

Durych, Jaroslav. *Gottes Regenbogen*. Translated by J. Patočka and F. Boldt. Bremen: Verlag K-Presse, 1975.
Evink, Eddo. "Patočka and Derrida on Responsibility." In *Analecta Husserliana LXXXIX*, edited by A.-T. Tymieniecka, 307–321. Dordrecht: Springer, 2006.
———. "The Relevance of Patočka's 'Negative Platonism.'" In *Jan Patočka and the Heritage of Phenomenology: Centenary Papers*, edited by E. Abrams and I. Chvatík, 57–70. Dordrecht: Springer, 2011.
———. "Horizons of Expectation: Ricoeur, Derrida, Patočka." *Studia Phaenomenologica* 13 (2013): 297–323.
———. "The Gift of Life: Jan Patočka and the Christian Heritage." In *The New Yearbook for Phenomenology and Phenomenological Philosophy XIV. Religion, War and the Crisis of Modernity: A Special Issue Dedicated to the Philosophy of Jan Patočka*, edited by L. Hagedorn and J. Dodd, 47–63. London: Routledge, 2015.
Falque, Emmanuel. *Crossing the Rubicon: Exploring the Borderlands of Philosophy and Theology*. New York: Fordham University Press, 2016.
Findlay, Edward F. *Caring for the Soul in a Postmodern Age: Politics and Phenomenology in the Thought of Jan Patočka*. Albany: State University of New York Press, 2002.
Frei, Jan. "Problém transcendence u Jana Patočky." Unpublished doctoral dissertation, Faculty of Arts, Charles University, Prague, 2014.
Gangle, Rocco, and Jason Smick. "Political Phenomenology: Radical Democracy and Truth." *Political Theology* 10 (2009): 342–363.
Gasché, Rodolphe. "European Memories: Jan Patočka and Jacques Derrida on Responsibility." *Critical Inquiry* 33 (2007): 291–311.
Gschwandtner, Christina M. *Postmodern Apologetics? Arguments for God in Contemporary Philosophy*. New York: Fordham University Press, 2013.
———. *Degrees of Givenness: On Saturation in Jean-Luc Marion*. Bloomington: Indiana University Press, 2014.
———. *Marion and Theology*. London: Bloomsbury T & T Clark, 2016.
Gubser, Michael. "Jan Patočka's Transcendence to the World." In *Asubjective Phenomenology*, ed. L. Učník, I. Chvatík, and A. Williams, 71–95. Nordhausen: Traugott Bautz, 2015.
Hagedorn, Ludger. "*Bewegung* als Leitmotiv von Patočkas Ideengeschichte." In *Andere Wege in die Moderne: Forschungsbeiträge zu Patočkas Genealogie der Neuzeit*, edited by L. Hagedorn and R.-M. Sepp, 10–25. Würzburg: Königshausen & Neumann, 2006.
———. "Auto-immunity or Transcendence: A Phenomenological Re-consideration of Religion with Derrida and Patočka." In *Phenomenology and Religion: New Frontiers*, edited by J. Bornemark and H. Ruin, 131–148. Stockholm: Södertörn University Publishers, 2010.

---. "Beyond Myth and Enlightenment: On Religion in Patočka's Thought." In *Jan Patočka and the Heritage of Phenomenology: Centenary Papers*, edited by E. Abrams and I. Chvatík, 245-262. Dordrecht: Springer, 2011.
---. "Kenosis: Die philosophische Anverwandlung eines christlichen Motivs bei Jan Patočka." In *Figuren der Transzendenz: Transformationen eines phänomenologischen Grundbegriffs*, edited by M. Staudigl and C. Sternad, 349-366. Würzburg: Königshausen & Neumann, 2014.
---. "Religion and the Crisis of Modernity." *IWM Post* (Winter 2014/15): 19-20.
---. "Christianity Unthought: A Reconsideration of Myth, Faith and Historicity." In *The New Yearbook for Phenomenology and Phenomenological Philosophy XIV. Religion, War and the Crisis of Modernity: A Special Issue Dedicated to the Philosophy of Jan Patočka*, edited by L. Hagedorn and J. Dodd, 31-46. London: Routledge, 2015.
---. "Fatigue of Reason: Patočka's Reading of *The Brothers Karamazov*." In *The New Yearbook for Phenomenology and Phenomenological Philosophy XIV. Religion, War and the Crisis of Modernity: A Special Issue Dedicated to the Philosophy of Jan Patočka*, edited by L. Hagedorn and J. Dodd, 181-198. London: Routledge, 2015.
---. "René Girard's Theory of Sacrifice, or: What Is the Gift of Death?" *The Journal for Cultural and Religious Theory* 15 (2015): 105-118.
Hagedorn, Ludger, and James Dodd. "Editors' Introduction." In *The New Yearbook for Phenomenology and Phenomenological Philosophy XIV. Religion, War and the Crisis of Modernity: A Special Issue Dedicated to the Philosophy of Jan Patočka*, edited by L. Hagedorn and J. Dodd, xv-xviii. London: Routledge, 2015.
Hála, Vlastimil. "Duchovní člověk a 'majitelé rozumu.'" *Filozofia* 62 (2007): 487-496.
Hanna, Robert. "Husserl's Crisis and Our Crisis." *International Journal of Philosophical Studies* 22 (2014): 752-770.
Hanyš, Milan. "Radikální nadcivilizace a ortodoxie: O některých nezamýšlených důsledcích teologie Pavla z Tarsu." In *Dějinnost, nadcivilizace a modernita: Studie k Patočkově konceptu nadciviliace*, edited by J. P. Arnason, L. Benyovszky, and M. Skovajsa, 271-287. Praha: Togga, 2010.
Hart, Kevin. *Postmodernism: A Beginner's Guide*. Oxford: Oneworld, 2004.
Härtel, Filip. "The Problem of Self-Fulfilment in the Philosophy of Jan Patočka." Unpublished thesis, Faculty of Arts, Charles University, Prague, 2012.
Havel, Václav. "Politics and Consciousness." Translated by E. Kohák and R. Scruton. *The Salisbury Review* 2 (1985): 31-38.
Havel, Václav, et al. "The Power of the Powerless." In *The Power of the Powerless: Citizens against the State*, edited by J. Kane, 23-94. London: Routledge, 2009.
Hazard, Paul. *La crise de la conscience européene 1680-1715*. Paris: Boivin, 1935.

Heidegger, Martin. "The Onto-theo-logical Constitution of Metaphysics." In *Identity and Difference*, translated by J. Stambaugh, 42–74. New York: Harper & Row, 1969.

———. "Nur noch ein Gott kann uns retten." *Der Spiegel* 30 (May 1976): 193–219.

———. *Nietzsche: The Will to Power as Knowledge and as Metaphysics*. Translated by D. F. Krell. New York Harper & Row, 1987.

———. "Modern Science, Metaphysics, and Mathematics." In *Basic Writings*, edited by D. F. Krell, 267–305. San Francisco: HarperCollins, 1993.

———. "The Question Concerning Technology in Heidegger." In *Basic Writings*, edited by D. F. Krell, 307–342. San Francisco: HarperCollins, 1993.

———. *The Fundamental Concepts of Metaphysics: World, Finitude, Solitude*. Translated by W. McNeill and N. Walker. Bloomington: Indiana University Press, 1996.

———. "Phenomenology and Theology." In *Pathmarks*, edited by W. McNeill, 39–62. Cambridge: Cambridge University Press, 1998.

———. "What Is Metaphysics?" In *Pathmarks*, edited by W. McNeill, 82–96. Cambridge: Cambridge University Press, 1998.

———. *Introduction to Metaphysics*. Translated by G. Fried and R. Polt. New Haven: Yale University Press, 2000.

———. *Being and Time*. Translated by J. Macquarrie and E. Robinson. Oxford: Blackwell, 2001.

Heisenberg, Werner. *Physics and Beyond: Encounters and Conversations*. Translated by A. J. Pomerans. New York: Harper & Row, 1971.

Hejdánek, Ladislav. "Nicota a odpovědnost." *Filosofický časopis* 39 (1991): 32–37.

Hejduk, Tomáš. "K Patočkově filosofii náboženství." In *Jan Patočka, české dějiny a Evropa*, 50–58. Semily: Státní okresní archiv Semily, 2007.

Hillebert, Jordan. "The Death of God and Dissolution of Humanity." *New Blackfriars* 95 (2014): 674–688.

Homolka, Jakub. *Koncept racionální civilizace: Patočkovo pojetí modernity ve světle civilizační analýzy*. Praha: Togga, 2016.

Husserl, Edmund. *The Crisis of European Sciences and Transcendental Phenomenology: An Introduction to Phenomenological Philosophy*. Translated by E. Carr. Evanston: Northwestern University Press, 1970.

———. *Ideen zu einer reinen Phänomenologie und phänomenologischen Philosophie*. The Hague: Martinus Nijhoff, 1976.

———. "Philosophie als strenge Wissenschaft." In *Aufsätze und Vorträge (1911–1921)*, edited by H.-R. Sepp and T. Nenn, 3–62. Dordrecht: Kluwer, 1986.

Janicaud, Dominique. *La phénomneologie éclatée*. Paris: Éditions de l'Eclat, 1998. English edition: *Phenomenology Wide Open*. Translated by C. N. Cabral. New York: Fordham University Press, 2005.

———. "The Theological Turn of French Phenomenology." Translated by B. G. Prusak. In *Phenomenology and the "Theological Turn": The French Debate*, 16–104. New York: Fordham University Press, 2000.

Jonkers, Peter. "God in France: Heidegger's Legacy." In *God in France: Eight Contemporary French Thinkers on God*, edited by P. Jonkers and R. Welten, 1–42. Leuven: Peeters, 2005.
Kant, Immanuel. *Critique of Pure Reason*. Translated by N. K. Smith. New York: St. Martin's Press, 1965.
Karfík, Filip. *Unendlichwerden durch die Endlichkeit*. Würzburg: Königshausen & Neumann, 2008.
Kearney, Richard. *Dialogues with Contemporary Continental Thinkers*. Manchester: Manchester University Press, 1984.
———. *Strangers, Gods and Monsters*. London: Routledge, 2003.
———. *The God Who May Be: A Hermeneutics of Religion*. Bloomington: Indiana University Press, 2001.
Koci, Martin. "Ein unbekannter Gott: Herausforderungen für die Systematische Theologie in einer postchristlichen und posttotalitären Gesellschaft." In *Diaspora als Ort der Theologie: Perspektiven aus Tschechien und Ostdeutschland*, edited by B. Kranemann and P. Štica, 169–187. Würzburg: Echter Verlag, 2016.
Kohák, Erazim. "Jak číst Patočku: Bibliografický úvod." *Proměny* 24 (1987): 24–33.
———. *Jan Patočka: Philosophy and Selected Writings*. Chicago: University of Chicago Press, 1989.
Lacoste, Jean-Yves. "Philosophy." In *Encyclopedia of Christian Theology*, Vol. 3, edited by J.-Y. Lacoste, 1234–1242. New York: Routledge, 2005.
———. *From Theology to Theological Thinking*. Translated by W. C. Hackett. Charlottesville: University of Virginia Press, 2014.
Landa, Ivan. "Patočka a negativní platonismus." In *Jan Patočka, české dějiny a Evropa*, 40–49. Semily: Státní okresní archiv Semily, 2007.
Landgrebe, Ludwig. "Jan Patočka." *Philosophy and Phenomenological Research* 38 (1977): 287–290.
Maggini, Golfo. "Europe's Janus Head: Jan Patočka's Phenomenological Elucidation of the Crisis of Modern European Civilization." *Epoché* 19 (2014): 103–125.
Margaroni, Maria. "Jacques Derrida." In *Encyclopedia of Postmodernism*, edited by V. E. Taylor and C. E. Winquist, 92–94. London: Routledge, 2001.
———. "Metaphysics of Presence." In *Encyclopedia of Postmodernism*, edited by V. E. Taylor and C. E. Winquist, 245–246. London: Routledge, 2001.
Marion, Jean-Luc. *God without Being: Hors-Text*. Translated by T. A. Carlson. Chicago: University of Chicago Press, 1991.
———. "Metaphysics and Phenomenology: A Summary for Theologians." In *The Postmodern God: A Theological Reader*, edited by G. Ward, 279–296. Malden: Wiley, 1998.
———. *Being Given: Toward a Phenomenology of Givenness*. Stanford: Stanford University Press, 2002.
———. *In Excess: Studies of Saturated Phenomena*. Translated by R. Horner and V. Berraud. New York: Fordham University Press, 2002.

———. "The 'End of Metaphysics' as a Possibility." In *Religion after Metaphysics*, edited by M. A. Wrathall, 166–189. Cambridge: Cambridge University Press, 2003.

———. "*Mihi magna questio factum sum*: The Privilege of Unknowing." *Journal of Religion* 85 (2005): 1–24.

———. *The Visible and the Revealed*. Translated by C. M. Gschwandtner. New York: Fordham University Press, 2008.

———. "The Phenomenality of the Sacrament." In *Words of Life: New Theological Turns in French Phenomenology*, ed. B. E. Benson and N. Wirzba, 89–103. New York: Fordham University Press, 2010.

———. *The Reason of the Gift*. Translated by S. E. Lewis. Charlottesville: University of Virginia Press, 2011.

———. *Negative Certainties*. Translated by S. E. Lewis. Chicago: University of Chicago Press, 2015.

Marx, Karl. "Theses on Feuerbach." In K. Marx and F. Engels, *The German Ideology*, edited by C. J. Arthur, 121–123. New York: International, 2004.

Masaryk, Tomáš G. *The Making of a State: Memories and Observations (1914–18)*. London: Allen & Unwin, 1927.

Mensch, James. *From Being to Knowing: A Postmodern Reversal*. University Park: Pennsylvania State University Press, 1996.

Michalski, Krzysztof. *The Flame of Eternity: An Interpretation of Nietzsche's Thought*. Translated by B. Paloff. Princeton: Princeton University Press, 2007.

Moran, Dermot. *Husserl's Crisis of the European Sciences and Transcendental Phenomenology: An Introduction*. Cambridge: Cambridge University Press, 2012.

Nancy, Jean-Luc. "Entzug der Göttlichkeit: Zur Rekonstruktion und Selbstüberschreibung des Christentum." *Lettre International* 76 (2002): 76–80.

———. *Dis-Enclosure: The Deconstruction of Christianity*. Translated by B. Bergo, G. Malenfant, and M. B. Smith. New York: Fordham University Press, 2008.

Naas, Michael. *Miracle and Machine: Jacques Derrida and the Two Sources of Religion, Science, and the Media*. New York: Fordham University Press, 2012.

Nietzsche, Friedrich. *On the Genealogy of Morals*. Edited by W. Kaufmann. New York: Vintage Books, 1967.

———. *The Will to Power*. Edited by W. Kaufmann. New York: Random House, 1968.

———. *The Gay Science: With a Prelude in German Rhymes and an Appendix of Songs*. Edited by B. Williams. Cambridge: Cambridge University Press, 2001.

———. *Thus Spoke Zarathustra: A Book for All and None*. Edited by A. del Caro and R. Pippin. Cambridge: Cambridge University Press, 2006.

Palouš, Martin. "A Philosopher and His History: Jan Patocka's Reflections on the End of Europe and the Arrival of the Post-European Epoch." *Thesis Eleven* 116 (2013): 77–98.

Palouš, Radim. "Patočkovo KRINEIN." In *Jan Patočka, české dějiny a Evropa*, 90–94. Semily: Státní okresní archiv Semily, 2007.

Paparusso, Ricardo. "Life, Technology, Christianity: Patočka's Sacrifice for Nothing and Its Economic-mythical Roots." In *Asubjective Phenomenology*, edited by L. Učník, I. Chvatík, and A. Williams, 187–198. Nordhausen: Traugott Bautz, 2015.

Patočka, Jan. Review of *Das Urchristentum im Rahmen der antiken Religionen*, by Rudolf Bultmann. *Křesťanská revue* 19 (1952): 311–315.

———. "Vom Ursprung und Sinn des Unsterblichkeitsgedankens bei Plato." In *Denken und Umdenken: Zu Werk und Wirkung von W. Heisenberg*, edited by H. Pfeiffer, 102–115. München: Piper, 1977.

———. *Jan Patočka: Philosophy and Selected Writings*. Translated by E. Kohák. Chicago: University of Chicago Press, 1989.

———. "Le christianisme et le monde naturel." Translated by E. Abrams. *Istina* 38 (1993): 16–22.

———. "Phénoménologie et ontologie du movement." In *Papier phénoménologique*, translated by E. Abrams, 29–52. Grenoble: J. Millon, 1995.

———. *Heretical Essays in the Philosophy of History*. Translated by E. Kohák. La Salle: Open Court, 1996.

———. *An Introduction to Husserl's Phenomenology*. Translated by E. Kohák. Chicago: Open Court, 1996.

———. *Sebrané spisy Jana Patočky, vol. 1. Péče o duši, I: Stati z let 1929–1952; Nevydané texty z padesátých let*. Edited by I. Chvatík and P. Kouba. Praha: Oikoymenh, 1996.

———. *Body, Community, Language, World*. Translated by E. Kohák. Chicago: Open Court, 1998.

———. *Sebrané spisy Jana Patočky, vol. 10. Komeniologické studie II: Texty publikované v letech 1959–1977*. Edited by V. Schifferová. Praha: Oikoymenh, 1998.

———. *Sebrané spisy Jana Patočky, vol. 2. Péče o duši, II: Stati z let 1970–1977; Nevydané texty a přednášky ze sedmdesátých let*. Edited by I. Chvatík and P. Kouba. Praha: Oikoymenh, 1999.

———. *Sebrané spisy Jana Patočky, vol. 3. Péče o duši, III: Kacířské eseje o filosofii dějin; Varianty a přípravné práce z let 1973–1977; Dodatky k Péči o duši I a II*. Edited by I. Chvatík and P. Kouba. Praha: Oikoymenh, 2002.

———. *Plato and Europe*. Translated by P. Lom. Stanford: Stanford University Press, 2002.

———. *Sebrané spisy Jana Patočky, vol. 4. Umění a čas, I: Soubor statí, předníšek a poznámek k problémům umění*. Edited by D. Vojtěch and I. Chvatík. Praha: Oikoymenh, 2004.

———. *Sebrané spisy Jana Patočky, vol. 12. Češi I: Soubor textů k českému myšlení a českým dějinám*. Edited by K. Palek and I. Chvatík. Praha: Oikoymenh, 2006.

———. *Sebranné spisy Jana Patočky*, vol. 13. *Češi II: Soubor textů k českému myšlení a českým dějinám; Nepublikované práce*. Edited by K. Palek and I. Chvatík. Praha: Oikoymenh, 2006.

———. *Andere Wege in die Moderne: Studien zur europäischen Ideengeschichte von der Renaissance bis zur Romantik*. Edited by L. Hagedorn. Würzburg: Königshausen & Neumann, 2006.

———. *L'Europe après l'Europe*. Translated by E. Abrams. Lagrasse: Verdier, 2007.

———. *Living in Problematicity*. Edited by Eric Manton. Praha: Oikoymenh, 2007.

———. *Sebranné spisy Jana Patočky*, vol. 6. *Fenomenologické spisy I: Přirozený svět; Texty z let 1931–1949*. Edited by I. Chvatík and J. Frei. Praha: Oikoymenh, 2008.

———. *Sebranné spisy Jana Patočky*, vol. 7. *Fenomenologické spisy II: Co je existence; Publikované texty z let 1965–1977*. Edited by P. Kouba and O. Švec. Praha: Oikoymenh, 2009.

———. *Aristote, ses devanciers, ses successeurs*. Translated by E. Abrams. Paris: J. Vrin 2011.

———. "Time, Myth, Faith." Translated by L. Hagedorn, 3–12; "The Dangers of Technicization in Science according to E. Husserl and the Essence of Technology as Danger according to M. Heidegger (Varna Lecture)." Translated by E. Kohák, 13–22; "On Masaryk's Philosophy of Religion." Translated by J. Rothbauer, 95–135. All in *The New Yearbook for Phenomenology and Phenomenological Philosophy XIV. Religion, War and the Crisis of Modernity: A Special Issue Dedicated to the Philosophy of Jan Patočka*. Edited by L. Hagedorn and J. Dodd. London: Routledge, 2015.

———. *The Natural World as a Philosophical Problem*. Translated by E. Abrams. Evanston: Northwestern University Press, 2016.

———. *Europa und Nach-Europa: Zur Phänomenologie einer Idee*. Edited by L. Hagedorn and K. Nellen. Freiburg: Verlag Karl Alber, 2017.

Pavlincová, Helena. "Polemiky Jana Patočky s novotomisty." In *Jan Patočka, České Dějiny a Evropa*, 69–75. Semily: Státní okresní archiv Semily, 2007.

Peacocke, John. "Heidegger and the Problem of Onto-theology." In *Post-Secular Philosophy: Between Philosophy and Theology*. Edited by P. Blond, 93–102. London: Routledge, 1998.

Pechar, Jiří. "Patočkova dekonstrukce metafyziky." *Literární noviny* 27 (1997): 7.

Peperzak, Adrian. "A Re-reading of Heidegger's 'Phenomenology and Theology.'" In *The Multidimensionality of Hermeneutic Phenomenology*. Edited by B. Babich and D. Ginev, 317–338. Heidelberg: Springer, 2014.

Petříček, Miroslav. "Mýtus v Patočkově filosofii." *Reflexe* 5–6 (1992): 6.1–6.15.

———. "Jan Patočka and Phenomenological Philosophy Today." In *Jan Patočka and the Heritage of Phenomenology: Centenary Papers*, edited by E. Abrams and I. Chvatík, 3–6. Dordrecht: Springer, 2011.

Powell, Jason. *Jacques Derrida: A Biography*. New York: Continuum, 2006.

Raschke, Carl. "Derrida and the Return of Religion: Religious Theory after Postmodernism." *The Journal for Cultural and Religious Theory* 6 (2005): 1–16.
Ratzinger, Joseph. *Truth and Tolerance: Christian Belief and World Religions*. San Francisco: Ignatius, 2004.
Reynolds, Jack. "The Implicit and Presupposed Theological Turn in Phenomenology." *Sophia* 47 (2008): 261–263.
Rezek, Petr. "Třetí životní pohyb u Jana Patočky jako problém intersubjektivity." *Filosofická reflexe* 4 (1990): 5.1–5.13.
———. *Jan Patočka a věc fenomenologie*. Praha: Oikoymenh, 1993.
Ricoeur, Paul. "Preface to the French Edition." In Jan Patočka, *Heretical Essays in the Philosophy of History*, translated by E. Kohák, vii–xvi. La Salle: Open Court, 1996.
———. "Jan Patočka: De la philosophie du monde naturel à la philosophie de l'histoire." *Studia Phaenomenologica* 7 (2007): 193–200.
Ritter, Martin. "Transcendence u Jana Patočky a problém oběti." In *Dějinnost, nadcivilizace a modernita: Studie k Patočkově konceptu nadciviliace*, edited by J. P. Arnason, L. Benyovszky, and M. Skovajsa, 201–215. Praha: Togga, 2010.
Rodrigo, Pierre. "Negative Platonism and Maximal Existence in the Thought of Jan Patočka." In *Jan Patočka and the Heritage of Phenomenology: Centenary Papers*, edited by E. Abrams and I. Chvatík, 87–97. Dordrecht: Springer, 2011.
Russell, Matheson. "Phenomenology and Theology: Situating Heidegger's Philosophy of Religion." *Sophia* 50 (2011): 641–655.
Schifferová, Věra. "Jan Amos Komenský—portrét filozofa." In *Patočka a novoveká filozofia*, edited by V. Leško, V Schifferová, et al., 105–128. Košice: Acta Facultatis Philosophicae Universitatis Šafarikinae, 2014.
Schinkel, Willem. "The Image of Crisis: Walter Benjamin and the Interpretation of 'Crisis' in Modernity." *Thesis Eleven* 127 (2015): 36–51.
Schrijvers, Joeri. *Ontotheological Turnings: The Decentering of the Modern Subject in Recent French Phenomenology*. Albany: State University of New York Press, 2011.
———. "Thinking Despite Everything? On Unknowing God, and the Common Concerns of Philosophy and Theology." *Modern Theology* 31 (2015): 666–675.
Shore, Marci. *The Taste of Ashes: The Afterlife of Totalitarianism in Eastern Europe*. New York: Broadway Books, 2013.
Simmons, Aaron J., and Bruce E. Benson. *The New Phenomenology: A Philosophical Introduction*. New York: Bloomsbury, 2013.
Simpson, Christopher. *Religion, Metaphysics, and the Postmodern: William Desmond and John D. Caputo*. Bloomington: Indiana University Press, 2009.
Skovajsa, Marek. "'Moderantní' nadcivilizace: nekonečná krize liberalismu a možnost jejího překonání." In *Dějinnost, nadcivilizace a modernita: Studie k Patočkově konceptu nadciviliace*, edited by J. P. Arnason, L. Benyovszky, and M. Skovajsa, 81–122. Praha: Togga, 2010.

Sladký, Pavel. "Negativní Platonismus jako případ sokratismu." *Filosofický časopis* 58 (2010): 753–756.

Sroda, Krzysztof. "Patočka, Platón a nesmrtelnost duše." *Filosofický časopis* 39 (1991): 357–362.

Sternad, Christian. "Spectres of the Sacred: Jan Patočka, or: The Hidden Source of Jacques Derrida's 'Phenomenology of Religion.'" In *The New Yearbook for Phenomenology and Phenomenological Philosophy XIV. Religion, War and the Crisis of Modernity: A Special Issue Dedicated to the Philosophy of Jan Patočka*, edited by L. Hagedorn and J. Dodd, 287–299. London: Routledge, 2015.

Svobodová, Zuzana. "Česká tradice křesťanské víry v Patočkově reflexi." In *Jan Patočka, České Dějiny a Evropa*, 59–68. Semily: Státní okresní archiv Semily, 2007.

Šrubař, Ilja. "Jsou dějiny morální? K Patočkově dialektice úpadku." In *Dějinnost, nadcivilizace a modernita: Studie k Patočkově konceptu nadciviliace*, edited by J. P. Arnason, L. Benyovszky, and M. Skovajsa, 57–80. Praha: Togga, 2010.

Tava, Francesco, and Darian Meacham, eds. *Thinking after Europe: Jan Patočka and Politics*. London: Rowman & Littlefield, 2016.

Tengelyi, László. "On the Border of Phenomenology and Theology." In *Phenomenology and Religion: New Frontiers*, edited by J. Bornemark and H. Ruin, 17–34. Stockholm: Södertörn University Publishers, 2010.

ten Kate, Laurens. "Intimate Distance: Rethinking the Unthought God in Christianity." *Sophia* 47 (2008): 327–343.

Thomson, Iain D. *Heidegger on Ontotheology: Technology and the Politics of Education*. Cambridge: Cambridge University Press, 2005.

———. *Heidegger, Art and Postmodernity*. Cambridge: Cambridge University Press, 2011.

Učník, Lubica. "*Esse* or *Habere*. To be or to have: Patočka's Critique of Husserl and Heidegger." *Journal of the British Society for Phenomenology* 38 (2007): 297–317.

———. "Patočka on Techno-power and the Sacrificial Victim (*Oběť*)." In *Jan Patočka and the Heritage of Phenomenology: Centenary Papers*, edited by E. Abrams and I. Chvatík, 187–202. Dordrecht: Springer, 2011.

———. "Patočka's Socrates: The Care for the Soul and Human Existence." *Investigationes Fenomenológicas* 4 (2013): 87–100.

Učník, Ljubica, Ivan Chvatík, and Anita Williams, eds. *Asubjective Phenomenology*. Nordhausen: Traugott Bautz, 2015.

Ullmann, Tamás. "Negative Platonism and the Appearance-problem." In *Jan Patočka and the Heritage of Phenomenology: Centenary Papers*, edited by E. Abrams and I. Chvatík, 71–86. Dordrecht: Springer, 2011.

Umlauf, Václav. "Tractate on God Almost Non-existing." *AUC Theologica* 3 (2013): 9–35.

Valéry, Paul. *La crise de l'esprit*. Paris. Éditions Manucius, 2016.

Vattimo, Gianni. *After Christianity*. Translated by L. D'Isanto. New York: Columbia University Press, 2002.

———. "The Christian Message and the Dissolution of Metaphysics." In *The Blackwell Companion to Postmodern Theology*, edited by G. Ward, 458–466. Malden: Blackwell, 2005.

———. "Toward a Non-religious Christianity." In John D. Caputo and Gianni Vattimo, *After the Death of God*, edited by J. W. Robbins, 27–46. New York: Columbia University Press, 2007.

———. "Nihilism as Postmodern Christianity." In *Transcendence and Beyond: A Postmodern Inquiry*, edited by J. D. Caputo and M. J. Scanlon, 44–48. Bloomington: Indiana University Press, 2007.

Veselý, Jindřich. "Jan Patočka a křesťanství." *Studia Philosophica* 60 (2013): 63–84.

———. "Mýtus v myšlení Jana Patočky." Unpublished doctoral dissertation, Protestant Theological Faculty, Charles University, Prague, 2014.

Vítek, Jan. "Patočkovo pojetí krize moderní doby a člověka: Duševní krize evropského lidstva." In *Jan Patočka, české dějiny a Evropa*, 175–181. Semily: Státní okresní archiv Semily, 2007.

Westphal, Merold. *Overcoming Onto-theology: Toward a Postmodern Christian Faith*. New York: Fordham University Press, 2001.

Williams, Anita. "The Meaning of Mathematical." In *Asubjective Phenomenology*, edited by L. Učník, I. Chvatík, and A. Williams, 227–251. Nordhausen: Traugott Bautz, 2015.

Wolfe, Judith. *Heidegger and Theology*. London: Bloomsbury, 2014.

Wrathall, Mark E., ed. *Religion after Metaphysics*. Cambridge: Cambridge University Press, 2003.

Wyschogrod, Edith, Jean-Joseph Goux, and Eric Boyton, eds. *The Enigma of Gift and Sacrifice*. New York: Fordham University Press, 2001.

Index

Absolute, 14, 22, 28, 37, 41, 100, 138, 169
  and gift, 185–86
  and God, 130, 170
  and modernity, 78, 86
  and philosophy, 31, 34–35, 44, 99, 136
  and sacrifice, 212–16
Aesthetics, 53, 74, 135, 136
Analogia entis, 98, 102
Aristotle, 32, 41, 47, 51, 95–97, 100, 101, 116, 145, 252n21
Arnason, Johann P., 76, 123, 125
Augustine, 25, 41, 43, 136, 206, 268n34

Balthasar, Hans Urs von, 43
Barth, Karl, 244n62
Bataille, Georges, 206
Being-in-the-world, 6–7, 23, 29–30, 44, 112, 125, 131–32, 152, 165, 167, 180, 194–95, 224–25, 228, 232, 235, 238
Bonhoeffer, Dietrich, 221
Brentano, Franz, 61
Bultmann, Rudolf, 2, 156–57, 165, 221

Caputo, John D., 3, 93–94, 104, 107–10, 115, 149, 156, 169, 172, 176, 188–90, 193, 197, 210, 221, 228
Catholicism, 50, 62–63, 81, 100
  and Patočka, 10–11, 245n92
Charter 77, 6, 8, 227, 271n3
Chorismos, 126–27, 136, 140, 171
Chrétien, Jean-Louis, 17, 19, 27, 41, 104, 228
Christ, Jesus, 93, 162, 180, 187–88, 201, 208, 210–23, 230, 270n75
Chvatík, Ivan, 10, 150, 165–66, 179, 196–97, 200, 205, 214
Comenius, Jan Amos, 1, 8, 59, 98
Comte, August, 63, 80, 90

Death of God, 106, 133, 152, 164–65, 197, 199, 205, 237
  and Michalski, 217–19
  and Nietzsche, 64–66
Deconstruction, 45, 69, 101, 106, 204
  and Christianity, 4, 17, 149–73, 199
  and metaphysics, 16, 93–94, 107–109
Democritus, 95–96
Derrida, Jacques, 4, 17, 41, 108, 138, 143, 147, 149, 169, 200, 216, 221, 228
  and Patočka, 175–98
Descartes, René, 8, 50, 52, 56, 59, 67, 99, 105

287

Dogma, 36, 62, 136, 168–69, 184, 195–96, 210
Dostoevsky, Fyodor, 163–64
Durych, Jaroslav, 240n20

Eckhart, 42, 43, 98, 108, 231, 234
Embodiment, 14, 232, 236
Enlightenment, 8, 30, 48, 50, 68–69, 99, 149, 151, 154, 232, 249n75
 and rationalism, 56–59, 67
Eschatology, 80, 230, 234, 236
Eternity, 62, 108, 111, 137, 236
 Eternity and Historicity, 116, 142
Europe, 5–8, 64–65, 90, 177, 182–83, 185, 189
 and crisis, 65–68, 87
 Four Seminars on Europe, 209, 211
 and Greek pillar, 184
 Plato and Europe, 183–84, 205
 and post-Europe, 7, 13, 16, 61, 89
Evink, Eddo, 15, 39, 127, 138, 185–89, 193, 200, 216, 217, 219, 236
Existential phenomenology, 9, 188, 235

Falque, Emmanuel, 41, 43, 44
Faith and Knowledge, 190–91, 266n79
Feuerbach, Friedrich, 80
Foucault, Michel, 137–38
Freedom, 9, 11, 37–38, 82–83, 109 146, 163, 169, 225
 experience of, 123–29
 and faith, 144
 and myth, 158
Freud, Sigmund, 48

Galileo, 52, 67, 59, 71
Gasché, Rodolphe, 183–85
Gelassenheit, 108
Gestell, 73–74, 91
The Gift of Death, 175–76, 183–201, 270n78

God, 23, 44, 140, 162–64, 194, 208–209, 220, 222, 230–31
 and modernity, 57, 59, 79
 and philosophy, 22
 Greek philosophy, 41, 53, 154, 177, 182
 and Christianity, 184, 196
Guilt, 25, 181

Hagedorn, Ludger, 15, 39, 150, 155, 165–67, 183, 185, 189–91, 194, 200, 210, 214, 216, 220, 236
Havel, Václav, 84, 240n15
Heidegger, Martin, 1–6, 110–12, 116, 130, 135, 140, 159–60, 228–29, 234, 254n52, 261n34, 266–67n90
 and *Destruktion*, 26, 101, 105
 and Hölderlin, 72
 and ontological difference, 11, 32, 105, 108, 193, 203, 209, 211–13, 220
 and ontotheology, 101–103, 195
 and *Phenomenology and Theology*, 23–27, 243n31
 and technology, 71–75, 91, 152–53, 201
Heisenberg, Werner, 88, 251n133
Hellenism, 64
Henry, Michel, 10, 17, 19, 27–28, 30, 41, 104, 147, 228
Heresy, 149–73, 183, 197, 200, 235
 and phenomenology, 27–28
 and theology, 17, 234, 236
Heretical Essays in the Philosophy of History, 9–11, 39, 42, 146, 150, 155, 162, 167, 169–70, 175–76, 180, 182–83, 185, 187, 190, 192–93, 230–31, 260n3, 264n22
Heteron, 129, 133, 135, 137–38, 143–46
Historicity, 112, 116, 128, 137, 153, 159, 186
 and faith, 142–45

Hromádka, Josef-Lukl, 2, 35, 244n62
Humanism, 8, 50, 99, 139, 151
Husserl, Edmund, 1, 3, 5-6, 8-9, 12, 19-20, 27-29, 48, 51, 54, 56, 61, 66-71, 74-75, 86, 88-89, 121, 152, 193, 201, 223, 229, 234, 234, 243n40

Immortality, 163, 165, 178, 218
Incarnation, 194, 220, 232-33, 236

Janicaud, Dominique, 2, 17, 20-21, 27-30, 40, 45, 103, 105, 119
Jaspers, Karl, 147
John of the Cross, 42
Judaism, 64, 84, 210

Kant, Immanuel, 57, 62, 87, 99, 126, 163-64, 193, 253n32,34, 266-67n90
Karfík, Filip, 41, 166, 212, 231, 236
Kearney, Richard, 93, 104, 171, 192, 228
Kenosis, 4, 199-201, 209-15, 217, 219-20, 223, 230, 269n59
Kierkegaard, Søren, 25, 41, 42, 169, 176
Kohák, Erazim, 8-9, 11-12, 56, 61, 86-89, 96, 111, 119-20, 123

Lacoste, Jean-Yves, 10, 14, 30, 40-45, 104, 135, 147, 228
Levinas, Emmanuel, 19, 27-28, 41, 121, 137-38, 182, 206, 228
Love, 62, 106-107, 110, 179, 181, 185-86, 213, 223

Marion, Jean-Luc, 3, 10, 17, 19, 27-30, 41, 115, 228
and metaphysics, 93-94, 103-10
and sacrifice, 199-201, 205-209, 215, 222-24

Marx, Karl, 48, 68
Marxism, 99, 193
Masaryk, Tomáš Garrigue, 8, 74, 85, 88-89, 163, 248n43
and religion, 61-66
Methodological atheism, 19, 25
Merleau-Ponty, Maurice, 28
Metaphysics, 3-4, 79, 85, 94-99, 108, 100-101, 110-17, 119-23, 126, 128-29, 132-37, 140, 229, 256n10
classical, 51, 95, 116
in Heidegger, 101-103
in Marion, 104-107
modern, 121, 143
and ontotheology, 103-11, 116, 237
Michalski, Krzysztof, 217-19, 270n79
Modernity, 51, 58, 64, 105, 154
and Cartesianism, 50, 53, 56, 59, 99, 163
and crisis, 49-50, 60, 62, 66-67, 70, 74-78, 85-92, 246n1
and question of meaning, 68, 78, 91, 195
Movements of Existence, 7, 159-60, 179, 186, 193, 232, 236, 261n33
Myth, 143, 157-59, 158, 178, 270n75
of God-man, 187, 210, 214-15
Mysterium tremendum, 170, 181, 187, 189

Nancy, Jean-Luc, 147, 149, 170-71, 199, 228
Natural world, 9, 68, 132, 155
and Christianity, 152-54
Natural World as a Philosophical Problem, 6-7, 187, 214
Negative Platonims, 115, 119-47, 196, 234
Nietzsche, Friedrich, 8, 33, 48, 61, 63-66, 74, 88, 102, 106, 119, 133, 138, 164, 172, 180, 199, 215, 246n1

Nihilism, 50, 61, 138, 151, 156, 164, 237
  and Nietzsche, 63–65
  and Sartre, 135, 140

Objectivity, 9, 55, 57, 61–64, 125, 127, 130–33, 139, 146–47, 207, 233–35
  and science, 36
  in Husserl, 66–69
  and metaphysics, 113–14, 122, 133
  and nonobjectivity, 128, 136–37, 140–44, 152

Paul the Apostle, 25, 43, 162–63, 180, 196
  and Pauline epistles, 81, 84, 210
Pascal, Blaise, 41–42, 98
Petříček, Miroslav, 137–38, 151, 167
Phenomenology of givenness, 107, 217–19, 224
Plato, 32, 51, 95–97, 116, 119, 124, 126, 128, 132, 177, 179, 196, 218, 252n21
Plato and Europe, 183–84, 205
Poetry, 60, 74, 91–92, 103, 153
Polemos, 203, 232, 238, 268n13
Positivism, 37, 50, 63, 99, 121
Postmodernity, 48, 50, 194, 236
Protestantism, 11, 50, 81, 100
Przywara, Erich, 245n92

Ratzinger, Joseph, 196
Reason, 50–60, 81, 87, 91–92, 109, 218, 249n75
  and Christianity, 90–92
  and metaphysics, 99, 109, 172
  and modernity, 42, 67–70, 75, 86, 89–90, 164, 235
  and science, 54–55
  crisis of, 3, 7, 49
Redemption, 80, 91, 144, 234
  as *das Rettende*, 74, 202

Religion without religion, 172, 182, 189, 192, 221
Responsibility, 173, 175–87, 190–95, 237
  and Christianity, 13, 17, 144, 167
  and sacrifice, 173
Resurrection, 165, 167, 194
Revelation, 19, 21–22, 24, 44, 93, 100, 115, 162, 164, 167–68, 185, 191, 203, 222, 235
Ricoeur, Paul, 9, 28, 188, 197

Sacred, 152, 161, 181, 190–91, 206
Sacrifice, 2, 4, 40–41, 65, 102, 173, 188, 197–98, 200–26
  and kenosis, see *Kenosis*
  and myth, 202
Scholasticism, 41, 43, 98–99, 100, 256n10
Secularization, 48, 54, 77, 79–80
Socrates, 38, 90, 95–97, 109, 116, 123, 138, 177, 201, 205, 217–19, 221, 227, 252n21
Solidarity of the shaken, 225, 238
Soul, 115, 153, 162, 163, 167, 178–80, 195, 218
  and care for the soul, 7, 13, 95, 170, 172, 177, 181, 186–88, 239n7
  and abysmal deepening of the soul, 166, 181–82, 187, 194, 215
  and open and closed soul, 59–60
  and dark night, 124
Souček, Josef B., 2, 42, 212
Supercivilization, 66, 70, 75–87, 90, 92, 256n10

Technology, 87, 91–92, 95, 205
  as danger, 201–202
  in Heidegger, 71–75
Theological turn and phenomenology, 2–5, 10, 13, 16, 20, 27–31, 37,

40–45, 60, 94, 103, 105, 107, 111, 121–22, 134, 149, 156, 169, 172, 197, 199–200, 206, 215–16, 223, 228–29, 236, 243n37, 252n21, 254n52
Theology, 19–21, 36, 227–36
  as fundamental theology, 44, 325
  as moral theology, 163–65, 171, 253n34
  in Heidegger, 23–27, 103
  in Lacoste, 41–43
  and negative Platonism, 133–37
  as negative theology, 17, 169, 171
  and philosophy, 3, 20–21, 23–45, 134, 145, 217
  and task of thinking, 1–4, 41–45, 135, 140, 146–47, 228, 252n21
Theória, 34, 52, 60, 69, 90, 115
  and modern theory, 42, 54, 57, 113, 252n21

Theresa of Avila, 43
Time, Myth, Faith, 142, 158
Titanism, 50, 63
Transcendence, 14–16, 30–31, 34, 36, 81, 125, 136, 144, 146, 212, 220, 229, 232–36, 271n7
  and freedom, 127–29, 225
Truth, 21, 32, 54–56, 72, 83–84, 96, 99, 121–22
  as in-adequacy, 129–33
  and objectivity, 36, 59, 63–64, 84, 132, 181
  living in, 1, 14, 97

Varna lecture, 201, 205, 209
Vattimo, Gianni, 93, 104, 149, 156, 172, 199, 210, 221, 228

War, 1, 7–8, 49, 51, 70, 175, 202
Westphal, Merold, 104, 238